26 Nov. 1984

26 Nov. 1984

DUMBARTON OAKS STUDIES

❧ XIV ☙

THE CHURCH OF THE PANAGIA KANAKARIÁ AT LYTHRANKOMI IN CYPRUS

ITS MOSAICS AND FRESCOES

Thomas

THE CHURCH
OF THE PANAGIA KANAKARIÁ
AT LYTHRANKOMI IN CYPRUS

ITS MOSAICS AND FRESCOES

A. H. S. MEGAW and E. J. W. HAWKINS

Dumbarton Oaks
Center for Byzantine Studies
Trustees for Harvard University
Washington, District of Columbia
1977

The Dumbarton Oaks Studies are published under the editorship of the Director of Studies and Faculty; Miss Julia Warner, Associate Editor; Mrs. Fanny Bonajuto, Research Associate for Publications (retired); Mrs. Nancy Bowen, Assistant Editor; Miss Frances Jones, in charge of Plate Layouts.

Distributed by
J. J. Augustin, Publisher
Locust Valley, New York

Library of Congress Catalogue Card Number 77–99267; ISBN 0–88402–074–6
Printed in Germany *at* J. J. Augustin, Glückstadt

FOR ELEKTRA AND HILDA

Preface

The circumstances in which this study was undertaken owe much to the efforts of His Beatitude Archbishop Makarios III and his immediate predecessors to preserve the architectural heritage of the archiepiscopal diocese in Cyprus. The Panagia Kanakaria was one of the first churches to receive their attention.

Dr. V. Karageorghis, Director of the Cyprus Department of Antiquities, has kindly given permission for this publication of the results of investigations carried out for the Department during repair of the church, which were supervised initially by the late T. Mogabgab and subsequently by ourselves and others. We are further in his debt for many photographs from the Department's negatives, some of which we have reproduced (figs. 23–25, 105, 107–11, and 128). Mr. K. Papageorghiou, Curator of Ancient Monuments, kindly communicated information about his investigations in 1966 and arranged for us to examine fallen fragments of mosaics found in his excavations in the church; he also supplied the photograph reproduced with his permission as figure 16. To them both and to Mr. A. Orphanou, the Department's Chief Foreman who was in charge of all the structural work on the church, we are indebted for facilities during numerous visits. We also owe much to Father Antonios Christophorou, parish priest of Lythrankomi, for his long-suffering cooperation; and to the staff of Mangoian Brothers in Nicosia for their careful handling of photographic problems.

The division of labor in the preparation of this monograph was broadly as follows. E. J. W. H. prepared the description of the mosaic, the section on the technique of the mosaic, and the description of the frescoes; he also took the photographs not otherwise acknowledged. The survey of the structure of the church is our joint work. The remaining chapters and the appendix were initially written by A. H. S. M., who also drew figures A–O. The entire text has, however, been agreed upon by both contributors.

This study has benefited greatly from our discussions with many colleagues. We are particularly grateful to Professors E. Kitzinger and C. Mango for very kindly reading the text and drawing attention to errors and omissions; for those that remain we alone are responsible. We are also indebted to many others who have assisted us with individual problems, particularly Dr. Ch. Bakirtzis, Dr. S. Brock, Dr. M. Christodoulou, Dr. R. Cormack, Prof. R. M. Harrison, Prof. A. D. Komines, Dr. T. Mark-Weiner, Mr. M. Ross, Prof. J. Rosser, Mme. M. Sacopoulo, Prof. I. Ševčenko, Prof. I. Shahid, Dr. Dorothy Shepherd, Mr. A. Stylianou, Dr. D. B. Vayiakakos, and Prof. K. Weitzmann. For their patient and perspicacious editorial attention to our manuscripts, our debt in particular to Mrs. Fanny Bonajuto, as well as to Miss Julia Warner, Mrs. Nancy Bowen, and Mrs. Mary Lou Masey, is gratefully acknowledged. Finally, we owe much to Dumbarton Oaks for support in the field, for hospitality in Washington, and for their undertaking publication of this monograph.

The approximate date of the setting of the apse mosaic of the Lythrankomi church can be determined only by comparison with other early mosaic decorations. In few cases are these closely datable from documentary sources, and several, such as the mosaics of the Salonica Rotunda, are the subject of wide differences of opinion. When first referring to them we have thought it necessary to subjoin a summary of recent views, and to indicate the chronology that we prefer and have adopted in estimating the place, in the general development, of the fragmentary mosaic here published in detail for the first time.

June, 1974   A. H. S. M.
                                                                              E. J. W. H.

Postscript

Our MS was nearly ready for the printer when Marina Sacopoulo's *La Théotokos à la mandorle de Lythrankomi* (Paris, 1975) appeared. Following an introductory description (composed without advantage of close examination), the author offers detailed argument in support of her thesis that the mosaic was conceived as an assertion of the Dual Nature doctrine in the face of Monophysite heresy, to which we have referred on page 77 f. *infra*; also, an estimate of the date of the setting of the mosaic, falling (like our own) in the second quarter of the sixth century and based on iconographic and stylistic analyses. In some respects, her inquiry has been pressed further than ours, but always with essentially the same chronological result. References to *La Théotokos à la mandorle*, as well as to certain works of other authors which appeared after this study was written, are given in the footnotes in square brackets. Whereas Mme. Sacopoulo illustrates a number of the comparanda to which we also refer, none are included in this volume; instead, available resources have been applied to illustrate fully an important monument which, at the time of writing, remains inaccessible as a result of the events of last summer.

August, 1975

Table of Contents

List of Illustrations

Frontispiece. Thomas (color)

LINECUTS

A. Sketch Plan of Carpas Peninsula
B. Section through Church, looking North
C. Plan of Church
D. Cross Section through Bema, looking East
E. Cross Section through Main Dome, looking East
F. Reconstruction of Pier-Basilica of First Restoration: a. Section, looking North; b. Cross Section through Bema, looking East; c. South Elevation; d. Cross Section through Nave, looking East
G. Composite Plan of Original Column-Basilica and Pier-Basilica
H. Plan of North Side of Bema
I. a. Intermediate Border. b. St. Polyeuktos, Border (restored) of Plaque Fragment. c. St. Apollinare, Border of Pierced Panel
J. Moldings of Original Basilica. I. Archivolt of North Window of Apse. II. Profile of Base
K. Outer Border, South Side
L. Detail of Foliage beside North Archangel's Wing
M. Central Composition, Restored
N. Alphabet of Mosaic Inscriptions
O. Facsimile of Painted Inscription

PLATE FIGURES

1. Cyprus, Lythrankomi, Panagia Kanakaria, View from South
2. South Clerestory Windows
3. View from West
4. View from Southwest
5, 6. Porch:
    5. View from Southwest
    6. Interior
7. West Gable
8. Inscription of Chrysanthos
9. West Door, Inscription on Jamb
10. View from Northwest
11. View from Northeast
12. Monastery (1970)

Abbreviations

FelRav Felix Ravenna

GBA Gazette des Beaux-Arts

IGLSyr Inscriptions Grecques et Latines de la Syrie, ed. L. Jalabert,
R. Mouterde, and Cl. Mondésert, 7 vols. (Paris, 1929–70)
ILN Illustrated London News
IRAIK Izvěstija Russkago Arheologičeskago Instituta vᶜ Konstantinopolě
IstMitt Istanbuler Mitteilungen, Deutsches Archäologisches Institut, Abteilung
Istanbul

JbAChr Jahrbuch für Antike und Christentum
JbBerlMus Jahrbuch der Berliner Museen
JbLw Jahrbuch für Liturgiewissenschaft
JdI Jahrbuch des Deutschen Archäologischen Instituts
JHS Journal of Hellenic Studies
JÖBG Jahrbuch der Österreichischen Byzantinischen Gesellschaft

Κρ.Χρον. Κρητικὰ Χρονικά
Κυπρ.Σπουδ. Κυπριακαὶ Σπουδαί

MAMA Monumenta Asiae Minoris Antiqua
Mansi J. D. Mansi, *Sacrorum Conciliorum nova et amplissima collectio*
MémInstCaire Mémoires publiés par les membres de l'Institut Français
d'Archéologie Orientale du Caire
MonPiot Monuments et Mémoires, publiés par l'Académie des Inscriptions et
Belles-Lettres, Fondation E. Piot

OCA Orientalia Christiana Analecta
OCP Orientalia Christiana Periodica
ÖJh Jahreshefte des Österreichischen Archäologischen Instituts in Wien
OrChr Oriens Christianus

PEQ Palestine Exploration Quarterly
PG Patrologiae cursus completus, Series Graeca, ed. J.-P. Migne
PO Patrologia Orientalis (Paris, 1903–   )
ProcAmPhS Proceedings of the American Philosophical Society

QDAP Quarterly of the Department of Antiquities in Palestine

RA Revue Archéologique
RAC Reallexikon für Antike und Christentum
RDAC Report of the Department of Antiquities, Cyprus
REB Revue des Etudes Byzantines
REG Revue des Etudes Grecques
*RendPontAcc Atti della Pontificia Accademia Romana di Archeologia, Rendi-
conti*
RepKunstw Repertorium für Kunstwissenschaft

RHR Revue de l'Histoire des Religions. Annales du Musée Guimet

RM Mitteilungen des Deutschen Archäologischen Instituts, Römische Abteilung

RQ Römische Quartalschrift für christliche Altertumskunde und [für] Kirchengeschichte

SBN Studi Bizantini e Neoellenici

SemKond Seminarium Kondakovianum

VizVrem Vizantijskij Vremennik

BOOKS AND ARTICLES

Ainalov, *Hellenistic Origins*: D. V. Ainalov, *The Hellenistic Origins of Byzantine Art*, trans. E. and S. Sobolevitch (New Brunswick, N.J., 1961)

Burke, "A Bronze Situla": W. L. M. Burke, "A Bronze Situla in the Museo Cristiano of the Vatican Library," *ArtB*, 12 (1930), 163–78

Ciampini, *Vetera Monumenta*: J. Ciampini, *Vetera Monumenta*, I–II (Rome, 1690–99)

Clédat, *Baouît*: J. Clédat, *Le monastère et la nécropole de Baouît*, MémInstCaire, 12, 1–2 (1904–6)

Cormack, "S. Demetrios": R. S. Cormack, "The Mosaic Decoration of S. Demetrios, Thessaloniki. A Re-examination in the Light of the Drawings of W. S. George," *BSA*, 64 (1969), 17–52

Cruikshank Dodd, *Silver Treasures*: E. Cruikshank Dodd, *Byzantine Silver Treasures* (Bern, 1973)

Deichmann, *Bauten und Mosaiken*: F. W. Deichmann, *Frühchristliche Bauten und Mosaiken in Ravenna* (Baden-Baden, 1958)

— *Geschichte*: F. W. Deichmann, *Ravenna: Geschichte und Monumente* (Wiesbaden, 1969)

Enlart, *L'art gothique*: C. Enlart, *L'art gothique et la Renaissance en Chypre*, I–II (Paris, 1899)

Forsyth-Weitzmann, *St. Catherine*: G. H. Forsyth and K. Weitzmann, *The Monastery of St. Catherine at Mount Sinai. The Church and Fortress of Justinian* (Ann Arbor, 1973)

Frantz, "Byz. Illum. Ornament": A. Frantz, "Byzantine Illuminated Ornament," *ArtB*, 16 (1934), 43–76

Galassi, "Musaici di Cipro": G. Galassi, "Musaici di Cipro e musaici di Ravenna," *FelRav*, 66 (1954), 5–37

Garrucci, *Storia*: R. Garrucci, *Storia dell'arte cristiana dei primi otto secoli della Chiesa*, I–VI (Prato, 1873–80)

Gerasa: *Gerasa, City of the Decapolis*, ed. C. H. Kraeling (New Haven, 1938)

Grabar, *Ampoules*: A. Grabar, *Ampoules de Terre Sainte (Monza-Bobbio)* (Paris, 1958)
— *Byzantium*: A. Grabar, *Byzantium, from the Death of Theodosius to the Rise of Islam* (London, 1966)
— *Iconography*: A. Grabar, *Christian Iconography, a Study of its Origins. The A. W. Mellon Lectures in the Fine Arts, 1961* (London, 1968)
— *Martyrium*: A. Grabar, *Martyrium: Recherches sur le culte des reliques et l'art chrétien antique*, I–II and album (Paris, 1943–46)
— *Sculptures*: A. Grabar, *Sculptures byzantines de Constantinople* (Paris, 1963)
Great Palace I: *The Great Palace of the Byzantine Emperors, Being a First Report on the Excavation Carried Out in Istanbul on Behalf of the Walker Trust, University of St. Andrews, 1935–1938* (Oxford, 1947)
Great Palace II: *The Great Palace of the Byzantine Emperors. Second Report*, ed. D. Talbot Rice (Edinburgh, 1958)

Hackett, *History*: J. Hackett, *A History of the Orthodox Church in Cyprus* (London, 1901)
Hill, *History*: Sir George Hill, *A History of Cyprus*, I–IV (Cambridge, 1940–52)

Ihm, *Programme*: Christa Ihm, *Die Programme der christlichen Apsismalerei vom vierten Jahrhundert bis zur Mitte des achten Jahrhunderts* (Wiesbaden, 1960)

Jeffery, *Monuments*: G. E. Jeffery, *Historic Monuments of Cyprus* (Nicosia, 1918)

Kitzinger, "Between Justinian and Iconoclasm": E. Kitzinger, "Byzantine Art in the Period between Justinian and Iconoclasm," *Berichte zum XI. Internationalen Byzantinisten-Kongress, München 1958*, IV,1 (Munich, 1958)
— *Römische Malerei*: E. Kitzinger, *Römische Malerei vom Beginn des 7. bis zur Mitte des 8. Jahrhunderts* (Diss. Munich, 1934)
Kleinbauer, "Mosaics of the Rotunda": W. E. Kleinbauer, "The Iconography and the Date of the Mosaics of the Rotunda of Hagios Georgios, Thessaloniki," *Viator*, 3 (1972), 27–107
Krautheimer, *Byz. Architecture*: R. Krautheimer, *Early Christian and Byzantine Architecture* (Harmondsworth, 1965)

Lazarev, *Istorija*: V. Lazarev, *Istorija vizantijskoj živopisi*, I (Moscow, 1947)
— *Storia*: V. Lazarev, *Storia della pittura bizantina* (Turin, 1967)
Levi, *Antioch Pavements*: D. Levi, *Antioch Mosaic Pavements*, I–II (Princeton, 1947)

Mango-Hawkins, "St. Neophytos": C. Mango and E. J. W. Hawkins, "The Hermitage of St. Neophytos and its Wall Paintings," *DOP*, 20 (1966), 119–206
Mas Latrie, *Histoire*: L. de Mas Latrie, *Histoire de l'Ile de Chypre sous le règne des Princes de la maison de Lusignan*, I–III (Paris, 1852–61)

Megaw, "Early Byz. Monuments": A. H. S. Megaw, "Early Byzantine Monuments in the Light of Recent Discoveries," *Akten des XI. Internationalen Byzantinisten-Kongresses* (Munich, 1960), 345–51

— "Vaulted Basilicas": A. H. S. Megaw, "Three Vaulted Basilicas in Cyprus," *JHS*, 66 (1948), 48–56

— "Metropolitan or Provincial?": A. H. S. Megaw, "Byzantine Architecture and Decoration in Cyprus: Metropolitan or Provincial?", *DOP* 28 (1974), 57–88

Megaw-Hawkins, "Perachorio": A. H. S. Megaw and E. J. W. Hawkins, "The Church of the Holy Apostles at Perachorio, Cyprus, and Its Frescoes," *DOP*, 16 (1962), 277–348

Megaw-Stylianou, *Mosaics and Frescoes*: *Cyprus: Byzantine Mosaics and Frescoes*, preface by A. H. S. Megaw, intro. by A. Stylianou (UNESCO World Art Series, 1963)

Orlandos, Βασιλική: A. Orlandos, Ἡ ξυλόστεγος παλαιοχριστιανικὴ βασιλικὴ τῆς μεσογειακῆς λεκάνης (Athens, 1952)

Papageorghiou, *Icons of Cyprus*: A. Papageorghiou, *Icons of Cyprus* (Paris-Geneva-Munich, 1969)

— *Masterpieces*: A. Papageorghiou, *Masterpieces of Byzantine Art in Cyprus* (Nicosia, 1965)

Peirce-Tyler, *L'art byzantin*: H. Peirce and R. Tyler, *L'art byzantin*, I–II (Paris, 1932–34)

ΠΠΔΚΣ, Β': Πρακτικὰ τοῦ πρώτου διεθνοῦς κυπρολογικοῦ συνεδρίου, 1969, Β', μεσαιωνικὸν τμῆμα (Nicosia, 1972)

Prelog, *Mosaïques de Poreč*: M. Prelog, *Les mosaïques de Poreč* (Ljubljana, 1959)

Rabbula Gospels: The Rabbula Gospels, Facsimile Edition of the Miniatures of the Syriac Manuscript Plut. I, 56 in the Medicaean-Laurentian Library, ed. and commented by C. Ceccelli, G. Furlani, and M. Salmi (Olten-Lausanne, 1959)

Rice-Gunnis, *The Icons of Cyprus*: D. and T. Talbot Rice and R. Gunnis, *The Icons of Cyprus* (London, 1937)

Sacopoulo, *La Théotokos à la mandorle*: M. Sacopoulo, *La Théotokos à la mandorle de Lythrankomi* (Paris, 1975)

Saqqara II: J. E. Quibell, *Excavations at Saqqara (1906–1907)* (Cairo, 1908)

Saqqara III: J. E. Quibell, *Excavations at Saqqara (1907–1908)* (Cairo, 1909)

Saqqara IV: J. E. Quibell, *Excavations at Saqqara (1908–1909, 1909–1910): The Monastery of Apa Jeremias* (Cairo, 1912)

Shepherd, "Tapestry Panel": Dorothy Shepherd, "An Icon of the Virgin: a Sixth-Century Tapestry Panel from Egypt," *The Bulletin of the Cleveland Museum of Art*, 56 (1969), 90–120

Smirnov, "Mozaiki": Ja. I. Smirnov, "Hristianskija mozaiki Kipra," *VizVrem*, 4 (1897), 1–93

Soteriou, Μνημεῖα: G. A. Soteriou, Τὰ βυζαντινὰ μνημεῖα τῆς Κύπρου, Α' (Athens, 1935)

Stylianou, *Painted Churches*: A. and J. A. Stylianou, *The Painted Churches of Cyprus* (Cyprus, 1964)

Torp, *Mosaikkene*: H. Torp, *Mosaikkene i St. Georg-Rotunden i Thessaloniki* (Oslo, 1963)

Van Berchem-Clouzot, *Mosaïques*: M. van Berchem and E. Clouzot, *Mosaïques chrétiennes du IV*[me] *au X*[me] *siècle* (Geneva, 1924)

Volbach, *Elfenbeinarbeiten*: W. F. Volbach, *Elfenbeinarbeiten der Spätantike und des frühen Mittelalters* (Mainz, 1952)

Volbach-Hirmer, *E. C. Art*: W. F. Volbach and Max Hirmer, *Early Christian Art* (London, 1961)

Wellen, *Theotokos*: G. A. Wellen, *Theotokos* (Utrecht-Antwerp, 1961)

Wilpert, *MM*: J. W. Wilpert, *Die römischen Mosaiken und Malereien der kirchlichen Bauten vom IV. bis XIII. Jahrhundert*, I–IV (Freiburg im Breisgau, 1916–19)

Xyngopoulos, Καθολικὸν: A. Xyngopoulos, Τὸ καθολικὸν τῆς μονῆς τοῦ λατόμου ἐν Θεσσαλονίκῃ καὶ τὸ ἐν αὐτῇ ψηφιδωτόν, in 'Αρχ.Δελτ., 12 (1929), 142–80

THE CHURCH OF THE PANAGIA KANAKARIÁ
AT LYTHRANKOMI IN CYPRUS

ITS MOSAICS AND FRESCOES

INTRODUCTION

The church of the Panagia Kanakaria adjoins the village of Lythrankomi in the Carpas peninsula (fig. A). The church and the substantial fragments it preserves from an early mosaic apse decoration were first studied by the Russian scholar Jakov Smirnov, who visited Cyprus in 1895. He had gone there in search of Byzantine mosaics, prompted by the inclusion of a Cypriot example in a ninth-century catalogue of wonder-working images. This purports to be part of the proceedings of a synod held by the three Eastern patriarchs, which were communicated to the iconoclast Emperor Theophilus.[1] Two years later Smirnov published an account of the Lythrankomi and Kiti churches and their mosaics.[2] He overlooked the third of the fragmentary apse mosaics surviving in Cyprus, preserved in the small church of Panagia tis Kyras near Livadia.[3] Since then, the mosaic in the Panagia Kanakaria has been discussed, or referred to, by a number of other scholars;[4] but in no case has a detailed study been attempted, such as Theodor Šmit devoted to that in the Panagia Angeloktistos at Kiti.[5]

After the Second World War, when the Archbishopric and the Antiquities Department of the Government of Cyprus undertook the systematic repair of the church, opportunities occurred for a closer examination of the structure

---

[1] See Appendix.

[2] Smirnov, "Mozaiki," 27–93. An abbreviated Greek translation by Arsenios Deliyannis was published in installments entitled Χριστιανικὰ μωσαϊκὰ τῆς Κύπρου, in Ἐκκλησιαστικὸς Κήρυξ (Larnaca, 1911), 43ff., 277ff., and 737ff. Brief notices of the church and its mosaic, without illustrations, had previously appeared: G. S. Frankoudis, Κύπρις (Athens, 1890), 411ff.; A. A. Sakellariou, Τὰ Κυπριακά, I (Athens, 1890), 106f.

[3] Cf. G. E. Jeffery, "Byzantine Churches in Cyprus," *Proceedings of the Society of Antiquaries of London*, 28 (1915–16), 123; *idem, Monuments*, 25; R. Gunnis, *Historic Cyprus* (London, 1936), 328; A. H. S. Megaw, *CARDA*, 1961, p. 13 and fig. 28; A. Papageorghiou, Ἡ παλαιοχριστιανικὴ καὶ βυζαντινὴ τέχνη τῆς Κύπρου, in *Ἀ.Β.*, 27 (1966), 167 and fig. 10; A. H. S. Megaw and E. J. W. Hawkins, "A Fragmentary Mosaic of the Orant Virgin in Cyprus," *Actes du XIVᵉ Congrès International des Etudes Byzantines, 1971*, III (Bucharest, 1976), 363–66.

[4] E. K. Redin, *Mozaiki Ravennskih cerkvej*, Zapiski Imp. Russkogo Arheologičeskogo Obščestva, 9. Trudy Otdelenija Arheologii Drevne-Klass. Vizant. i Zapadno-evrop., 2 (St. Petersburg, 1897), 262; E. Dobbert, in *RepKunstw*, 21 (1898), 105; Enlart, *L'art gothique*, I, 401–3; D. V. Ainalov, *Ellenističeskija osnovy vizantijskago iskusstva*, Zapiski Imp. Russ. Arh. Ob., 12. Trudy Otd. Arh. Drevne-Klass. Vizant. i Zapadno-evrop., 5 (St. Petersburg, 1901), 187f.; *idem, Hellenistic Origins*, 244; G. Millet, "L'art byzantin," in André Michel, *Histoire de l'art*, I (Paris, 1905), 170; C. Diehl, *Manuel d'art byzantin* (Paris, 1910), 190; O. M. Dalton, *Byzantine Art and Archaeology* (London, 1911), 367, 384–87; Th. I. Šmit, Παναγία Ἀγγελόκτιστος, in *IRAIK*, 15 (1911), 219; O. Wulff, *Altchristliche und byzantinische Kunst*, II (Berlin, 1914), 432, 553, and fig. 369; N. P. Kondakov, *Ikonografija Bogomateri*, I (St. Petersburg, 1914), 240–42; II (1915), 316f.; Jeffery, "Byzantine Churches," 118; *idem, Monuments*, 261ff.; O. M. Dalton, *East Christian Art* (London, 1925), 283f.; E. Weigand, in *BZ*, 32 (1932), 68; O. Wulff, *Bibliogr.-kritischer Nachtrag zu Altchr. und byz. Kunst* (Potsdam, n. d. [1935]), 73 (note to p. 553); G. A. Soteriou, Τὰ παλαιοχριστιανικὰ καὶ βυζαντινὰ μνημεῖα τῆς Κύπρου, in Πρακτικὰ τῆς Ἀκαδημίας Ἀθηνῶν, 1931, pp. 478, 487; *idem, Μνημεῖα*, pl. 61; Gunnis, *Historic Cyprus*, 332; S. Bettini, *La pittura bizantina. I mosaici*, I (Florence, 1939), 44; Grabar, *Martyrium*, II (Paris, 1946), 229; Lazarev, *Istorija*, 60.

[5] Šmit, Παναγία Ἀγγελόκτιστος, 206–39.

and its decoration.[6] Of these the writers were able to take advantage over a period of several years. It fell to Megaw, as head of the Department, to direct the work, which in 1950 exposed a substantial area of the mosaic previously concealed.[7] Provisional cleaning and consolidation of the mosaic by the Department's staff followed in 1952,[8] and thorough repair of the apse in 1954.[9] Hawkins completed the conservation of the mosaic during visits to Cyprus in 1952, 1961, and 1966, by arrangement with the Byzantine Institute and Dumbarton Oaks. After initial experiments in the presentation of the bare plaster in the lost areas,[10] he finalized their treatment in 1970 and took the photographs used in this publication.

During the consolidation and cleaning of the mosaic no part of it was removed from the structure. Occasionally, during cleaning of the tesserae, a few of them found loose were reset in the sockets they had formed in the plaster bed. No trace of any earlier cleaning or restoration was observed. Consequently, where it is preserved, the mosaic remains in its first state, retaining the texture of the original setting. The surviving areas have suffered some deterioration through the flaking off of the gold and silver caps from a number of the glass tesserae representing these colors, which now give instead a dark, almost black tone. Elsewhere, the coloring has been lost as a result of the erosion of the pigments with which a number of white marble and stone tesserae were originally tinted, in order to provide colors not otherwise available. Despite these defects and the disappearance of large areas, the composition and character of the decoration are not in doubt.

[6] Damage caused by an earthquake in 1941 had earlier led to the insertion of concealed reinforced concrete collars round the dome and the east end. In 1949 this system was extended to the west end in conjunction with other repairs; *CARDA*, 1949, p. 12.

[7] *CARDA*, 1950, p. 12 and fig. 26; A. H. S. Megaw, "The Mosaics in the Church of Panagia Kanakaria in Cyprus," *Atti dell'VIII Congresso internazionale di Studi bizantini, Palermo 1951* (= *SBN*, 8) (Rome, 1953), 199f.

The illustration of the border of medallions containing busts of the Apostles, for the first time in these publications, was followed by some further discussion of our mosaic; Galassi, "Musaici di Cipro," 5–37; A. Grabar, "The Virgin in a Mandorla of Light," *Late Classical and Mediaeval Studies in Honor of Albert Mathias Friend, Jr.* (Princeton, 1955), 307; A. H. S. Megaw, "Early Byzantine Art in Cyprus," Κυπριακὰ Γράμματα, 21 (1956), 175; A. Amman, *La pittura sacra bizantina* (Rome, 1957), 40–42; Megaw, "Early Byz. Monuments," 348; *idem*, in *EUA*, III (1958), col. 67; Ihm, *Programme*, 59f., 188f.; Wellen, *Theotokos*, 153; Megaw-Stylianou, *Mosaics and Frescoes*, 6, 11f., pls. I–II; Stylianou, *Painted Churches*, 23–27; Papageorghiou, *Masterpieces*, 10–12 and pls. IV–V; Grabar, *Byzantium*, 135; Papageorghiou, Ἡ παλαιοχριστιανικὴ καὶ βυζαντινὴ τέχνη (*supra*, note 3), 167 and fig. 9; Lazarev, *Storia*, 86 and figs. 64 and 65; D. I. Pallas, article Ψηφιδωτά, in Θρησκευτικὴ καὶ ᾿Ηθικὴ ᾿Εγκυκλοπαιδεία, 12 (Athens, 1968), cols. 1160–63; Maria Soteriou, Βυζαντιναὶ τοιχογραφίαι μοναστικῆς τέχνης τῆς Κύπρου, in ΠΠΔΚΣ, Β΄, 244–47; Megaw, "Metropolitan or Provincial?", 73f.; G. Matthiae, "Mosaici di Cipro," *CorsiRav* (1972), 253–65; Silvia Pasi, in *FelRav*, fasc. 105–6 (1973), 150f., 161ff.

[8] This "first-aid" was carried out by Elias Markou and Kakoulis Georghiou. They also assisted Hawkins during his initial visit.

There is no foundation for the belief that the mosaic is now preserved in the Nicosia Museum (cf. Wellen, *Theotokos*, 153). Two small sections of the outer border found detached were taken to the Museum in 1961, in preference to reattaching them to the structure at a point not visible from the floor.

[9] *CARDA*, 1954, p. 12.

[10] First, on uncolored plaster, with painted outlines linking the preserved sections of mosaic: cf. *CARDA*, 1961, p. 13 and fig. 2; Megaw-Stylianou, *Mosaics and Frescoes*, pls. I and II; Papageorghiou, *Masterpieces*, pl. V,2. Secondly, gold-toned plaster with missing features indicated by pale tones of flat color; e.g., our pl. 80. Finally, dotted outlines only on a plain ground.

During his later work Hawkins was assisted by Costas Zaferiades (1966), subsequently by Yiannis Makrides, and throughout by Christos Tsourtsos.

By contrast, the architecture of the church itself has been confused by numerous drastic restorations. Since it is of some interest and since the published plans have added further confusion,[11] the present account and discussion of the mosaic are preceded by a description of the building and an analysis of its structural history. Also included is a summary account of the remains of fresco decoration in various parts of the building. They are ill-preserved and relatively late in date, but they are helpful at several points in clarifying the structural vicissitudes of the church. It remains to sketch the historical background to these in the light of the few references to the name Kanakaria in documentary sources.

The church and the scant remains of the monastery which it once served stand in open country on the north side of the branch road by which Lythran-komi and other villages on the southward slope of the Carpas are reached (fig. A).[12] In its original form, the church is likely to have served an Early Christian successor to the ancient settlement on the ridge to the north.[13] To that Christian settlement the structures observed by Hogarth to the east of the church could well have belonged.[14] Its remains provided a handy source of stone for the numerous restorations of the church, to judge by reused blocks such as that at the northeast corner with the mortar-grip channels cut on its exposed bed (fig. 20).

The settlement, which was some three miles from the coast, evidently survived the initial Arab incursions of the mid-seventh century, if we may judge by the reconstruction of the initial basilica in a style of architecture to be associated with the "dark ages" that followed. After the treaty of 688 between Justinian II and Abd-el-Malik, by which Cyprus was neutralized, the Island lay beyond effective imperial jurisdiction. This condition prevented enforcement of the iconoclast edicts, and to this we owe the survival, in varying states of preservation, of the three early apse decorations in the Island.

A second restoration of the church, when a dome was added, attests revival of the community some time after the reestablishment of Byzantine rule in the Island (965). There are structural reasons to place this restoration in the twelfth century, a period of relative prosperity in Cyprus with much church

---

[11] Smirnov, "Mozaiki," 68; Enlart, *L'art gothique*, I, 402, fig. 268; Soteriou, Μνημεῖα, fig. 20.

[12] This branch road follows the line of an old carriage road along the peninsula to Rizokarpaso. It parts at Leonarisso from the new main road which proceeds through Ayios Andronikos to Yialousa and along the north coast (see fig. A).

[13] On this site, known to him as "Kafkalia," see E. Gjerstad, in Κυπριακὰ Χρονικά, 2 (1924), 250. He also reported a Bronze Age cemetery in the same area at "Chalasmata": *Studies in Prehistoric Cyprus* (Uppsala, 1926), 10.
The remains in this area known to A. A. Sakellarios as Ἄκρη were tentatively identified by him with the place of that name in Cyprus listed by Stephanus of Byzantium (Τὰ Κυπριακὰ [*supra*, note 2], I, 106f.); but for this there is a better candidate on the coast. Alternatively, the settlement which the church served may be identifiable with Erythra, Ἐρυθρὰ κώμη, from which S. Menardos derived Lythrankomi (Τοπωνυμικὸν τῆς Κύπρου, in Ἀθηνᾶ, 18 [1906], 348). The recorded distance of Erythra from Salamis-Constantia seems to fit (cf. Chr. J. Pantelides, in Κυπριακὰ Χρονικά, 2 [1924], 178f.).

[14] D. G. Hogarth, *Devia Cypria* (London, 1889), 71f. These remains have disappeared in subsequent leveling. Others of Late Roman to Early Byzantine date have lately been recorded in the same area, "northwest of Lythrankomi" (Papageorghiou, in ᾿Α.Β., 28 [1967], 349).

building, reflecting the island's new strategic importance following the inroads of the Seljuks in Asia Minor and the foundation of the Crusader States. But it is not until well after the establishment of the Latins in Cyprus itself (1191) that we find any written references to Kanakaria.

The place must have been well known under this name in the early fifteenth century, if not earlier. It is used in the *Chronicle* of Makhairas as a point of reference to locate the village of Ayios Andronikos in the same neighborhood, where the tomb of St. Photeini was discovered: εἰς τὴν Ἀκροτίκην εἰς τὴν κώμην τοῦ ἁγίου Ἀνδρονίκου τῆς Κανακαρίας.[15] A Paris MS preserves the same formula in a marginal note recording the burning of Ayios Andronikos by Turkish raiders in 1451.[16] By this time Kanakaria, like nearby Lythrankomi, was a *casal* of the Lusignan Royal Domain. They are separately listed in the inventory of its possessions in the anonymous *Relatione del regno di Cipro* compiled for the Venetian Government some years after it had secured the Island in 1489.[17] Both villages are also separately named on some of the earliest detailed maps of Cyprus.[18]

---

[15] Leontios Makhairas, § 34, ed. R. M. Dawkins (Oxford, 1932), I, 32. Kanakaria is here named in order to distinguish this village of Ayios Andronikos (which is about four miles distant from it to the northwest) from the other villages of the same name in Cyprus. The Venice recension of the *Chronicle* was probably written by Makhairas about 1426 (ed. Dawkins, II, 16). But in this section the version of the *Chronicle* which he followed was probably using the earlier Pseudo-Cyriac, a Cypriot hagiographic source of which a sixteenth-century extract in the British Museum MS 34554 preserves the subject matter of Makhairas, §§ 8, 9, 30, 31, and 32. If the continuation of this hagiographical excursus, where Kanakaria is mentioned (also the cure of Peter I at Meniko), derives from the same source (cf. R. M. Dawkins, "On a Hagiographical Source used by Leontios Makhairas," Κυπριακά Χρονικά, 11 [1935], 22), the currency of the name can be put back at least to the late fourteenth century.

In a parallel passage, Florio Bustron, who used the same sources as Makhairas, has: *Al Carpasso, cioè al casal Coma fu trovata una Santa Photini ...* (*Chronique de l'île de Chypre*, ed. R. de Mas Latrie, in *Mélanges historiques*, V, Collection de documents inédits sur l'histoire de France [Paris, 1886], 34). The words "of St. Andronicos of Kanakaria" evidently dropped out of his text after *Coma*.

On Ἀκροτίκην (Ἀκροτικήν in § 448), see Dawkins' note 1 on Makhairas, § 34 (*op. cit.*, II, 65). With the reference to this place in § 654, compare *Avrotichia* in the corresponding passage in Strambaldi (*Chroniques d'Amadi et de Strambaldi*, ed. R. de Mas Latrie, II, Collection de documents inédits sur l'histoire de France, 1ᵉ série. Histoire politique [Paris, 1893], 269 and note 4, where Ἀκροτήρι is presumed).

[16] τον αγιον Αδρονικον τις Κανακαριας, in Paris MS 1626, fol. 75 (J. Darrouzès, in Κυπρ.Σπουδ., 23 [1959], 43 f., no. 52).

[17] Venice, Bibl. Marciana, MS Contarini Q2. Misc. no. 11 (Mas Latrie, *Histoire*, III, 508). Sir George Hill pointed out that the *Relatione* must have been written between 1510 and 1521 (*History*, III, 765 note 1). A Greek translation of a version of this document copied by Franco Bustron in 1533 was published by N. G. Kyriazis, in Κυπριακά Χρονικά, 13 (1937), pp. 4–44, with the same list of casals in the bailiwick of Carpasia on p. 38.

Canacharia should not be equated with Karcha (which was sold to Filippo Mistachiel *ca.* 1464–68, according to Florio Bustron) as has been suggested (Smirnov, "Mozaiki," 67). The village of Karcha is situated on the north slope of Mt. Yaila.

[18] Most of the printed maps which show both villages derive from Ortelius' double folio copper-plate *Cypri insulae nova descript* (Antwerp, 1573); but this was itself copied from a now rare Venetian map engraved by Iacomo Franco about 1570, on which both "Canacaria" and "Setracomi" appear in similar positions and in the same spelling as on the later maps (A. and J. Stylianou, "An Important Venetian Map of Cyprus," Κυπρ.Σπουδ., 34 [1970], 145–58; A. Stylianou, "The Old Cartography of Cyprus," ΠΠΔΚΣ, Β′, 237 ff.). The information on these maps issued at the time of the Turkish conquest would have been taken from earlier sources. In fact, Kanakaria may be concealed in the name "Caldaria" in a more or less appropriate position on Matteo Pagano's woodcut *Isola di Cipro* (Venice, 1538); also on its derivatives: G. F. Camocio's copperplate map (Venice, 1566), and Ortelius' first map of the Island, in *Theatrum orbis terrarum* (Antwerp, 1570).

There is no documentary indication of the status of the church itself under the Lusignans, as distinct from the village and surrounding lands to which it gave its name. According to local tradition, the church was once shared by Orthodox and Catholics. It is perhaps significant that the south aisle was reconstructed in more substantial masonry datable, as we shall see, to the early years of Frankish rule. Latin chapels in otherwise Orthodox churches were not uncommon in rural areas of Cyprus under the Lusignans.[19]

The third restoration, which left the church in its present state in all essentials, followed the gradual recovery of the Greek Church in Cyprus during the fifteenth century as the fortunes of the Lusignans declined and the Frankish nobility and clergy dwindled. The Venetian takeover accelerated this recovery, and this final restoration of the Panagia Kanakaria takes its place among much rebuilding or repair of Greek churches in the early years of Venetian rule. It was in this restoration that the lunette over the south door received a fresco of the Virgin and Child labeled "the Mother of God, the *Kanakaria*" (fig. 128).

Under the Venetians the Royal Domain remained in existence, though many of the villages were sold to raise money.[20] There is some indication that by about 1540 Lythrankomi had been sold, but not Kanakaria.[21] However, even if the status of the latter remained unchanged until the Turkish conquest in 1570–71, the church and the *casal* would most probably have passed at that juncture into the hands of the revived Orthodox diocese of Famagusta. Here as elsewhere, following the extermination of the Latins, the Greeks could exploit the dispensations under which they were allowed in most cases to retain their churches and to recover their ecclesiastical properties.[22] The monastery may have been established at this time.

Early in the seventeenth century, when the see of Famagusta was suppressed upon the reestablishment of that of Kyrenia, the monastery would have passed to the jurisdiction of the Archdiocese. It survived as an active monastery until the late eighteenth century, to judge by the inscription of 1779 over the west door in which Chrysanthos is styled "Monk and Abbot," and by an entry made the following year in the property register of the Archbishopric recording repairs to "the church and rooms."[23] Kanakaria is included among the

---

[19] The Panagia Angeloktistos at Kiti provides a good example: Enlart, *L'art gothique*, II, 440f.

[20] Hill, *History*, III, 777f.

[21] The catalogue of villages in Cyprus extracted from a MS entitled *Trattato del Regno di Cipro*, formerly in the Library of G. Leimonides, which was published in Greek translation by N. G. Kyriazis (in Κυπριακὰ Χρονικά, 13 [1937], 51f.), lists in Carpasia 44 casals, including Lythrankomi, and 12 *prastii*. Seven of the casals appearing among the possessions of the Royal Bailiwick in the *Relatione* (see *supra*, note 17), including Kanakaria, and two of the *prastii* are not mentioned in this *Trattato*. It seems probable that when the latter was composed these still formed part of the *Dominio*, as the Venetians called it, and that the author was listing only villages outside it. As to the date, it seems probable from Kyriazis' description that the Leimonides MS is a version of the compilation of Francesco Attar, which is datable *ca.* 1540 (Mas Latrie, *Histoire*, III, 493 note 1. His extracts do not include the catalogue of villages).

[22] Hill, *History*, IV, 308–10.

[23] Fol. 1079, under the year 1780, quoted N. G. Kyriazis, Τὰ μοναστήρια ἐν Κύπρῳ (Larnaca, 1950), 122.

monasteries under the jurisdiction of the Archbishopric in the list published in 1788 by the Archimandrite Kyprianos.[24] Indeed, it continued to be described officially as a "monastery" into the present century,[25] though Smirnov in 1895 observed that the monks had long since departed. From the mid-nineteenth century, if not earlier, its lands have been leased as a farm, originally to individual monks and latterly to lay tenants.[26] While the village of Kanakaria disappeared, that of nearby Lythrankomi survived and, although it had a smaller church of its own, it took over the Panagia Kanakaria as its principal parish church.[27] In conseqence the "monastery" has sometimes been referred to as the *Panagia tou Lythrankomou*.[28]

Smirnov and Enlart observed what the latter calls a "trône pontifical en pierre" at the back of the main apse,[29] and local tradition asserts that the church was once the seat of a bishop. This tradition can hardly be connected with the Orthodox prelate who under the Lusignans was subordinated to the Latin bishop of Famagusta and obliged to live in "Carpasia."[30] For it is usually assumed that he resided at Rizokarpaso, the successor settlement to the ancient city of Carpasia. Furthermore, at a time when the *casal* of Kanakaria formed part of the Lusignan Royal Domain it could hardly have been the seat of an Orthodox bishop. For the Byzantine period there is no record of any bishopric in the Carpas other than Carpasia itself. Consequently, the supposed episcopal character of the Panagia Kanakaria must have arisen simply from the survival until the present century of the throne in the apse. We shall see that this feature probably derives from the initial arrangement of the apse at a date when such thrones in apses were not restricted to bishops' churches.

As to the name *Kanakaria*, Menardos, who gave the dialect version Κανακαρκά, grouped it among names deriving from images of the Theotokos with special characteristics, but he went no further.[31] Smirnov was mistaken in believing

[24] Archimandrite Kyprianos, Ἱστορία χρονογραφικὴ τῆς νήσου Κύπρου (Venice, 1788), 392; p. 584 in the Nicosia edition of 1902.

[25] Hackett, *History*, 365. Hackett was in Cyprus in the nineties. Elsewhere (p. 331) he includes Kanakaria in his list of suppressed monasteries leased to monks or priests who cultivated their properties.

[26] Kyriazis (Τὰ μοναστήρια ἐν Κύπρῳ, 122) quotes a three-year lease to the monk Gregory signed by Archbishop Cyril on December 1, 1852. C. P. Kyrris has located other documents of this sort concerning the "monastery" of Kanakaria in the archives of the Archbishopric, which he plans to publish.

The change in status may have occurred before 1815 to judge by inscriptions of that year on icons in the screen of the church: of Athanasios, *exarchos* of the Archbishopric, on the icon of the Theotokos; of John, monk and *epistates*, on two others.

[27] Already in 1895: Smirnov, "Mozaiki," 67.

[28] Hogarth, *Devia Cypria* (*supra*, note 14), 71f.

[29] Enlart, *L'art gothique*, I, 402. The throne is shown on Smirnov's plan, approached by a broad flight of straight steps (Smirnov, "Mozaiki," 68) and was seen in 1914 (Jeffery, *Monuments*, 263), but it was subsequently removed. The steps and throne shown in our figure G have been copied from Smirnov's plan, which is also the basis for their reconstruction in section and elevation in figure F.

[30] The reduction of the Orthodox hierarchy to four subordinates of the four Latin bishops was instituted in 1222, when the places where they were to have their seats were also fixed. In accordance with these repressive measures, we find a bishop "Joachim de Carpasio" accompanying Germanos Pesimandros in 1260 on his mission to Pope Alexander IV, a mission which provoked confirmation of the measures in the *Bulla Cypria* (Mansi, XXIII, cols. 1037–46; Hackett, *History* 114f.; Hill, *History*, III, 1058ff.).

[31] Menardos, Τοπωνυμικὸν τῆς Κύπρου (*supra*, note 13), 381.

the root alien to the Greek language,[32] for κανάκι is a known Byzantine word for *caress*,[33] which survives in Cyprus as κανάτζιν,[34] and this offers an acceptable derivation. For the common suffix -άρις makes κανακαρέα in the Byzantine feminine form, whence κανακαρία of the earliest record of the name, in the *Chronicle* of Makhairas. Commenting on this passage, Dawkins evidently had in mind the primary meaning of κανακάρης, -άρισσα in modern Greek: *beloved*;[35] for he translates: *darling*.[36] In this derivation the sense is rather *the Theotokos who caresses (the Child)*, which matches such better-known titles of the Virgin as the *Glykophilousa*. "The Kanakariá" would thus belong to the class of titles denoting qualities of the Theotokos, which, after those originating in place-names, is the commonest in Cyprus.[37] It is no impediment to this interpretation that *Kanakaria* is so rare.[38] And if it is argued that a title appropriate to an affectionate pose marries ill with the ceremonious *Hodegetria* formula which it accompanies in the lunette fresco, it must be remembered that types and titles are notoriously liable to confusion and that in any case the title *Kanakaria* is demonstrably older than the fresco. Initially it may have been attached to some portative icon representing the Virgin and Child quite differently, and different also from the existing principal icon of the church, which is treasured as a rainmaker.[39]

Four other explanations of the name have been put forward:

I. Smirnov noted the occurrence of the place-name *Canacar* in Syria.[40] The transplantation of a Syrian name is plausible, since migration from the mainland to Cyprus is well attested under both the Byzantines and

---

[32] "Mozaiki," 65 f.

[33] F. Du Cange, *Glossarium ad Scriptores mediae et infimae Graecitatis* (Lyons, 1688), *s.v.* κανάκι.

[34] Sakellariou, Τὰ Κυπριακά, II (Athens, 1891), 572; P. Xioutas, in Κύπρ.Σπουδ., 1 (1937), 135 f., where he uses it to give the explanation of *Kanakaria* here preferred.

[35] The secondary meaning *only son* or *only daughter* is equally unhelpful. Κανακάρης also occurs in Greece today as a family name.

[36] Makhairas, ed. Dawkins, II, 65, note 2 on § 34.

[37] C. Spyridakis, in Κύπρ.Σπουδ., 7 (1943), 4. The Byzantine feminine ending survives also in Πορταρέα, a homonym for the Πορταΐτισσα: Ph. Koukoules, Ἐπίθετα τινὰ τῆς Θεοτόκου, in Ἡμερολόγιον τῆς Μεγάλης Ἑλλάδος (1932), 438.

[38] For a chapel τῆς Κανακαρκᾶς at Akanthou, see N. Kyriazis, Ναοὶ καὶ παρεκκλήσια καὶ ἐπώνυμα τῆς Παναγίας ἐν Κύπρῳ, in Πάφος, 10 (1945), 136. No other occurrence of the title in Cyprus is mentioned in similar published lists, e.g., Timotheos P. Themelis, Αἱ ἐπονομίαι τῆς Παναγίας ἐν Κύπρῳ (Jerusalem, 1926); M. Christofides, Τὰ ἐπώνυμα τῆς Παναγίας ἐν Κύπρῳ, in Κυπριακὰ Γράμματα, 14 (1949), 92 ff.; N. Kyriazis, Ἐπώνυμα τῆς Παναγίας (Larnaca, 1950).
Nor has the title been traced in Greece, though we have not had access to some items in D. B. Vayiakakos' long bibliography covering the period 1833–1962 ([Athens, 1966], 193 f.). No use of it by the hymnographers was recorded by S. Eustratiades, Ἡ Θεοτόκος ἐν τῇ ὑμνογραφίᾳ (Paris, 1930). The long list of titles of the Panagia published by Timotheos, Bishop of Jordan, suggests that *Kanakaria* was restricted to Cyprus (Μεγ. Ἑλλ. Ἐγκυλοπαίδεια², 19 [Athens, 1932], 496 f.).

[39] Cf. Rice-Gunnis, *The Icons of Cyprus*, 170. It is still customary to take the principal icon to the sea in times of drought, not only in Lythrankomi and neighboring villages in the Carpas but also in other coastal areas of Cyprus.
The present icon of the Theotokos is an Italianate panel named "The Kanakaria." It follows the mosaic rather than the lunette fresco so named in portraying the Child frontally on Mary's lap. It bears an inscription of Athanasios, Exarch of the Archbishopric, and the date 1815.

[40] Smirnov, "Mozaiki," 66 note 1, quoting Eutychius of Alexandria, *Annales*, trans. E. Pocock (Oxford, 1658), II, 491, whence PG, 111, col. 1146. *Kanâkar* in the original Arabic text, ed. L. Cheikho, II (Beirut, 1909), 75.

the Lusignans,[41] in particular the settlement of Maronites, before the Frankish conquest and initially in the Carpas.[42] Other place-names in this part of Cyprus, such as Kantara, have been regarded as importations by Arabic-speaking immigrants.[43] But it is doubtful if Smirnov would have made this suggestion if he had referred to Du Cange.

2. Smirnov rejected a derivation from the Turkish *kan* (blood) + *akar* (flowing), which was suggested to him by the monk who was tenant of Kanakaria at the time of his visit in 1895. This was doubtless inspired by the story of a mosaic of the Theotokos in Cyprus from which blood miraculously flowed when an Arab weapon struck it (see Appendix).[44] For the monk produced his copy of the 1885 edition of the *Thesaurus* of Damaskenos of Thessaloniki and pointed out to Smirnov the version of the story which that work contains.[45] He would have been proud to attach to his church a miracle which is only vaguely localized, "in the south part" of the Island, and he was probably the originator of the local "tradition" which in a variety of forms connects it with the Lythrankomi church. The earliest version we know was published in 1890,[46] after the appearance of the first modern edition of the *Thesaurus* and only a few years before Smirnov's visit. Enlart was evidently given the same explanation when he visited the church only a few months after Smirnov,[47] and it has since been given further currency.[48]

This derivation is improbable for a place-name current in Cyprus well before the Turkish conquest, when there can have been few Turkish speakers in the neighborhood apart from occasional Turcopole mercenaries; it lacks the support of any independent indication that the story of the wonderworking mosaic concerns the Lythrankomi church; and even if the story current in the ninth century could be attached to it, this might have given rise at that time to a Greek name such as τοξευθεῖσα or even an Arabic equivalent, but not conceivably a Turkish.

3. Pharmakides rejected this popular explanation and, recognizing the Byzantine character of the church, suggested a derivation from the name of some illustrious but now forgotten founder, Kanakaris.[49] But

---

[41] A massive migration of fugitives from Arab persecution in 813 is recorded in Theophanes, a. M. 6305 (Bonn ed., 778f.; ed. de Boor, 499). Cf. Hill, *History*, I, 292.

[42] Hill, *History*, I, 305, and II, 3.

[43] *Ibid.*, I, 272 note 1.

[44] Smirnov, "Mozaiki," 66, note 1.

[45] *Ibid.*, 11.

[46] Frankoudis, Κύπρις (*supra*, note 2), 411f. In this version, the story is moved to the early years of Turkish rule, the mosaic becomes an icon, and the church is built to commemorate the miracle!

[47] Cf. "Notre-Dame Sanglante," in Enlart, *L'art gothique*, I, 401. The rendering "Bleeding Heart" must originate in the same derivation: Themelis, Αἱ ἐπονομίαι τῆς Παναγίας ἐν Κύπρῳ, 22.

[48] Kyriazis, Τα μοναστήρια ἐν Κύπρῳ (*supra*, note 23), 122; Stylianou, *Painted Churches*, 27; A. I. Dikigoropoulos, "The Church of Cyprus during the Period of the Arab Wars," *The Greek Orthodox Theological Review*, 11 (1965–66), 270 note 161.

[49] X. P. Pharmakides, Κυπριακά σκηνογραφήματα (Famagusta, 1922), 65. His version of the tradition still concerns a Turk but is closer in some other respects to the account of the miracle in Damaskenos, which he quotes verbatim (p. 67).

it is hazardous to project this contemporary Greek family name back to the Byzantine period.

4. Papacharalambos, on the other hand, preferred a derivation from καμουχᾶς, the name for a patterned woven fabric which he says was formerly used to cover precious icons. He presumes an intermediary καμουχαρκά.[50] This suggestion has found no favor.

---

[50] G. Papacharalambous, Ἡ μονὴ Μαχαιρᾶ καὶ Κανακαριᾶς, ἡ παραγωγὴ τῆς ἐπωνυμίας των, in Κυπριακὰ Χρονικά, 10 (1934), 311.

PART ONE

The Church and Its Structural History[51]

THE EXTERIOR

A forecourt precedes the church, entered not from the road, but from the west through a wide gateway in a crumbling wall. It is closed on the south side by a two-storey building of traditional Cypriot style, of which the western end is now ruinous (fig. 12). Below are stone-built stables and storerooms opening off a covered portico behind an arcade of low, pointed arches; in two cases the arches are carried on large, reused limestone bases, cut down to fit their present positions (fig. 15). Above, and reached by an external staircase, are the main rooms with walls of plastered masonry and a flat mud roof. On the opposite, northern side of the forecourt and on higher ground a few ruinous structures of one storey complete the surviving ancillary buildings. But at many points traces of other, earlier structures can be seen, including some suggestive of a range of rooms along the west side of the forecourt and of a predecessor of the arcade on the south. To the east the church stands alone, surrounded by a modest burial ground, now disused, which can also be entered directly from the road through an opening in its enclosure wall. This has long been a normal approach to the church, for it opens opposite a domed porch outside the south door (fig. 1).[52] The semicircular lunette above this door preserves, thanks to the protection of the porch, a fresco of the Theotokos holding the Christ Child on her left arm and inscribed Μή(τη)ρ | Θ(εο)ῦ ‖ ἡ Κανα|καρηᾶ (fig. 128).[53] The domical vault of the porch is carried on pendentives and semicircular arches supported on four columns with crude cushion capitals (figs. 5 and 6). The two inner shafts stand on stone capitals, which were exposed during Mr. Papageorghiou's investigations in 1966 (fig. 16). The other two are engaged on their outer sides to piers of masonry.[54]

For the rest, the south wall is featureless. Its rather rough coursed masonry gives place to large ashlar blocks at the entrance and at the two extremities.

---

[51] Observations made by Megaw in the course of conservation work up to 1959 and during subsequent visits with Hawkins are here incorporated; also the results of A. Papageorghiou's later investigations as recorded in 'A.B., 29 (1968), 12–15. The adjoining building has since been restored.

[52] The former low and narrow doorway in the enclosure wall is illustrated in Stylianou, *Painted Churches*, fig. 2. The new burial ground lies outside the enclosure, to the north.

[53] See *infra*, p. 158 ff..

[54] The northeast column is of marble and 2.375 m. high (upper diam. 0.32 m.). The others are of limestone and two of them, 2.41 m. and 2.42 m. in height, are probably the complete lower parts of columns constructed in two sections. Their upper diameters are 0.42, 0.43, and 0.44 m. Their total height with the upper sections would have been about 3.60 m., if normally proportioned. Prior to the repairs of 1966 (*CARDA*, 1966, p. 9), the two outer columns, which were leaning critically outward, had been reinforced by encasing masonry, shown in Soteriou, Μνημεῖα, pl. 32a, and Stylianou, *Painted Churches*, fig. 2.

It rises, uninterrupted by any windows, to a cornice of thin stone slabs, slightly projecting. A straight joint in the upper part of the masonry near the west end indicates that in its present form the south wall of the narthex was completed rather later than the remainder. This wall incorporates a buttress at the west end, one of four added to the west wall. At the east end its masonry is homogeneous with that of the present apse of the diaconicon.

The roof of the south aisle follows the curvature of its masonry barrel vault. Beyond it rises the upper part of the nave wall, where five small clerestory windows have been almost totally blocked by raising the aisle roof to its present high level (fig. 2).[55] Between and immediately above the windows the masonry is a rough assemblage of rather large reused blocks. Somewhat west of the center point rises a low gable of rather neater construction, pierced by a pair of roundheaded windows. This gable terminates a short transverse vault which buttresses, on the south side, the square base of a rather tall dome. This has a plain circular drum constructed in rubble masonry, except where four narrow windows with pointed heads open at the cardinal points; here reused dressed blocks are employed. The modern tiled roofing of the nave follows the curvature of the main barrel vaults converging on the dome, and at the east end rises at the center to cover the domical vault over the bema.[56]

The western aspect of the church is enhanced by a subsidiary dome on the central bay of the narthex (figs. 3 and 4), though by masking the window in the west gable of the nave it further darkens an already ill-lit interior. This dome has a plain cornice and windows in its cylindrical drum at the cardinal points, the east excepted, and four matching niches between them. The west wall is provided with a low central arch of segmental form, above the entrance door, supporting a gable of very low pitch (fig. 7). This is carried on a pair of buttresses, themselves additions to the west wall, and performs the function of a shallow porch. The doorway itself is now covered with a plain stone lintel, which is seen internally to be a clumsy repair. The jambs, which evidently belong to the same repair, are edged with a simple roll molding and are capped by molded brackets. Above the lintel a stone 0.425 m. wide has been inserted conforming with the curvature of the arch. On it is the following inscription, in deeply cut letters filled with pitch, which doubtless relates to the repair of this entrance among other works (fig. 8):

1779 Χρυσάνθου	1779 Chrysanthos,
ἱερομονάχου καὶ καθη-	monk and abbot,
γουμένου · δαπάνης · τῆς ἱκοδ(ο)μ(ῆ)ς	defrayed the cost of this building
μαρτήου · 15.	March 15

---

[55] The easternmost of these windows has also been blocked by internal additions. The rectangular recess above it is unexplained.

[56] Except over the bema, where some early *stroteres* had survived, the roof surfaces were formerly finished with lime concrete. The roof of the apse was tiled in 1954 to protect the mosaic, the rest of the church in 1966 (*CARDA*, 1966, p. 9).

On a stone of the south jamb of the door, on its west face, have been roughly cut the words Μήτηρ (Θεοῦ ἡ) Κανακ(α)ρ(ι)ᾶ. In this position the stone belongs to the repairs of 1779, but with the inscription it could have featured previously in some other part of the monastery (fig. 9). The west wall leans outward and has been reinforced by two more buttresses at either end.[57] Two stone capitals and a base lie close to the west door (figs. 7, 13, 17, and 18); they are discussed below.

The north elevation differs from the south in that the aisle wall is considerably lower and is pierced by three narrow windows, as well as a narrow door (figs. 10 and 11). There is a change in the masonry at a point about 0.70 m. above the threshold of the door. The lower masonry is rougher and extends to a point in line with the outside face of the west wall of the church proper. Beyond this point, the north wall of the narthex is of different construction and is differently aligned. But the straight joint between them is so placed as to attest a *reprise* in a single phase of construction. At the foot of the narthex section, as in the remainder of the wall, there are a few courses of rougher masonry. These may survive from some predecessor of the present narthex. In the upper part of the nave wall, in addition to the windows in the added gable flanking the dome, there are two more of the lower, earlier series.[58] There were doubtless others before the west part of this wall was reconstructed.[59]

The east end is dominated by the large semicircular apse (fig. 11). This is constructed, to an external radius of 6.50 m., of large slabs of dressed stone set on edge and bedded in gypsum, quite unlike the rougher lime-built masonry of the other walls.[60] There are some irregularities: on the north side the face diverges from the normal radius in an almost straight line (see plan, fig. C) and below the shallow eaves the masonry follows a polygonal rather than a semicircular plan (fig. 23). During the repair of the apse in 1954, it was seen that the semidome is likewise constructed of squared slablike stones set in gypsum in regular and rather deep courses. It was found that the central window had at some time been enlarged. The other two windows had been

---

[57] An ugly belfry had been built (in 1888, according to Smirnov, "Mozaiki," 71) on the low gable above the door, but to one side. This masked the narthex dome, and was removed during the repairs of 1950. The single bell was transferred to the more modest construction then added above the northwest corner of the narthex (fig. 3), where the existing buttress was enlarged to carry it (*CARDA*, 1950, p. 12 and figs. 14–15).

[58] Previously blocked with masonry, these were reopened during the repairs of 1949 (*CARDA*, 1949, p. 12).

[59] The masonry in this part is comparatively recent, certainly subsequent to the construction of the gable.

[60] Formerly, but not originally, the apse was even larger. For when the original apse wall, only 0.86 m. thick, showed signs of weakness, it was on three successive occasions ringed with an outer sheath of new masonry, bringing the final thickness to 1.85 m. In 1954 two concealed collars of reinforced concrete were inserted in the original apse wall, one just below the cornice and the other just above the windows. This made it possible, by removing the additions, to expose and repair the original masonry and reopen the lateral windows, which had been walled up (*CARDA*, 1954, p. 12). The slab-shaped blocks employed in the original masonry range from 0.42 to 0.56 m. in height, from 0.42 to 0.90 m. in width, and from 0.16 to 0.30 m. in thickness. In a binding course above the window arches these slabs are bedded flat.

walled up and had suffered damage in this process; but enough remained to establish their original form and positions, and that on the north side retained a section of its molded archivolt (fig. 24). The windows were notably wide in proportion to their height, and set unusually low in the apse wall.[61]

The lateral apses do not conform with the main one, nor with each other, save in that all three are semicircular. That of the diaconicon (fig. 1) to the south is indeed constructed of squared blocks of large size, but here the apse wall, in comparison with that of the main apse, is disproportionately thick (0.98 m.), its window disproportionately small, and its construction neater. That it abuts the initial addition to the main apse (see plan, fig. C) indicates its relatively late date. This diaconicon apse is larger than that of the prothesis to the north (fig. 11). Here the masonry, only 0.60 m. thick, appears to be homogeneous with that of the north wall, and it is unlike that of the main apse. The small central window indicates that this apse also is later than the main one.

When the church is viewed from the east, it is apparent that not only do the lateral apses differ from each other, but the aisles which they close are unsymmetrical, the south aisle being considerably higher than the other. In fact, although at first sight the church presents an agreeably homogeneous exterior appearance, closer examination reveals that this is the result not of any uniform design but of the fortunate compatibility of a long series of reconstructions, additions, and repairs. How complex was its structural history is apparent only in the interior; but thanks to the use of the same material in works of different dates and to their execution throughout in conformity with the rudiments of Byzantine style, the final result, externally at least, is surprisingly well integrated.

THE INTERIOR[62]

The narthex extends low barrel vaults to north and south from the domed central bay (fig. 26). Built against the west wall of the church, these vaults, for convenience of construction, spring from a series of blind arches of semicircular form, a feature repeated in the west wall in order to increase the abutment it opposes to the outward thrust of the vaults.[63] The effective span was thus reduced by about 1.10 m. In the dome bay, wider wall arches corresponding to the span rise to the height of the lateral vaults, together with which they carry the pendentives supporting the high drum (figs. 26 and 27). This last impinges on the west wall of the church so that the opening on this side is replaced by a deep internal recess, corresponding with the windows on the other sides.

[61] The northern one is 1.35 m. high by 0.76 m. wide. That the windows are nearer to the ground than is usual is not due to any raising of the level outside the apse. For the photograph in fig. 11 was taken after the accumulations in this area were removed in 1966, approximately to the interior floor level (Papageorghiou, in 'A.B., 29 [1968], 14).

[62] Throughout this section, reference should be made to the plan and sections in figures B–E.

[63] The recesses in the west wall, which had been blocked up, were reopened in the repairs of 1950, when the modern wall plaster of the narthex was also removed except at the crown of the vaults. The windows of the dome were reopened at the same time (CARDA, 1950, p. 12).

There are some scant remains of frescoes on the east wall. Elsewhere, where the original pointing is intact, straight joint-lines have been scribed on it, or painted in red. The plates set in the plaster at the crown of the lateral vaults derive from some renovation of this part of the church (figs. 21 and 22). They include specimens of what has been called "drip-painted" ware. Examples found in the Athenian Agora come from contexts for which an eighteenth-century date is indicated.[64] Although this type of interior decoration appears to have been in vogue in Cyprus at an earlier date, at the Panagia Kanakaria the introduction of the plates may well have been part of the work of Abbot Chrysanthos recorded in the inscription of 1779 above the west door.

There is a narrow window in each of the end walls of the narthex but there are no others except for those in the dome. Three doorways originally communicated with the church but that into the north aisle was suppressed in some repair. The jambs of the corresponding entrance to the south aisle are without rebates for a door. The wide central opening which leads from the domed bay of the narthex into the church proper preserves its original north jamb, a single block with a shallow rebate (fig. 27). The other jamb and the lintel were restored in the recent repairs; whether originally the lunette above the lintel was glazed as at present is open to doubt.

THE NAVE

Entering the nave, which is very ill lit, one is struck by the complex articulation of its side walls (figs. 37 and 38). Setting aside for a moment the latest additions, it is seen that these walls, which are constructed with lime mortar, are pierced by very small arches communicating with the aisles, only 1.20–1.25 m. broad and now 2.85–2.95 m. to the crown of the arch (figs. 30 and 37).[65] Against the inner faces of the piers which supported these arches stood a series of engaged pilasters, 0.45 m. wide and projecting 0.18 to 0.20 m. The tops of these pilasters have nowhere survived and in some cases the pilasters themselves have been cut away (fig. 30). But on the south wall one of these pilasters can be seen extending higher than the top of the adjoining clerestory window (fig. E), over 6.0 m. from the present floor. In view of this height, the meager thickness of the clerestory walls (0.60 m.), and the lack of lateral abutment, the pilasters cannot have carried transverse arches across the nave, such as were employed in the vaulted basilicas of the Carpas.[66] Instead, they would have provided additional support for the ends of the main trusses of a wooden roof. Spaced at intervals of 2.10 m. center to center, the pilasters divided the nave into four narrow bays. These were followed at the east end by a wider fifth bay, now closed off from the bema by a modern wooden icon

---

[64] Alison Frantz, "Turkish Pottery from the Agora," *Hesperia*, 11 (1942), 12, fig. 23, no. 2, and for the date p. 3.

[65] The original height may have been reduced by subsequent raising of the floor level, though the extent of this is unknown.

[66] E.g., those partly preserved in the ruined Asomatos church at Aphentrika (Soteriou, Μνημεῖα, pl. 12; Megaw, "Vaulted Basilicas," 48–56, fig. 1).

screen (fig. 31). The larger arches in the lateral walls of this wider bay still exist, partly obscured on both sides by later masonry. They are 1.58 to 1.65 m. wide and 3.0 m. high. Between the pilasters and well above the arches several of the original clerestory windows are visible; where not completely masked by later masonry they had all been blocked up. Wherever possible they have been reopened during the recent repairs (figs. 29, 30, and 28, below the beam). The sill of the north window of the wider fifth bay where seen in the interior (fig. 31) is now lower than those to the west (fig. B). But on the exterior, where the masonry is intact, there is no appreciable difference.[67] On the walls above the arches, on the piers, and on the arches themselves are some remains of fresco decoration.

These lateral walls of the nave belong, as we shall see, not to the original church, but to what may be called the first restoration. They are far from parallel, but converge toward the west, as indicated on the plan (fig. C). The width at the icon screen is 5.40 m. compared with 5.15 m. at the most westerly point that can be measured.[68]

The existing west wall of the nave with its wide entrance door (fig. 29) seems to correspond, at least in its lower parts, with the lateral arcades and clerestory of the first restoration. But the gable in its present form is almost certainly contemporary with the gables later added to the north and south walls. In the west gable is a cruciform window (fig. 29). It is set rather high, but even so it has been almost entirely masked by the construction of the narthex dome outside it. At the east end, the nave of the first restoration was divided from the bema by a massive "triumphal arch." Its springings are visible on the west face high above the modern icon screen (fig. 36). The central part of the arch has fallen but the springings are supported by masonry resting on the much smaller existing "triumphal arch" (figs. 36 and 113).

When in due course the timber roof of the first restoration fell, it was not again restored. Instead, in what we call the second restoration, alternate piers were reinforced on the inside by heavier pilasters, three on each side of the nave. The two eastern pairs are 0.70 to 0.75 m. wide and project 0.75 to 0.80 m. from the wall face, concealing the slender pilasters which form part of the original piers. Those in the angles formed by the arcades and the west wall were linked to the next of the added pilasters by semicircular arches against the lateral walls of the nave (fig. 29). These arches spring from points 3.65 m. above the floor and now rise in their subsided state to 5.25 m. above the present floor.[69] Over the space between these arches, a barrel vault was constructed to cover the two westernmost bays of the earlier scheme. In this way the span at the west wall was reduced to 3.60 m. This vault of the second

---

[67] On the south side where the tops of all five clerestory windows are visible externally, they are substantially of the same size and at the same level.

[68] The wider span at the east end was determined by the width of the bema, which of necessity conformed with the opening of the wide central apse of the original building.

[69] In the case of the north arch the amount of subsidence from the original regular semicircle is serious, not less than 0.20 m. For this reason this arch has been underpinned with an inner one, resting on additions to the masonry on either side (fig. B).

restoration, backed by the repaired masonry of the earlier nave walls, is essentially what survives today.[70]

At the same time, at the other end of the nave, two smaller lateral arches were turned between the easternmost of the added pilasters and the abutments of the "triumphal arch" (fig. 31). These arches of small span spring from points 4.25 to 4.30 m. above the present floor, considerably above the springings of the wider western arches. But the short barrel vault covering the space between them, corresponding to the wider fifth bay of the original scheme, rises to the same height as the western vault, now some 7.70 m. above the floor.

The approximately square area between these two sections of barrel vault (3.62 and 3.78 m. by 3.70 and 3.80 m.), occupying the third and fourth bays of the earlier scheme, must have been covered by a dome from the time of this second restoration. The lateral arches of this section rise to a height corresponding with that of the vaults to east and west and with them form the normal genesis for pendentives, drum, and dome. The bottom of the southwest pendentive and the springing of the dome arches below it are visible in figure 28, top right. This is not to say that the existing dome was the first in this position. The present dome shows no signs of settlement or other distortion which would justify the elaborate system of secondary arches and tie-beams with which it is supported. The lateral arches and the ends of the vaults which match them have all been underpinned with inner arches of much crisper masonry resting on additions to the main pilasters (figs. 28–30). Wooden beams resting on sharply projecting moldings at the springing level and at points about 2.00 m. below provided two timber collars linking the four points where the weight of the dome is concentrated. It seems most probable that after collapse of the first dome the substructure which had supported it was strengthened in this way before the existing dome was erected on it. These were the principal structural changes in what we call the third restoration.

The scheme adopted for the nave in the second restoration is that normal in the "domed-hall" churches, popular in Cyprus in the twelfth century and later, in which the lateral arches of the dome constitute short sections of barrel vaulting engaged to the side walls and closed externally by gable ends.[71] It corresponds to the central section of a domed church of the normal "inscribed-cross" type, a standard form for larger churches in Cyprus after the Byzantine recovery in the tenth century.[72] In the Panagia Kanakaria, where aisles existed, the adoption in the second restoration of the full apparatus of the "inscribed-cross" type was evidently inhibited by the survival to a good height of the walls of the earlier nave. Nevertheless, the aisles evidently did require reconstruction at the same time.

[70] Enlart's suggestion that these secondary pilasters were part of an initial articulation of large bays (L'art gothique, 402, fig. 268) was made when the interior was plastered. It must be rejected now that the masonry has been exposed.

[71] Cf. the parecclesion of the Holy Trinity in the monastery of St. Chrysostom (Soteriou, Μνημεῖα, fig. 33, where, however, the lateral recesses of the west bay are not shown); for the date of its construction by the dux Eumathius Philocales, see C. Mango and E. J. W. Hawkins, in DOP, 18 (1964), 335 ff.; for a corrected plan and section, see Megaw, "Metropolitan or Provincial?", 84, fig. 1.

[72] A good example in the Carpas is the now ruinous church of St. Philo on the site of Carpasia (Soteriou, Μνημεῖα, fig. 6 and pl. 10).

THE AISLES

Indeed, it is questionable whether any part of the barrel-vaulted aisles as we see them today survives from the first restoration. If the nave had a timber roof in this restoration, and this, we have seen, is most probable, it is virtually certain that the aisles also were similarly reroofed at that stage. In the case of the north aisle, the lower part of the outer wall, where it is of larger and rougher masonry, may survive from the first restoration. On its inner face there is no trace of the pilasters which would probably have been provided to carry transverse arches if the aisle had been vaulted at that stage (fig. 32).[73] On the other side of the aisle, the piers of the nave arcade are masked by the masonry added to support the present aisle vaults (fig. 33), but at no point does this masonry appear to have been adjusted to preexisting pilasters. This added masonry, the upper part of the north wall, and the barrel vault they carry are homogeneous. They doubtless replaced the timber roof of the first restoration, when that over the nave was replaced by the existing barrel vaults and the first dome. In this second restoration the width of the north aisle was so reduced (minimum 2.17 m.) that in the aisle proper two transverse arches carried on corbels were considered adequate support for the vault (fig. 32). Only the third arch at the entrance to the prothesis was carried on pilasters, but this was not for structural reasons but rather to define the change of function at this point, where, for the same reason, there is a change of one step in the floor level (fig. 33). The three small windows in the north wall are slightly narrower at the top than at the bottom, and like the small door they correspond approximately to the articulation of the nave arcades. In the west wall of the aisle there is an arched recess above a blocked doorway (fig. 32). The doorway was narrow, not much over 0.80 m. wide, which is the width of the entrance door on the north wall of the aisle, and like that door it seems to have been covered by a lintel. This suggests that the west wall belongs, like the rest of the north aisle we see today, to the second restoration. The recess must have been designed as a window, but it is too low to clear the roof of the narthex and too high to open beneath its vaulting. This is not the only indication that, although the narthex and the north aisle in their present form both belong to the second restoration, the aisle was completed first. No traces of fresco decoration survive in the north aisle; but on the south side, as in the narthex, some scribed joint-lines are visible on the added masonry where it retains its original pointing, also some zigzag scribing.

[73] Even in the smaller Asomatos basilica at Aphentrika the vaulted aisles have such pilasters: Megaw, "Vaulted Basilicas," figs. 2 and 3. Here the aisle width is *ca*. 2.30 m. compared with a minimum 2.61 m. in the Panagia Kanakaria (measuring from the piers of the first restoration). Only in the yet smaller Sykha church with an aisle span of under 2.00 m. are the pilasters suppressed and the transverse arches carried on corbels (*ibid.*, figs. 11 and 12).

If the lower part of the present north wall of the Panagia Kanakaria survives from, or corresponds in position with, that of the first restoration, and if that wall was of the same thickness as the west wall, the aisle would have been some 0.25 m. wider, as shown in the restored plan, figure G. Across this wider span the thinner wall could only have carried a timber roof. It will be noted on the plan in figure G that in this position the wall of the first restoration would have been constructed immediately outside the position of the original north wall (as restored in that plan), the optimum position for constructing it on a new foundation.

The south aisle, including the south wall, was probably rebuilt at the same time with a similar barrel vault, but much of it subsequently required reconstruction for the third time. For below the springing of the present vault on the north side can be seen the vault springing of the second restoration and, at an appropriate level below it, the corbels which carried its two transverse arches (fig. 35). The tops of these earlier corbels are 2.60 m. above the floor, as are those in the north aisle, and they are set in masonry added against the nave arcade of the first restoration, precisely as in the north aisle. The crown of the present south aisle vault is a meter higher than that of the north aisle, even when allowance is made for the difference in floor level.[74] The present transverse arches of the south aisle are pointed, unlike those of the north aisle. The vault itself is parabolic rather than pointed and the semidome of the apse has the same compromised form in elevation (fig. 34), in order to merge with its semicircular plan. The well-cut large blocks of which the apse is built contrast with the inferior masonry of the prothesis apse. The south wall, unlike the outer wall of the north aisle, is entirely without windows and it is much thicker.[75] The only opening is the door, which is not only larger and more elaborate than the north entrance door but, unlike the latter, it is quite unrelated in its position to the openings of the nave arcades. On the other hand, its masonry is integrated with that of the porch outside it. As we see it today, the south aisle is largely a reconstruction in more massive masonry of the lower vaulted aisle of the second restoration. Only at one point in the south wall is the inferior masonry of the second restoration incorporated in it. This is at the west end near the floor, where it is partly concealed by a plain buff-colored plaster. This recurs at the corresponding point in the north aisle, where, as elsewhere, it is found on masonry of the second restoration. From the decoration of the south aisle in this earlier phase a fresco of an archangel survives much effaced on the north wall (fig. 90; see *infra*, p. 150). Opposite it, on the later south wall, are the remains of two superimposed panels representing St. George (fig. 99), on the later of which is a graffito dated 1598 (fig. 127; see *infra*, pp. 152f., 158).

The west wall of the south aisle is unlike that of the north aisle. The door into the narthex is arched and wider, and there is no window recess above it (fig. 35). The door arch was turned on centering supported on the tops of the jambs, as were those of the arcades of the first restoration, to which, like that of the west door of the nave, it probably belongs.[76]

The two aisles extend on either side of the bema, unbroken in construction up to the east wall. In the north aisle, however, we have already noted a

---

[74] The floor of the north aisle is 0.15 m. above the level in the nave and south aisle.

Throughout the church the floor is paved with local *marmara*, well squared in the nave and some other areas and clearly recent, elsewhere a random "crazy paving." At no point does it throw light on the history of the building.

[75] Thickness of the south wall 1.10 m., of the north wall 0.74 m.

[76] Assuming that the door was in the middle of the wall, this gives a fixed point for the south wall of this restoration. If at the east end the south aisle were given the same width as that indicated for the north aisle, this second south wall would have been constructed immediately outside the first, as restored in figure G, as in the case of the north wall.

transverse arch on pilasters corresponding with the west limit of the bema to mark the entrance to the prothesis. But in the reconstructed vault of the south aisle it is only a transverse arch on corbels that marks off the diaconicon to the south of the bema (fig. 34). As in the prothesis, the floor of the diaconicon is raised one step above the rest of the aisle and the small passage in its north wall, on the transverse axis of the bema, makes it clear that from the time of the first restoration the area to the south functioned as part of the sanctuary. A corresponding passage may be inferred leading to the prothesis, but on this north side the previous arrangements were obliterated when the functions of the prothesis were transferred to the niches improvised in the northeast corner of the bema.[77]

If it is correct, as argued above, to dissociate even the north aisle (the earlier of the two, as we see them today) from the first restoration, it follows that neither of the lateral apses can belong to that stage. The present apses are constructed on the axes of the existing aisles, their conches concentric with the existing vaults. Those of the first restoration would have been centered a little closer to the bema walls of that phase, when the latter had not yet been concealed and the spans reduced. It follows, a fortiori, that no part of the original east wall is to be seen in the parabemata; indeed, there is no visible evidence that lateral apses existed in the first state of the church. Basilicas with only one apse are known in Cyprus, but only a few, and none of them in the Carpas.[78] There, the basilica excavated in the Ayia Trias quarter of Yialousa[79] is, as we shall see, close to ours in size, in its stone colonnades, and probably in date; so close that it would be surprising if the original Kanakaria basilica did not share with it the feature of lateral apses also.[80] These would have been repeated in the first restoration, though no part of the lateral apses of that phase either is visible today.

THE BEMA[81]

The bema itself is now covered by an irregular dome without clearly defined drum or windows. Wider from north to south than on the east-west axis, it

---

[77] When this was done, the passage was blocked and a new one was crudely cut on the splay a little to the west, through the masonry of the first reconstruction. The masonry of the second reconstruction (through which the passage would have extended, as on the south side), after insertion of a very flat half-arch to support its upper courses, was entirely cut away at ground level to permit formation of the new prothesis niches (fig. B).

[78] Kourion (Megaw, "Early Byz. Monuments," 346, fig. 25; though here there are rectangular pastophoria); Marathovouno (A. Papageorghiou, Ἡ βασιλικὴ τοῦ Μαραθοβούνου, RDAC, 1963, p. 85, fig. 1); Ktima (BCH, 88 [1964], 374).

[79] For a summary report on the initial excavations by A. I. Dikigoropoulos, see ArchRep, 1957, p. 50. On subsequent campaigns by A. Papageorghiou, see reports in BCH, 88 (1964), 372–74; 90 (1966), 386; 91 (1967), 363; in ILN, March 1975, 79f.; and in ʼΑ.Β., 25 (1964), 155f.; 27 (1966), 159f.; 28 (1967), 78–83, with a plan, p. 79, fig. 1.

[80] Although the original basilica may have had lateral apses, they have not been indicated in figure G in the absence of any tangible evidence. The probable position of the apse closing the north aisle, if there was one, is indicated by broken lines in figure H.

[81] The bema, like the east end of the nave, retains considerable remains of fresco decoration and where this is lost the masonry remains concealed by whitewashed plaster. In consequence, the structural history of this part of the church is less easy to disentangle.

is supported on somewhat crude pendentives, which bring the plan at the springing of the dome to a rectangle with rounded corners (fig. C). The pendentives rise from four arches, of which that to the east is more sharply pointed than the others and underpins the front of the conch of the original apse. This eastern arch springs from two substantial secondary pilasters, one on either side, which reduced the span of the entrance to the apse from 4.78 m. to 3.10 m. Above the arch which they support, the masonry was carried up to the crown of the conch, concealing the front part of the mosaic.[82] Much of the rest of it is masked by the arch when seen from the nave (fig. 38).

The arch on the west side, now of irregular parabolic form, is of similar span (2.95 m.) and height and, in addition to supporting the dome, likewise serves a secondary purpose, that of supporting the remains of the "triumphal arch" of the first restoration. The western edges of the two lateral sections of this earlier arch are visible from the nave, above a fresco of the Annunciation (fig. 36). This arch appears to have been rebuilt at least once. Its original springings, about 0.50 m. below those carrying the surviving sections of the arch, are 5.25 m. above the present floor of the nave (fig. 31). Even from these lower springings the arch would have risen to a height of 7.75 m. above the nave floor, well above that of the conch containing the mosaic, the crown of which would originally have been less than 7 m. above the same point. Consequently, it is virtually certain that the superstructure of the bema in the first restoration would have cleared the conch, and the present obstruction of the mosaic would have been avoided at that stage.[83] To the north and south the bema was bounded in the first restoration by solid walls, the thickness of which (0.90 m.) can be seen in the passage leading to the diaconicon; it exceeds that of the nave walls (0.72 m.). The width of the "triumphal arch" was almost certainly the same.[84]

These massive features on north, south, and west presuppose, in the first restoration, some taller and possibly heavier superstructure for the bema than the timber roof indicated for the nave. The space it covered was even more elongated (5.00 by 3.05) than that covered by the present dome. Nothing has survived to indicate how this space was covered. By far the simplest method would have been to raise the walls enclosing it to support a tiled timber roof with a transverse ridge, high enough for its western eaves to clear the ridge of the nave roof (fig. F, a). In the circumstances of the first restoration it is probable that this simplest solution would have been preferred. On the other hand, if the existing roof of the bema can be accepted as some guide to what it replaced, a pair of lateral arches could have reduced the elongation of the space to be roofed to proportions which would admit of a domical covering

[82] In 1950 the masonry above the arch was cut away to expose the hidden sections of the mosaic (fig. 39).

[83] In its present state, what appears to be the crown of the "triumphal arch" is quite flat. The probability is that this part had collapsed prior to the construction of the underpinning arch in the second restoration, after which the gap was filled by the masonry of the present flat section (fig. 36).

[84] The width of the visible western edge (0.35 m.) and the width of the later arch underpinning its invisible eastern part (0.57 m.) together add up to 0.92 m.

in the first restoration also.[85] Whatever form it took, the superstructure of the bema at this stage would have been high enough to leave the view of the mosaic from the nave entirely unobstructed and to allow windows to be opened in its lateral walls, and even above the apse.

What we see today (figs. B and D) derives from a later reconstruction, which substantially reduced both the height and the width of the bema. The excessive width was first reduced by adding 0.60 m. of masonry inside the existing side walls, while lateral arches were then added at the same height as those newly constructed to east and west, in order to reduce the base of the dome almost to a square. The occasion when these changes were made was probably the same which saw the replacement of the timber roof over the nave by a vaulted system carrying a dome, what we have called the second restoration. However, the pointed form of the arch at the entrance to the apse and the irregularity of that under the "triumphal arch"—the others are more or less semicircular—suggests that there were some further but minor changes in this part of the church, perhaps in preparation for the execution of the surviving fresco decoration in the third restoration.

THE MAIN APSE

The windows open rather low in the apse wall, the height of the sill of the intact north window being just over 1.60 m. above the floor. This does not seem to be due to any raising of the interior floor level, for a test made below the bema floor in 1966 revealed no earlier floor at a lower level.[86] A simple plaster cornice marks the beginning of the conch, though its curvature actually starts from a point 0.22 m. above the cornice. We have already noted that both wall and conch were constructed of stone slabs set in gypsum mortar. The manner in which the exterior contour of the apse on the north side diverges from the semicircle to end in a straight face (fig. H) is curious, but not unparalleled.[87]

After the supporting arch had been constructed under the front of the conch in the second restoration—perhaps immediately after—the pilasters which support it were considered inadequate for their second function. This was to contain the eastward thrust of the north and south arches of the bema dome, which spring from the west face of the same pilasters. They were reinforced in two ways, which made further encroachments into the area of the apse. At the base of each, the triangular space lying between the pilaster

---

[85] Such lateral arches would have sprung necessarily from the spandrels on the east side of the "triumphal arch" to those on the original east wall flanking the conch and would have been segmental in form. It is possible that the solid walling 0.60 m. thick later constructed against the north and south walls of the bema (see *infra*) served to fill in such putative lateral arches of the first restoration. In that case the final dimensions of the bema superstructure at that stage would have been 3.05 by 3.80 m. If the elongation of the rectangle was reduced in this way it could, alternatively, have been covered with a pyramidal timber roof.

[86] Papageorghiou in 'A.B., 29 (1968), 15. Indeed, the floor in the apse may formerly have been at a higher level, for Smirnov recorded features there which have since been removed (see *infra*).

[87] Such is the outline of the apse of the fifth-century Martyrium at Seleucia: *Antioch-on-the-Orontes*, III (Princeton, 1941), plan X.

and the wall of the apse was filled with masonry to a height of 1.15 m. from the floor, forming a "shelf" on either side (fig. B). Above these "shelves" segmental arches were thrown to points close to the window jambs, and on these arches raking buttresses were constructed up to the height of the apse cornice. It is clear that at this stage the lateral windows of the apse had not been blocked. It was doubtless at this stage that the apse wall was thickened externally for the first time, and that the windows were reformed as twin openings of the characteristic Middle Byzantine form. The mullion of the south window, which is shown on Smirnov's plan, no longer exists; but the plastered springing of the inner end of one of the pair of small arches which it supported has survived.

During the work carried out by the writers in 1961, a probe was made behind the pilaster which carries the north end of the arch underpinning the front of the conch. The purpose was, by examining the point of contact between the north wall of the bema and the north side of the apse, to confirm that the apse is indeed of earlier date than what we have called "the first restoration." The results are shown in the accompanying plan (fig. H). An open straight joint was found to separate the masonry of the north wall from that of the east wall close beside the original opening into the apse. The north wall of the bema is indeed secondary, since it was seen to abut the plastered face of the east wall. Pursuing this plastered face, it was seen to turn westward, at a point 0.20 m. in from the face of the secondary masonry, round an unfluted limestone column shaft, half of which is immured in the east wall.[88] Its diameter could not be measured, but assuming that the bema wall, which is 0.90 m. thick, embraces the column equally on both sides, the diameter would have been some 0.50 m. at this point, about 1.30 m. above the estimated level of its base. This accords reasonably well with the lower diameter of the two capitals outside the west door (0.49 and 0.50 m.). Consequently, these and the other similar capitals almost certainly formed part of one or another of the colonnades of the initial wood-roofed, three-aisled basilica from which the apse and its mosaic have survived, and in which the immured column served as the eastern respond of the north colonnade.[89] The five surviving bases, which are discussed below, doubtless also belong to these colonnades.

On figure C are indicated the various outer shells of masonry added to strengthen the apse wall, which were all removed in 1954 after consolidation of the original structure. The photograph in figure 23 was taken during removal of the added masonry. The first addition was constructed on a footing of the original apse wall projecting only 0.20 m. from the face above (figure 25, at the bottom) and it tapered to nothing about a meter below the top; we have seen reason to assign it to the second restoration. The next addition, the most substantial, masked the lateral windows and is clearly later than the second

[88] In that part where it has always been concealed by the masonry of the east wall, the column retains a stucco dressing, indicating that it was a *spolium*.

[89] The three limestone shafts reused in the porch seem too small to belong to these colonnades; for their dimensions, see note 54 *supra*.

restoration, in which the lavish reinforcement of the pilasters within the apse avoided those windows. It was 0.64 m. thick and constructed with a lime mortar containing much red earth. This suggests a late date, possibly as late as the works of 1778. The lateral openings now became internal niches, flanking a single central window. Since this is the state in which the apse is shown in Smirnov's plan, the last addition 0.33 m. thick and built with modern lime mortar must, like the walling up of the lateral "niches," have formed part of the works of 1920.

THE PLAN OF THE ORIGINAL BASILICA (fig. G)

The question arises: does any part of the present west wall survive from the original basilica? To judge from the proportions of comparable basilicas, this seems improbable. Since the position of one of the eastern responds is known, the span, measured between the center-lines of the colonnades, can be estimated at 5.90 m. The existing west wall is not parallel to the chord of the apse, but the mean distance between the east and the west walls is almost exactly 15.00 m. As the following table shows, this distance would make the initial intercolumniations, which could hardly have been less than six in number, rather small in proportion to the size of the church. The four basilicas listed, all of them in the Carpas and with similar stone colonnades in their original state, show that nave span and length were not in a fixed proportion. As the span increased the proportion tended to become more elongated (only the Yialousa basilica is exceptionally short in proportion to its span), and as the length of the church increased so did the width of the intercolumniations.

	Span	Length	Proportion	Intercolumniations
Panagia, Syka	4.80 m.	12.30 m.	1:2.56	5 of 2.46 m.
Asomatos, Aphentrika	5.50	15.00	1:2.73	6 of 2.50*
Panagia Kanakaria	5.90	(16.00) (15.00)	(1:2.71) (1:2.54)	(6 of 2.66) (6 of 2.50)
Ayia Trias Yialousa	6.90	17.30	1:2.51	6 of 2.88
Panagia, Aphentrika	7.80	22.20	1:2.85	8 of 2.77

* By elongating the responds the intercolumniations were actually reduced to 2.40 m. In all cases the measurements are taken from published plans and are only approximate.

In order to conform, the length of our nave would have had to be about a meter longer than at present, giving a similar elongation to that of the rather smaller Asomatos basilica, but with wider intercolumniations; while both elongation and intercolumniations would have been less than in the larger Panagia Aphentrika. The existing west wall is consequently unlikely to preserve any part of the corresponding west wall of the original basilica. At no point does its masonry conform with the slab construction of the apse, which is used in the Aphentrika churches also, and not only in the apses.[90]

Excavation in the forecourt could doubtless establish whether the original basilica had the usual narthex and atrium. Since they have been found nearby in the only slightly larger basilica near Yialousa,[91] they are to be expected at Kanakaria also. In that case the three stone shafts reused in the porch, which are too small for the nave colonnades, might well come from the atrium peristyle.[92] When the level outside the north wall of the existing church was reduced in 1966, a wall running parallel to it at a distance of about 3.00 m. from it was found to continue to a point beyond the western limit of the present building.[93] If this survives from some annex of the original basilica it attests the existence of, at least, a narthex.[94] Lateral annexes, which probably served as catechumena, are a common feature of early basilicas in Cyprus.[95]

A distinctive feature of the apses of some of these early basilicas is the connection of the central and lateral apses by narrow passages passing through the solid masonry between them. These are found both in the great basilica attributed to St. Epiphanius at Salamis-Constantia[96] and in the first state of those on humbler scale at Aphentrika;[97] also, in quite a different part of the Island, in the recently excavated basilica at Soli.[98] Had such passages existed in conjunction with lateral apses in the Panagia Kanakaria, some trace of the openings into them would have shown on the apse wall (at the back of the niches reserved on either side in the raking buttresses), even though this remains plastered. Their presence would also have been apparent on the

---

[90] Megaw, "Vaulted Basilicas," 53, fig. 10. The present west wall of the Lythrankomi church belongs rather to the first restoration, for it is perpendicular to the somewhat oblique axis of the nave of that phase. If our position for the first west wall is correct, the second was built on new foundations just inside it, a most reasonable procedure.

[91] For a plan, see Megaw, "Metropolitan or Provincial?", 70, fig. D.

[92] They seem too large for gallery colonnades. Galleries are not otherwise attested, though there is evidence for them in the Ayia Trias basilica (Dikigoropoulos' report in *ArchRep*, 1957, p. 50; Papageorghiou's report in *BCH*, 88 [1964], 372–74).

[93] Papageorghiou, in 'A.B., 29 (1968), 14, shown in our figure G.
The relationship of this wall to the first basilica is confirmed by its alignment, almost exactly perpendicular to the original east wall. In the restoration of the first basilica in figure G, its axis has been made parallel to this wall, and its aisles and narthex have been made proportionate to those of the Ayia Trias basilica.

[94] The rougher masonry at the base of the north wall of the existing narthex, which we have remarked is possibly earlier than the remainder, can have nothing to do with the first narthex. Its oblique alignment, perpendicular to the existing west wall (see fig. G), clearly originated in the first restoration.

[95] On both sides: basilica at Kourion (Megaw, "Early Byz. Monuments," 346, fig. 25); on one side: basilica at Ayia Trias (see note 91 *supra*).

[96] Megaw, *ArchRep*, 1956, p. 30, fig. 2, and 1957, p. 49, fig. 3; *idem*, "Metropolitan or Provincial?", 63, fig. A.

[97] Megaw, "Vaulted Basilicas," 49, fig. 2, and 51, fig. 7.

[98] Plan in *BCH*, 94 (1970), 227, fig. 142. Similar passages have also been exposed in the remains of a large basilica incorporated in the monastery church of Panagia Archeiropoietou at Lambousa: Papageorghiou, in 'A.B., 25 (1964), 213.

exterior; for there they require a straight face of wall between the central apse and each of the lateral ones, well eastward of the point where their circumferences would meet, a feature lacking in the Lythrankomi church. The lateral passages are lacking also in the Ayia Trias basilica, where the side apses are well preserved. Some change in ritual may have made the passages of the early basilicas unnecessary, but if so this was prior to the developments which led to the adoption, probably in the sixth century, of the semicircular synthronon.[99] The lack of any trace of the passages in the Panagia Kanakaria is consequently no proof that initially it had only one apse. However, in the absence of any positive indications for them, no lateral apses are shown on the plan in figure G; but the probable position of the apse (if any) closing the north aisle of the original basilica is shown in broken line on figure H.

THE DATE OF THE ORIGINAL BASILICA

Although so little is preserved, there are a few features which taken together suggest a construction date not later than the close of the fifth century. The use of stone for the colonnades is in itself an indication of relatively early date. At Salamis-Constantia the great basilica commonly attributed to St. Epiphanius has stone bases, drums, and capitals, and it is only for the early sixth century that the Campanopetra basilica provides evidence of colonnade construction in imported marble.[100] In the sixth century marble colonnades were normal, at least in coastal areas, if we may judge by the three basilicas on Cape Drepanum.[101] Of the other basilicas in the Carpas with stone colonnades, that excavated at Ayia Trias near Yialousa is the most comparable as it is only slightly larger than ours. Its mosaic floor when first discovered was observed by Dikigoropoulos to include a motif not found in Antioch after the second half of the fifth century.[102] The two basilicas at Aphentrika are not later, since they have the apparently early feature of passages linking the three apses,[103] found in St. Epiphanius' basilica also,[104] but which is lacking at Ayia Trias. It is also lacking in the Syka basilica, where the semicircular

---

[99] E.g., Peyia, Basilica I, sixth century (Megaw, "Early Byz. Monuments," 349, fig. 26); Campanopetra basilica at Salamis-Constantia (*BCH*, 94 [1970], 262, fig. 119). In this last case the synthronon is probably secondary, like that in St. Epiphanius' basilica (Megaw, "Archaeology in Cyprus, 1954," *JHS*, 75 [1955], Suppl., 33). In the case of the Syka basilica, another example with lateral apses but no passages, it has not been established whether or not the synthronon is contemporary with the initial construction.

[100] Datable approximately by the fine "Theodosian" capitals (J. Pouilloux, "Fouilles à Salamine de Chypre, 1964–68," *RDAC*, 1969, p. 47 ff., fig. 3).

[101] For Basilica I with typical sixth-century marble acanthus capitals and floor mosaics, see Megaw, "Early Byz. Monuments," 348, and pls. XXXIX–XL; for Basilica II with rudimentary Ionic impost capitals, *ArchRep*, 1955, p. 45; for Basilica III with impost capitals, *JHS*, 74 (1954), 175.

[102] An example in Bath D is illustrated by Levi, *Antioch Pavements*, I, 427, fig. 161. Cf. *ArchRep*, 1957, p. 50. Papageorghiou, who completed the excavation of the Ayia Trias basilica, reports that the ambo and the posts and panels of the sanctuary screen were of stone. He also favors a construction date in the fifth century: 'A.B., 27 (1966), 159–60.

[103] Megaw, "Vaulted Basilicas," figs. 2 and 7. A stone post from the presbytery screen (Papageorghiou, in 'A.B., 26 [1965], 94) indicates a construction date for the Asomatos Church before marble furniture became prevalent.

[104] See note 96 *supra*, and for the same feature at Soli and Lambousa, note 98 *supra*.

synthronon may thus be part of the original plan.[105] This and the presence of ambon fragments and other furniture of marble[106] indicates that Syka alone of these stone-colonnade basilicas may be as late as the sixth century.

The original Lythrankomi basilica, on the other hand, does not belong to the time of the semicircular synthronon, for there are no indications that it ever had one. Instead, the lost features which Smirnov planned, and which are shown dotted in figure C and reconstructed in figures F and G, indicate that here the layout of the bema and apse was of the earlier type. It is true that Smirnov himself considered that the broad flight of three straight steps, which led up in the apse to the throne on the higher level, was a secondary arrangement replacing a semicircular synthronon.[107] But such steps are a usual adjunct of the earlier disposition of the clergy in the bema, on two lateral benches facing each other on either side of the altar table. Broad flights of steps were found, for example, in the fifth-century basilicas A and B at Nikopolis, where, since they had to reach a much higher level, they started from the chord of the apse.[108] Elsewhere, where the difference in level was less, the steps rose from a rectangular recess cut into the platform which filled the apse.[109] The Lythrankomi apse approximated the second of these arrangements for, according to Smirnov's plan, the steps were withdrawn well to the east of the chord, so that only a small area was floored at the higher level. That these steps were ancient and in all probability contemporary with the original construction is suggested by the survival in the Acheiropoietos church at Lambousa of a comparable though shallower, rectangular recess in the raised floor of the apse of the original fifth-century basilica.[110] At Lythrankomi, the retention of this early arrangement would fit a construction date in the late fifth century, but hardly in the sixth century, when the semicircular synthronon prevailed. The masonry throne that still existed eighty years ago in the

---

[105] Megaw, "Vaulted Basilicas," fig. 12.

[106] *Ibid.*, fig. 13.

[107] Smirnov, "Mozaiki," 71.

[108] Basilica A, Soteriou, in 'Αρχ.'Εφ. (1929), 206, fig. 37; Basilica B, *ibid.*, 202, fig. 33, and Orlandos, Βασιλική, 494, fig. 454. In both these cases the apse floor must have been raised some two meters above the floor level at the altar-table in order to pass over a passage leading round the wall of the apse from the north to the south side of the bema.

In the episcopal basilica at Stobi, the lateral clergy benches have survived because the presence of the *confessio*-crypt below the wooden floor of the apse (see R. Egger, in *ÖJh*, 24 [1929], 63) precluded their replacement by a semicircular synthronon. Here also we may presume that a broad flight of steps, but of wood and cutting into the ceiling of the crypt, rose behind the altar to the higher level in the apse indicated by the ambulatory colonnade in the crypt.

[109] E.g., the two fifth-century basilicas at Nea Anchialos in Thessaly. These lack the semicircular passage of the Nikopolis examples and like Kanakaria had only three steps, though in a Π-shaped arrangement: Basilica A, Soteriou, in 'Αρχ.'Εφ. (1929), 21, fig. 17 and pl. B': Basilica B, *ibid.*, 112, fig. 155, and 121, figs. 165 and 166. In its first state the apse of the Bargala basilica was similar, but with the steps along the east side of the recess only, as recorded by Smirnov at Lythrankomi: Blaga Aleksova and C. Mango, "Bargala: A Preliminary Report," *DOP*, 25 (1971), 270 and fig. 24.

On the bishop's throne as the sole feature in such apses, see Orlandos, Βασιλική, 496.

[110] Soteriou, Μνημεῖα, fig. 15. In this case the floor is raised only one step above the bema, and if this was the original arrangement it was probably dictated by the presence of the lateral passages into the parabemata (not shown on Soteriou's plan).

The arrangements within the main apse of the Ayia Trias basilica were obliterated when the apse wall was robbed to the foundations (Papageorghiou, in 'A.B., 29 [1968], 9).

Panagia Kanakaria can also have been, like the steps, a survival from the original arrangement, since evidence for a throne in the same position in fifth-century apses is not lacking.[111]

Of the original layout in the bema to the west of the apse there is no evidence. The marble column reused in the south porch seems disproportionately large for a ciborium,[112] and it can hardly be cited against a construction date before the sixth century, when marble furniture became normal even in remote locations. In any case, a ciborium with marble columns could have been introduced as part of the embellishment, perhaps a generation after the construction of the church, when the mosaic was set (see *infra*, p. 30).

Only one section of molding remains in position: that over the north window of the apses (fig. J, 1). Nothing comparable with this coarse profile has been published from Cyprus, and those in Syrian churches are more sophisticated. There, such moldings often extend to the sill or run from window to window at the level of the arch springs.[113] But late fifth-century examples can be cited in which the molding is limited to the arches of individual windows, as at Lythrankomi.[114]

The bases, of which five have survived, are of tall proportion: 0.735 m. square at the base and 0.50 to 0.55 m. high (figs. 13–15). Their exiguous profile gives a diameter of 0.67 m. at the top (fig. J, 11). Since the column used as the northeast respond is a *spolium* it is possible that bases and columns alike were taken from some earlier building. But it is to be noted that a significant detail of the base profile, the canted fillets above and below the cavetto, can be matched in Christian monuments of the fifth century.[115] The flat seating on the top of the base, measurable in only one case, is 0.63 m., which would take a column matching that used for the respond (est. diam. 0.50 m.) if it had the usual apophyge at the bottom.

The two capitals reused as bases in the porch (fig. 16) are similar to one of those outside the west door (fig. 18) and there is a fourth of the same type, but very worn, outside the west gate (fig. 19). The only other surviving, that to the south of the west door, is of the same form but its acanthus leaves are treated rather more naturalistically (fig. 17), perhaps the work of a more conservative craftsman. These capitals vary little in height (0.535 to 0.55 m.) and the lower diameters (0.49 to 0.50 m.) would fit the top of shafts similar

---

[111] E.g., in Basilica A at Nea Anchialos (Soteriou, 'Αρχ.'Εφ. [1929], 26). Neither there, where Basilica C is larger, nor at Kanakaria is this feature proof of "cathedral" status.

[112] For dimensions, see *supra*, note 54.

[113] E.g., Bizzos' church at Ruwêha: *Syria: Publications of the Princeton University Archaeological Expeditions to Syria, 1904–5 and 1909*, II, B, pt. 3 (Leyden, 1909), pls. xv and xviii.

[114] St. Phocas at Basufân (491–92), a window in the south wall: *ibid.*, pt. 6 (Leyden, 1920), 286, fig. 306.

[115] On bases at Thala in Tunisia (Orlandos, Βασιλική, 270, fig. 218,3 and 5, from Gauckler); on a door architrave of the baths at Meriamlik which are probably contemporary with the adjoining late fifth-century domed church (E. Herzfeld and S. Guyer, *Meriamlik und Korykos*, *MAMA*, II [Manchester, 1930], 87, fig. 85, and for the date, 86); on mullions of the transept basilica *extra muros* at Korykos (*ibid.*, 121, fig. 123). This last was originally dated in the late sixth century (*ibid.*, 126) but it is certainly pre-Justinianic (cf. R. Kautzsch, *Kapitellstudien* [Berlin-Leipzig, 1936], 89); Krautheimer includes it with the fifth-century monuments (Krautheimer, *Byz. Architecture*, 85).

A fifth base of similar profile was exposed in the forecourt of the Panagia Kanakaria during the investigations of 1966.

to the northeast respond (0.50 m. near the bottom), allowing for normal diminution. There is thus no reason to doubt that the capitals belong to the basilica from which the apse and the respond have survived, and the variation in detail suggests that they were locally carved for that building. They provide useful evidence for the date at which it was constructed, particularly as they follow the normal form of acanthus capital with four leaves in each of two rows. The development of this style of capital, which has been studied by Kautzsch,[116] is complicated by contemporary use of both marble and stone and of both conservative and experimental designs; also, in the provinces, by the time lag between imported examples and their local derivatives. The locally carved limestone capitals of the churches at Meriamlik in Cilicia probably offer the fairest comparison in the circumstances. A mullion capital from the apse of the basilica of St. Thecla has a geometricized leaf treatment with a broad central rib rather similar to that of the four Lythrankomi capitals, as in figure 18.[117] The reconstruction to which this Meriamlik capital belongs was dated by Guyer in the decade 460–70.[118] But our capitals, to judge by the flatter form and sharper outlines of the leaves, evidently belong to a somewhat later stage in the process of desiccation. The upper part of the Meriamlik capital is not preserved, but the full apparatus of inner and outer helices, which the Lythrankomi capitals retain, is also found on one face of a stone mullion capital of the later North Church at Meriamlik.[119] This has the further interest that the leaves on its other face copy the heavily drilled *acanthus spinosa* of the "Theodosian" type of capital. Ample models of this treatment on marble capitals were available at Meriamlik in the nearby domed church,[120] which must have been erected about 480 if it is indeed the Emperor Zeno's thank offering for his victory over the usurper Basilicus in 476, as Guyer supposed.[121] A comparison of moldings established that the North Church is the later of the two, and a date for it around 500 has been proposed.[122] In the light of these Cilician examples it should not be wide of the mark to assign the Lythrankomi capitals to the closing years of the fifth century. The more naturalistic treatment of the fifth capital (fig. 17) cannot inpose an earlier dating on its companions.

This conclusion may be checked to some extent by comparison with the fine marble capitals from Basilica A at Philippi, provided that allowance is made for the time lag between practices in a major city close to Constantinople and a remote provincial settlement. They were not available to Kautzsch but, applying his principles, Lemerle dated them precisely "around 500,"[123] which

---

[116] Kautzsch, *Kapitellstudien*, 5–115. He does not cite any capital exactly the same as ours.
[117] Herzfeld and Guyer, *Meriamlik und Korykos*, 12f. and figs. 11–13.
[118] *Ibid.*, 32; for Weigand's contrary view, see note 121 *infra*.
[119] *Ibid.*, 74, figs. 67–69.
[120] *Ibid.*, 60, fig. 59.
[121] *Ibid.*, 74. E. Weigand regarded the rebuilding of the basilica of St. Thecla as Zeno's work and dated the domed church in the period 460–70 (*Deutsche Literaturzeitung*, 54 [1933], Heft 52, col. 2471 ff.).
[122] Herzfeld and Guyer, *Meriamlik und Korykos*, 77.
[123] P. Lemerle, *Philippes et la Macédoine orientale* (Paris, 1945), pl. XI and p. 406.

fitted the other finds and has been generally accepted.[124] Here the stylization of the acanthus is more developed than on our capitals and the inner helices are suppressed. But such differences do not exclude contemporaneity in capitals so dissimilarly situated. Thus the capitals and the architectural characteristics of the church alike suggest a construction date in the last years of the fifth century.

Apart from confirming the columnar character of the original basilica, the probe on the north side of the apse revealed an unexpected feature: a pilaster 0.46 m. wide and of 0.10 m. projection southward in the line of the east wall (fig. H). This doubtless once carried an arch of similar width across the front of the conch. Such pilasters and arches are common features of early basilicas in North Syria.[125] The original, very thin gypsum plaster on the apse wall extended onto this pilaster. Subsequently, however, the pilaster was concealed altogether by filling the angle beside it with plaster to form an even curve, which gave the apse a semielliptical form. It is this secondary plaster which extends to the respond formed by the immured column; it consequently relates to the basilica in its original form. The reason for concealing the pilaster very probably arose from a similar and simultaneous suppression of the arch it carried, which the setting of the mosaic would have occasioned: for, otherwise, the arch would have cast disfiguring shadows onto the mosaic round the front of the conch and would have excluded the program actually adopted, for this has a border with Apostle medallions much wider than the concealed arch.[126] It follows that an interval elapsed between the building of the basilica and the setting of the mosaic, though it need not have been a long one. If the original construction is datable to the closing years of the fifth century, the terminus a quo provided for the mosaic by examination of the structure it adorns must be placed somewhat later.

THE FIRST RESTORATION (fig. F)

Almost without exception, the chronology of the subsequent restorations of the church can be fixed only on the evidence of style. The original wood-roofed basilica with colonnades is unlikely to have survived the Arab incursions of the mid-seventh century, which the archaeological evidence from other sites and the historical sources alike indicate were extremely destructive. In any case the first restoration, which gave the building the character indicated in figure F, a–d, is unlikely to have antedated them, for, prior to the first raids, imported marble columns and capitals would almost certainly have been used, as in many buildings of the sixth and early seventh centuries in Cyprus. The recourse to pier-arcades of squared stone set in lime mortar is a reflection, on

---

[124] E.g., Krautheimer, *Byz. Architecture*, 97.

[125] In early fifth-century examples, such as the Kasr-il-Benat convent church (*Syria: Princeton Univ. Arch. Exped.* [*supra*, note 113], II, B, pt. 5 [Leyden, 1912], 218, ill. 222), as well as later, such as Kal'at Sim'an (*ibid.*, pt. 6 [Leyden, 1920], pl. XXIV).
Our discovery of the initial wall face beside the pilaster established that the internal radius of the apse was 2.60 m. and was struck from the same point (0.16 m. west of the chord) as the external curvature.

[126] The evidence of later replastering of the apse wall is also noteworthy. The next layer after that which concealed the pilaster continued onto the masonry of the first restoration, and more followed before construction of the arch underpinning the front of the conch in the second.

the one hand, of the rise of Arab sea power which curtailed, if it did not actually end, the traffic in Proconnesian marble, and, on the other, of local impoverishment which precluded renewal of columns and capitals in stone.[127]

The excavation in 1956–58 of an annex of the basilica of St. Epiphanius at Salamis-Constantia provided some confirmation that in Cyprus this use of lime-built piers instead of columns may be characteristic of the early phase of the period following the first Arab raids. After the destruction of the great basilica, this annex between it and its baptistery was rebuilt as a church, in the form of a three-aisled basilica with small square piers and a timber roof, for piers and walls were alike too weak to carry a vaulted superstructure. Later, it was rebuilt a second time with a series of three domes over the nave and barrel vaults over the aisles.[128] The first reconstruction with pier-arcades could be as early as the years around 700, as the excavator suggested.[129] In the case of the vaulted basilicas in the Carpas, where the pier-arcades were of well dressed masonry set in lime mortar, the most likely time for their erection would be immediately after the destruction of their wood-roofed predecessors, perhaps in the devastating initial Arab incursion when the eastern part of the Island suffered most.[130] At that juncture maintenance or reestablishment

[127] Basilicas with pier-arcades are known at an earlier date; but in Cyprus, if we can judge by that excavated at Marathovouno, they are distinct in that the squared piers are built of rough masonry set in and plastered with gypsum, to which base and other moldings were added in the same material (Papageorghiou, in *RDAC*, 1963, pp. 88 and 100, where this basilica is dated to the fifth or sixth century. Exceptionally, the responds on the east wall were in the form of engaged half-columns). Limited resources may have precluded the use of columns, whether of stone or marble, where gypsum was readily available.

At some time, the basilica which preceded the domed church of the Panagia Angeloktistos at Kiti was similar. A gypsum-built respond attached to the east wall, which carries remains of an acanthus capital carved in plaster, and the bases of the two easternmost piers of the nave arcades were exposed in 1959 (*BCH*, 84 [1960], 296ff. and fig. 75). Subsequent examination has satisfied us that the apse was originally undecorated, and that it had been discolored by fire before the addition of the plaster of which the acanthus capital forms part. The setting of the mosaic followed, but doubtless was executed during the same restoration, to which the gypsum-built pier-arcades may also have belonged (cf. Megaw, "Metropolitan or Provincial?", 74 and note 72).

[128] Excavated by A. I. Dikigoropoulos; see *ArchRep*, 1957, p. 49 and fig. 3.

[129] Dikigoropoulos suggested that the building of the pier-basilica might have been connected with the return in 698 of those Cypriots whom Justinian II had attempted to settle on the Hellespont. On conditions in Cyprus after its demilitarized neutrality had been agreed in the treaty of 688, see R. J. H. Jenkins, "Cyprus between Byzantium and Islam, A. D. 688–965," *Studies Presented to D. M. Robinson*, II (St. Louis, 1953), 1007–14.

[130] Cf. Megaw, "Vaulted Basilicas," 54–56. The tenth-century dating there preferred was subsequently abandoned; see *EUA*, III (1958), col. 187, *s.v.* "Afendrika." After the first Arab expedition of 648/49 was withdrawn on the reported approach of the imperial fleet, the island had a brief respite until 653/54, when the second expedition caused further devastation and established a garrison on the island. It is uncertain whether this survived the crisis following the murder of the Caliph Uthman in 655/56, when Muawiya had to concentrate his forces for his struggle with Ali. Dikigoropoulos argues that it was probably withdrawn then and that Cyprus enjoyed a few more years of peace under Byzantium (*RDAC*, 1940–48, p. 98). At this juncture the Empire, despite the naval disaster of 655, was able to exact humiliating terms from Muawiya in 659. On the other hand, Papageorghiou believes that the Arab garrison which was withdrawn under the Caliph Yazid (680–83) had been continuously maintained since 653/54 ("Les premières incursions arabes à Chypre et leurs conséquences," Ἀφιέρωμα εἰς τὸν Κωνσταντίνον Σπυριδάκιν [Nicosia, 1964], 152–58; cf. N. Oikonomaki, Ἡ ἐν Κύπρῳ Ἀραβοκρατία κατὰ τὰς ἀραβικὰς πηγάς, in ΠΠΔΚΣ, Β', 194).

The initial reconstructions could, then, have been undertaken between 649 and 653 and, whether or not favorable conditions for rebuilding again obtained for a few years after 656, the political if not the economic circumstances of Cyprus around 685 and after 698 would have permitted further church reconstruction.

of effective Byzantine control would still have been expected and the withdrawal from such coastal settlements as that at Aphentrika, which was general
later, might not yet have been contemplated.

Apart from its timber-roofed nave and aisles, the Panagia Kanakaria, in this
second phase of its history, was in another respect closer to the wood-roofed
pier-basilica at Salamis-Constantia than to the vaulted basilicas: both have
lateral walls in the bema, pierced by small archways indicating a fully
developed tripartite sanctuary. The wider arches of the bay immediately west
of the bema (fig. F, a) shows that already at this stage some form of barrier
below the "triumphal arch" extended across the aisles also, as does the present
icon screen. In the reconstruction of the Aphentrika and Syka basilicas the
pier-arcades continue to the east wall, as the colonnades which they replaced
had done. This was the normal arrangement of fifth-, sixth-, and early seventh-
century column-basilicas in Cyprus, as elsewhere; and it was followed in those
pier-basilicas which are contemporary with them.[131] It is arguable that those
of the later pier-basilica reconstructions which have continuous arcades
antedated those with tripartite sanctuaries, in which case the vaulted basilicas
at Aphentrika and Syka might have been erected as early as the brief respite
after the withdrawal of the first Arab expedition of 648/49. The years around
700 suggested for the basilica with bema walls at Salamis-Constantia would be
suitable also for the first restoration of the Panagia Kanakaria, which shows
a similar development.

Monuments outside Cyprus do not provide any very satisfactory terminus
a quo for the prevalence of the walled bema. Although this was a usual feature
of domed churches from the later sixth century, its adoption in three-aisled
basilicas was erratic. In Syria that at Qalb-Louzeh, if it is to be dated ca. 500,
offers an early example in conjunction with pier-arcades of the large-arch
type.[132] But in the approximately contemporary basilica of St. Sergius at
R'safah-Sergiopolis the arcades continue to the apse;[133] likewise in the
basilica dated 602 at Shêkh Slemân with pier-arcades of narrow bays, as at
Lythrankomi, which are rare in Syria.[134] In Asia Minor, the west church at
Alahan, which is of Justinianic if not earlier date, had a walled sanctuary
separated by a transverse arch from the colonnaded nave.[135] In the area of
Constantinople, the wood-roofed basilica at Nessebar (Mesembria), a seaport
where the appearance of pier-arcades would suggest a relatively late date,
they nevertheless continue to the east wall.[136] So also in the vaulted basilicas

---

[131] E.g., that at Marathovouno; see *supra*, note 127.

[132] J. Lassus, *Sanctuaires chrétiens de Syrie* (Paris, 1947), 76, fig. 38 and pl. XXXIV; Krautheimer, *Byz. Architecture*, 113, fig. 45.

[133] Lassus, *op. cit.*, 32, fig. 17; Krautheimer, *op. cit.*, 114, fig. 114.

[134] *Syria: Princeton Univ. Arch. Exped.*, II, B, pt. 6 (Leyden, 1920), 338, ill. 386.

[135] For an up-to-date plan, see M. Gough, in *AnatSt*, 18 (1968), 161, fig. 1. Reviewing the various dates from the fourth century onward which have been proposed for the Alahan complex, Gough preferred a mid-fifth-century date for the west church, assuming that it would have been completed before the hospice contributed by the Tarasis who died in 462 (*ibid.*, 17 [1967], 45–47).

[136] For the plan, see A. Rašenov, *Eglises de Mesembria* (Sofia, 1932), fig. 3; for the date, *BCH*, 84 (1960), 244 ff., where discoveries indicating a sixth to seventh-century date are reported.

of St. George in Astypalaea,[137] at Belovo in Bulgaria,[138] and at Tolmeita in Cyrenaica,[139] all of which, unlike the examples at Aphentrika and Syka in Cyprus, seem to have been constructed *ab initio* in this form and some of them not later than the sixth century. Only in Yugoslavia does it seem possible to distinguish among modest wood-roofed pier-basilicas a development from continuous arcades associated with the early type of clergy benches[140] to examples with the walled bema,[141] a development parallel to the appearance in major column-basilicas datable within the sixth century, such as the cathedral of Caričin Grad,[142] of the fully tripartite sanctuary of some domed churches. It can at least be said that there is nothing anachronous in assigning the first restoration of the Panagia Kanakaria with its walled bema to the years around 700, even though basilicas rebuilt at a later date with continuous pier-arcades are known.[143]

We have to deduce from the greater thickness of the bema walls that the present windowless dome replaced some form of high superstructure erected in the first restoration.[144] This second state of the Kanakaria church, combining a high transverse roof over the bema (if not a dome or a pyramidal roof) with wood-roofed nave and aisles (fig. F), brings it into relation with other basilicas incorporating a higher roof or dome over the sanctuary. The original Apostoleion, known only from the description of Eusebius,[145] may be regarded as their archetype. Several of the surviving examples are datable before the mid-seventh century.[146] Consequently, the introduction of a transverse roof

[137] P. E. Lazarides, in Πεπραγμένα τοῦ Θ.' Διεθ. Βυζ. Συνεδρίου: Ἑλληνικά, Παραρτ. 7 Α' (Athens, 1955), 237, fig. 2.

[138] A. Grabar and W. Emerson, "The Basilica of Belovo," *BByzI*, 1 (1946), 45, fig. 2; Krautheimer, *Byz. Architecture*, 194 ("late sixth century") and pl. 107A.

[139] The "Fortress Church" reexamined by C. H. Kraeling, in *Ptolemais, City of the Libyan Pentapolis* (Chicago, 1962), 97 ff., where he proposed a mid-fifth-century date. Krautheimer's dating in the sixth century is preferable (*Byz. Architecture*, 194 and pl. 107B).

[140] E.g., the southwest church at Caričin Grad (D. Mano-Zisi, in *Starinar*, 9–10 [1958–59], 295 ff., fig. 1; R. F. Hoddinott, *Early Byzantine Churches in Macedonia and South Serbia* [London, 1963], fig. 144) and that at Suvadol (F. Mesesnel, in *Actes du IVᵉ Congrès intern. des Etudes byzantines*, II = *BIABulg*, 10 [1936], 186, fig. 124; Hoddinott, *op. cit.*, fig. 128).

[141] At Kalaja near Radinovac (Hoddinott, *op. cit.*, fig. 103) and at Prokuplje, where alone the bema walls are pierced by entries into the pastophoria (*ibid.*, fig. 105); compare the basilica at Hissar Bania near Philippoupolis, Trontchef's plan of which is reproduced by Orlandos, Βασιλική, 185, fig. 149, from *Annuaire du Musée et de la Bibliothèque Nationale de Plovdiv*, 1935–36, p. 107, fig. 80.

[142] Hoddinott, *op. cit.*, fig. 131; Krautheimer, *Byz. Architecture*, fig. 76(A). Cf. the late sixth-century remodeling of the Pirdop basilica in Bulgaria where a dome is postulated (*ibid.*, 181; Hoddinott, *op. cit.*, 206, fig. 132).

Comparable also is the rock-cut pier-basilica at Midye in Thrace, where the separation of bema and pastophoria from nave and aisles is well defined. Nicole Thierry favors a date for this monument in the sixth century (*CahArch*, 20 [1970], 75).

[143] E.g., the reconstruction dated 812 of the basilica at Alakilise in Lycia cited by Smirnov ("Mozaiki," 70, note 1). See M. Harrison, in *AnatSt*, 13 (1963), 125, fig. 3 and 126 ff., with earlier bibliography.

[144] Nothing seems to have been done at this stage to reinforce the front of the conch, which would have carried the east wall of the superstructure (see fig. G). Later, some resulting subsidence led to the construction of the existing arch to support the crown of the conch, which is now some 0.30 m. below its original position.

[145] Eusebius, *Vita Constantini*, IV.58 ff. (*PG*, 20, col. 1209 f.). For a recent discussion, see Krautheimer, *Byz. Architecture*, 46 and 320 note 4.

[146] Early examples are the basilicas in the two monasteries at Sohag, where domes have replaced the original timber roofs over the "crossings" (*ibid.*, 89, with bibliography, 327 note 33), and the Ilissus basilica in Athens (G. Soteriou, in 'Αρχ.'Εφ. [1919], 3, fig. 3; restored plan in Orlandos, Βασιλική,

of the type we have inferred over the bema in the first restoration of our church around 700 would not be surprising.

THE SECOND RESTORATION

The introduction of a dome and vaults over the nave and the reconstruction of the aisles with barrel vaults could best be associated with the general adoption of domed-type churches in Cyprus. The normal inscribed-cross type with a single dome may well have been rare in Cyprus before the reestablishment of Byzantine rule in 965. No surviving example is demonstrably earlier than the eleventh century and the majority appear to be of the twelfth century, to which the second restoration of the Lythrankomi church could reasonably be assigned.

The widespread damage to the church which necessitated such extensive rebuilding can hardly have spared the bema. After the subsidence of the apse conch and of the "triumphal arch" and the collapse of whatever structure had roofed the space between them, the bema would have been reroofed at the same time as the rest, in all probability in the form which we see today. We have seen that the construction of the existing narthex is to be connected with the same phase of the building's history. We have also assigned to this phase the first additional leaf of masonry sheathing the exterior of the main apse, which doubtless received the polygonal outline of its topmost courses at this time. This second restoration can hardly be later than the twelfth century in view of its purely Byzantine character and the indications that part of the building again required attention in the thirteenth (see *infra*). The earliest fresco fragments which cover or are otherwise related to the walls of this restoration include the figure of St. Barbara in the north arcade (figs. 91 and 96) and an archangel on the north wall of the south aisle (fig. 90). These doubtless belong to a general redecoration of the restored building. Their style is considered below and is consistent with a twelfth-century date for the restoration of which they formed part.

Two distinctive architectural features of the second restoration also point to the twelfth century. The cruciform window in the west gable (fig. 29) recalls the cruciform recess surrounded by a molding (and perhaps originally conceived as a window) in the north gable of the Holy Trinity chapel in the monastery of St. Chrysostom, which is now known to be an addition of the *dux* Emathius Philocales, probably in the second decade of the twelfth century.[147] Secondly, the curious profile of the bema dome with a sharper curvature at the crown (figs. B, D) is repeated in another windowless dome in Cyprus, that of the church of the Holy Apostles at Perachorio, for which the style of its frescoes suggests a construction date in the third quarter of the twelfth century.[148]

185, fig. 148). In the latter also, the precise form of the superstructure carried by the four massive piers is unknown (cf. Krautheimer, *Byz. Architecture*, 92). Closer to our period but still before the mid-seventh century is the cathedral of Sofia, though here the nave and aisles were covered by groin vaults (*ibid.*, 184, fig. 72, plate 93, and bibliography, 340 note 29).

[147] *CARDA*, 1958, fig. 16; on the date, see Mango and Hawkins, in *DOP*, 18, pp. 335–38.

[148] Megaw-Hawkins, "Perachorio," 282, fig. a, and, for the date, 348.

The dangerous dislocation of the nave walls and the collapse of the "triumphal arch" prior to the second restoration, when the whole super-structure of the bema must also have fallen, are strongly indicative of an earthquake. There are two recorded in the mid-twelfth century: the first in 1157, which was particularly severe over the greater part of Syria and the Orient,[149] and one in Cyprus a few years later which, according to St. Neophytos, destroyed fourteen churches in the district of Paphos alone.[150] Damage caused by one or other of these may well have been the occasion of the second restoration of the Panagia Kanakaria.

The next major undertaking was another reconstruction of the south aisle, embracing the diaconicon apse and almost the entire south wall, including that of the narthex. The combination of the pointed arches supporting the new vault with higher proportions and more massive construction suggests the influence of Frankish practice; but the Comnenian style of the earliest fresco fragments on the new south wall, which survive from the first of two superimposed panels of St. George (figs. 97–100), would hardly admit of a date after the thirteenth century (see *infra*, p. 152 f.).

At the west end of the south aisle a fragment of the south wall of the second restoration was retained, but this was concealed externally by the masonry of the reconstruction, which increased the wall thickness to 1.10 m. (see plan, fig. C). The earlier south wall of the narthex was evidently retained *in toto* though it is concealed both inside and out by added masonry, which brings the thickness here to 1.41 m. The buttresses against the west wall of the narthex were added at the same time.

The first St. George painted in the reconstructed south aisle is not matched by any of the other surviving fresco fragments, but it is earlier in style than those in the dome bay of the nave on the north side, which attest a partial redecoration before the third major restoration. These fragments from a Last Judgment (figs. 101, 104, and 105) and the rather crude soffit designs connected with them (figs. 102 and 103) are tentatively assigned to the fourteenth century (see *infra*, p. 153 ff.). The relationships of the first St. George panel, as well as the architectural indications, permit us to assign the reconstruction of the south aisle to the thirteenth century.

THE THIRD AND LATER RESTORATIONS

The last major restoration of the church included the reconstruction of the dome on new supporting arches and a general redecoration, from which

---

[149] Hill, *History*, I, 311 note 1, quoting Yusuf ibn Toghribirdi, in *Receuil des Historiens des Croisades. Historiens Orientaux*, III, (Paris, 1884), 508 f.

[150] This occurred at the beginning of the Saint's sojourn in his hermitage near Paphos, to which he retired on June 24, 1159: Ἀνάμνησις περὶ σεισμῶν, § 10 (ed. Delehaye, *AnalBoll*, 26 [1907], 211). Not long after, Neophytos was visited by a monk from Antioch who told him of the earthquake (probably that of 1157) which had thrown down the great church there, killing the patriarch and many of his congregation: *ibid.*, § 11 (ed. Delehaye, 211 f.). On the simultaneous impact of earthquakes in Syria and Cyprus, see E. Oberhummer, *Die Insel Cypern* (Munich, 1903), 141.

The state of the mosaic in the twelfth century may be gauged to some extent by the very much better preservation of those parts which were concealed by the arch constructed across the front of the conch in the second restoration. The greater part of the main composition may then also have been largely intact, especially in the lower areas which are now entirely blank.

have survived all the existing frescoes in the bema and the majority of those elsewhere. This redecoration extended onto the new arches under the dome (fig. 132) and the style of the painting to some extent fixes the date of the structural work. This last series of frescoes includes the Theotokos Kanakaria in the south porch and the later of the superimposed panels of St. George in the south aisle. The graffito on this panel with the date 1598 (fig. 127) provides a terminus ad quem for the whole operation. The proportions of the dome and the style of the frescoes suggest that this phase coincided with the widespread restoration and rebuilding of Orthodox churches throughout the Island in the early years of the Venetian occupation.[151] It is probable that much of this activity around 1500 was occasioned by the serious earthquake of 1491, when part of the cathedral of St. Sophia and many other buildings in Nicosia were thrown down and damage was caused in all parts of the Island.[152]

The dome, damaged again by 1750,[153] was doubtless repaired by Abbot Chrysanthos in 1779. Apart from general maintenance such as replastering the interior wherever the frescoes had fallen (the ceramic plates in figs. 21 and 22 were almost certainly inserted during his repairs), he must have undertaken some structural work at the west end to justify inserting his inscription there. This would have included the reconstruction in their present form of the main entrance and its lintel, above which the inscription is set (fig. 8). At the other end of the church, the second external addition to the thickness of the wall of the main apse, which was of rather poor construction, may well have been built as late as Chrysanthos' time.

The date 1859 on the cross surmounting the dome over the nave does not relate, so far as we know, to any major repair work elsewhere. But the cross itself is of interest for the inscriptions on its west face. In addition to the year at the base and the normal abbreviation in capitals for Ἰησοῦς Χριστὸς νικᾶ at the center, the name of the mason who carved it is recorded in both Arabic and Greek. Upper arm (Arabic script): *Jurjīūs*; north arm (Arabic script): *al-masīhī*, "The Christian"; lower arm (monogramatically in Greek capitals): Γεώργιος (fig. 133). Evidently he was a Maronite.

The belfry of 1888 was almost certainly an isolated addition.

The repairs of 1920 reported by Gunnis[154] were concerned with the main apse, where a crack in the semidome was reported in June 1914 to let in daylight at the feet of the Virgin.[155] They evidently included removal of the bishop's throne and the wide steps shown on Smirnov's plan leading up to it; also further strengthening of the apse wall by filling up the internal recesses, which were all that remained of the lateral windows, and by making the third and final external addition to its thickness.[156]

---

[151] A notable example is the catholicon of the monastery of St. Neophytos, datable about 1500: Mango-Hawkins, "St. Neophytos," 203.

[152] Oberhummer, *Die Insel Cypern*, 143; Hill, *History*, III, 819.

[153] In 1750, A. Drummond saw only a drum: *Travels Through Different Cities* (London, 1754), fig. 7.

[154] Gunnis, *Historic Cyprus*, 332.   [155] Jeffery, *Monuments*, 262.

[156] The recesses appear on Smirnov's plan ("Mozaiki," 68) but not on that made in 1931 for Soteriou (Μνημεῖα, fig. 20), where the throne seen by Jeffery in 1914 (*Monuments*, 262) is also missing, and where the apse wall is 0.30 m. thicker than on Smirnov's plan.

PART TWO

The Mosaic

DESCRIPTION

The apse, in plan, is a little less than a semicircle, and the conch in consequence less than a quarter sphere. Owing to the distortion in several directions its present measurements are a poor guide to its original form and dimensions. It is estimated that the depth of the apse as constructed was 2.44 m. against an estimated radius of 2.60.[157] The pilasters which projected on either side reduced the span of the opening in the east wall, and when the face of the apse wall was subsequently made to line up with these (as shown in fig. H) in preparation for the setting of the mosaic, the apse and the conch with it assumed in plan an irregular, elliptical form. The conch at this stage, when the mosaic was set, would have been some 2.44 m. deep, 4.78 m. wide, and 2.66 m. high.

The mosaic decoration treated the whole of this irregular conch area as a unity, insofar as it was framed by a uniform Irisated Border, arching round the front edge of the conch and passing along the top of the apse wall, just above the cornice (figs. 41 and 42). But the mosaicist divided the area within this border into two distinct parts. He limited the main composition to the inner part of the conch and treated the remainder as if it were the soffit of a quite separate arch (fig. 39). This dichotomy served to mask the change in curvature from that of the conch as originally constructed to the sharper curve where the plaster bed was lined up with the soffit of the arch carried by the two pilasters. On the other hand, the series of mosaic borders served to underline the structural function of the fore-edge of the conch: to support the part of the east wall above it, a function which explains the original subordinate masonry arch now concealed by the mosaic. The soffit of the "arch" of mosaic was decorated with a broad band enriched with a series of medallions containing busts of the apostles. This Apostle Border, so arranged that the portraits could be seen without distortion only from either side of the apse (figs. 41 and 42), bears no integral relationship to the main representation in the conch, which has to be viewed from the body of the church. Perhaps for this reason these two main elements of the decoration were separated from each other by an Intermediate Border, of purely ornamental character.

The front edge of the conch, where it meets the vertical inner face of the east wall, doubtless formed a sharp angle in the masonry of the original supporting arch; but this edge was rounded off in the plaster beds of the

---

[157] The curvature of the apse wall both inside and out was centered at a point about 0.16 m. westward of the line of the inner face of the east wall.

mosaic. Onto the inner part of this "bull-nose" the outer edge of the Irisated Border extended. The remainder was covered by yet another border, the Outer Border as it is here called, of which little can be seen, but which doubtless extended onto the vertical face of the east wall to embellish the front of the arch over the entry to the apse.

What other mosaics decorated the east wall above and on either side of the apse cannot now be determined, for what survives of the wall face is entirely concealed by the secondary vaulting over the bema. That there were mosaics on this wall face is certain. During Mr. Papageorghiou's investigations in 1966, tests made below the present floor in front of the altar-table and just behind it produced some small pieces of plaster bed with the tesserae still in place, the largest not more than 0.10 m. square. Some of these had fallen from the conch, but several have gold tesserae set at an angle to the surface. This technique occurs nowhere in the surviving parts of the apse decoration, and in other Early Byzantine mosaics it is found exclusively on vertical surfaces. In addition, tesserae of a grey Proconnesian marble not observed in the conch are included, and those pieces which appear to come from repeating patterns cannot be matched in the borders preserved in the apse. However, the mosaic decoration of the wall above the apse was probably part of a single undertaking with that of the conch. Included in this find were tesserae of white marble dipped in red earth color which, as we shall see, are of frequent occurrence in the main composition and its borders.

The Outer Border will be described first, then the Irisated Border, the Apostle Border (p. 40), the Intermediate Border (p. 48), and finally the main composition in the conch (p. 49).

The Outer Border (fig. 43 left, and fig. K)

Little of this border has survived *in situ* and that little is all along the inner edge, next to the Irisated Border, and is confined to the lower sections on either side: up to 0.80 m. on the south, up to 1.30 m. on the north. However, when the masonry of the second restoration which had entirely concealed these remnants was partially removed, two substantial fragments were found detached on the south side, fallen into a cavity between the original surface and the addition designed to support it.[158] The two detached fragments join and the larger fits what is preserved *in situ*, with the result that at one point virtually the full width of the border is known and the entire scheme of its design can be reconstituted (fig. K).

The border would have been some 0.22 m. wide inclusive of an edging of a single row of purple-black tesserae on either side. The design comprises a series of quadrangular forms repeated in different colors to represent the ends of roof joists seen from below in isometric projection. These are filled out with triangles suggestive of the sections of ceiling or coffers between them. The

---

[158] The cavity is visible in figure 48. The detached fragments were lodged in the Cyprus Museum at the time of their discovery in 1961.

"joists" alternate in direction and would have formed a zigzag border round the fore-edge of the conch. They are colored alternately green and red, each in two tones. The two tones are counterchanged: thus the lowest green "joist" has a dark side and a light green underside whereas the next green "joist" has a dark underside. A sequence of four "joists" thus formed the repeating design unit, about 0.95 m. high, in which the alternate lighting accentuated the trompe l'oeil effect. For the greens and reds, glass tesserae were used except for the lighter tone of red, which was provided by white marble dipped in red earth pigment now largely lost. Within these areas of green and red there is some gradation of tone; in particular, the edges of the "joists" are often accentuated with one or two rows of tesserae of a lighter or darker tone.

The joist ends are edged with a single row of gold, inclusive of which they are 0.10 m. wide by 0.12 m. high. In all cases a yellow marble provides the ground color and each is decorated with four petals of olive-brown glass radiating to the corners from small centers of the same color with a single yellow marble tessera in the middle. A group of four olive-brown glass tesserae is set in each quarter of the ground. In the triangles only dark blue glass and a cream-colored stone are used, those preserved are decorated with an "ivy leaf" bud in the latter material with a single tessera of the same in the spaces on each side. Dark blue glass is also used for the outer edgings along the sides forming the obtuse apex of each triangle.

The section of the inner edge of this border preserved on the north side of the apse follows the same color scheme.

The Irisated Border (figs. 43, 48, and 52)

This has been exposed on both sides of the apse. On the south side it can be seen returning below the Apostle Border to extend as a horizontal border at the base of the conch, a little above the cornice (fig. 52). Here it is 0.155 m. deep. The tesserae are set diagonally throughout. On the north side of the conch twenty-two were counted in one diagonal row; on the south twenty-six were counted in another. The tesserae range in color from red on the inner edge, passing through pink, white, yellow, and green to dark green (in places blue) on the outer. On the inner edge the border is outlined by a single row of brown tesserae set normally; and wherever it is fully preserved it is separated on both sides from the borders which adjoin it by a single row of white. Below and adjoining the two lowest medallions of the Apostle Border on both sides, the red of the Irisated Border is formed of red glass tesserae,[159] but above this the mosaicist has employed instead white marble tesserae once tinted with red pigment, most of which has been lost.

At the bottom of the conch this Irisated Border was separated from the plaster cornice by an additional border of crowstep pattern. Here, into a ground of white marble tesserae projects a row of pyramids each four tesserae

---

[159] On the north side the first row of the red glass tesserae along the inner edge is set normally, not diagonally.

high, formed normally of glass tesserae alternately red and green. The only preserved section is under the south end of the Apostle Border (fig. 52). The most easterly of the pyramids appeared at first sight to be missing, because here white tesserae were used. However, close inspection revealed that in the interstices between the tesserae of this pyramid the plaster of the setting bed is red in color. It is evident that white marble tesserae dipped into a red pigment, now eroded, had been used for this particular pyramid.

The Apostle Border (frontispiece, figs. 48, 49, 53–72, and color figs. 137–43)

The band enriched with medallions containing busts of the apostles forms an arch across the front of the apse. It is 0.49 m. wide between the outer edges of the dark background. The medallions are so spaced that there would have been thirteen in all. The central one at the crown of the arch is missing, as are the two uppermost medallions on the south side, and some of the others are damaged. The medallions are linked by a narrow stem edged with yellow marble and formed by two rows of green glass tesserae of two tones. Formalized acanthus foliage grows out from this stem to frame the medallions. On either side of the stem the foliage is folded to form a series of waists between the medallions, whence it extends pointed leaves into the spandrel areas. Everywhere it is outlined with a row of dark purple tesserae. The dark ground in the remaining areas is formed of dark blue tesserae in the outer (west) half of the band and of purple in the inner half, except in the lowest inner spandrel on the north where dark translucent tesserae are used. Scattered in these background areas are rosettes, stars, and other small motifs of white marble with red center points: a red glass tessera in one case but elsewhere white marble dipped in red pigment. Glass tesserae of four tones are used in the foliage, ranging from olive-green through light green and yellow-green to yellow on the highlights, which are edged with a row of ochre-colored marble. Many of the leaves end in sharp spines, which are particularly well defined on the south side (figs. 48, 65, and 69).

The medallions are 0.45 m. in diameter, inclusive of the outline, for which purple-brown is used, that of Paul alone excepted. Within the outlines the medallions on the north side are bordered with single rows of light olive-brown glass and white marble; on the south side the corresponding borders are of light olive-brown and a paler shade in the inner row. The names of the apostles are divided into two groups of letters set vertically on either side of their nimbi in dark purple tesserae; a slightly darker purple-black is used on the south side. The grounds of the medallions, with one exception, are blue, for which light blue and pale blue glass and white marble tesserae are used. These are shaded from a dark tone above the right shoulder of each apostle[160] to a light tone above the left shoulder, to suggest the concave form of the clipeus which each medallion represents, lit from the apostle's right in each case.

[160] Exceptionally, in the cases of Matthew and Jude above their right shoulders the blue ground is edged with a single line of pale purple, which returns a short way up the outline of the nimbus.

Exceptionally, for the ground of Paul's medallion, the top one on the north side, light purple tesserae are used. This distinction was no doubt repeated in the missing topmost medallion on the south side, the appropriate position for Peter. Paul's medallion is exceptional in another respect: the colors used elsewhere for the outline (purple-brown) and the circle of tesserae next to it (light olive-brown) are interchanged.

All the nimbi are outlined with a single row of white marble tesserae, within which there is a single row of yellow glass, except in the cases of Paul and Andrew (the two uppermost on the north side), whose nimbi have the white marble outline alone. In the case of Andrew this simplification was necessary to provide extra space to do justice to his usual hair style, standing on end. In each case the field of the nimbus is of gold tesserae laid in concentric circles except for a single row following the outline of the head. The gold tesserae average about 0.009 m. square, but they are very irregular and include some triangular pieces.

All the apostles wear a himation over a chiton of differing color. The latter is shown as fitting loosely at the neck, of which a rather large area is exposed; in several cases there is a fold in the neckline. In every case the himation hangs well over the left shoulder, but only just covers the right. The four evangelists carry Gospels, of which little more than the top edge is seen. No two evangelists adjoin each other and their Gospels give variety to what could have been a monotonously uniform series of busts. In fact, the series is varied in other ways also, quite apart from the differentiation of the heads. In some cases an underfold of the himation is shown drawn across the chest from the left shoulder (e.g., Andrew, fig. 55), in others only the chiton is seen below the vertical overfold (e.g., Matthew, fig. 59); and both these treatments are further diversified by variation of the chiton neckline. Where identical combinations of these treatments occur in two busts (e.g., Andrew and Bartholomew; Matthew and Luke) they never adjoin each other. In the same way, repetitions in the colors of the garments are avoided in adjoining medallions. On the north side, although purple is twice used for the himation (Andrew and Thomas), no combination of colors is repeated here; and not one of those used on this side recurs among the four surviving busts on the south side of the arch. Exceptionally, tones of the same color (blue) are used for the chiton in three adjoining medallions on the south side (Philip, Luke, and James).

The heads, which are about two-thirds life-size, are strongly outlined with purple or purple-black tesserae; the ears also in the three lowest medallions on the north side, whereas on the south the ears lack this definition and those of James are not outlined at all. Purple and purple-black are used also for eyebrows and for the lashes and pupils of the eyes, for moustaches, and for the shadow lines along the noses and between and below the lips. For the lighter flesh tones white, cream, and pink marbles and orange-vermilion glass are used. For the shadows light purple glass tesserae are employed. In several cases (Paul, Philip, and James) a slight shadow over the bridge of the nose is rendered by a small group of yellow glass tesserae. In the four lower heads on the north side, there is a group of pale blue tesserae in the same place. The head of Bartholomew alone lacks this treatment. On the south side, the shading on the faces and necks is stronger, and here darker purple glass tesserae are used. In all the faces the tesserae are smaller than elsewhere, and reach a minimum of about 0.004 m. square. On both sides the lighting is from the viewer's left. In all the apostles on the south side the neck is heavily shaded on the other side. In almost every case the left shoulder is shaded and shows dark against the lighter tones of blue used in the adjoining area of the blue background, whereas the other shoulder stands out light against the darker tones of the shadowed side of the clipeus above it. But in most cases some reverse lighting is also indicated. For example, the fold of the himation hanging vertically from the left shoulder casts a shadow on the neck and on the under-fold, or on the chiton where this is not covered. These reverse shadows may be conceived as cast by reflected light from the brighter section of the clipeus.

Paul, much damaged, heads the group on the north side of the arch and is followed by Andrew, Matthew, Jude, Mark, and Thomas. On the south, the two missing medallions at the top would have figured Peter and John; below survive Philip and Luke, though damaged, followed by James and Bartholomew. They will be described in the order of seniority in which they are arranged.

Peter

Missing, with the whole of the top medallion on the south side.

Paul. [Π|Α]|Υ||[Λ|Ο|C] (figs. 53 and 57)

Badly damaged, in the top medallion on the north side. Only a few tesserae of the ground are preserved above the shoulders: light purple on the right, purple on the left interrupted by dark purple tesserae forming what is evidently the lower part of the letter Υ, of the type with a cross bar. The chiton is light blue with darker blue shading and white marble highlights; the himation white with light blue shadows. Enough of the head is preserved to leave no doubt of the identification: high furrowed brow and pointed beard, purple shaded by purple-black.

John

Missing, with the whole of the second medallion on the south side.

Andrew. Α|Ν|ΔΡ|Ε||Α|C (figs. 53, 55, 56, and color fig. 141)

The second on the north side, this medallion lacks a section of its rim on the right, where the ground is very light passing from white through very pale purple to pale blue. The chiton is white with some pink tesserae and light blue shadows; its folded neckline is of dark red glass.[161] Pale purple tesserae are used for the slight shadow cast by the head on the neck. The himation is pale purple with purple shadows and white marble highlights; it is draped well across the chest below the fold which hangs over the left shoulder.

Andrew's wild and flowing hair is parted in the middle and fills much of the area of the nimbus. Hair, beard, and eyebrows are all light blue shadowed with dark olive and dark translucent glass tesserae. For the features and the outline of the head purple and purple-black are used and there are light purple shadows below the eyebrows, along the nose, and below the eyes. The irises of the eyes are light blue and the whites, as in the whole series, are of white marble except for a single pale blue glass tessera below each iris. A few dark red tesserae are used at the inner ends of the upper eyelashes, below the nose, and in the lips, and a single tessera of the same color is at the lowest point of the left cheek, providing a sharp contrast to the adjoining blues in the beard and moustache.

Philip. [ΦΙ |ΛΙ |Π] ‖Π |Ο |C (figs. 54 and 58)

Of this medallion, the third on the south side, rather less than half is preserved, the part that was protected by the underpinning arch. The apostle's chiton is light blue; his himation is light brown with yellow highlights and darker brown shadows, and like Andrew's it is drawn across the chest below the part of this garment hanging over his left shoulder. His dark hair recedes from a furrowed brow and like his pointed beard is rendered with purple tesserae shaded with black. On the rather strongly lighted face and neck the shaded areas are purple; above the bridge of the nose there is a small group of yellow tesserae. The eyes were light brown. For the tear duct, below the nose, and on the lips red tesserae are used; but not so many, nor of so bright a color as in the heads on the north side of the arch.

Matthew. M |A |T ‖Θ |E |O |C (figs. 59, 60, and color fig. 139)

This medallion, the third from the top on the north, is complete except for a few tesserae missing from the apostle's left ear and from the part of the nimbus immediately below it. Like the other evangelists, Matthew carries his Gospel in the form of a codex, of which only the upper part is seen. It is outlined with tesserae of dark translucent glass, which are also used to shadow the gold clasps. The edges are of dark red glass mixed with tesserae of white marble which were originally tinted red. The chiton is pale olive lit with white marble and shaded with purple; it has a loose fold in the dark blue neckline. The himation is yellow-brown lit with yellow glass tesserae and outlined with dark translucent glass, except on the apostle's right shoulder; there it is highlighted against the adjoining darker area of the ground, where the blue is edged with a single row of pale purple tesserae. Although the other shoulder

---

[161] Except for one of white marble, doubtless formerly pigmented with red.

is heavily shaded, no part of the neck is represented in shadow; this is exceptional.

Matthew's dark hair is shown closely cropped and with a short fringe; like his short, slightly pointed beard it is rendered in various tones of purple shadowed with purple-black. The chin is bare below the mouth. The features are again strongly outlined and in the face the usual three colors of marble are thrown into relief with glass tesserae, dull olive-green, pale brown, and purple, to give fullness to the cheeks and roundness to the brow. The latter is further defined by the usual shadow between the eyebrows, here rendered by a group of pale blue tesserae. A little dark red glass is again used for the tear ducts in the eyes and below the tip of the nose: also at the corners of the lips, which are otherwise of pink marble. A lighter tone of red is used for the contour of the chin. The eyes are olive-green and the whites are marble with pale blue glass at the center. The ears are outlined with dark translucent glass.

Luke. [Λ |O |Y] ‖ K |A |C (figs. 54, 61, and 62)

Much has fallen from the left, inner side of this medallion, the fourth from the top on the south side, but the rest, including the greater part of the head, was revealed in good condition when the supporting arch was removed. There is some irregularity in the gold tesserae of the nimbus, normally set in concentric rows. The chiton is of light blues with the usual loose fold in the purple neckline. The himation, now white, was evidently red originally. For over the left shoulder and above the Gospel the outlines are of red glass and in the interstices of the marble tesserae between these outlines the plaster of the setting bed is red. Some of the white marble tesserae on the other shoulder still have traces of red paint on the surface. The Gospel book is outlined against the chiton with blue. The clasps are red and white. The cover is red bordered with gold and the edges of the pages are light purple and white (probably once tinted red).

Luke's hair, with a line of curls across the brow, his moustache, and short beard are all rendered with purple tesserae, outlined and shaded with black. The chin is again bare below the mouth. The face has purple shadows, rather strong down the left side. On the furrowed brow and down the left side of the nose an unusual half-shadow technique is used: olive-green and pink tesserae alternating in a single row. On the other side of the nose olive-green and red alternate. The eyes have olive irises and the usual black pupils. As in the case of Philip, isolated red tesserae are used for the tear ducts and on the lips.

Jude. Θ |A |Δ ‖ Δ |E |O |C (figs. 63, 64, and color fig. 143)

This medallion, the fourth on the north, is undamaged. The apostle wears a light purple chiton with translucent tesserae for the darkest shadow; the straight neckline is of dark red and purple. The himation is olive-green with white marble lights and is edged with dark translucent glass on the shaded shoulder, on the other with a line of pale purple tesserae which extends somewhat erratically along the lower periphery of the nimbus. As in the case of Matthew, the meager shading of the neck with purple tesserae does not match the stronger light and shade of the himation.

In form and coloring the head is close to that of Matthew; but here the beard is exiguous, ending in two incipient points, while the hair recedes steeply above the temples. Though the nose shadow again indicates a stronger light from the apostle's right, both sides of the face are shaded. Further relief is given by the skillful use of rather orange-pink marble, notably on the cheeks, on the contour of the chin, on the lips, and, as an intermediate tone, down the ridge of the nose. A few of the dark red tesserae are again used for the tear ducts, below the nose, and on the lips; and, exceptionally, they are used with purple for the irises.

James. I |A |K |O ‖B |O |C (figs. 65, 66, and color fig. 142)

The edge of this medallion is missing on the unprotected side and a few tesserae from the ground and the nimbus have also fallen. Fifth on the south side, James wears a pale blue chiton with darker blue shadows and highlights rendered with white marble. For the straight neckline purple tesserae are used, shading to dark purple. The himation is brown shaded and outlined with purple, except on the right shoulder where, as on the lighted folds elsewhere, a lighter brown is used. The neck is heavily shaded with purples. Exceptionally, a number of yellow tesserae are used on the throat.

His close-cropped hair and rounded beard are blue and light blue with white lights and outlines in shades of dark blue. Below the furrowed brow, a weak shadow between the eyebrows is formed by a group of yellow tesserae, a color used in this position only in two other cases (Paul and Philip). The whites of the eyes are shaded on one side to give them a slightly oblique direction. The irises are purple. The tear ducts are indicated by a single red tessera.

Mark. M |A |P ‖K |O |C (figs. 67, 68, and color fig. 140)

This undamaged medallion is the fifth on the north side. Mark's light purple chiton has a fold in the dark purple neckline. His pale blue himation has white lights and is drawn well across the chest below the fold which drapes over his left shoulder. For his Gospel book the same colors are used as for Matthew's, but here gold tesserae are used not only for the clasps but also on the small section of the front cover, which is visible here and reveals the gold edging that is even more clearly seen on Luke's Gospel. Here, between the clasps, the top edge of the book is rendered with a mixture of dark red glass and white marble tesserae which have lost their red pigment; on the other edge only the glass tesserae are used.

Mark is portrayed with a broad head, dark hair, and bushy beard for which purple and brown glasses are used. The neck, rather heavily shadowed with light purple elsewhere, is light below the chin. The face, including the brow below the bowed hairline, is shaded with pale purple, and dull olive-green is used at the left temple. The eyebrows are purple and the upper lashes purple-black except for the innermost tessera in each case, which is dark red. The irises are dark purple and the lower lashes dull olive green; a pink marble tessera represents the tear duct of the right eye.

Bartholomew. B |A̧ |P̧ |ΘΩ ‖Λ |O |ME |OC (figs. 69 and 70)

This medallion, the lowest on the south side, lacks part of the rim on the inner side, where the second and third letters of the name are also damaged. A vertical crack passes through Bartholomew's right ear and has removed part of the beard below it. The chiton is yellow with light yellow lights and light brown shadows; it has a loose fold in the purple neckline. The himation, drawn well across the chest from the left shoulder, is pale blue with white marble lights. The left shoulder is outlined with translucent tesserae to set off the garment from the light blue ground.

The head is narrow and is given a spare appearance by shadows under the cheekbones and by unusually heavy shading to suggest deep-set eyes. The dark hair recedes steeply above the temples leaving a prominent central tuft; the beard ends in small twin points. Both hair and beard are rendered with purple tesserae outlined with purple-black. The same colors are used in the eyebrows, which are exceptionally thick: at one point three rows of dark purple tesserae are used. The irises of the eyes are purple, and the whites are broken by a single pale blue tessera, as in the eyes of all the apostles on the north side. Red is used for the tear ducts and in the outline of the left ear. The patch of blue or yellow tesserae above the bridge of the nose, a distinctive feature of all the other heads, is here lacking. The marble tesserae in the face are all eroded and now sunk below the original surface, which is maintained by those of glass. Two white tesserae in the upper lip were undoubtedly pigmented red.

Thomas. Θ |Ω ‖M |A |C (frontispiece, and figs. 71, 72)

This medallion, the lowest on the north side, is undamaged. Thomas wears a pale blue chiton with white lights; the exposed section of the neckline is straight as in only three other cases (Paul, Jude, and James). The purple himation is draped well across his chest below the fold which, as usual, hangs vertically from his left shoulder; its lighted folds are light purple. Unlike most of the apostles on this north side, Thomas's neck is shaded above his left shoulder. The dark hair, for which dark purple and olive glasses are used, recedes above the temples on either side of a central tuft, yet Thomas is portrayed as a youth with incipient moustache and beard. This has offered the mosaicist more scope to give relief to the face by using light and shade, especially around the mouth, in contrast to the flatter treatment of some of the other faces, notably that of Jude. The irises of the eyes are dark purple.

The whole series of medallions is thus rather consistent in coloring and execution. Even the lighting from the viewer's left, which gives the impression that the apostles on the south side are illuminated by the radiance of the central image, is retained on the north side also, so that here the source of light appears to be in the body of the church. On the other hand, there are some minor differences. The medallions on the two sides are differently edged (white within light olive-brown on the north, olive-green within light purple on the south); the apostles on the south are more sharply shadowed and their faces thrown into higher relief than those opposite them. If this is taken as evidence of the work of different hands, it remains improbable that one hand set the entire north side and another the whole of the south. There is, indeed, a certain sameness about the faces of Matthew, Jude, and Thomas on the north side: the dark red for the tear ducts and the light blue to give a slight shadow between the eyebrows. But in this last respect Paul provides an exception, for yellow tesserae are used at this point, as in the heads of Philip and James on the south side. These three heads have another detail in common: the necklines of their chitons are straight. However, this treatment is repeated in two other cases on the north side (Jude and Thomas), and the other treatment, a zigzag line representing a loose fold in the neckline, is likewise found on both sides. No rigid distinction can therefore be drawn between the two sides of the arch as regards traits of workmanship.

In the lettering of the names, while there is little variation in the basic letter forms (fig. N), it is possibly significant that where *alpha* occurs on the south side the bar is horizontal, whereas the bars of all the six examples in the north medallions are oblique to a greater or lesser degree. On the other hand the simple *mu* is used in the bottom medallions on either side (Thomas and Bartholomew) but in the two other occurrences of this letter, both on the north side (Matthew and Mark), the point of the angle-bar is carried down by an additional tessera almost to the bottom of the letter. The Thomas medallion differs from those immediately above it also in the use of heavier shading, a characteristic of the four heads preserved on the south side; and this heavier shading extends to the neck, which in other medallions on the north side (Matthew and Jude) is conspicuously flat. These differences do not appear to follow any logical pattern; nor do they detract from the unity of the whole border. But it does seem reasonable to suggest that, after the sketching out of the whole design of the border on the fresh plaster, the main framework and the secondary areas were set by more than one assistant, and that those who worked on the north section were in some respects slightly out of step with their colleagues working on the south side. The master himself would doubtless have set the busts, and the variations in detail probably arose from his desire to avoid monotonous repetitions, and perhaps to some extent were determined by the colors of the tesserae immediately at hand at any moment.

The Intermediate Border (figs. 44, 46, 47, 49, 50, color fig. 138, and fig. I, a)

This border is 0.17 m. wide inclusive of the single rows of white marble tesserae which divide it from the Apostle Border on the one hand and the main composition on the other. In design it represents a jeweled band comprising a series of precious stones *en cabochon*, alternately green squares (set diagonally) and blue circles. In both cases varying tones suggest their curvature and they are outlined with a single row of dark blue-black tesserae enclosed within one of gold to represent the setting. The green tesserae are arranged in a chevron pattern round a yellow highlight at the bottom of the square and range from yellow-green to dark green at the top. The blue are set concentrically in four rows ranging from dark to light blue round a central white tessera.[162] The spaces between the stones are filled by iris flowers, whose stems emerge upward and downward from the apexes of the square jewels and are flanked by rectangular, meander-like tendrils. The stems are green where they reach the flowers and lighten, through light dull olive-green to yellow where they spring from the points of the squares. The tendrils similarly darken from yellow where they emerge laterally from the base of each stem, through light green and dull olive to a medium green at the extremities of their coils. The flowers are represented with five petals and in each unit of the design converge on the circular blue jewels. They comprise three blue standards at the top with stigmas between them and a fall on either side below. The central standards are of a pale, cold blue and the others of a darker value of the same color. The stigmas, green at the base, terminate in yellow tips. The falls have been treated as if they were leaves and are rendered by three rows of medium green, for which a darker green or blue is sometimes substituted in the middle row.

On the north side, where this border is best preserved, the background on which these motifs are set is red, comprising central groups of dark red glass tesserae edged with a single row of marble tesserae. These last follow the outlines of both the jewels and the flowers, including the stigmas and the stems with their lateral tendrils. This edging of the areas of red ground is normally of marble tesserae, now showing their natural white color but originally tinted with a dark red pigment. This is suggested in the best preserved area by the occasional use of the marble tesserae in areas where in corresponding parts of the design the dark red glass tesserae are used. Furthermore, in the small section preserved at the crown of the conch (fig. 50) the central square jewel is edged with dark red glass, while the area of ground which this edging limits is filled with the white marble tesserae which have lost their red tinting. In addition, while the tendrils which immediately adjoin this central jewel on the south side are of the same shades of green as before, for the ground between their meanders a dark red glass, not white marble,

---

[162] The length of each unit, from the center of one square jewel to the center of the next, is 0.69 m. There would have been five repeats on each side, starting with one of the square jewels, complete, at the bottom. The central square jewel is preserved at the crown of the conch (fig. 50).

is used. Again, in the ground areas round the petals of the flower of the same unit the reverse of the treatment on the north side is seen: for these areas are outlined with dark purple-brown glass and for the most part filled with bleached white marble. Consequently, it is beyond doubt that, initially, the ground of this border was red throughout.[163] It follows that of the two rows of white marble on either side of the border only the outermost row on each side was originally white; the tesserae of the inner row were almost certainly tinted with a red color before they were set to form part of the red background. This would, in consequence, have been much more prominent than at present, and would have provided a bold band, predominantly red in color, to form an effective divider between the two very diverse areas of the decoration on either side of it. On the other hand, the irises and their adjuncts would have appeared much more delicate than in the present confusing condition of the mosaic. In the photograph reproduced in figure 47 the white marble tesserae which have lost their red coloring have been retouched to show the original state of the border, so far as this can be represented in monochrome.

The Main Composition (fig. 40, and fig. M)

The main area of the decoration, which occupies the inner part of the conch and is considerably less than a quarter-sphere, has been much distorted by subsidence of the structure it adorns. It was separately framed by a dark brown band three tesserae wide[164] consisting of two rows of translucent glass tesserae (probably trimmed from the glass plates, amber in color, which were used in the manufacture of the gold-capped tesserae) and, on the inside, one row of purple-black glass. This band is preserved on the north side and at the summit of the conch, divided from the Intermediate Border by a single row of white marble tesserae. It doubtless continued round the bottom of the conch, above the Irisated Border. The central position was occupied by a large mandorla surrounding a representation of the Virgin, enthroned and holding the Christ Child on her lap. Outside the mandorla and flanking this central image two attendant archangels stood in a conventional landscape with a uniform gold ground for sky and including two palm trees symmetrically disposed.[165]

---

[163] The different ways in which the red glass and the red-tinted marble tesserae were combined in the two areas may have been predetermined simply in order to vary the texture of the border. Alternatively, they could be regarded as evidence that the two areas were set by different hands.

[164] At the crown this band is now 2 m. above the horizontal section restored in paint at the bottom. The maximum width between the restored vertical sections of the brown band is now 4.68 m. The original measurements of the area assigned to the main composition were probably close to 2.41 and 4.38 m. respectively.

[165] Some small fragments which had fallen from the central area of the mosaic were discovered when Papageorghiou made a sounding below the floor in 1966 ('A.B., 29 [1968], 15). The largest of these is about 0.10 m. square and, like some of the others, evidently belongs to the robes of one of the archangels; but a cursory examination suggests that it will not be possible to determine the exact position of any of these fragments in the large vacant areas from which they had fallen.

The Gold Ground

This does not extend to the brown band enclosing the whole composition; instead, four rows of marble tesserae set parallel to the band provide an inner intermediate zone, yellow in color (figs. 44 and 50). Round the lower part of the conch proper the mosaic is nowhere preserved, but the yellow zone probably continued inside the brown band on either side to the bottom; for on the north side the yellow tesserae survive at a height only about 0.85 m. above it. Here the two inner rows of tesserae are of yellow marble, the next of yellow alternating with white, and the outer row next to the brown band of white marble alone (fig. 44). At the crown of the conch, the only other point where this edging of marble tesserae is preserved, all four rows are of yellow marble (fig. 50). The tesserae of the gold ground, of average size 0.010 by 0.008 m., are normally set in horizontal rows. At the crown they form concentric segments of circles, the centers of which lie outside the brown framing band, about the middle of the Intermediate Border (fig. 50). At the sides, the edges of the gold ground were set differently, evidently to mask the transition between it and the yellow band; on the preserved north side there are four rows of tesserae set parallel to the yellow band, the outer one of yellow glass, the two inner ones of gold, while the intermediate one has an alternation of these two colors. At many points in the areas of gold sky it is apparent that the plaster setting bed was painted with a dark red earth color.

There are some other exceptions to the rule of setting the gold tesserae in horizontal rows. Round the mandorla there are two rows set against its outline (fig. 51), two rows also follow the outline, the nimbus, and the top of the inner wing of the north archangel (fig. 75). Other outlines attracted a single row of gold tesserae: the foliage and trunks of the palm trees, the arm and hand of the south archangel, and the palm leaf below these (fig. 77). In a few other places, where only narrow areas of the ground are seen, for convenience the outlines are followed, for example, outside the tip of the outer wing of the north archangel (fig. 44). It is noteworthy that, above the latter area, the outermost part of the wing oversails the limits of the gold ground and covers much of the yellow band as well.

The North Archangel (figs. 73–76, and color fig. 134)

The head, a little less than life size,[166] is represented in a slightly oblique view and the set of the wings, with the point of the right one extending behind toward the corner of the conch but the other concealed by the body, also suggests that the whole figure is conceived in a slightly oblique view, advancing toward the central image. The left arm must have been bent at the elbow with the hand holding the staff, the upper part of which is preserved. The right hand, if we may judge from the preserved right forearm of the other attendant, would have been extended toward the Theotokos and Christ, and necessarily in a position roughly below the archangel's head (see fig. M).

---

[166] Height 0.24 m., from the hair fillet to the chin.

The nimbus[167] is of silver tesserae (most of which show black, having lost their metal caps) edged with single rows of white marble, dull light blue glass, and, on the outer circumference, dark translucent glass. Except for a single row following the outline of the hair, the silver tesserae are set in concentric rows. The abundant curly hair has a prominent central parting and is rendered in purple glasses, those of lighter tone giving the highlights on the outer side. The hair fillet is blue and its ends float over the white outline of the nimbus.

For the flesh tones of the face, ears, and neck, marble tesserae of three colors are used, white, cream, and pink, shaded with light purple glass of three values. Across the forehead a few yellow glass tesserae are used. The use of relatively large tesserae (the smallest average about 0.05 m. square) imposed a somewhat impressionistic treatment, but this has been exaggerated by the bleaching of white marble tesserae originally pigmented, probably with bright red. These are used on the right side of the face and neck, where not only is the pigment lost but the marble itself has started to disintegrate. There are two more in the upper lip, used beside a tessera of dark red glass, and single ones below the tip of the nose and on the lower lip. The parting of the lips is in dark purple and the shadow below the lower lip in a lighter purple. Heavy shading under the chin and down the inner side of the neck suggests sharp lighting from a point outside the apse to the north. The eyebrows are drawn with double rows of dark purple near the nose, thinning to a single row and a lighter purple toward the temples. A single row of the darker tone extends from the inner eyebrow to define the shaded side of the nose. This outline becomes lighter below the nose and ends with a small tessera of dark red glass to indicate the shadow of the right nostril. On the ridge of the nose it is shaded by a line in which light olive glass alternates with the pink marble; a similar counter-change technique is used in the row of tesserae which limits the other side of the nose, where purple and a darker olive glass alternate. The pupils of the eyes, which are turned sharply toward the Theotokos, are of purple-black and the irises of purple glasses; the whites are of marble with a single pale blue glass tessera on the shadow side in each case. The eyelashes are in purples and the upper eyelids end in dark red glass toward the nose, where the lowest tesserae indicate the tear ducts.

The wings, which are outlined with dark purple, are represented as brown on the outer surface and blue on the underside. The fore-edge is rendered in three values of brown highlighted with a row of yellow marble. For the underside three values of blue are used with purple glass, the latter in four values for feather texture and shadow. A row of light blue tesserae is used to set off the shaded contour of the left shoulder and upper arm.

Blue chiton and light olive-brown himation comprise the costume. The former has a broad clavus and a small fold in the rather low neckline. Five values are used for the chiton ranging from the palest blue to dark blue. The darkest is used for the line of shadow cast on this garment (including the

---

[167] Diameter 0.33 m.

clavus) by the oblique section of the himation. Some silver and the palest value of purple are employed in the fold in the neckline and in short lines to give the highlights on the folds toward the shoulder. In this position gold tesserae are used on the clavus, otherwise rendered in four values of brown. The himation is drawn obliquely across the chest to the left shoulder where a small section of the vertical underfold is seen. It is presumably this that reappears below the oblique section and covers the upper part of the left arm; one end of the garment would doubtless have hung below the forearm. On the other side a small segment of this underfold hangs over the right shoulder, whence it would have passed under the right arm to form the oblique overfold. No more of this is preserved but, having passed obliquely across the back also, it would have reappeared wound round, and hanging down from the waist, as suggested in figure M. Most of the outlines of the himation are of dark translucent glass; some purple is used along the right shoulder, and the fold drawn obliquely across the chiton is highlighted with white marble against the row of dark blue glass giving the shadow on the undergarment. Elsewhere the himation is rendered with five values of light olive-brown glass and some white marble for the highlights. The rather repetitive fold treatment on the oblique section is varied at the lower side, where a strongly lighted fold prevents the shaded edge of the overfold from merging with the dark area below the armpit.

The gold staff has a small spherical head and, contrary to the lighting of the figure itself, it is shaded with dark red glass along the outer side, indicating that here at least the central image, if not the mandorla, is the source of light. The dark red shadow extends onto the spherical head, where light brown is used on the inner side and gold tesserae, most of which have lost their metallic faces, give a highlight at the center.

The South Archangel (fig. 77)

Only the right forearm and the greater part of the open hand are preserved, extended and half-raised in recognition of the central group. The lighting is here from the center, the cuff of the loose sleeve of the chiton casting a heavy shadow on the forearm. The flesh tones are again provided by white, cream, and pink marbles, in some cases rendered by tesserae as small as those used for the faces. Dark translucent glass is used between the fingers and below the elbow, dark purple-brown and two shades of light purple glass for the shadow cast by the sleeve on the forearm. A line of medium purple glass gives the upper contour of the thumb and wrist but this changes to dark blue where the upper part of the forearm is silhouetted against the trunk of a palm tree.

The sleeve of the light blue chiton is very loose and short, in modern parlance three-quarter length; though the cuff is perhaps represented as turned back. Five values of blue glass are used together with a couple of lines of silver for highlights. On the edge or fold of the cuff above the forearm the first row of tesserae has medium blue and silver alternating.

The Trees (figs. 73, 74, 77, 78, and fig. L)

The tree trunk, which rises behind the forearm of the south archangel and is masked at its base by drooping foliage, belongs to a palm tree of which otherwise only the topmost fronds are preserved, close to the apex of the mandorla at the crown of the conch (fig. 50). The vertical top shoot is preserved, a second bending away from it on the inner side, and, on the other side, what is probably the top frond of the group which formed the first branch; these in olive-browns and light green with dark translucent and purple glasses in the upper and right outlines, and dark turquoise on the left. The trunk (fig. 77) is outlined by a row of blue-green tesserae on the inside with a row next it in which the same color is alternated with a lighter value (below the wrist with dark green). There follows, for the highlight, a row of olive-green. The horizontal striations of the bark are rendered with glass tesserae which form both vertical and horizontal rows. The horizontal rows are alternately of light and dark tones and within each row the tones darken as the shaded side of the trunk is reached. Thus in the lighted section of the trunk, olive-green alternates vertically with light green, then olive-brown with dark green and finally dark olive-brown with dark blue-green, while dark purple alone is used for the outline of the shaded outer side. The lower part of the trunk is masked by a large, fan-shaped palm leaf, not all of which is preserved (fig. 77). This is outlined in dark turquoise and the central stem from which the fronds radiate is of the same color. The fronds range from yellow through light green to dull blue-green. This leaf springing as a sucker from the base of the palm tree (doubtless there would have been a whole group of them) would have helped to fill the triangular space between the inner outline of the lower part of the angel and the edge of the mandorla (see fig. M).

A good deal has survived of the foliage at the top of the corresponding palm tree on the north side, but less of its trunk. The latter appears below the archangel's left wing parallel to the staff, which masks its outer edge (fig. 73). The inner outline is blue-green and next to the staff there is a row of dull olive-green; between these, olive-greens and blue-greens alternate with lighter greens in horizontal rows, each of three tesserae, to give the texture and cylindrical form. Of the foliage are preserved: the small vertical shoot at the top, the entire first fan-shaped leaf on the outer side, and parts of the second with fronds extending almost to the nimbus of the archangel (fig. 74). Yellow at the center of the leaves, the foliage darkens through light greens and light blues to an outline of purple-black. These drooping leaves make it clear that the two trees do not represent the usual date palm but are inspired rather by the fan-leaved palm.

Behind the north archangel, filling the triangular space which would have remained between his right thigh and the outer wing, was a smaller tree or shrub. Some of the dense foliage of its outer profile is preserved close to the tip of the wing (fig. 44). The character of this foliage may be judged from the drawing in figure L, which is based on a tracing. The leaves, which are small and pointed, are rendered in green and blue-green glasses, with blue-black for the darkest shadows and bright yellow-green for the brightest highlights. The small area of foliage which is preserved includes no trace of fruit or flowers, but is suggestive of an orange tree.

No part of the terrain in which the trees grow is preserved.

The Mandorla (fig. 78)

The mandorla enclosing the central figures is preserved at seven points: the obtuse angle at the top (fig. 51); a large section on the north side somewhat above the midpoint (fig. 74) and extending to the throne (fig. 82); a smaller section on the south side, at the edge, rather lower down (fig. 77); in three areas outside the south profile of the throne, adjoining the cushion (fig. 81), between the Virgin's nimbus and the top of the throne (fig. 80), and adjoining the upright (fig. 83); also a small group of six tesserae along the top of the throne on the north side. The maximum width would have been 1.82 m.;[168] the height, more approximately estimated, would have been 2.45 m. It is represented by concentric zones of blue and blue-green framed by an irisated border, which originally ranged from dark red on the inner edge to dark blue-green on the outer.

The frame is set off from the rest of the mandorla by a row of dark red glass edged by a row of marble tesserae on either side. These marble tesserae now show their natural white color but, if the color of the plaster bed in which they were set is a reliable guide, they were once tinted red. For, where some of the tesserae are missing in the top section, the plaster bed is red, not only where the dark red glass tesserae have fallen but also on either side where marble tesserae are missing (fig. 51).[169] The frame is bordered on the outer edge by a row of dark blue-green glass. Between these edgings the tesserae of the frame itself are all set in diagonal rows with, on the average, fourteen to each row. Outermost in each row are three of dark blue-green glass, then one each of blue-green and middle green, followed by two of light green and one of yellow-green. Next, and commonly ninth in each row, is a single gold tessera.[170] The remaining six tesserae are of white marble formerly tinted red. This is indicated by the red color on the plaster bed where this is preserved but where the diagonally set tesserae have fallen from it at the apex of the mandorla (fig. 51). It is confirmed by the inclusion of a single dark red glass tessera among the

---

[168] At present it is 0.03 m. wider as a result of the crack in the structure which has amputated the right arm of the Theotokos.

[169] Exceptionally, to the left of the apex the outer concentric row of marble tesserae is lacking and the diagonal setting of the main frame area extends to the edging of dark red glass. Now, there is independent evidence that the innermost diagonal tesserae were red (see *infra*), which confirms that those of marble set normally outside the red glass tesserae were also red. There is no such confirmation in the case of the row along the inside of the red glass tesserae; so the possibility that this row was always white cannot be excluded, despite the fact that it was set in an area of plaster colored red.

[170] The well preserved north section is here described. On the south section smaller tesserae are used and the gold tessera is the tenth, eleventh, or even twelfth. At the top of the mandorla, where larger tesserae are used, the gold tessera comes seventh or eighth in each row.

marble ones, and by the remains of red paint on one of the latter, in both cases in the long section of frame preserved on the north side (fig. 74).

It follows that in two respects the present state of the mandorla frame is deceptive. In the first place, the division between the inner zones and the frame may have been much less emphatic; even the white line now dividing them may not have existed. Secondly, the present indication of a bright lighting on the frame itself from the interior is quite false; what highlight there was fell at the middle of the band, where the gold tesserae mark the transition from pale red to yellow-green.

The concentric zones within the frame on the north side are of darker tones than on the south where, especially close to the throne and cushions, more tesserae of light tones are used. The mandorla, then, is not conceived as a source of light, but rather as a tangible object, in the form of the concave back of a shield, itself illuminated from a source to the north. For the rim appears to cast a dark shadow on this north side, against which the highlighted upright of the throne back stands out effectively, while the light catches the south side to provide a brighter background to the shaded edge of the upright on this side. The treatment of the clipei in front of which the busts in the Apostle Border are represented is thus exactly repeated in this mandorla-clipeus.

Where the zones of the mandorla are complete to the north of the throne, they are three in number and appear to represent concentric undulations. Each is graded from the darkest blue at the outside to turquoise, though the light area of the third is masked by the throne back. The outer zone has ten concentric rows of glass tesserae in four values of blue,[171] the next has fourteen in the same four values with a fifth of paler turquoise added, the third in the widest part has seven rows in the three darkest values. At the apex of the mandorla a small section of the outermost zone is preserved—only the first eight rows, all of dark values of blue.

On the south side a small section of the zone next to the frame preserves parts of seven rows of tesserae of which only the outermost four are of dark values. Close beside the top of the throne back and outside the end of the cushion the light inner edge of the second zone is preserved. Here there are four rows all of values lighter than those used on the north side. The third zone is here seen to be the last. Departing from the concentric setting normally followed in preserved areas, the lighter tones of this zone are set in rows following the contours of the cushion and the upright of the throne back. The purpose was clearly to ensure that the adjoining areas of the mandorla would be light enough for these shaded contours to stand out against them. The process was carried to the extreme against the top of the upright, where the rows of light blue tesserae following its contour pass right across the dark area of the innermost zone of the mandorla to merge with the lighter inner edge of the middle zone (fig. 83).

---

[171] Three rows of dark blue, two of blue, three of dark turquoise, and one of blue.

Above the throne back the normal concentric setting is resumed and the innermost zone is seen gradually brightening to the lightest of blues against the red rim of the nimbus of the Theotokos. On the north side only a few dark blue tesserae of the innermost zone survive, along the top of the throne back.

The Throne (fig. 79)

Apart from the back, which is preserved almost completely, only a small section of the throne has survived: on the south side, below the cushion. At the bottom of the cushion (fig. 81) the small group of gold and dark translucent tesserae set in three slightly oblique rows evidently belong to the cushion (see *infra*). Close below them (fig. 85) is a fragment of rectangular decoration in light blue centered with translucent glass and bordered with light brown. This doubtless belongs to the jeweled fore-edge of the seat of the throne. Lower down are a few more light brown tesserae set in a vertical line, probably to draw the outer edge of a drape covering the seat of the throne and hanging down in front. For this edging continues upward and conceals part of the jeweled fore-edge of the seat. The triangular area inside this edging extends to the footstool (fig. 84), where it is again edged with light brown along the silver top of the stool. The whole of this triangle is filled with white marble tesserae set in vertical rows and originally pigmented with red. This drape on which the Theotokos sits thus matched in color the material covering the back of the throne, where similar tinted marble tesserae were used.

The back is of the lyre form, bounded by two curved uprights evidently represented as of ivory (figs. 82 and 83). Their basic white color is given by white marble with the palest tones of glass for shading (on the south side of both uprights) grading to very pale olive-green, outlined on the shaded side with a single line of dark translucent glass. The south upright is also defined on the inner side by a single row of the same, which tapers from the bottom and disappears before the top is reached. This, with the shading and the curved drawing of the horizontal lines in the decoration, suggests the curvature of the tusks from which the uprights would have been made. Delicate inlaid decoration is represented by rectangular, diamond, and S-shaped forms between the horizontal divisions, in which only green glass is used and with great restraint.

Between the uprights the whole area of the back is set in vertical rows of white marble tesserae which were originally tinted with red pigment. The mosaicist evidently conceived the throne as covered by a single loose piece of fabric draped over the back, extending onto the seat (under the cushion) and hanging down in front, where it appears behind the footstool, rendered in precisely the same way as it is on the back.

The Cushion (fig. 81)

On the north, no part of the cushion has survived; but on the south it is complete except for the lower outline. It is represented as having an approximately cylindrical central part and a hemispherical end with a terminal medallion, the two parts separated by an ornamented seam. Both parts are rendered in white marble tesserae, but whereas those of the end were always seen in their natural color, in the central section this was graded into red by using similar white marble tesserae which had been dipped into a red earth color. A red area would thus have framed the contour of the Virgin's robes on either side, virtually continuous from the top of the throne to the footstool. On the cushion the tinted tesserae were set in curved rows near the figure, where despite their eroded state they appear somewhat darker in tone. Here, we may presume, tesserae colored with darker reds were used to give a shadow suggesting sharp curvature at the point where the cushion would have been compressed. The concentric setting would have facilitated the gradation from dark to lighter reds and ultimately white. A general effect approximating that of shot silk seems probable.

Three rows of dark blue glass represent the vertical seam between the central and terminal sections of the cushion; the middle row grades to brighter blue to provide a highlight suggesting curvature. At the bottom of the central section a few gold and dark translucent glass tesserae survive, set in three rows rising slightly toward the end of the cushion. To judge by the representation of gold-thread embroidery round the terminal medallion (see *infra*), these may belong to a horizontal seam with similar adornment.

The upper contour of the cushion is of translucent glass which starts as a single row but splits into two toward the terminal medallion, perhaps suggesting the gathers of the fabric at this point. The center of the medallion, which surely represents embroidery, is set with yellow and green glasses outlined in dark purple. This is bordered by a double row of gold shading at the top through yellow to light brown, and by an outer edging of dark green, brightened at the center with lighter green. Against the green edging are pairs of silver tesserae muted at the top by a pair of pale blue glass. By these changes of color the mosaicist rendered the sparkle of gold and silver embroidery where the curvature of the cushion would have caught the light.

The Footstool (fig. 84)

In contrast to the rest of the central composition, which is seen in strict frontality, the square footstool was represented in steep perspective, with one of its angles to the front. This unusual diagonal position was determined by the proximity of the lower point of the mandorla, to the curvature of which the two visible sides of the footstool would have conformed (fig. 78). None of its angles is preserved but parts of the upper edges survive on three sides to establish its form. These edges are drawn with silver tesserae and are well defined by a double row on the north forward side and by a single row on the south rear side, the latter running at an even steeper angle giving a reverse perspective. Only a few tesserae survive on the line of the south forward edge, but these leave no doubt of its front angle and of the square form of the footstool. The top surface is represented as covered with cloth of gold and has gold tesserae along the edges, where it would catch the light, shading through yellow and yellow-brown to light brown glass next to the robes. This gives the shadow beneath the robes in front, as well as that cast by the figure on the south side. Toward the missing south angle, gold and yellow fingers are alternated to give a highlight.

Much of the north forward side of the stool is preserved. For the ground light brown glass is used. The alternating square and oval cabochon jewels have their mounts and claws drawn in gold tesserae. The square jewels are green at the center and the oval ones are of white marble which originally were doubtless pigmented with red. All the jewels are shaded with dark purple glass. Groups of four silver tesserae are set in vertical pairs to represent pearls between the jewels.

The Theotokos (fig. 79)

Except for the head, virtually the whole of the south half of the figure is preserved. On the other side a vertical crack in the structure has caused great damage. In the upper part the contour of the right arm is intact to below the elbow and almost exactly balances the curve of the other arm. But the crack which cuts through the shoulder has opened a gap in the mosaic about .03 m. wide which disguises the narrow proportions of the figure. Originally the width from elbow to elbow was only 0.61 m. compared with a height of 1.50 m. from the chin to the bottom of the robe between the feet, resulting in very elongated proportions for a seated figure.[172] The lower part of the north side of the figure is lost (except for the foot), including the right hand. However, the position of this cannot have differed greatly from that of the left hand, since the curvature of the arm as far as it is preserved is so similar and the symmetry of the figure in other respects so well balanced. The left hand extends almost vertically downward to cover the outer part of Christ's left knee. The other would probably have touched His right leg below the raised knee. The Theotokos wears a blue maphorion which nearly covers a purple chiton, seen only over the lower parts of the legs and partly covering the feet.

Of the head little is preserved: only the left cheek, a small part of the right side of the chin, with much of the neck on this side. Part of the dark blue maphorion has survived where it borders the left (south) side of the head,[173] as well as the adjoining section of the nimbus.[174] The nimbus is edged with an outer row of dark red glass, within which are single rows of medium green and silver. The field is of gold tesserae set concentrically.

[172] The estimated height of the head above the chin is 0.26 m., and this is a maximum figure, which gives a total height of nearly six heads, almost as tall a proportion as some standing figures of the Theotokos (cf. that in the Rabbula Gospel, fol. I^b, six and one-half heads).

[173] Here the outermost four rows of tesserae evidently represent the vertical, hood-like fold hanging a little away from the face with a lighter tone for its north edge; the remainder, the heavily shadowed cavity between this and the cheek.

[174] The photograph published by Smirnov ("Mozaiki," pl. II) shows a further part of the nimbus above the head, on a small section of the mosaic now lost, which in his time extended from the existing section at the top of the mandorla almost to the outline of the maphorion.

In the face and neck, white, cream, and pink marbles are used for the lighted flesh tones. The shaded contour of the left cheek is of light blue glass with a row of paler blue within it, which color appears again among the pink marble where the shadow lightens. The shadow under the chin on the other side of the face is given by bright purple glass. The same marbles are used in the left hand (fig. 81), where thumb and fingers are outlined in dark translucent glass. The shadow cast on the hand by the cuff is rendered in pale purple and light olive brown.

The neck is fully exposed, and it is clear from what is preserved that if anything intervened between it and the edge of Christ's nimbus it could have been no more than a single row of blue glass tesserae, representing the edge of a fold of the maphorion passing below the chin (fig. 80). No part of the neckline of the purple chiton can have appeared here. Likewise, its left sleeve is completely concealed by the fold of the maphorion over the wrist. The undergarment only appears where it drapes the lower part of the legs in ample folds, and almost conceals the feet (fig. 84). Four values of purple glass are used to draw the folds, which hang almost vertically between the legs. Above the left foot they are interrupted by five gold tesserae set obliquely to form a cross. The dark blue hem of the garment follows a sinuous line to reveal the slippers which cover the feet. They are rendered in white marble tesserae, a few of which retain a reddish tint; no doubt they were dipped in a red earth pigment before they were set.

The maphorion hangs down over the left knee in numerous concentric folds almost to the cross on the chiton (fig. 84). Below the hoodlike section round the head it is represented as hanging rather loosely, but it is gathered tightly on the forearms to give several folds at the elbows. Four values of blue glass are used, the darkest not only for fold shadows but also in a single row to set off the contours of the hand and of the figure and nimbus of Christ.

The Christ Child (figs. 85–89, and color figs. 135–36)

The figure of Christ[175] is preserved in entirety except for a loss at the top of the nimbus and the damage caused by the crack which passes down its extreme edge on the north side. A Child rather than an Infant, He sits on the lap of the Theotokos, the center point of the whole composition. While the head faces rigidly to the front, below the head the figure presents no such symmetry but rather a complex balance of swinging curves and oblique accents. The exposed part of the blue chiton opens an oblique movement which is barely arrested by the sharp bend in the right arm. The right knee is raised well above the other and the hands are in an answering oblique relationship, holding the scroll of the New Law between them. The left hand is covered by the cream-colored himation, the folds of which provide further contrapuntal rhythms, but everywhere in reasonable conformity with the anatomy they clothe.

[175] Height 0.96 m. from the top of the head to the bottom of the left foot, just over six times the height of the head (0.155 m.).

The cross nimbus (fig. 88)[176] is edged with an outer row of green glass within which are single rows of dark red and silver, both of which are interrupted by the arms of the cross. The ground is of gold tesserae set concentrically. The arms of the cross are silver, outlined with the dark red glass, except at the ends.

The hair (fig. 89) is outlined in dark translucent glass, as are the ears and the sides of the head and neck. The hair itself, represented as curly but brushed down to an irregular fringe, is of light brown glass lit by yellow tesserae, which in a few places break the outline. For the flesh tones white, cream, and pink marbles are used, as in the other heads, with light purple glass for the shadow down the nose and below the chin. This last color is used to draw the arching eyebrows, together with a few tesserae of a very dark purple, a color used also for the upper eyelashes, the pupils of the eyes, the shadows below the nostrils, and at the parting of the lips. Dark red glass is used for the shadow below the tip of the nose. The whites of the eyes are of white marble with a single pale blue tessera in each to give the shadow. The irises are of light brown glass, used also on the lower eyelids, for the middle tone on the nose, and for the shadows below the lower lip and on the neck. Single tesserae of the rare orange vermilion glass are used for the ends of the upper eyelids nearest the nose, on the left nostril, and on the upper lip. Despite these subtleties, few tesserae of very small size are used, the smallest being about 0.004 m. square, and their shapes and sizes are very irregular.

The same marbles are used in the right forearm and hand (fig. 86) as in the face, with dark translucent glass for the shaded lower contours, including the fingers. Along the upper contour the marble tesserae are thrown into relief by a dark shadow on the himation. The shadow below the knob of the ulna is an indication of the attention paid to anatomical detail. Here a few tesserae of orange vermilion glass are used with a couple of pale purple, a color also used to give the shadow cast by the sleeve. On the feet, where the foreshortening of the right foot is notably successful, light brown glass is introduced for intermediate shadows and purple for the shaded outlines. The soles and thongs of the sandals are of gold shadowed with dark red glass (fig. 87).

The pale blue tones of the chiton (fig. 88) are shaded with medium blue tesserae in the folds and a darker blue where it is covered by the oblique fold of the outer garment. The highlights are silver: near the right shoulder, on the fold in the neckline, which is drawn in dark translucent glass, and on the folds gathered back from the forearm. The clavus is of gold tesserae near the shoulder, shading to yellow and brown; it is edged with red.

The cream color of the himation evidently represents a natural wool of a finer quality than is suggested by the light brown of the archangel's garment. The highlights are of white marble, the middle tones of pale brown and dull olive glasses, and the shadows of darker olive brown. The dark outline below the segment appearing on the right shoulder is of dark translucent glass. Another heavy shadow is drawn on the oblique folds from the left shoulder in

[176] Diameter 0.245 m.

dark olive brown to set off the lighted upper contours of the forearm, hand, and scroll. This shadow would suggest that the scroll is held tight against the garment to form a receding fold, but this is not well adjusted to the treatment below the scroll where the folds on which the scroll should cast a shadow are unexpectedly highlighted. The lower contour of the oblique folds of the garment, so prominent on the archangel's left shoulder, is here omitted above the scroll. Elsewhere the folds are more logical. The end of the himation which covers the left hand is seen below the scroll, covering the upper arm also, the inner edge well defined; it reappears above the oblique fold at the neck and (having passed across the back) emerges to form the segment on the right shoulder; thence the garment passes (unseen) below the right arm to reappear in the bunched folds which rise obliquely to the left shoulder and there pass out of sight. The same folds return to the front of the figure to encircle the waist, whence the lower edge is here seen hanging down as far as the feet. Finally, since the figure is complete, some indication of the second end of the himation could be expected, and it is perhaps represented by the folds passing across Christ's lap and disappearing over His left thigh.

The scroll (fig. 86) is of white marble along the upper edge, shading through pale blue glass to light blue on the underside. The crossed thongs are drawn in dark purple glass.

THE THEME

The Main Composition

a. The Image of the Incarnation

In the Byzantine sphere, well before Iconoclasm, the image of the Theotokos as a symbol of the Incarnation had become the favorite theme for apse decorations. It was chosen for three surviving early apse mosaics in Cyprus, though with varying iconography. Elsewhere, the ravages of Iconoclasm and later losses have spared no other examples in mosaic, and the record of what has been lost is meager. It is possible that a figure of the Theotokos had been inserted into the originally plain gold conch of St. Sophia in Istanbul, only to be thrown down during the controversy.[177] It is quite certain, on the other hand, that the post-iconoclastic apse figure in the church of the Dormition at Iznik (Nicaea), which was destroyed in 1924, was in the nature of a restoration of one that had formed part of the original decoration of this seventh-

---

[177] The inscription on the front edge of the semidome refers to images which the Iconoclasts had cast down, and there is a suggestive passage in the homily delivered by the Patriarch Photios at the dedication of the existing image of the Theotokos. But close examination of the mosaic itself has produced no evidence either to confirm or refute the suggestion that a pre-iconoclast figure or figures had previously occupied this position. Virtually the entire gold ground was remade when the ninth-century figure was set (C. Mango and E. J. W. Hawkins, "The Apse Mosaics of St. Sophia at Istanbul. Report on Work Carried Out in 1964," *DOP*, 19 [1965], 147f.). On Heisenberg's tenuous thesis that Justin II embellished Justinian's church with figure mosaics, see C. Mango, *Materials for the Study of the Mosaics of St. Sophia at Istanbul*, DOS, VIII (Washington, D.C., 1962), 93.

century church.[178] In Salonica, the basilica of St. Demetrius preserved until the fire of 1917 a mosaic of the Virgin and Child enthroned between angels and flanked by saints. Though not in an apse, this votive panel is thought to have reflected an apse mosaic, and it is best regarded as part of the first decoration of the fifth-century basilica, but not the first part of it to be completed.[179]

Other early mosaics figuring the Theotokos are known to have existed. The earliest in the surviving record, dating from 473, was that in the shrine added to the basilica in the Blachernae monastery by Leo I and the Empress Verina

---

[178] On the evidence for a pre-iconoclast figure, see P. A. Underwood, "The Evidence of Restorations in the Sanctuary Mosaics of the Church of the Dormition at Nicaea," *DOP*, 13 (1959), 239f., confirming a suggestion of Kitzinger, "Between Justinian and Iconoclasm," 16, note 59.

The shape of the excision made when the cross was substituted was such that the original can only have been a standing figure (Underwood, *op. cit.*, fig. 1), while the Hand of God and the rays at the apex of the conch, together with the paraphrase of Ps. 110:3 encircling them, ... ἐκ γαστρὸς πρὸ ἑωσφόρου ἐγέννησά σε, make it clear that the Theotokos held the Child before her. It is also established that the two pairs of archangels on the side walls of the bema featured in the pre-iconoclast program (*ibid.*, 242).

A date for the original construction and decoration of the church in the seventh century fits both the indications of the brickwork (in the view of Krautheimer, *Byz. Architecture*, 206f.) and the style of the closure panels and monograms (E.Weigand, *Deutsche Literaturzeitung*, 48 [1927], Heft 53, col. 2601 ff.; H. Grégoire in *Byzantion*, 5 [1929–30], 287ff.). T. Ulbert, in a recent study of the panels, accepts a building date around 700 (*IstMitt*, 19/20 [1969/70], 346). [An earlier date, perhaps as early as the end of the sixth century, has been suggested: C. Mango, *Byzantine Architecture* (New York, 1976), 172.]

[179] For an illustration in color and a recent discussion with bibliography, see Cormack, "S. Demetrios," 26ff. and pl. 7; for the relation of this composition to apse schemes, *ibid.*, 30, though the close parallel to the early encaustic icon of the Theotokos with angels and saints in the Sinai monastery (K. Weitzmann *et al.*, *Icons from South Eastern Europe and Sinai* [London, 1968], pls. 1–3) suggests a panel painting intermediary.

Cormack argues forcefully (*op. cit.*, 45ff.) in favor of assigning the aisle mosaics to the original decoration of the fifth-century basilica, against the dating around 600 preferred by Kitzinger ("Between Justinian and Iconoclasm," 22).

The construction date of the basilica is unknown, but useful indications are given by those capitals which remain in position in parts of the building untouched by the seventh-century fire, and by others used in the subsequent reconstruction, which may reasonably be assigned to the first phase. Kautzsch considered that none of them was earlier than the third quarter of the fifth century (*Kapitellstudien*, 72–75). In more recent studies an earlier dating is preferred (J. Kramer, *Skulpturen mit Adlerfiguren an Bauten des 5. Jahrh. n.Chr. in Konstantinopel* [Cologne, 1968], 65f.; Maria Panayiotides, Βυζαντινὰ κιονόκρανα μὲ ἀνάγλυφα ξῶα, in Δελτ.Χριστ.'Αρχ.'Ετ., 6 [1972], 91–94: "a little before 441"). These capitals and the discovery in the building of stamped bricks similar to those used in the walls of the city and in the conversion of the Rotunda (see note 197 *infra*) points to the third quarter of the fifth century (W. E. Kleinbauer, "Some Observations on the Dating of St. Demetrios in Thessaloniki," *Byzantion*, 40 [1970], 40), which is within the wider bracket of earlier estimates (e.g., M. and G. Soteriou, Ἡ βασιλικὴ τοῦ ἀγ. Δημητρίου Θεσσαλονίκης [Athens, 1952], 264–47: in the middle or second half of the fifth century). Kleinbauer does not take up Krautheimer's speculation (*Byz. Architecture*, 91) that an earlier fifth-century basilica, from which the apse survives, was rebuilt in the last years of the century.

M. Vickers has proposed the date 447/48 (or soon after) for the construction of the basilica. He suggests that it was built to enshrine relics of the patron saint taken to Salonica upon Attila's capture of Sirmium, which many scholars regard as the original center of the Demetrius cult, and, secondly, that some of the stamps on bricks recovered from the basilica record an indication corresponding with that year. The basilica would in that case belong (with the walls, the Rotunda conversion, the Acheiropoietos basilica, and other buildings where similarly stamped bricks have been found) to a virtual reconstruction of the city, which in 442/43 had become the seat of the prefect of Illyricum (M. Vickers, "Sirmium or Thessaloniki? A Critical Examination of the St. Demetrius Legend," *BZ*, 67 [1974], 337–50; *idem*, "Fifth-Century Brickstamps from Thessaloniki," *BSA*, 68 [1973], 337–50).

The mosaic decoration would have started in the sanctuary, and since elsewhere it was carried out piecemeal as a series of separate votive panels, a date around 500 for the lost aisle mosaics may not be far from the mark.

to receive the *maphorion* of the Virgin. Here, with the imperial donors on either side, the Theotokos was represented enthroned, and thus almost certainly with the Christ Child on her lap.[180] A figure of the Virgin and Child enthroned was the centerpiece of a similar mosaic group in the apse of Justinian's church of St. Sergius at Gaza; this had been completed before 536 and is known from the description in Choricius' first encomium on Bishop Marcian, which was composed before that year. The titular Saint was shown approaching from the right to present the Emperor to the infant Christ. The Bishop, who was also portrayed, presumably figured in a second procession approaching the throne from the other side.[181] These compositions centered on the Theotokos reflect another type of *praesentatio*, grouped round a figure of Christ, of which the surviving examples are in the West and date from the sixth century,[182] but which had its roots in much earlier imperial ceremonial and iconography.

It has been inferred that a major image of the Theotokos in mosaic of a rather different type adorned the main apse of Justinian's reconstruction of the basilica at Bethlehem.[183] But this, as we shall see, rests mainly on a description of the mosaics on the façade in a ninth-century MS which is in some respects suspect, and on the assumption that these reflected others within the building.

If the list is extended to representations in fresco, we can include the only pre-iconoclast apse decoration featuring the Theotokos to be found in Istanbul, that discovered in 1935 in the ruins of Odalar Camii and assigned to the seventh century. It had been overpainted and is known only from an indifferent drawing.[184] The several examples in fresco found in the sanctuary niches of the ruined chapels excavated at Bawit and Saqqara indicate how widespread was the popularity of the theme in the East in the sixth and seventh centuries. To these Coptic niche frescoes we shall return.

In the West, although many more early apse decorations have survived or are known from descriptions, representations of the Virgin and Child are

---

[180] The description is preserved in Paris. gr. 1447, fols. 257–258, published by A. Wenger, in *REB*, 10 (1962), 54 ff. Cf. A. Grabar, *L'iconoclasme byzantin* (Paris, 1957), 21 ff. The Empress was portrayed kneeling and holding in her arms her grandson, the future Leo II, whose mother Ariadne was also represented. A second manuscript, Palat. gr. 317, has variant readings, which in some cases are to be preferred and have been used in C. Mango's English translation, in *The Art of the Byzantine Empire 312–1453: Sources and Documents* (Englewood Cliffs, N.J., 1972), 34 f.

[181] *Laudatio Marciani*, I.29–31, ed. Foerster-Richtsteig (Leipzig, 1929), 7 ff. The passage is quoted in Ihm, *Programme*, 193; English translation in Mango, *Sources and Documents*, 62.

[182] E.g., the apse mosaic of SS. Cosmas and Damian in Rome, between 526 and 530 (Ihm, *Programme*, 137 f. and pl. XII,2; G. Matthiae, *Mosaici medioevali delle chiese di Roma*, II [Rome, 1967], illus. 78).

[183] Most recently: Ihm, *Programme*, 52 ff.

[184] P. Schazman, "Des fresques byzantines récemment découvertes par l'auteur dans des fouilles à Odalar-Camii, Istanbul," *Atti del V Congresso intern. di Studi bizantini, Roma 1936*, II (= *SBN*, 6 [1940]), 372 ff. and pl. CXXI, whence Ihm, *Programme*, pl. XVII,2. He mentions traces of an earlier version of the same subject, which would explain some apparent inconsistencies in the published drawing. The importance of this example of the enthroned Virgin and Child between archangels lies, as Matthiae has stressed (*CorsiRav* [1972], 262), in the localization of the formula in Constantinople itself.

proportionately fewer and some of them may be attributable to specific Eastern influences. The earliest may have been almost contemporary with the acknowledgment of Mary as the Mother of God at the Council of Ephesus (431). For it is commonly assumed that the original apse decoration in S. Maria Maggiore in Rome, probably of the time of Sixtus III (432–40), included a central figure of the Virgin;[185] while another is well attested for the mosaic similarly placed in Bishop Symmachus' contemporary basilica at Capua.[186] The earliest surviving example is the apse mosaic of about 540–50 in the basilica at Poreč (Parenzo), which clearly owes much to Byzantium. Here the flanking processions of saints and patrons, including Bishop Eufrasius offering a model of his church, evoke Choricius' description of those in St. Sergius at Gaza.[187] In Ravenna a similar mosaic figuring the Virgin and Child enthroned, to whom a model was offered by the founding bishop (probably accompanied by other figures), was set in the apse of S. Maria Maggiore by Bishop Ecclesius (521–32).[188]

These are exceptions among a larger number of Western apses with focal images of Christ. Even in Ravenna under Byzantine rule (after 540) the theme of the Redeemer is preferred: in the apse mosaic from S. Michele in Affricisco (dedicated in 545)[189] and also in the apse of S. Vitale, now regarded as part of Bishop Maximian's work.[190] Nor does sixth-century Rome offer any example, unless we include the fragmentary *Maria Regina* fresco on the east wall of S. Maria Antiqua, for which a date in the first half of the century is now

[185] The inscription on the entrance wall, quoted with bibliography in Ihm, *Programme*, 132–35, is now thought to refer specifically to the apse mosaic. On the case for a slightly earlier dating, drawn from Krautheimer's cautious statements on the chronology of the church and its decoration, see T. Klauser, in *JbAChr*, 15 (1972), 120–35.

[186] The Virgin and Child enthroned, apparently without accompanying figures. For a tentative reconstruction, see Ihm, *Programme*, fig. 10, with sources and literature on p. 177ff; G. Bovini, "Mosaici paliocristiani scomparsi di S. Maria Capua Vetere," *CorsiRav*, 14 (1967), 35–42.Another lost mosaic, on the east wall of S. Maria della Croce at Casaranello, may have represented the Virgin and Child. For in 1913–14 the upper part of a central nimbus without cross or christogram was exposed on a blue ground (R. Bartoccini, "Casaranello e i suoi mosaici," *FelRav* [1934], 173, fig. 14; G. Bovini, "I mosaici di S. Maria della Croce di Casaranello," *CorsiRav*, 11 [1964], 36). Most scholars assign the surviving nonfigural mosaics to the fifth century, but Wilpert (*MM*, I, 18), preferred the sixth, and it is with floor mosaics of that century that the motifs used best accord.

[187] Peirce-Tyler, *L'art byzantin*, II pl. 60, G (good detail of the Theotokos); B. Molaioli, *La basilica eufrasiana di Parenzo* (Padua, 1943), fig. 10; Prelog, *Mosaïques de Poreč*, figs. on pp. 1–3; Ihm, *Programme*, pl. XV,2. On the "Syrian" style of the mosaic, see Lazarev, *Istorija*, 58; idem, *Storia*, 75. Matthiae, on the other hand, believes that, occidental features apart, the Poreč mosaic is attributable to the direct influence of Constantinople itself (*CorsiRav*, 19 [1972], 262). Iconographic conformity with orthodox Chalcedonian doctrine suggested to J. Maksimović that the decoration of the basilica was conceived as an expiation of Eufrasius' Monophysite leanings, for which he had been reproved by the Pope ("Ikonografia i program mozaika u Poreću," *ZVI*, 8,2 [1964] [= Mélanges Georges Ostrogorsky, II] 247–60). In that case it would have been carried out *ca.* 550.

[188] For sources and literature, see Ihm, *Programme*, 173.

[189] Now in the Staatlichen Museen in Berlin; see K. Wessel, *Das Mosaik aus der Kirche S. Michele in Affricisco zu Ravenna* (Berlin, 1955); idem, "Il mosaico di San Michele in Africisco," *CorsiRav*, 8 (1961), 369–92; Ihm, *Programme*, 161–63, where the earlier literature is given; Deichmann, *Geschichte und Monumente*, 221ff. and figs. 211–17.

[190] Deichmann, *Bauten und Mosaiken*, pl. VIII and fig. 351; Grabar, *Byzantium*, figs. 147 and 149 (color). In Deichmann's view, now widely accepted, the entire decoration of the sanctuary is a unity, executed after 540, though by different teams of mosaicists: *Geschichte und Monumente*, 226f. and 249–56. Cf. Ihm, *Programme*, 163–65 with earlier bibliography.

preferred.[191] This representation of the Virgin in the guise of a Byzantine empress cannot indeed be matched in the East, but if it was painted after the occupation of the city by Belisarius in 536 it could well have been executed under strong Eastern influence, for the church is structurally connected with the Palatine, the seat of Byzantine government.[192]

Even in the East, at the time when the growing attention paid to Mary in theology, liturgy, and popular piety found official sanction at Ephesus, images of the Virgin seem to have had no comparable place in church art.[193] It was only subsequently, as churches dedicated to the Theotokos multiplied in Constantinople,[194] that the figure of Mary seated on the throne of God with the Christ Child on her lap, as at Lythrankomi, became accepted and was propagated as the appropriate symbol of the Incarnation.

The emergence of the Theotokos in Byzantine art as the normal counterpart of Christ is well illustrated by the "five-compartment ivory diptychs," where with their attendants they occupy the two central panels. It has been suggested that these and the upper panels, usually filled by flying angels holding a central wreathed cross, reflect mosaic decorations respectively in and above the apses of contemporary churches.[195] However, the decoration of these diptychs is more reasonably derived from secular equivalents bearing imperial portraits, as Grabar has argued,[196] and for the rest may have owed as much to contemporary Christian panel painting as to monumental art. Such inter-relations notwithstanding, the similarity of the themes adopted in apse decoration, panel painting, and other media is attributable rather to dependence on officially approved formulae conceived in the tradition of imperial iconography. In any event, it seems that in the Byzantine sphere by the end of the fifth century Christ and the Theotokos were equally acceptable as the

---

[191] Reconstructions in W. de Grüneisen, *Sainte Marie Antique* (Rome, 1911), fig. 105, whence C. R. Morey, *Early Christian Art* (Princeton, 1953), fig. on p. 172, and *idem, Mediaeval Art* (New York, 1942), fig. on p. 90; Wilpert, *MM*, IV, pl. 134. P. J. Nordhagen, in view of his chronology for the later strata of frescoes on the "palimpsest wall," favors a date in the first half of the sixth century: "The Earliest Decorations in Santa Maria Antiqua and their Date," *ActaIRNorv*, 1 (1962), 53–72; P. Romanelli and P. J. Nordhagen, *Santa Maria Antiqua* (Rome, 1964), 32, with good details in pls. 14–17. Stylistically, C. Bertelli places the Maria Regina in an early phase of that "petrification" of forms which was to culminate in the mosaics of San Lorenzo (579–90): "Icone di Roma," *Stil und Überlieferung in der Kunst des Abendlandes, Akten des 21. Intern. Kongr. für Kunstgeschichte in Bonn 1964* (Berlin, 1967), 100.

The first move to establish the Christian cult in major buildings in the area of the Forum was the conversion of the *Templum sacrae urbis* as the church of SS. Cosmas and Damian under Felix IV (526–30). The conversion of the *vestibulum* of the imperial palace on the Palatine as a church of St. Mary is thus unlikely to have been undertaken much before the fourth decade of the century. Nor is it likely to have been much later than that; for the subsequent reconstruction of the building with the addition of the apse which damaged the Maria Regina panel is now known to have followed as early as the reign of Justin II (565–78), three of whose coins were buried underneath one of the columns (R. Krautheimer, *Corpus Basilicarum*, II, iii [Vatican City, 1962], 254–55, 264).

[192] Cf. G. McN. Rushford, "S. Maria Antiqua," *BSR*, 1 (1902), 11.

[193] Wellen, *Theotokos*, 139.

[194] On the foundation of the original basilica of the Virgin at Blachernae by Pulcheria, probably between 450 and 453, and that in Chalkoprateia, also of the mid-fifth century, *ibid.*, 143 and sources quoted in notes 13–18.

[195] C. Ossieczkowska, "Gli avori a cinque placche e l'arte imperiale romana," *Atti del V Congr. intern. di Studi bizantini*, II, 327; Ihm, *Programme*, 3 and 54.

[196] Grabar, *Iconography*, 80.

central figure for apse compositions. The prevalence, in this position, of the Incarnation image came with the development of Byzantine domed architecture, which provided a superior location for the figure of Christ. The fifth-century conversion of the Salonica Rotunda supplies the earliest example of Christ as the centerpiece of a dome composition of which anything survives.[197] In the sixth century, as domed churches multiplied, the Theotokos became the more usual occupant of the apse, a development which matched her growing veneration in Constantinople, ultimately as guardian of the city and Queen of Heaven.[198]

[197] Pending appearance of a full publication, the best presentation of the Rotunda mosaics is in Torp, *Mosaikkene.*

For the Second Coming interpretation, see A. Grabar, "A propos des mosaïques de la coupole de Saint Georges à Salonique," *CahArch,* 17 (1967), 64–66, and Kleinbauer, "Mosaics of the Rotunda," 27 ff. Maria Soteriou's case for a glorification of *Christus Victor* is less convincing: Προβλήματα τῆς εἰκονογραφίας τοῦ τρούλλου τοῦ ἁγ. Γεωργίου Θεσσαλονίκης, in Δελτ.Χριστ.'Αρχ.'Ετ., 6 (1972), 191–204. The zone above the martyrs, where only feet are preserved (not less than 24 figures and not more than 36, Torp calculates), is variously assigned to angels (*op. cit.,* 195, and Kleinbauer, *op. cit.,* 41–44), to the 24 Elders of the Apocalypse (F. Gerke, *Spätantike und frühes Christentum* [Baden-Baden, 1967], 171), or to apostles and prophets (E. Dyggve, "Fouilles et recherches faites en 1939 et en 1952–53 à Thessaloniki," *CorsiRav,* 2 [1957], 83; H. P. L'Orange and P. J. Nordhagen, *Mosaics* [London, 1966], 21).

That the mosaics were not set before the mid-fifth century, and probably soon after, has been argued by M. Vickers ("The Date of the Mosaics of the Rotunda at Thessaloniki," *BSR,* 38 [1970], 183–87). His argument, accepted by Kleinbauer but not by Paola Cattani (*La rotonda e i mosaici di San Giorgio a Salonicco* [Bologna, 1972], 31 f. and 110), rests on the approximate contemporaneity of the Rotunda conversion and the walls of the city (bricks with the same stamps are used in both) and the assignment of the walls to the Hormisdas who became *praefectus praetorio orientis* in 448–50 (first proposed by H. Koethe, in *JdI,* 48 [1933], 197 ff.). His dating would receive effective support if the letter A in association with a monogram of the letters ENT on brickstamps recorded (with other types) for both the walls and the Rotunda (also Archeiropoietos, St. Demetrius, and St. Sophia) does indeed stand for the first year of an indiction, for a new indiction began in September 447 (M. Vickers, "Fifth-Century Brickstamps from Thessaloniki," *BSA,* 68 [1973], 292).

Torp's dating of the mosaics *ca.* 400 or earlier (following Dyggve) arose from Tafrali's attribution of the walls to an earlier Hormisdas, who was in the city in 380. But Vickers has pointed out that this date is impossible for the walls since they incorporate *spolia* from the hippodrome, which was still in use in 390 ("The Date of the Walls of Thessalonia," *Istanbul Arkeoloji Müzeleri Yıllığı,* 15 [1969], 313–18; "Observations on the Chronology of the Walls of Thessaloniki," Μακεδονικά, 12 [1972], 229–33). The objections put forward by Weigand (*BZ,* 39 [1939], 116–45) to dating the mosaics earlier than *ca.* 500 have been answered by Kleinbauer ("Mosaics of the Rotunda," 68–78), who is satisfied that the associated sculpture (including the ambon in Istanbul) and the mosaics are stylistically compatible with a conversion date in the third quarter of the fifth century (*ibid.,* 107). Since Torp established that the mosaics were set immediately after the conversion, this conclusion is not in conflict with the use of bricks of the type made for the walls of the city *ca.* 442–50; for of these, surplus supplies may have been available over a long period. It brings this superb mosaic decoration into the period of major building activity in the city after it became the seat of the prefect of Illyricum in 442–43 (cf. Vickers, "Sirmium or Thessaloniki?" [note 179 *supra*], 338).

The paleography of the inscriptions is unhelpful, since it does not exclude the earlier dating for the mosaics (see G. Gounaris, Αἱ ἑορταστικαὶ ἐπιγραφαὶ τῶν ψηφιδωτῶν τοῦ Τρούλου τοῦ ἁγ. Γεωργίου [Rotunda] Θεσσαλονίκης, in Μακεδονικά, 12 [1972], 201–26). The inscriptions differ from those in the *Tribelon* mosaics of the Acheiropoietos basilica, but these are not strictly comparable since they are on a smaller scale and were not designed to be seen from the ground (C. Diehl, M. Le Tourneau, and H. Saladin, *Les monuments chrétiens de Salonique* [Paris, 1918], 57; otherwise unpublished). Consequently, the weight of present evidence indicates that the two series of mosaics are approximately contemporary. Those of the Acheiropoietos could be as early as *ca.* 460, quite apart from Vickers' interpretation of the brickstamps (see note 179 *supra*), since the building is linked by its capitals to the Studios basilica, now known to have been completed in 453/54, not 463, from Mango's rereading of *AnthPal,* 1,4. [Cf. C. Mango, Byzantine Architecture (New York, 1976), 352 note 6].

[198] See A. Frolow, "La dédicace de Constantinople dans la tradition byzantine," *RHR,* 127 (1944), 61–127. For the "Queen of Heaven," compare the passage in a *kontakion* on the Synaxis of the

It so happens that the two best preserved early apse mosaics in the East both have Christ as the central figure: that in the church of Hosios David in Salonica, the former Latomon monastery, which represents a conflation of the visions of Ezekiel and Isaiah, who are portrayed as witnesses, and is probably a work of the late fifth century;[199] and that in Justinian's basilica in the monastery of St. Catherine on Mt. Sinai which, contrary to what could be expected in a church dedicated to the Theotokos, represents the Transfiguration.[200] Furthermore, since the description by Choricius of a second

Theotokos attributed to Romanos Melodos: Βασιλίδα σε ὁρῶ, βασιλέως μητέρα (Ρωμανοῦ τοῦ Μελωδοῦ ῞Υμνοι, ed. N. B. Tomadakis, II [Athens, 1954], ρκά, item 131 of Patmos, cod. 212, fol. 127ʳ).

On the other hand, there is no warrant for the suggestion that in our mosaic the Theotokos has usurped Christ's place on the Globe of the World (Ihm, *Programme*, 60 and restoration in fig. 12; Wellen, *Theotokos*, 153; Pallas, Θρησκευτικὴ καὶ ᾿Ηθικὴ ᾿Εγκυκλοπαίδεια, 12, col. 1161, fig. 120; Matthiae, "Mosaici di Cipro" [*supra*, note 7], 262; Silvia Pasi, in *FelRav*, 105–6 [1973], 163). This error originated in Smirnov's description ("Mozaiki," 79). No globe is represented.

[199] Volbach-Hirmer, *E. C. Art*, pls. 134–35; Grabar, *Byzantium*, fig. 140. For the identification of the witnesses as Ezekiel and Isaiah (not Habakkuk or Zechariah), see Ihm, *Programme*, 46 and bibliography on 184; also F. Gerke, "Il mosaico absidiale di Hosios David di Salonicco," *CorsiRav*, 11 (1964), 179–99. In another interpretation it is John on Patmos who, as the New Testament witness, balances Ezekiel: J. Snyder, "The Meaning of the 'Maïestas Domini' in Hosios David," *Byzantion*, 37 (1967), 143–52.

The dating in the last decades of the fifth century first proposed is now widely accepted (Xyngopoulos, Καθολικὸν, 171f. and 179). Morey's attempt to date it to the seventh century (*Byzantion*, 7 [1932], 331ff.) is not. Weigand proposed a date about 500 (*BZ*, 33 [1933], 211ff.), and more recently Lazarev proposed the early sixth century (*Istorija*, 49 and 283f.; *Storia*, 47). Kitzinger also prefers a date somewhat later than that originally proposed ("Between Justinian and Iconoclasm," 23f.), but in relation to his dating of the aisle mosaics in St. Demetrius to *ca.* 600. If the latter are instead to be assigned to the initial decoration (see note 179 *supra*), a late fifth-century date for the Hosios David apse is more acceptable, particularly in view of certain affinities with the mosaics in the Rotunda, for which a date in the mid-fifth century or soon after is now proposed (see note 197 *supra*). Gerke's dating of this mosaic to the early fifth century rested in part on Dyggve's now generally rejected opinion that the Rotunda was decorated in the reign of Theodosius I (Gerke, "Il mosaico absidiale," 179ff.).

[200] The color plates in Forsyth-Weitzmann, *St. Catherine*, supersede the illustrations in earlier publications: G. A. Soteriou, Τὸ μωσαϊκὸν τῆς Μεταμορφώσεως τοῦ καθολικοῦ τῆς Μονῆς Σινᾶ, *Atti dello VIII Congr. intern. di Studi bizantini*, II (Rome, 1953), 246ff.; K. Weitzmann, "The Mosaic in St. Catherine's Monastery on Mt. Sinai," *ProcAmPhS*, 110 (1966), 392–405. Contrary to earlier opinions (e.g., A. Guillou, in *MélRome*, 68 [1955], 226ff.), close examination has proved the mosaic to be virtually intact in its original condition (Weitzmann, *op. cit.*, 398f.; cf. I. Ševčenko, "The Early Period of the Sinai Monastery in the Light of Its Inscriptions," *DOP*, 20 [1966], 291–61). The dedication of the church to the Theotokos is given by Procopius (*De aedificiis* V.viii.i.4–9), who names Justinian as its builder.

The church was unfinished at Theodora's death in 548, since she is referred to as "the late Empress" in the inscriptions on the boards masking the roof beams (Ševčenko, *op. cit.*, 255ff., nos. 4 and 5). But it must have been completed in the fifties, whichever of the dates indicated for the composition of *De aedificiis* is preferred (553–55 or 558–60). If the setting of the mosaic followed the building of the church without much delay and was completed before Justinian's death in 565, which is Weitzmann's view (*op. cit.*, 405 and note 24; Forsyth-Weitzmann, *St. Catherine*, 11), the apse decoration must have been completed in that year. The inscription forming part of the mosaic (Ševčenko, *op. cit.*, no. 7) bears the name of the Abbot Longinus and the indiction year 14. The date 550/51 is excluded since it falls in the abbacy of George, who died in 552 (cf. V. Benešević, in *Byzantion*, 1 [1924], 154). The next indiction year 14 began on September 1, 565, shortly before Justinian's death on November 13. This must be accepted as the date of the completion of the mosaics if Benešević was correct in identifying the Abbot Longinus of the inscription with the Isaurian abbot ("Isauros") who, probably between 561 and 568, built a hospital in the monastery with contributions from the Pope (*Byzantion*, 1, pp. 155–64).

On the other hand, if the mosaic did not form part of the initial undertaking it could have been set in 580/81, when the name of the reigning abbot is unknown, or in some even later fourteenth indiction year falling in the abbacy of a Longinus unknown to history. This later dating would suit Kitzinger's *praesentatio* mosaic in Gaza, that in the church of St. Stephen, makes no mention of the Theotokos, it has been suggested that here an enthroned Christ may have been the central figure.[201] Nevertheless, the Theotokos was gradually accepted as the proper subject for the apse of a church and, although the Lythrankomi mosaic is probably the earliest surviving example, it evidently belongs to a rather advanced stage in this process of acceptance. For apart from varying details of iconography, which are considered below, there were clearly some differences of conception and function among the several apse representations of the Theotokos which we have listed. To the extent that these differences represent successive stages in the development of this theme, and insofar as these stages can be fixed in time, the place of our mosaic in this development can be determined.

The mosaic in the Blachernae shrine certainly served a subsidiary commemorative purpose, that of glorifying its imperial patrons; and a similar secondary function characterized the mosaic in St. Sergius at Gaza, where the sacred figures were flanked by lateral groups including living persons. The surviving mosaic at Poreč (Parenzo) is in the same tradition, reflecting court ceremonial. But here it is noteworthy that the Theotokos, like the Redeemer at S. Vitale, is isolated from the other figures by escorting archangels. The mid-sixth-century apse compositions in the West evidently conformed with a Byzantine prejudice against representing donors, or even patron saints, in direct communication with Christ. For archangels attended the enthroned Theotokos in the pre-Justinianic (in our view) St. Demetrius aisle mosaics,[202] where, furthermore, the suppliants for whom the patron saint mediates are of much smaller stature. It has been assumed that already in the Blachernae composition of 473 also the angel guards were included, though the surviving description does not mention them.[203]

This Byzantine practice was followed in Ostrogothic Ravenna, where in Theodoric's mosaics in S. Apollinare Nuovo the enthroned figures of Christ and the Theotokos, here facing each other on the walls of the nave (but probably reflecting apse compositions), were each guarded by two pairs of

---

view that in style the mosaic may be related to an abstract current in the post-Justinianic art of Constantinople ("Between Justinian and Iconoclasm," 29). In that case considerable time would have elapsed since the dedication of the church, and the puzzlingly insignificant role given to the Theotokos in the decoration could be explained to some extent (cf. G. H. Forsyth, "The Monastery of St. Catherine," *DOP*, 22 [1968], 14 and note 17).

The indiction year 14 beginning 1 September 595 is excluded since either John Climacus or his brother George was abbot at that time (see Beneševič, *op. cit.*, 169f.). Consequently, if the year 610/11 is ruled out as too late, the choice remains between 565, the most probable, and 580/81.

[201] Ihm, *Programme*, 194 with references. The second encomium on Bishop Marcian, where it is mentioned, has been dated to the year 548.

[202] Angels also escorted the Virgin where she was portrayed as intercessor in the adjoining Maria cycle of the same series of votive mosaics (spandrel E): Cormack, "S. Demetrios," pls. 4 and 8. On the date, see note 179 *supra*.

[203] E.g., Grabar, "The Virgin in a Mandorla of Light" (*supra*, note 7), 310. On this image set up by the two patricians who brought the maphorion to Constantinople, see *supra*, note 180. Likewise, it has reasonably been suggested that the angel guards were present in the apse of St. Sergius at Gaza: Ihm, *Programme*, 193.

angels, as the processions headed by Theodoric and his family approached them.[204]

In the category to which the Lythrankomi composition belongs, no subsidiary figures other than the archangels are allowed to dilute the doctrinal message of the Incarnation.[205] As to the date when the portrayal of donors and patron saints side by side with the deity passed out of favor, there is some indication in the western series of apse mosaics with Christ as the central figure. In that from S. Michele in Affricisco in Ravenna, the accompanying figures are restricted to Michael and Gabriel alone,[206] and in this respect, the lost mosaic of S. Agata Maggiore in Ravenna was similar.[207] The former church was dedicated in 545, a few years after Byzantine authority was established in the city. The S. Agata mosaic was probably a close contemporary.[208] The suppression of the commemorative element in these mosaics may be connected with the establishment of Byzantine rule,[209] in which case this development in apse compositions would have originated somewhat earlier in Byzantium itself. Similar indications are offered by the fragmentary *Maria Regina* fresco in S. Maria Antiqua, insofar as it can be regarded as a substitute for an apse

[204] Deichmann, *Bauten und Mosaiken*, pls. 112–19; Volbach-Hirmer, *E. C. Art*, pl. 152. The group of the Virgin and Child enthroned formed part of the first decoration, unlike the adjoining figures of the Magi inserted with the processions of martyrs under Bishop Agnellus (556–69): Deichmann, *Geschichte und Monumente*, 175; and cf. G. Bovini, in *Studi Romagnoli*, 3 (1952), 19–26, in *RQ*, 3/4 (1953), 251, and in *Atti dello VIII Congr. intern. di Studi bizantini*, II, 55–87; also C.-O. Nordström, *Ravennastudien* (Uppsala-Stockholm, 1953), 55–87. The church was erected by Theodoric (493–526) but it is not known when its decoration was completed (Deichmann, *op. cit.*, 170). Some authorities assign the mosaics to the last years of his reign (e.g., Lazarev, *Storia*, 77). But it is probable that the Theotokos group, to which one of the processions commemorating the royal foundation of the church was directed, belonged to an early phase of the decoration.

[205] The lower part of our mosaic has fallen and it has been suggested, in order to explain the presence of a mandorla, that other figures were there represented, such as the Magi (Grabar, *Martyrium*, II, 229). But the tentative restoration in fig. M shows that there is really no room for other figures. On the other hand, where the Magi were included in representations of the Adoration, as on the ampullae, their presence did not impose isolation of the Theotokos in a mandorla.

[206] See *supra*, note 189. This is one of the few cases where the angel escorts are named. In the Lythrankomi church there is no trace of such labels among the surviving fragments and it is unlikely that they ever existed; for above the head of the Theotokos, where her identification could be expected, the mosaic is largely intact and contains no sign of it. We refer to the Lythrankomi angels, and also to those in comparable compositions such as that at Poreč, as archangels. The warrant for this lies in those examples where the figures flanking "Holy Mary" are labeled Michael and Gabriel. Such are the sixth-century Cleveland tapestry icon (see *infra*, note 230); the Kiti mosaic, for which a date in the late sixth century is now suggested (Megaw, "Metropolitan or Provincial?", 74–76); and the fresco traces in the shrine of the Theotokos built against the east wall of the cathedral of Gerasa (*Gerasa*, 208 and 473).

[207] Known from a drawing by Cesare Pronti reproduced by Ciampini, *Vetera Monumenta*, I, pl. XLVI, whence Ihm, *Programme*, pl. VII, 2.

[208] The part of the apse from which the mosaic fell in 1688 dates from the time of Archbishop Agnellus (557–70) at the latest (M. Mazzotti, "La basilica ravennate di Sant' Agata Maggiore," *CorsiRav*, 14 [1967], 250). It has been assigned to the episcopate of Victor (538–45) by G. Bovini, "Mosaici parietali scomparsi," *FelRav*, 69 (1955), 7; *idem*, "Note sull'antica decorazione musiva di S. Agata Maggiore a Ravenna," *CorsiRav* (1956), ii, 23–28. For a recent discussion, see Silvia Pasi, "Mosaici ravennati col tema dell' 'Imagine votiva della Maestà,'" *FelRav*, 105–6 (1973), 143 ff.

[209] The apse mosaic in S. Vitale does not conform with this view if it is indeed part of Bishop Maximian's work (see note 190 *supra*). But that being so, overriding factors have in any case to be postulated to explain the portrayal of Ecclesius rather than his successors, who were more concerned than he with the construction and decoration of the bema.

decoration, and as a reflection of Byzantine practice painted soon after 536. For here again there were attendant archangels but no subsidiary figures.[210]

The next stage in the development, in which the archangels also were excluded and the Virgin and Child alone were figured in the apse, was reached by the seventh century, if we may judge by Hyakinthos' original mosaic decoration in the church of the Dormition at Iznik (Nicaea), where the archangels were relegated to the side walls of the bema.[211] Yet the conception which prompted this isolation, which was implicit in the prayer of intercession in the liturgy and, perhaps later, in the phrase ἀνωτέρα ἀγγέλων,[212] was evidently already a factor when the Kanakaria mosaic was set; for here the angels are isolated from the central visionary image by its enclosure in a mandorla, though we shall see that this device probably performed another function also.

Finally, and remote from the earlier conceptions but certainly before Iconoclasm, the Virgin alone stood in the apse with arms raised in supplication, a formula which presupposes a major image of Christ elsewhere in the church. Of this the only early example in the East is provided by the very fragmentary apse mosaic in the Livadia church.[213] This solitary figure evidently derives from representations of the Ascension, where the Virgin stands among the apostles, through intermediary, multifigure compositions such as that in the oratory of S. Venanzio in the Lateran (642–50), where an orant Virgin, very similar to that of the Livadia church, occupies the central position below the bust of Christ emerging from the clouds.[214] The connection between the isolation of the orant in the apse and the localization of the Christ in Glory as the crowning centerpiece in domed churches is not in doubt.[215]

These successive stages in the development of the Theotokos theme in apse compositions can hardly have followed each other everywhere simultaneously.

[210] See *supra*, notes 191 and 192. Even if it is correct to regard the crowning of the Virgin as a Roman development (cf. Marion Lawrence, "Maria Regina," *ArtB*, 8 [1925], 150 ff.), this representation undoubtedly reflects official empress portraits such as that of Ariadne on the diptych leaf in Florence (Grabar, *Byzantium*, fig. 318).

Insofar as early panel painting and mural decoration were related, it is noteworthy that in the early eighth-century icon of the crowned *Madonna della Clemenza* in S. Maria in Trastevere, which was probably modeled on an older panel, the attendant archangels alone figure in the main register; the donor, Pope John VII, is relegated to the foot of the throne as a suppliant: J. Beckwith, *Early Christian and Byzantine Art* (Harmondsworth, 1970), pl. 77. For a full study of this icon, see C. Bertelli, *La Madonna di Santa Maria in Trastevere* (Rome, 1961).

[211] See *supra*, note 178.

[212] The phrase is at least as old as Joseph the Hymnographer; see Eustratiades, Ἡ Θεοτόκος ἐν τῇ Ὑμνογραφίᾳ (*supra*, note 38), 8. The wording of the liturgy is τὴν τιμιωτέραν τῶν Χερουβὶμ καὶ ἐνδοξοτέραν ἀσυγκρίτως τῶν Σεραφίμ.

[213] See *supra*, note 3. The apse is older than the present domed church, whose bema walls conceal part of the mosaics which flanked the apse on the east wall. Remains of marble furniture incorporated in the secondary structure indicate a relatively early date for the church to which the mosaic belongs. The orant figure was adopted, albeit in the guise of *Maria Regina*, as the focal image in the oratory added to Old St. Peter's by Pope John VII in 706, now in Florence in the church of S. Marco (P. Nordhagen, "The Mosaics of John VII [705–707 A.D.]," *ActaIRNorv*, 2 [1965], 124 ff. and pls. I–IV. The entire composition is known only from Grimaldi's drawings, reproduced in Wilpert, *MM*, I [text], 390, fig. 128, and van Berchem-Clouzot, *Mosaïques*, figs. 266 and 269). This presupposes Byzantine examples of the orant Virgin of earlier date (cf. Ihm, *Programme*, 63), which makes it permissible to assign the Livadia mosaic to the seventh century.

[214] Van Berchem-Clouzot, *Mosaïques*, 199–203; Ihm, *Programme*, pl. XXIII, 2 and p. 144 ff.

[215] *Ibid.*, 108 ff.

The decision taken at the Council of Ephesus opened the way for such representations at a time when figural church decoration on a monumental scale was still in its infancy, and the practice in the various centers could have been widely different. But by the sixth century the authority of Constantinople was so well established that, even when allowance is made for the preferences of local patrons and particular workshops, a reasonable degree of conformity is certain. The place of the Lythrankomi composition in the development is thus some guide to the date when it was set. Since the earlier practice of portraying the Theotokos in company with living persons was still followed in St. Sergius at Gaza, erected and decorated between 527 and 536, it would be hazardous to place our mosaic substantially earlier than that. It could be argued, however, that commemorative elements would have survived longer in churches where, as at Gaza, official patronage would count for much. On the other hand, if the mosaic in Hosios David, the former Latomon monastery, in Salonica is a work of the late fifth century,[216] apse programs of purely theological content may have been no novelty in Cyprus before Justinian came to the throne, even if monastic churches were leaders in this respect. It has been suggested that the basis of the Hosios David apse program, an apocalyptic *Maiestas* with liturgical overtones, was a creation of Egyptian monasticism.[217]

Without necessarily accepting this hypothesis, it must be admitted that, even if the frescoes in the chapels at Bawit and Saqqara, where the *Maiestas* is a favorite subject, are of a humble provincial character and relatively late date, some of them must reflect monumental compositions in the lost apses of the main churches of these monasteries and of other churches in Egypt.[218] Secondly, even if the mid-sixth century, the main period of construction and decoration at Bawit and Saqqara,[219] is accepted as a terminus a quo for the chapels, it must be conceded that in such a conservative milieu some of their niche frescoes could well reflect monumental models of earlier date. From whatever source the Hosios David mosaic was inspired, it seems to represent a tradition of apse decoration with purely theological content current already before 500 which, whether or not it was specifically monastic, would explain the gradual elimination of commemorative elements from apse mosaics in the first half of the sixth century.

The Egyptian frescoes are most relevant to the theme of the Lythrankomi mosaic when they reveal the impact of monumental apse compositions featuring the Theotokos; particularly since, to a degree not shared with Coptic architecture and sculpture, "Christian wall-painting in Egypt kept in line

[216] See *supra*, note 199.
[217] Ihm, *Programme*, 47 ff.
[218] Cf. Grabar, *Byzantium*, 173.
[219] H. Torp, "Byzance et la sculpture copte du VIᵉ siècle à Baouît et Sakkara," *Synthronon*, Bibl. des Cahiers Archéol., II (Paris, 1968), 11–27, arguing from the capitals locally made in imitation of Justinianic models datable to the second quarter of the sixth century; *idem*, "The Carved Decorations of the North and South Churches at Bawit," *Kolloquium über spätantike und frühmittelalterliche Skulptur*, II (Mainz, 1970), 35–41. At Saqqara the coin evidence suggested a *floruit* from *ca.* 550 to *ca.* 750: Milne, in *Saqqara*, IV, 37. The niche frescoes have been assigned to the end of the sixth century by K. Wessel, *Koptische Kunst. Die Spätantike in Ägypten* (Recklinghausen, 1963), 180.

with the practices current in other Mediterranean lands."[220] In the two-zone niche frescoes of the Bawit chapels figuring a conflation of the vision of Ezekiel with the Byzantine Ascension, the orant Virgin normally stands among the apostles in one or other of the poses known to sixth-century iconography.[221] But in two cases the apostles flank an enthroned Virgin with the Child on her knee, an intrusion in a composition evoking the Ascension which surely derives from independent Incarnation programs.[222] In a third, below the usual vision of Ezekiel, the apostles give place to a commemorative assembly of local saints, two of whom boldly take precedence over one of the archangels guarding the enthroned Virgin and Child.[223] Similar intrusions of commemorative groups, doubtless reflecting some local equivalent of the Gaza apse mosaics, were found in the lower zones of two of the niche frescoes of the Saqqara monastery.[224] Even closer to hypothetical Gaza-type models are those Saqqara frescoes where the enthroned Virgin and Child with two archangels and two patrons (Jeremias and Enoch) constitute the entire program.[225] Finally, equivalents of the Lythrankomi mosaic may well have inspired the lower zone compositions in which the local saints are absent,[226] as well as those niche frescoes where the enthroned Virgin and Child, attended by the archangels alone, replaces the Vision of Ezekiel as the main subject.[227] We may infer that the painters who worked in these Egyptian foundations were no strangers to major apse decorations featuring the Theotokos both as the centerpiece of a ceremonial group of commemorative character and also as an image of the Incarnation accompanied only by the angel guards. As to the probable date of their models, since even the relative chronology of the Bawit and Saqqara frescoes has not been securely established, little can be said; but it is permissible to conclude that apse compositions akin to that of the Panagia Kanakaria were to be seen in Egypt as early as the mid-sixth century, if not earlier. This is not to say that they would normally have represented the Theotokos in the Lythrankomi formula, with the Child on her lap in a strictly frontal position. In fact the surviving representations in the Coptic frescoes show the Child differently—on one or the other of the Virgin's

[220] Grabar, *Byzantium*, 122.

[221] Frontal: as in the "Ascension" miniature in Rabbula's codex and on the reverses of the Monza ampullae 1, 10, and 11, and Bobbio ampulla 13, in the numbering of Grabar, *Ampoules*; Bawit chapel 17 (reproduced side by side with the Rabbula miniature in Ihm, *Programme*, pls. XXII, 1, and XXIII, 1). The fresco in Bawit chapel 20 is similar but with local saints instead of apostles (J. Maspéro and E. Drioton, *Fouilles exécutées à Baouît*, MémInstCaire, 59 [1932, text] and 2 [1943, plates], pp. X–XI and 10 with pls. XXXI–XXXIV). Profile: as on the reverses of Monza ampulla 16 and Bobbio ampulla 19; Bawit chapel 46 (Ihm, *Programme*, pl. XXIV, 1).

[222] Bawit chapel 6 (Cairo, Coptic Museum, no. 1220) and Bawit chapel 42 (conveniently illustrated in Ihm, *Programme*, pl. XXV, 1 and 2).

[223] Bawit chapel 3 (Clédat, *Baouît*, 13f. and 23f. with pls. X and XII, 1); cf. Ihm, *Programme*, 199f.

[224] Saqqara chapel F (*Saqqara*, II, 67 and pl. LIX); Saqqara cell 1733 (*Saqqara*, IV, 22; cf. Ihm, *Programme*, 208).

[225] Saqqara cell 1719 (*Saqqara*, IV, 134 and pl. XXIII, lower figure); cell 1724 (*ibid.*, 23; cf. Ihm, *Programme*, 207). Comparable were two Bawit frescoes, in chapels 7 and 8 (Ihm, *Programme*, 200f.).

[226] Saqqara cell 1723 (*Saqqara*, IV, 23, 135 and pl. XXV); cell 1727 (*ibid.*, 22, 134 and pl. XXIV).

[227] Bawit chapel 28 (Ihm, *Programme*, pl. XVIII); Saqqara chapel A (*Saqqara*, II, 64, 81 and pls. XLI, XLIII).

knees or held in the crook of one arm, a preference that has been connected with Egyptian representations of Isis and the infant Horus.[228] But the frontal pose also was current in Egypt in monumental church decorations reproducing the Byzantine Incarnation formula, if we may judge by its appearance in a series of limestone reliefs preserved in the Coptic Museum,[229] and in a tapestry icon in the Cleveland Museum which there is good reason to connect with apsidal compositions.[230]

In respect of the axial position and frontal pose of the Child, another parallel to our mosaic has been postulated in the Holy Land; for, though no comparable monumental example has survived there, one such did exist in mosaic on the façade of the basilica of the Nativity at Bethlehem, if a plausible account of it can be accepted. This is preserved in a catalogue of miraculous images included in what purports to be a copy of a synodical letter addressed to the Emperor Theophilus in 836 by the three Eastern Patriarchs.[231] This mosaic was included because, we are told, it was the costume of the Magi there figured that caused the Persians to spare the church in 614. The mosaic represented the Nativity, the Theotokos, and the Adoration, and the wording of the text—Θεομήτορα ἐγκόλπιον φέρουσα τὸ ζωοφόρον βρέφος—is appropriate only for an enthroned Virgin with the Child on her knee before her. Even if the letter is in some details suspect, this description in a ninth-century MS of a prominent composition above the entrance to one of the principal loca sancta, which the writer's contemporaries would have been able to check from other sources, is unlikely to be a fabrication. But although it establishes the existence at Bethlehem of a portrayal of the Theotokos in mosaic comparable with that at Lythrankomi, and of early Justinianic date,[232] there the similarity of the two compositions must have ended; for in the text there is no mention of attendant angels, and there is reason to believe that this Bethlehem façade composition was arranged somewhat as that on the ivory pyxis in Vienna.[233] It follows that the synodical letter, if such it be, provides scant support for the speculation that the façade mosaic reproduced the composition of a hypothetical mosaic of the Lythrankomi type in the main apse of the Bethlehem basilica.[234]

[228] Cf. Ihm, *Programme*, 65f.

[229] No. 8006 (M. E. 8704) with flanking archangels: J. Beckwith, *Coptic Sculpture* (London, 1963), pl. 113. In two others, nos. 7814–15, figures usually identified as Peter and Paul are introduced on either side between the throne and the archangels: *ibid.*, pls. 111 and 112.

[230] Shepherd, "Tapestry Panel," 90–120.

[231] I. Sakkelion, Ἐκ τῶν ἀνεκδότων τῆς Πατμιακῆς Βιβλιοθήκης. Ἐπιστολὴ τῶν ἁγιωτάτων πατριαρχῶν Χριστοφόρου Ἀλεξανδρείας, Ἰὼβ Ἀντιοχείας, Βασιλείου Ἱεροσολύμων πρὸς τὸν Βασιλέα Θεόφιλον, in Εὐαγγελικὸς Κήρυξ, 8 (Athens, 1864), 157f. (29f. in reprint [Athens, 1964]); republished with an introduction by L. Duchesne, "L'iconographie byzantine dans un document grec du IXe siècle," *Roma e l'Oriente*, 5 (1912–13), 283ff. The authenticity of this letter is discussed *infra* (see Appendix).

[232] Eutychius, *Annales*, PG, 111, col. 1070; Arabic text, ed. L. Cheikho, I (Beirut, 1906), 201f.; English trans. in W. Harvey *et al.*, *The Church of the Nativity* (London, 1910), 59.

[233] Volbach, *Elfenbeinarbeiten*, no. 199, pl. 58. It is hoped that this suggestion will be enlarged upon in another place.

[234] Cf. Ihm, *Programme*, 52ff. There is no merit in the suggestion that, contrary to the specific indication of the letter (τῷ πρὸς δύσιν ἔξωθεν μέρει), the mosaic of the Adoration it mentions was not on the façade, but in the main apse: B. Bagatti, *Gli antichi edifici sacri di Betlemme* (Jerusalem, 1952), 12f.

It is not now possible to connect the Bethlehem façade mosaic at all closely with the obverse of the Dumbarton Oaks gold medallion, where below a Theotokos of the Lythrankomi type are small scenes of the Nativity (with the shepherds) and the Adoration.[235] The medallion can no longer be regarded as a pilgrim's souvenir, modeled on the mosaic,[236] for it is established that it was struck in the imperial mint at Constantinople, probably not before the last quarter of the sixth century.[237] But since the Theotokos is here flanked by the archangels the medallion proves how deeply rooted and enduring was this formula for the Incarnation theme.

Smirnov, who wrote before the medallion was found, connected the Lythrankomi composition with the Bethlehem façade by means of the Adoration scenes on the silver ampullae from the Holy Places preserved in Monza and Bobbio.[238] Ainalov, who developed the theme that the representations on the ampullae reflected monumental mosaics at the Holy Places, believed (erroneously, we now know) that the prototype of the ampullae Adorations, which give prominence to the shepherds, was not the façade mosaic but a mosaic in the grotto of the Nativity.[239] For us, the relevance of these ampullae does not lie in their Adorations as such but primarily in the portrayal of the enthroned Virgin and Child in accordance with the frontal formula of the Lythrankomi mosaic and, secondly, in the presence of the two angels; though on the ampullae the angels are either above the flanking groups of adorers and pointing to the huge central star, as on Monza 1,[240] or actually carrying the star in a clipeus, as on Monza 3.[241] On the other hand, the grotto mosaic at Bethlehem, known to Ainalov only from the twelfth-century account of Phocas,[242] cannot now be related to the mosaic in the Panagia Kanakaria. Some remains of it were discovered in 1944 and these clearly belong to a normal Byzantine twelfth-century Nativity.[243]

Later writers focused attention on the apses of the great basilicas erected to commemorate events in the life of Christ as probable receptacles for authoritative monumental representations of those events and on the prob-

---

[235] M. Ross, "A Byzantine Gold Medallion at Dumbarton Oaks," *DOP*, 11 (1957), 247–61.

[236] J. Strzygowski, in *OrChr*, 5 (1915), 96 ff.

[237] Ross, "A Byzantine Gold Medallion," 252. P. Grierson has since suggested (*DOP*, 15 [1961], 221 ff.) that the medallion was struck for presentation to high officials on the occasion of the baptism of Tiberius' son Theodosius, probably on the feast of the Epiphany in 584.

[238] Smirnov, "Mozaiki," 91–92.

[239] Ainalov, *Hellenistic Origins*, 235.

[240] Grabar, *Ampoules*, pls. I–II.

[241] *Ibid.*, pl. VIII.

[242] PG, 133, cols. 957–60; English trans., *The Pilgrimage of Joannes Phocas*, Palestine Pilgrims Text Society [London, 1889], 31 f., quoted in Harvey *et al.*, *The Church of the Nativity* (*supra*, note 232), 65 f.

[243] C. N. Johns, "Discoveries in Palestine since 1939," *PEQ* (1948), 100 and pl. VIII. What little survives matches the description of Phocas well enough and there can be little doubt that it was set at the same time as the twelfth-century mosaics in the basilica, to which Ephraim's inscription of 1169 in the bema belongs (Harvey *et al.*, *The Church of the Nativity*, 43 f.).

An earlier mosaic decoration in the grotto is mentioned by the Russian pilgrim Daniel (*Pravosl. palest. sbornik*, 3 and 9 [1885], 65; French trans. in B. de Khitrowo, *Itinéraires russes en Orient* [Geneva, 1889], 40; English trans., *The Pilgrimage of the Russian Abbot Daniel*, Palestine Pilgrims Text Society [London, 1888], 40, quoted in Harvey *et al.*, *The Church of the Nativity*, 63). If it included any figure subject at all, this also is likely to have been a Nativity.

ability that the ampullae reflect them.[244] But in his detailed study of the ampullae Grabar sets out the difficulties in this hypothesis: the lack of any text describing such apse mosaics, and the variations in the scenes on the ampullae themselves, which conflict with the concept of a single authoritative apsidal model. Furthermore, although the ampullae were made locally for pilgrims to the Holy Places, Grabar recognizes their dependence as regards their decoration on the imperial art of Constantinople exemplified in sumptuous metalwork, medallions, and jewelry, and as regards their style on an equally alien "Greek" figural tradition.[245] In that case, the ampullae, which date from the middle or second half of the sixth century,[246] are of prime importance as a reflection of Constantinopolitan art in the time of Justinian; secondly, they indicate that this was the dominating influence on silversmiths working in the Holy Places in the sixth century, which may be no less true of the mosaicists working there under Justinian;[247] indeed, the ampullae can now be related to the work of those mosaicists only insofar as both were reflections of contemporary metropolitan practice.

This reassessment of the art of the ampullae implies that the frontal formula for the Theotokos used in both the Lythrankomi and the Bethlehem mosaics was well-established in the capital at the time they were set. And since the entire Lythrankomi treatment of the Incarnation theme (the mandorla alone excepted) appears on one of the ampullae,[248] as well as on the obverse of the Constantinopolitan medallion, the Byzantine origin of this treatment is confirmed.[249]

If, then, everything points to Constantinople as the source of the Lythrankomi formula for the propagation of the dogma of the Incarnation, when did its adoption for apse decorations become general? The Hosios David apse in Salonica indicates the use of the conch for compositions of purely theological content before the end of the fifth century. By that time, the adoption of our Incarnation formula as the optional subject for apse decorations, at least in Constantinople, seems certain if Theodoric's nave mosaic in S. Apollinare Nuovo was indeed modeled on an apse composition, for the nave decoration was very probably among the first sections to be completed. The evidence of the Theotokos panel in the lost aisle mosaics of St. Demetrius in Salonica is less satisfactory, for the presence of saints and votaries seems to preclude direct modeling on an apse mosaic of our type. Such a prototype

---

[244] Grabar, *Martyrium*, II, 111 ff. and 164. B. Bagatti, "Eulogie Palestinesi," *OCP*, 15 (1949), 162, raises reasonable doubts concerning the existence of any such apse mosaics at an early date. Cf. Ihm, *Programme*, 3 and note 9, 54, 85, 122 ff.

[245] Grabar, *Ampoules*, 45–50.

[246] *Ibid.*, 14.

[247] The Patriarch Eutychius' story of Justinian's displeasure at the manner in which the Basilica of the Nativity had been constructed may be no more than a folktale, but it conforms with other indications of a rather strict control of provincial affairs in his time by the central government (for references, see note 232 *supra*).

[248] Monza 4: Grabar, *Ampoules*, pl. x.

[249] Ainalov preferred to relate the ampulla Monza 4, and with it the Berlin ivory diptych and the Kanakaria mosaic, to some hypothetical Palestinian image of the Virgin and Child (Ainalov, *Hellenistic Origins*, 244).

may be postulated in Rome for the *Maria Regina* fresco soon after 536, by which time others may have appeared in Egypt to inspire those of the somewhat later niche frescoes which approximate our type, as well as the Cleveland tapestry and the limestone reliefs which are even closer. Cyprus would not have been a late recipient. It lay on the sea route to the East and there is evidence that its independent hierarchy looked to Constantinople for the embellishment of its churches already in the early sixth century.[250] Consequently, on its theme alone, the Lythrankomi mosaic need be no later than the third decade of the sixth century.

b. The Mandorla

There is no sixth-century parallel for the mandorla in which the Virgin and Child are isolated in the Lythrankomi apse. This device had long been in use to denote the divinity of Christ, having originated as a representation of the luminous cloud by which the Glory of the Lord was revealed, according to passages in both the Old and the New Testament.[251] A notable early example is the lunette mosaic discovered in 1960 in the catacomb of Domitilla, where the enthroned Christ is isolated in a circular mandorla from the seated figures of Peter and Paul on either side.[252] When, after the Council of Ephesus, it became permissible to introduce formal representations of the Virgin and Child in such focal positions, it would have been understandable, though theologically improper, to embrace the Theotokos within the accepted symbol of Christ's divinity. It may be significant that the only surviving pre-iconoclastic example is in the East, where Mary was held in exceptional esteem; though it must be assumed that the presence of the mandorla in our mosaic reflects no conscious deification of Mary. On the other hand, if Grabar is correct in deriving the portrayal of the Virgin within a mandorla in Romanesque frescoes from Early Christian prototypes, the practice must have extended to the West also at one time.[253] A link is perhaps provided by the frescoes datable to the second quarter of the ninth century in the chapel of St. Lawrence at the source of the Volturno.[254] But this and a rare post-iconoclastic, Eastern example at Kizil Tchoukour in Cappadocia,[254a] where the mandorla is used as at Lythrankomi, are too remote and too late to help in the interpretation of

---

[250] To judge by the "Theodosian" capitals of Proconnesian marble used in the Campanopetra basilica at Salamis-Constantia; see *supra*, note 100. The advance of the Constantinopolitan influence in Cyprus is separately considered in Megaw, "Metropolitan or Provincial?", *passim*.

[251] Cf. F. van der Meer, *Maiestas Domini* (Vatican, 1938), 255–65; O. Brendel, "The Origin and Meaning of the Mandorla," *GBA*, 25 (1944), 5 ff.; Grabar, "The Virgin in a Mandorla" (*supra*, note 7), 307 ff.

[252] A. Ferrua, "*Qui Filius diceris et Pater inveniris*, Mosaico novellamente scoperto nella catacomba di S. Domitilla," *RendPontAcc*, 33 (1960–61), 217, fig. 5. He dates it not later than the pontificate of Damasus, 366–84.

[253] Grabar, "The Virgin in a Mandorla," 305 ff.

[254] E. Bertaux, *L'art dans l'Italie méridionale*, I (Paris, 1904), 97, fig. 34. Here, while the entire image of the Virgin with the Child before her on her lap is enclosed in a circular mandorla, this questionable practice is mitigated by isolating the Child in a separate elliptical mandorla-clipeus. But elsewhere in the same chapel a mandorla encloses the Virgin alone (*ibid.*, pl. III,3).

[254a] N. and M. Thierry "Eglise de Kizil-Tchoukour," *MonPiot*, 50 (1958), 130 and fig. 18. This and other frescoes in the north chapel are datable to the ninth or early tenth century (*ibid.*, 146).

the mandorla in the Panagia Kanakaria; and comparable representations in post-Byzantine icons portraying the Theotokos in glory must also be set aside.[255]

The appearance of the mandorla in other early apse programs is the best explanation of its presence in that adopted at Lythrankomi. Grabar has underlined its importance as a diagnostic of the historic theophanies such as the Transfiguration, as represented in the Sinai mosaic, and the Ascension; and he has indicated its appropriateness in a composition such as ours, regarded as a miraculous vision proclaiming the supreme theophany of the Incarnation.[256] On the other hand, the function of the mandorla to designate the celestial context of a visionary theophany, while isolating the vision from its witnesses, established a formula for apsidal representations of Christ in Majesty.[257] Initially, the central mandorla encircling the Redeemer was flanked by the witnesses of the Old Testament apocalypse, as in the Hosios David apse.[258] When, in the apse program more closely related to the Ascension and thereby to the Second Coming, the two attendant figures are Michael and Gabriel,[259] it is easy to see how the mandorla could have been retained together with the archangels, almost automatically, upon the introduction of the Theotokos into the apse in substitution for Christ in Glory. In the same way the inexpert craftsman who fashioned the Grado reliquary lid carried into his portrayal of the enthroned Theotokos the cross scepter held in her right hand from some corresponding figure of Christ which served him as model.[260] Yet, in the case of the Lythrankomi apse, the undoubted competence of the mosaicist and the lack of other signs of innovation suggest that the presence of the mandorla was no accident. That, on the contrary, it had a specific, propaganda purpose has been argued by one scholar.

Marina Sacopoulo has brought the use of the mandorla in our mosaic into relation with the bitter doctrinal controversy over the divine and human aspects of Christ.[261] The dual nature formula which prevailed at the Council of Chalcedon in 451 was long exposed to the reaction of the Monophysite

[255] E.g., an icon in the Byzantine Museum, Athens (V. Cotta, Περὶ σπανίας παραστάσεως τῆς Θεοτόκου ἐπὶ εἰκόνος τοῦ Βυζαντινοῦ Μουσείου Ἀθηνῶν, in Ἀρχ.Ἐφ. 1937, pt. 2, 673–86). [If the unusual marginal representation of the Trinity in the Utrecht Psalter, which M. Sacopoulo cites and illustrates (La Théotokos à la mandorle, 100 and fig. 64), was indeed taken from the supposed fifth-century model for this MS, the representation of the Virgin and Child within a mandorla would have been a recognized symbol for the Second Person well before the setting of the Lythrankomi mosaic, notwithstanding the adoption of the Hodegetria iconography in the psalter.]

[256] Grabar, Martyrium, II, 203 and 212f. Cf. Ihm, Programme, 95ff., and Wellen, Theotokos, 153.

[257] Ihm, Programme, 42ff.: "The Liturgical Maiestas."

Where a cross appears in an apse encircled by a mandorla the cross should be understood to represent Christ: e.g., in S. Apollinare in Classe (Deichmann, Bauten und Mosaiken, pl. XIV).

[258] See supra, note 199.

[259] Bawit chapel 6 (Ihm, Programme, pl. XXV, 1); Bawit chapel 17 (ibid., pl. XXV, 2). The flanking archangels reappear in the seventh- or eighth-century apse fresco of the cave church at Dodo in Georgia (ibid., 192 and pl. XIV, 2). Compare the mosaic from S. Michele in Affricisco where, however, there is no mandorla (see supra, note 189).

[260] Grabar, Byzantium, fig. 358.

[261] Marina Sacopoulo, "Mosaïque de Kanakaria (Chypre). Essai d'exégèse de la 'mandorla'," Actas del VIII Congreso intern. de Arqueología cristiana (Barcelona, 1972), 445f. [See now, more fully, idem, La Théotokos à la mandorle, esp. 102ff.]

doctrine entrenched in Syria and Egypt. In Cyprus, geographically in the frontline of Orthodoxy, it would not be surprising to find the normal proclamation of the Incarnation in an apse decoration conceived in terms of Chalcedonian doctrine.[262] For Mme. Sacopoulo, the nature of the *Theanthropos* is declared at Lythrankomi, on the one hand by the humanity of Mary embracing the Christ Child, and on the other by encompassing the whole image in a mandorla of divine glory.

Considered simply as a device to enhance a focal image, the mandorla in the Lythrankomi mosaic can be related to some other representations of the Virgin and Child in which a conch served a similar purpose. Grabar has observed that the Theotokos on the ambon from the Salonica Rotunda is so placed in her niche that the conch which crowns it serves as a sort of aureole.[263] The special significance of the conch in official portraiture is evident when it appears above Constantine II in the Calendar of 354[264] and above Theodora in the S. Vitale mosaic, and when it serves instead of a clipeus or a nimbus.[265] Apart from the ambon relief, the conch appears above so many representations of the Virgin and Child, including the *Maria Regina* fresco and the sixth-century miniature of the Adoration annexed to the Etchmiadzin Gospel,[266] that its significance as a symbol of majesty can hardly be doubted.

If the practice of enclosing the Virgin and Child in a mandorla enjoyed a similar vogue it was short-lived; for it is lacking even in closely related representations such as the Dumbarton Oaks medallion. It would quickly have been appreciated how inappropriate it was to extend to Mary a symbol of divinity proper only to Christ. We have seen that in monumental art, at least from the seventh century, the archangels could be isolated from the image of the Incarnation without using a mandorla by placing them on either side of the bema, as in the church of the Dormition at Iznik (Nicaea).[267] In this arrangement the gold ground of the conch, freed from all landscape elements, itself served as an aura of glory embracing both Mother and Child,

---

[262] The position of the Island in the dispute is illustrated by the appointment as a bishop in Cyprus of Philoxenos the Younger, formerly a Monophysite bishop in Syria, after he had accepted the tenets of Chalcedon at the synod over which Justinian presided in 532. See K. Chatzipsaltis, in Κυπρ.Σπουδ., 27 (1963), 69ff. For an inscription of Justinianic appearance naming an Archbishop Philoxenos, probably to be equated with Philoxenos the Younger, see T. B. Mitford, in *AJA*, 65 (1961), 120 no. 20 and pl. 45; J. and L. Robert, in *REG*, 75 (1962), 211.

[The scant evidence for Monophysite penetration in Cyprus is exploited by M. Sacopoulo (*La Théotokos à la mandorle*, 78ff.), who suggests that the Lythrankomi composition may reflect the defeat of the Monophysites at the synod of 536 and Justinian's condemnation and exile of their leaders the same year. If that could be proved, the setting of the mosaic would be fixed in that year or soon after.]

[263] Grabar, *Sculptures*, 82.

[264] Known only from Pieresc's drawing: Grabar, *Iconography*, fig. 253. Compare the conch in the pediment above Asturius in the consular diptych in Darmstadt (*ibid.*, fig. 203).

[265] For clipeus, on the sarcophagus with the resurrection of Lazarus in the Lateran Museums (*ibid.*, fig. 27); for nimbus, on the diptych of the consul Anastasius in Paris (*ibid.*, fig. 159) and on Maximian's throne at Ravenna (Volbach-Hirmer, *E. C. Art*, pls. 228–29).

[266] Lydia A. Dournovo, *Miniatures arméniennes* (Paris, 1960), 39. The conch reappears on the Berlin ivory panel (Volbach-Hirmer, *E. C. Art*, pl. 225) and on a crude limestone relief in the Coptic Museum (Beckwith, *Coptic Sculpture* [*supra*, note 229], pl. 113). Compare the radial flutes on the nimbus of the Virgin on another Coptic relief (*ibid.*, fig. 112).

[267] See *supra*, note 178.

but without involving any suggestion of Mary's divinity. Earlier, and evidently within the sixth century, insofar as it was desired to stress the divinity of Christ in an Incarnation formula, this was achieved by surrounding the Child alone in a small mandorla-clipeus. In mural painting, apart from one of the niche frescoes in the Saqqara monastery,[268] the earliest surviving example of this expedient in conjunction with an enthroned Theotokos of the Lythrankomi type is as late as the eighth century,[269] but it appears in the early miniature of the Adoration annexed to the Etchmiadzin Gospels.[270] Its use with a standing figure of the Virgin is also attested before the close of the sixth century by a lead seal of Maurice Tiberius.[271] A similar desire to accentuate the divinity of Christ alone may explain the portrayal of the Child on a shield held by Mary on her left knee.[272] If these later expedients are indeed a result of objections to embracing Mary within the mandorla of Christ, then this feature also confirms that our mosaic is likely to belong to a relatively early phase in the development of the Theotokos apse program. The surviving landscape elements, to which we now turn, point to the same conclusion.

c. Landscape Elements

The two prominent palm trees set the scene of our composition in Paradise. That this was their normal symbolism is clear from their frequent association with the Four Rivers.[273] This setting was not invented for representations of the Theotokos, but was taken over from earlier apsidal images of Christ, whose heavenly kingdom was rendered in terms of the biblical Paradise.[274] That the Lythrankomi mosaicist chose the fan-leaved palm, rather than the common feather-leaved date palm of Western mosaics, does not invalidate this imagery.[275] What is noteworthy is that these elements of the heavenly

---

[268] Cell 1723: *Saqqara*, IV, pl. xxv.

[269] In the group of the three Holy Mothers in S. Maria Antiqua painted under Pope Paul I (757–67): Wilpert, *MM*, IV, pl. 194; Grabar, *Byzantium*, fig. 180. Cf. A. Weis, "Ein vorjustinianische Ikonentypus in S. Maria Antiqua," *Römisches Jahrbuch für Kunstgeschichte*, 8 (1958), 17–61.

[270] See *supra*, note 266.

[271] N. Lihačev, *Istoričeskoe značenie italo-grečeskoj ikonopisi. Izobraženija Bogomateri* (St. Petersburg, 1911), pl. IV, 13. Cf. Kondakov, *Ikonografija Bogomateri*, II (1915), (note 4 *supra*), 128 ff. with fig. 49, a similar seal of Heraclius. These imperial seals do not support the view that the type originated in Syria, where, as in Egypt, the known examples are later. They include a miniature of the Syriac MS Paris, Bibl. Nat., Syr. 341, fol. 118 (Omont, "Peintures de l'Anc. Testament dans un MS Syriaque du VII ou VIII siècle," *MonPiot*, 17 [1909], 93 and pl. VI, 7) and a seventh-century half-length icon in the Sinai monastery (G. Soteriou, Εἰκόνες τῆς Μονῆς Σινᾶ, I [Athens, 1956], 42 f. and fig. 28).

[272] Bawit chapel 28 (Ihm, *Programme*, 203 and pl. XVIII, 1); the same in Saqqara cell 1723 (*Saqqara*, IV, 23, 135 and pl. xxv). On the derivation of this type from imperial iconographic sources such as the diptych of 480, on which the consul Basil is portrayed on a shield held by Victory (R. Delbrueck, *Die Consulardiptychen* [Berlin, 1929], pl. 6, v); see Grabar, *Martyrium*, II, 176; Ihm, *Programme*, 61.

[273] Already in the *Traditio Legis* apse in S. Costanza (Grabar, *Iconography*, fig. 101). Compare the evidently Eastern example of the association on a lead vessel from Tunisia (*ibid.*, fig. 39). [On the palm as a sacred tree and a symbol of everlasting life, see M. Sacopoulo's excursus, *La Théotokos à la mandorle*, 22 ff.]

[274] Perhaps already in the first apse decoration of Old St. Peter's, if this was followed in the medieval replacement featuring two large palm trees, which Grimaldi recorded (Ihm, *Programme*, pl. VI, 1 with references on p. 22 note 37). Cf. Grabar, "The Virgin in a Mandorla" (*supra*, note 7), 310.

[275] Christa Ihm's restoration of feather-leaved date palms in our mosaic is unwarranted (*Programme*, fig. 12), although this date palm is usual in Eastern representations also; e.g., those on a relief in the Istanbul Archaeological Museum (Peirce–Tyler, *L'art byzantin*, pl. 165).

landscape must have been quite prominent in his composition. For although nothing survives from the lower part of our mosaic, where such features would be most likely to occur, enough remains to show that they were very generously used throughout the background areas. The palms rose almost to the apex of the conch and, to judge by that on the south, suckered profusely at the base to fill the voids on either side of the mandorla. The other trees evidently occupied much of the vacant spaces outside the archangels, extending almost to the tips of their outer wings. The elaborate hilly landscapes of the Hosios David apse, rising into minimal areas of cloudy blue sky, belong to a different tradition; but, like the parklike country of which we have glimpses in the earlier mosaics of St. Demetrius, they underline a predilection for landscape in the pre-Justinianic period.

The use of palm trees as dividing elements in figure compositions from the Byzantine area is attested by the bronze situla in the Museo Cristiano for the fifth century,[276] and the palm trees separating the apostles in the Arian Baptistery in Ravenna indicate the currency of this device in mosaics of the early sixth. On the other hand, despite its reappearance in the Justinianic processions inserted into the nave mosaics of S. Apollinare Nuovo, there are many indications of a tendency in the course of the sixth century to reduce landscape elements in apse compositions to a minimum. The apse of SS. Cosmas and Damian (526–30) is the latest in which palm trees are featured,[277] and, apart from the altogether exceptional treatment in S. Apollinare in Classe, landscape by the mid-sixth century is reduced to the suggestion of a meadow with a sprinkling of flowers. Such are the meager indications of the heavenly locale of the assemblies in the apses of S. Vitale and of the Poreč (Parenzo) basilica. The gold ground, which had replaced the terrestrial blue, itself evoked the perpetual light of Heaven and made any other indication of the setting superfluous. The ubiquitous gold even eliminated any suggestion of Mt. Tabor in the Sinai mosaic, and in the seventh century landscape elements were almost everywhere suppressed. Our mosaic clearly antedates this process, which was evidently well under way in the time of Justinian.

In this respect, as in some others, more than one of the frescoes in the Bawit chapels probably reflect pre-Justinianic models, for in these the figures are set against tree-filled backgrounds. The palms, banal in Egypt, are replaced by citron trees,[278] which is one of the reasons for identifying as such the tree

---

[276] Burke, "A Bronze Situla," 63 ff., figs. 1–3. The traces of the preliminary sketch below the head of the phoenix in the Salonica Rotunda mosaics are interpreted by Torp as the top of a palm tree (Torp, *Mosaikkene*, 36 f., fig. on p. 39; cf. Kleinbauer, "Mosaics of the Rotunda," 34 ff.). This raises the possibility that there was a series of palm trees separating the figures in the zone below the flying angels.

[277] W. Oakeshott, *The Mosaics of Rome* (London 1967), pl. XII. The palms are lacking in S. Theodoro, which is somewhat later, while in S. Apollinare in Classe, expelled from the apse, a single date palm occupies each of the narrow panels on either side of it (Ihm, *Programme*, pl. XX, 2). The fresco in the oratory of St. Felicitas, in the baths of Titus, known only from drawings (*ibid.*, pl. XXVI, 3), was exceptional in featuring two palms if it was painted as late as the seventh century, as Grabar has suggested (*Martyrium*, II, p. 17; cf. Ihm, *Programme*, 147).

[278] Chapel 17: Ihm, *Programme*, pl. XXIII, and a good detail in Grabar, *Byzantium*, fig. 189; Chapel 28: Clédat, *Baouît* (2), 154 and pls. XCVI, XCVIII.

below the outer wing of the north archangel in our mosaic (fig. L). It is significant that these particular frescoes are close to known Byzantine compositions, whereas those which have plain backgrounds and could be expected to derive from later models are precisely those which feature the characteristic Coptic interpolation of an enthroned Virgin and Child in place of the orant figure of the Ascension prototypes.[279]

We may then reasonably conclude that, while the presence of the mandorla places our mosaic relatively early in the development of the Theotokos apse program, the prominence given to the trees of the Paradise landscape is particularly indicative of the early Justinianic, if not the pre-Justinianic, period.

The Apostle Border

There remains to be considered the question whether the Apostle Border has any significant relationship with the main composition. It has been noted that these two elements in the decoration cannot be viewed together, and that they are rather emphatically separated by the Intermediate Border. That their association is fortuitous might be inferred from the conjunction of a similar medallion border with a very different representation in the Sinai mosaic and with no dividing ornamentation between them.

However, it is not true that, irrespective of the subject of the main composition, this assembly of apostles was the invariable decoration of the underside of the apse arch in the sixth century. In the apse in S. Vitale and in the mosaic from S. Michele in Affricisco ornamental borders take its place; though in the latter, apostles may be represented symbolically by the doves in the loops of the garland.[280] In S. Vitale there is an apostle border of the Lythrankomi type, but it decorates not the apse arch but that at the entrance to the presbytery. Since in both these churches the apse mosaics figure the Redeemer, it might be suggested that the apostle medallions were the normal accompaniment of a main representation, not of Christ but of the Theotokos. But against this is the fact that the Poreč apse does not conform. The apostles are indeed represented close by, as a row of standing figures on the wall above the apse, six on either side of Christ,[281] but the medallions on the soffit of the apse arch are occupied by a series of female martyrs.

In the circumstances, the explanation of these many representations of the apostles in one form or another, whether on the soffit of the apse arch, on the wall above it, or elsewhere in the sanctuary, appears to lie not so much in their significance in relation to the various apse themes with which they are associated, but rather in their location in the sanctuary. In that case we could well ask whether they derive from the early practice of figuring the apostles in the apse itself, on either side of Christ. Examples of this apse

[279] Chapel 6 (Coptic Museum, Cairo): Ihm, *Programme*, pl. XXV, 1; Chapel 42, *ibid.*, pl. XXV, 2.
[280] See *supra*, note 189.
[281] See *supra*, note 187.

program in the West, surviving or recorded, are of various types.[282] They include representations of the Twelve seated with Christ the Teacher, as in the chapel of S. Aquilino in the church of S. Lorenzo in Milan,[283] or standing and acclaiming the enthroned Christ, as in the lost apse mosaic of S. Agata dei Goti in Rome which is known from drawings and datable between 460 and 470.[284] Catacomb frescoes and sarcophagus reliefs provide antecedents for both themes. The representation of the Twelve on such objects as the bronze situla in the Museo Cristiano[285] and the tapestry icon seen by Arculf in Jerusalem, which figured Christ with the apostles,[286] attest the currency of the theme in the Byzantine sphere. That there also it was employed as an apse program is to some extent borne out by the surviving seventh-century mosaic of the *Traditio legis* at Zromi in Georgia, though it figures only Peter and Paul.[287] In any case, the apostles would have been familiar figures in Eastern apses if, as seems probable for the reasons indicated below, their programs included the purely Eastern theme of the Second Coming rendered in terms of the Ascension.[288] On the introduction of other themes into the apse it would have been natural to retain the apostles in alternative positions nearby, and that is precisely where they are found, unless they remain in the conch itself, transformed into twelve lambs and subordinate to a new theme as in the apse mosaic in S. Apollinare in Classe. However that may be, it would have been recognized that the Twelve were singularly appropriate occupants for these positions close to the altar-table, as an evocation of the Last Supper,[289] to the extent that their relevance to the apse themes which they accompanied seems in some cases to have been a secondary consideration.

In the particular case of the Lythrankomi mosaic, the association of the apostle medallions with a main image of the Incarnation may not be accidental. For those niche frescoes at Bawit in which, below Christ in Glory, Mary is figured among the apostles presuppose major apsidal models following the Constantinopolitan Ascension—Second Coming formula. From these the program in the Panagia Kanakaria would have logically evolved: by removing Christ in glory to a superior position, by enlarging and transforming the orant Mary into a visionary Mother of God, and by accommodating the attendant apostles in the medallion border. It is true that no Early Byzantine

---

[282] Ihm, *Programme*, 5 ff.

[283] *Ibid.*, pl. I, 1, with bibliography on p. 158. While opinions differ on the date of the church, a fifth-century date for the mosaic is generally accepted.

[284] Ihm, *Programme*, 153 f. and pl. IV, 1.

[285] See *supra*, note 276.

[286] Discussed by E. Kitzinger, with references, in *DOP*, 8 (1954), 97. When Arculf saw it about the year 670 it was already old enough to be represented as the handiwork of the Virgin.

[287] Ihm, *Programme*, 38, fig. 7, and p. 191 f.

[288] A connection between apostle borders of the Lythrankomi type and Ascension iconography is well demonstrated by the pair of gold phylactery medallions from Adana in Istanbul (Grabar, *Iconography*, fig. 248). In the border are busts of the Twelve, six on either side of the central vertical axis, divided at the top by a bust of Christ and at the bottom by a bust of the Virgin.

[289] The distinction between the disciples and the apostles was not always clearly drawn. Before the λάβετε, φάγετε in the Liturgy, the priest's preceding words are ἔδωκε τοῖς ἁγίοις μαθηταῖς καὶ ἀποστόλοις εἰπών. By the sixth century the theme of the Communion of the Apostles was well developed, to judge by its representation in the Rossano codex and on the Stuma and Riha patens.

apse decoration has survived which follows the Ascension—Second Coming formula preserved on the ampullae;[290] nor can the ampullae any longer be considered satisfactory evidence of a prototype in the apse of the basilica of the Ascension at Jerusalem;[291] and against the existence of such early prototypes it could be argued that the earliest visible evidence of a mural mosaic evoking the Ascension is not in an apse but in a dome, that of the Second Coming in the Salonica Rotunda. Yet, in the same monument the immediately post-iconoclastic fresco of the Ascension, in the conch of the apse,[292] must surely reflect some early apsidal model; for it is quite out of step with the preference for the Theotokos theme in apses at the time when it was painted.[293] Likewise, when the Ascension appears in the apses of later provincial churches in Cappadocia and Trebizond this may well reflect a pre-iconoclastic rather than a contemporary metropolitan practice.[294]

Supporting evidence from a mid-sixth-century representation is provided by the Cleveland tapestry icon, which Dorothy Shepherd reasonably regards as ultimately derived from just such apse decorations.[295] Here the upper zone, containing only the mandorla of the enthroned Christ supported by two flying angels, is even closer to the Byzantine versions than is the apocalyptic *Maiestas* of the Egyptian frescoes; and the lower zone, while portraying the Theotokos enthroned with the Child as in the more Coptic of the Bawit frescoes, provides a remarkable link with the Lythrankomi mosaic by translating the accompanying apostles to a series of busts in border medallions. While the ultimate dependence of the tapestry on some major apse mosaic of the Ascension—Second Coming theme is probable, the narrow format of the Theotokos group suggests that, as in the case of the aisle panel in St. Demetrius, Salonica, the relationship may have been at two removes, with a panel painting as the intermediate model. Nevertheless, it is unlikely that either a panel painter or a weaver working "not long after the middle of the sixth century" would have adopted this abridged representation of the apostles on his own initiative.[296] Rather does the tapestry imply the existence of earlier apsidal prototypes in Egypt, in which the Theotokos-Incarnation program

[290] On the reverses of Monza 1, 10, 11, 14, and 16 (Grabar, *Ampoules*, pl. IIIff.).

[291] On this hypothesis, see Ihm, *Programme*, 95 ff.; on the metropolitan rather than local inspiration of ampulla iconography, see Grabar, *Ampoules*, 47 ff.

[292] A. Xyngopoulos, Ἡ τοιχογραφία τῆς Ἀναλήψεως ἐν τῇ ἀψίδι τοῦ ἁγ. Γεωργίου Θεσσαλονίκης, in Ἀρχ.Ἐφ. (1938), 32–53.

[293] E.g., that in St. Sophia in Istanbul, that formerly in the church of the Dormition at Isnik (Nicaea), and that in St. Sophia in Salonica itself.

[294] Xyngopoulos, *op. cit.*, 48, with references in notes 2 and 3. Add now the Ascension decorating the apse of the Mescidi Kilise at Amastris, the construction of which is assigned to the second half of the ninth century (S. Eyice, in *CahArch*, 7 [1954], 103 and 105).

Part of what is evidently a pre-iconoclastic example has been exposed in the main apse of the Panagia Drosianē in Naxos. In the lower register there are traces of standing apostles with trees between them and, above the throne built in the center of the apse, the nimbed head of the Virgin between small full-length angels, who turn toward the apostles (M. Chatzidakis, in Ἀρχ.Δελτ., 22 [1967], Χρονικά, 29; N. Drandakis, in *Athens Annals of Archaeology*, 3 [1970], 416 f.).

[295] Shepherd, "Tapestry Panel," 104 ff.

[296] The awkwardly placed and blundered names of the apostles on the tapestry attest the hands of copyists, not initiators.

was combined with an apostle border akin to those of the Lythrankomi and Sinai mosaics; also that such prototypes represented an evolution—a Byzantine rather than a local evolution—from earlier apse programs following the ampullae formula, which the Bawit niche frescoes reflect and the Salonica Rotunda apse fresco revived. In the apsidal composition from which the tapestry derives, the upper zone portrayal of Christ in glory borne by the flying angels might well have been placed on the east wall above the apse, the optimum position in a basilica (corresponding to the cupola of a domed church), where Christ is represented in several Western examples.[297] This would explain why the apostle medallions do not extend to that part of the tapestry frame which borders the upper panel, but encircle the Theotokos alone, as they would have done on the apse arch of the hypothetical prototype and as they do in the Lythrankomi mosaic. Now we know that our mosaic extended onto the wall above the apse,[298] and in this position no subject is more probable than the same group which on the tapestry is isolated in the upper panel—the crowning group of the Eastern Ascension—Second Coming conflation, a precursor of the Pantocrator of later Byzantine programs.[299] However that may be, the busts in the border of the Cleveland tapestry icon do suggest that their relationship to the Theotokos is meaningful at Lythrankomi also, the purpose being to evoke the assembly of witnesses in the Byzantine Ascension formula and thereby surround the visionary image of the Incarnation with overtones of the Second Coming.

Two of the three missing medallions of the apostle border were undoubtedly occupied by Peter and John. The third, at the apex of the arch, probably contained a cross. In fifth-century Salonica we find the cross used as a central motif for an arch soffit,[300] and also at the center of the mosaic border on the front edge of the apse arch in Hosios David.[301] It is a cross that fills the corresponding medallion of the apostle border of the Sinai mosaic,[302] and in Cyprus it appears in the same position in the border of the apse mosaic in the Kiti church.[303] In these last cases, it has more than one function, which would apply equally in our mosaic: viewed in relation to the main composition proclaiming Christ's humanity, the cross as the instrument of redemption affirms his other, divine nature; secondly, suspended above the altar-table, the cross specifically evokes the sacrifice on Calvary.

[297] In the Poreč (Parenzo) basilica and S. Michele in Affricisco (see *supra*, notes 187, 189).

[298] See *supra*, p. 38.

[299] The flying angels in the same position in the Sinai basilica must derive from some such prototype, though here, since the mandorla of the transfigured Christ occupies the conch, their function is different (Forsyth-Weitzmann, *St. Catherine*, pls. cxii, B, cxxiii, B). They each offer orb and scepter to the Lamb of God in a small central medallion, on the significance of which see Weitzmann, "The Mosaic in St. Catherine's Monastery on Mt. Sinai" (*supra*, note 200), 401.

[300] E.g., in soffits of the Acheiropoietos basilica (Diehl, Le Tourneau, and Saladin, *Monuments chrétiens* [note 197 *supra*], 56, fig. 26 and pl. ix, 2); also in one recorded by W. George at St. Demetrius (Cormack, "S. Demetrios," pls. 4 and 8).

[301] A. Xyngopoulos, Καθολικὸν, 160, fig. 20.

[302] Forsyth-Weitzmann, *St. Catherine*, pl. clii.

[303] Papageorghiou, *Masterpieces*, pl. i.

The only alternative to a cross in the missing central medallion of the Lythrankomi border is suggested by the two apostle borders in Ravenna, where a bust of Christ occupies the central position: on the arch at the entrance to the bema in S. Vitale[304] and on the sanctuary arch of the Archiepiscopal Chapel.[305] In this position a bust of Christ is less satisfactory visually than a cross. The bust is seen erect only when viewed from the west; a cross with equal arms is seen correctly both thus and also when viewed with the apostles below it from either north or south. Finally, if we are correct in postulating a Christ in Glory for the wall above the apse of the Panagia Kanakaria, a bust of Christ in the apostle border would constitute an improbable tautology.

Without certainty on these points and with the lower part of the main composition entirely destroyed, we cannot grasp all the subtleties of meaning implicit in the Lythrankomi program. By contrast, the many overtones in the almost perfectly preserved mosaic in the Sinai monastery have led Weitzmann to picture the cleric commissioning a Byzantine apse mosaic at pains to make it "as meaningful as possible by going beyond the literary and narrative depiction of a Christological event, and superimposing various additional layers of meaning which would reinforce the faith of the devout, as well as appeal to the learned."[306] It is clear that the program chosen for our mosaic likewise went beyond the simple affirmation of the basic theme, the dogma of the Incarnation. It provides various echoes of the liturgy, for which it was the setting. It glorifies the Mother of God in visual terms cognate with the wording of the Commemoration and the Prayer of Intercession, and it gives prominence to the "holy, glorious, and most honorable apostles," so qualified in the same prayer. We have also observed that it provides probably intentional overtones of the Second Coming. If it falls short of the Sinai mosaic in such subtleties, this is only to be expected of one set substantially earlier, even taking the earliest possible date for the Sinai apse (565).[307] Indeed, the comparative simplicity of the Lythrankomi mosaic is in line with the indications of a pre-Justinianic *floruit* for the program adopted.

ICONOGRAPHY

The Main Composition

While the theme adopted for the main composition in the Lythrankomi apse was probably normal in the East before the time of Justinian, the fact that no earlier apse decoration of this type has survived gives special interest to the iconographic formulae in which it was rendered. The symmetry of the whole composition and the frontality of the central group conform with and doubtless stem from the traditions of secular art in the service of the imperial court. The attendant archangels match the flanking figures which

[304] Deichmann, *Bauten und Mosaiken*, pl. 311 (much restored).
[305] *Ibid.*, pl. 220. The Christ at the summit of the west arch is modern.
[306] Weitzmann, "The Mosaic," 400f. See *supra*, note 200.
[307] See *supra*, note 200.

are almost as constant in Byzantine official portraiture as were supporters in the heraldry of a later age. Such are the figures of his two Caesars on the *multipla* of Constantine.[308] Such, in the sixth century, are the personifications of Constantinople and Rome on the ivory diptych of Magnus,[309] and of Megalopsychia and Phronesis in attendance on Anicia Juliana on the dedication page of the Vienna Dioscorides.[310]

The central figure of the Virgin enthroned with the frontal Child on her lap conforms with what was probably the first formula officially adopted when "autonomous" images of the Theotokos became permissible after the Council of 431 at Ephesus.[311] It is arguable that this formula derived from earlier representations of Mary in New Testament scenes, in some of which she holds Christ straight before her.[312] But comparable mother and child formulae belong also to the tradition of official secular portraiture,[313] from which the Early Christian iconographers inevitably borrowed. Whatever its immediate antecedents, it seems probable that the type represented in the Panagia Kanakaria was officially adopted for the autonomous image in the mid-fifth century. That would explain the persistence of this archetypal formula in the age of Justinian and later, both in isolation as a symbol of the Incarnation[314] and, when appropriate, as the centerpiece of a narrative scene. For the profile formula for the Adoration in which Mary holds the Child in her outstretched arms toward the approaching Magi[315] is often abandoned on the

---

[308] Cf. Maria R. Alföldi, *Die Constantinische Goldprägung* (Mainz, 1963), nos. 111–13, 438–40 and pls. 16–18. As a prototype for the enthroned Theotokos between angels on the Dumbarton Oaks medallion, which, but for the mandorla, follows the Lythrankomi formula, Grierson cites (*DOP*, 15, p. 223f.) the nimbate Empress Fausta, with an infant on her lap, enthroned between personifications on the medallion probably struck in 312 to celebrate the birth of her eldest son [reproduced in Sacopoulo, *La Théotokos à la mandorle*, fig. 59].

[309] Dated 518: Paris, Cabinet des Médailles (Grabar, *Byzantium*, fig. 326).

[310] *Ca.* 512: Vienna, National Library, Med. gr. 1 (*ibid.*, fig. 214).

[311] Wellen, *Theotokos*, 147ff. The possibility that autonomous images existed even earlier is posed by the battered fragment in the Istanbul Archaeological Museum (inv. 5639), evidently representing the Theotokos with the Child on her left arm and datable to the time of Thesodosius I (H.-G. Severin, "Oströmische Plastik unter Valens und Theodosius I.," *JbBerlMus*, 12 [1970], 240 and fig. 18). However, this fragment comes from a series of conch-headed niches separated by twisted columns and could well belong to a representation of the Adoration (possibly on a sarcophagus) akin to that on the ambon from Salonica discussed below. [For a study of the pre-iconoclastic iconography of the Virgin Enthroned, see A. Cutler, *Transfigurations: Studies in the Dynamics of Byzantine Iconography* (University Park, Pa., 1975), 10ff.]

[312] Some examples of Adorations (not all of them earlier than 431) which conform in this respect are cited by V. Lazareff, "Studies in the Iconography of the Virgin," *ArtB*, 20 (1938), 49. But two fourth-century representations of this scene are far removed from the hieratic treatment at Lythrankomi and portray the Child as a naked infant. One is on the late-fourth-century silver reliquary from S. Nazaro Maggiore in Milan (Volbach-Hirmer, *E. C. Art*, pl. 112). The other is on the marble crater in the Museo Nazionale, Rome, where the Theotokos *lactans* is flanked by three Magi on either side: a vessel which Severin (*op. cit.*, 211f.) has lately demonstrated to be a Constantinopolitan work of the time of Valens.

[313] E.g., the relief on a funerary stele in Aquileia (Grabar, *Iconography*, fig. 92).

[314] The influence of the enthroned type, which was frequently revived after the iconoclast period, is seen also in the iconography of the standing Theotokos with the Child held before her, but awkwardly as if still seated on her lap, notably in the icon (supposedly the Nikopea) preserved in St. Mark's in Venice. [A preferable identification of this icon with the Kyriotissa has recently been proposed: M. Tatić-Djurić, "L'icone de Kyriotissa," communication to the XVe Congrès International d'Etudes Byzantines (publication forthcoming).]

[315] As on the early fifth-century sarcophagus in S. Vitale, Ravenna (Volbach-Hirmer, *E. C. Art*, pl. 179), and the silver pyxis in the Louvre (*ibid.*, pl. 120).

ivories and ampullae of sixth-century date in favor of a symmetrical iconography centered on a frontal Theotokos.[316] Already in the fifth century, probably in the third quarter, the complex Adoration relief on the great semicircular ambon from the Salonica Rotunda suggests that the later symmetrical treatments evolved by interpolation of the frontal formula commonly adopted for the autonomous image; for the niche containing the Theotokos is isolated from those in which the Magi approach, and in such a way as to suggest that they do so from both sides.[317]

In any event, the battered relief of the Theotokos on the ambon is the earliest surviving monumental example of the type represented in the Lythrankomi mosaic. When comparing the two versions, it should be remembered that there can be no direct iconographic connection between our mosaic and representations of the Adoration. The suggestion that the Magi could have been figured in the now destroyed lower part of the Lythrankomi composition has already been rejected (*supra*, note 205). Nor is there any conclusive evidence that the Adoration was ever portrayed in an apse decoration.[318] That the Lythrankomi Theotokos and the ambon relief have a common ancestry in a frontal formula adopted after the Council of 431 is suggested by what we know of a third monument, somewhat later than the ambon: the Theotokos panel of the lost aisle mosaics of St. Demetrius in Salonica.[319]

In the ambon relief, unlike the two mosaics, the Virgin has no nimbus: though, as we have noted, by placing the head at the center of the conch (those of the Magi are lower) its flutes and scallops serve as a form of aureole. The representation of the Virgin without a nimbus in conjunction with a nimbed Christ links the relief with the early miniature of Mary acclaiming the Child on her arm on a fragment of the Alexandrian Chronicle in Moscow.[320] Christian iconography only gradually adopted the nimbus, which had long been a symbol of majesty for the emperor, and initially for Christ alone. Even in the sixth-

---

[316] Cf. Wellen, *Theotokos*, 148. There are two types: three Magi balanced by three shepherds (e.g., on the ampulla Monza 3: Grabar, *Ampoules*, pl. 8), or two Magi balanced by the third and one angel (e.g., the British Museum ivory panel: Volbach-Hirmer, *op. cit.*, pl. 222).

[317] *Ibid.*, pl. 78; well described in G. Mendel, *Musées Impériaux Ottomans. Catalogue des sculptures grecques, romaines et byzantines*, II (Constantinople, 1914), 399 f.; most recently in Grabar, *Sculptures*, 80–84. The character of the acanthus on the pilaster capitals and cornice are some indication of its date. Around 500 (*ibid.*, 83) may be too late if, as seems likely, it was carved as part of the original furniture of the Rotunda upon its conversion into a church. For this a dating in the third quarter of the fifth century is now preferred (see *supra*, note 197).
The Magi appear twice in separate processions. The first is below the left staircase (with one of the shepherds) in a wooded landscape, ending with the leader in the left panel of the façade. He was separated from the Theotokos in the right panel by the open bay below the central platform, which has not survived. The second procession, below the right staircase, figures the three in a curtained interior and is completed on the curving side of the ambon where, in a niche forming a sharp angle with that containing the Theotokos, are the leader and an accompanying angel. For a reconstruction of the entire ambon, see Orlandos, Βασιλική, figs. 518–19.

[318] On some hypothetical examples, see Ihm, *Programme*, 52 ff.

[319] See *supra*, note 179.

[320] Grabar, *Iconography*, fig. 64. Likewise on a Coptic limestone relief, where the iconography of the ambon is closely followed, the Child has a cross nimbus and the head of the Virgin is set in a conch (Beckwith, *Coptic Sculpture* [see *supra*, note 229], pl. 113).
On the triumphal arch mosaics in S. Maria Maggiore in Rome, while celestial personages are nimbed, the Virgin of the Annunciation, though arrayed as an empress, is not (Grabar, *Byzantium*, fig. 161).

century Theotokos groups it is not uncommon for neither Mother nor Child to be nimbed, notably in the group of ivory carvings of the Adoration often attributed to Syria.[321] In the Lythrankomi mosaic, in common with all sixth-century monumental examples, both figures are nimbed,[322] as they were already in the St. Demetrius aisle mosaic. In this, as in other respects, our mosaic is at home among the monuments of the early sixth century rather than their predecessors.

In some details of the Virgin's pose our mosaic does not conform with the two earlier examples. Although her right forearm and hand are not preserved, they could hardly have been placed otherwise than as indicated by the broken line in figure M. In any case the hand could not have been placed on the Child's right shoulder, the normal place for it in the sixth century,[323] and earlier if we may judge by the ambon; for in our mosaic Christ's right shoulder is fully preserved and there is no trace of any hand upon it (fig. 88). Curiously, in the St. Demetrius aisle mosaic the normal position was reversed to show the Virgin's left hand on Christ's left shoulder, a variant perhaps to be explained by the local character of these panels and by their relatively early date.[324] But the different treatment at Lythrankomi is no vagary of the mosaicist; for, by placing the Virgin's arms symmetrically with the hands extended downward, he conformed with several representations of the Theotokos in sixth-century Adorations. These are found both on the Monza ampullae[325] and on two ivory panels of the sixth-century group commonly attributed to Syria: one in the John Rylands Library at Manchester,[326] part of the diptych of which the complete leaf from Murano is the primary example of the group,[327] and the other in the British Museum.[328] Two features of the Virgin's costume found in some other Theotokos groups are lacking in the Lythrankomi mosaic. The first, the kerchief held in the left hand in the *Maria Regina* and Turtura frescoes in Rome,[329] is absent in all early Eastern

---

[321] E.g., the Adoration panels in the British Museum (see *infra*, note 328) and Manchester (see *infra*, note 326), the Berlin diptych leaf (Volbach-Hirmer, *E. C. Art*, pl. 225), and the Vienna pyxis, which combines Nativity, Adoration, and Flight into Egypt (O. Wulff, *Altchristliche und byzantinische Kunst*, I [Berlin-Neubabelsberg, 1913], fig. 188; Volbach, *Elfenbeinarbeiten*, no. 199, pl. 58).

[322] Likewise on the ampullae and the Dumbarton Oaks medallion.

[323] E.g., in the Poreč apse (details in Peirce–Tyler, *L'art byzantin*, II, pl. 60, b; Prelog, *Mosaïques de Poreč*, color illus. on p. 3), and on the Berlin ivory panel (Volbach-Hirmer, *Early Christian Art*, pl. 225).

[324] The figure in the S. Apollinare Nuovo nave mosaic is even more exotic: the Virgin raises her right hand as an orant and with her left clasps Christ's left forearm.

[325] Monza 2 (Grabar, *Ampoules*, pl. 4) and Monza 3 (*ibid.*, pl. 8).

[326] Dalton, *Byz. Art and Archaeology* (*supra*, note 4), fig. 114; Volbach, *Elfenbeinarbeiten*, pl. 39 no. 2.

[327] Volbach-Hirmer, *Early Christian Art*, pl. 223.

[328] *Ibid.*, pl. 222. The same position of the Virgin's arms recurs on the Vienna pyxis (see *supra*, note 321).

[329] For the Turtura panel in the catacomb of Commodilla: Grabar, *Byzantium*, fig. 176. The date 528 (*ibid.*, 167) does not relate to this fresco which, as Kitzinger suggested, is rather to be placed in the seventh century (Kitzinger, *Römische Malerei*, 22 f.; cf. E. Weigand, in *BZ*, 37 [1937], 467 note 8) and possibly is contemporary with the figure of Luke close by, of *ca.* 684 (G. Matthiae, *Pittura romana del medioevo*, I [Rome, 1965], 149 f.). At that time when a "Justinianic revival" has been postulated both in Byzantium and Rome (see *infra*, note 514a), the kerchief and other features of this Turtura fresco may reflect sixth-century practice. For *Maria Regina*, see *supra*, note 191.

representations. The second is the girdle, the end of which appears hanging down in front, below the maphorion, in the St. Demetrius aisle mosaic and in the Poreč apse. The girdle is to be expected in the iconography of Constantinople, for it was a treasured possession of the Chalcoprateia church and tradition claimed it had been in the city since the time of Arcadius. It is significant that elsewhere it figures in few of the earlier monuments. As at Lythrankomi, the girdle is lacking in the S. Apollinare Nuovo mosaic, in the Turtura fresco, in all three of the ivory panels in Berlin, London, and Manchester; even on the Salonica ambon and the encaustic Sinai icon, both of which are considered to be Constantinopolitan. The appearance of the girdle in the Poreč apse, the Rabbula Gospels,[330] and Bawit chapel 17 suggests that its representation was unusual in the provinces before the middle of the sixth century. If so, this would weigh in favor of an earlier date for our mosaic.

As a result of the loss of the Virgin's right forearm and the area below, it is not certain (though it is probable) that the robes on this side followed a simple outline similar to that preserved on the other. In the reconstruction in figure M, it has been assumed that they did. If this is correct, a feature of some seated Theotokos figures of early date was lacking: one end of the maphorion falls so that the hem, which is sometimes fringed, forms a series of diminishing zigzag folds. This treatment was usual in the case of the standing Virgin, and is a feature of the orant figure on the ampullae, in Bawit chapel 17, and in the Ascension and Pentecost miniatures of the Rabbula Gospels. In the "Hodegetria" miniature of this MS the zigzag folds hang over the arm carrying the Christ Child (and they are retained in the seated version of this early Hodegetria in Bawit chapel 6). In some representations of the enthroned Theotokos of the frontal type these folds reappear, notably in the St. Demetrius aisle mosaic and in the nave mosaic of S. Apollinare Nuovo, as well as in later examples including the Turtura fresco, the Berlin ivory, and the Poreč mosaic. With the exception of the Ravenna mosaic, which is exotic in many respects, all of these monuments display a standard contrapposto: the zigzag folds fall on the opposite side to the hand which holds Christ's shoulder. Since neither hand of the Lythrankomi Virgin supports the Child in this way, it is most probable that in the area now lost below her left elbow the profile matched that preserved on the other side. This simpler formula, in which both hands were extended downward and there were no zigzag folds, is found in the Adorations on the ivory panels in London and Manchester and in those on the ampullae Monza 2 and Monza 3; and since the relief on the ambon from Salonica conforms as regards the absence of the zigzag folds, it is likely to represent the earlier iconography. Consequently a date early in the sixth century is again indicated for the Lythrankomi Theotokos.

---

[330] The "Hodegetria" miniature on fol. 1ᵛ, facsimile in *Rabbula Gospels*; the girdle is also worn by the orant Virgin in the Ascension miniature of the same MS (Grabar, *Iconography*, pl. 1).

The cross-nimbus of Christ (fig. 89) is found in the earliest examples of the Theotokos group, the ambon from Salonica[331] and the St. Demetrius aisle mosaic, and recurs in most of those of the sixth century.[332] The coloring in the Lythrankomi mosaic, silver cross arms on a gold nimbus, corresponds with that in the Theotokos mosaic in S. Apollinare Nuovo, whereas in the aisle mosaic of St. Demetrius the cross arms were gold on a gold ground,[333] as they are in the nimbus of Christ, set probably somewhat earlier, in Hosios David.

The pose of Christ with the right knee raised and the left foot turned out[334] marks an advance on the rather artless treatment in the ambon relief, where the knees are level. In this respect our mosaic conforms with the less rigid poses in sixth-century monuments, where, however, a reverse position is more usual, with the left knee raised and the right foot turned out.[335]

More crucial is the position of the hands, holding the roll in the manner characteristic of antique philosopher figures (figs. 86, 88). This was frequently copied in Early Christian iconography, as well as in contemporary secular portraiture,[336] but it was seldom retained in sixth-century figures of the Christ Child.[337] Our mosaic is not remarkable so much for the retention of the roll, which though relatively archaic[338] remained a fairly constant feature in comparable Theotokos groups, but rather for the position of the right hand clasping the upper end of the roll. For already in the St. Demetrius aisle mosaic the right hand was raised in front in the stereotyped orator's gesture

---

[331] The arms of the cross are not visible on published photographs, but are shown on Garruci's drawing (Garrucci, *Storia*, VI, pl. 426, 1, whence Morey, *Early Christian Art*, fig. 111). In mosaic, the first recorded appearance of the cross nimbus was in the central medallion on the face of the apse arch of S. Sabina, *ca.* 430 (Ciampini, *Vetera Monumenta*, I, pl. 47).

[332] The cross had been used in Constantinople in representations of Christ alone from the early fifth century, to judge by the Psamathia relief in Berlin (Volbach-Hirmer, *E. C. Art*, pl. 73), but not invariably; the nimbi of the figures in the Rotunda dome in Salonica (Torp, *Mosaikkene*, fig. on p. 37) and the Sinai Transfiguration are plain. The cross is also lacking in the nimbus of the Child in the *Maria Regina* fresco in S. Maria Antiqua and in that of the later Turtura panel in the catacomb of Commodilla.

[333] Clearly indicated in N. K. Kluge's drawing, in *IRAIK*, 14 (1909), pl. 3.

[334] On the significance of the differentiation of the feet as a hallmark of familiarity with the classical tradition, see A. Cutler, "The Lord's Out-Turned Foot and the Problem of Classical Influence in Medieval Art," *L'arte* (1968), 83–95.

[335] E.g., the Poreč mosaic, the *Maria Regina* fresco, and the Berlin ivory diptych leaf. As might be expected in an earlier example, the St. Demetrius mosaic did not conform, for though it was the left foot of the Child that was seen from the side, as at Lythrankomi, it was not the right knee but the left that was raised. Exceptionally, the British Museum Adoration ivory retains a rigidly symmetrical pose. [The sandals are of the type normal in sixth-century representations, as M. Sacopoulo observes (*La Théotokos à la mandorle*, 20 ff. and fig. 28), following W. de Grüneisen (*Sainte Marie Antique* [*supra*, note 191], 201 note 6). In this type the front of the sole is attached by a strap passing between the toes, which forms a T-junction with the horizontal ankle strap. In earlier representations a strap across the toes is fixed to the sole on either side.]

[336] See Grabar, *Iconography*, 33, and compare the author portrait in the *Virgilius Romanus* (Vat. Lat. 3867, fol. 14ʳ) dated by Weitzmann to the first half of the fifth century: *Akten des VII. intern. Kongr. für Chr. Arch.*, Trier, 1965 (Vatican City, 1969), 272 with note 60, pl. 146, fig. 23.

[337] One occurrence is in the *Maria Regina* fresco (see *supra*, note 191), though here the roll is replaced by a codex, while in this detail the seventh-century Turtura panel (see *supra*, note 329), like the Lythrankomi mosaic, follows the earlier iconography.

[338] Cf. Grabar, *Sculptures*, 10. On the roll, see also T. Michels, "Christus mit der Buchrolle," *OrChr*, 29 (1932), 138 ff.

of allocution (not as yet conceived as blessing),[339] and this was the normal position in the sixth century, with the roll held vertically between the lowered left hand and the knee.[340] The retention of the classical position of the hands in the Lythrankomi mosaic is another feature at variance with what may be regarded as the normal metropolitan iconography of the sixth century. It also weighs against assigning our mosaic to a date far advanced in that century; for it certainly represents the initial Byzantine iconography to judge by its appearance in the earliest monumental example, the ambon from Salonica, if Garrucci's drawing is reliable.[341] A late example of the scroll held obliquely between the two hands of the Child is the Cleveland tapestry icon. But even this was probably woven not long after the middle of the sixth century,[342] and the apse mosaics from which Miss Shepherd reasonably derives it[343] would have been set somewhat before.

Notable also are the differences in the form and coloring of the Christ Child's garments. At Lythrankomi, an ample himation of "natural" color highlighted with white reveals the pale blue chiton only on the right arm and below the neck (color fig. 135). In the St. Demetrius aisle mosaic gold tesserae were used for the outer garment, also in the Poreč apse, and the same gold is represented by yellow paint in the *Maria Regina* and Turtura frescoes. Secondly, only in the lost Salonica panel did the hem reach to the feet, as it does in our mosaic. In the other cases, which are the latest in date, the lower part of the undergarment is seen. Such also is the treatment in the S. Apollinare Nuovo mosaic (though here both garments are white); likewise in the ambon relief and the three ivory panels[344] the hem of the himation passes obliquely above that of the chiton. The more voluminous outer garment in our mosaic and its cream color, like the manner in which the roll is held, attach it to an earlier tradition. On the other hand, the retention of white robes for Christ after gold had become general is attested by the Sinai mosaic, where, however, a deep gold hem is introduced.

The wide-sleeved chiton revealing a bare forearm is another distinctive detail attaching our figure to the early type of Christ-Philosopher. For in most groups of the Virgin and Child either the chiton has long sleeves tight at the wrist, as in the St. Demetrius aisle mosaic and the London and Berlin ivory panels, or, as in Western examples such as the Poreč mosaic and the *Maria*

[339] The figure was damaged, but Cormack, using all surviving records, was satisfied about this detail (Cormack, "S. Demetrios," 25). On the gesture, see T. Michels, "Segensgestus oder Hoheitsgestus?", *Festschrift für Alois Thomas* (Trier, 1967), 277–83.

[340] In the Poreč mosaic (Prelog, *Mosaïques de Poreč*, color illus. on p. 3), the Bawit frescoes (chapel 28), on the three ivory panels and the Vienna pyxis as well as on the ampullae. Exceptionally, the roll is lacking and the right hand is extended sideways in both the S. Apollinare Nuovo Theotokos mosaic and the Adoration miniature of the Etchmiadzin Gospels.

[341] Some recent photographs suggest conformity with the position of the hands that prevailed in the sixth century. But the relief is now so weathered that more reliance should be placed on the earlier observations, including the drawing in Garrucci, *Storia*, VI, pl. 426, 1 (whence Morey, *Early Christian Art*, fig. 111). In Mendel's careful but later description (*Catalogue des sculptures* [*supra*, note 317], II, 399), the gesture of the right hand is considered indistinguishable.

[342] Shepherd, "Tapestry Panel," 115.

[343] *Ibid.*, 105.

[344] See *supra*, notes 326–28.

Regina fresco, if the chiton has the wide three-quarter sleeve it exposes the long tight sleeve of an under tunic. In the seventh century the Turtura fresco provides a close Western parallel for the bare wrist of Christ in our mosaic, and this fresco could well have been modeled on an imported Eastern panel painting. Certainly, in figures of the mature Christ the bare forearm is occasionally seen in the sixth century in the East, notably on the Riha and Stuma patens. Erica Cruikshank Dodd has established that the Stuma paten, datable to 577 or 578, is the work of the Syrian silversmith Sergius who donated it, despite its imperial control stamps. However, we cannot cite the bare forearm of the Child among the deviations from Constantinopolitan iconography which reveal our mosaicist's attachment to the tradition of Antioch; for it is also established that Sergius' Communion scene, though executed on an imported blank, was modeled in many respects on the slightly earlier Riha paten, the unquestionable product of a Constantinopolitan workshop.[344a]

Iconographically, by far the most striking feature of this figure is that it represents not an infant but a grown child. In stature alone it is exceptional. We have noted that the Virgin is unusually elongated, yet the Child is proportionately even taller. His height is substantially more than half that of the Virgin, whereas it is less than half in all comparable sixth-century versions. Nor in any of these do we find the features so strongly delineated. The impression of maturity they give to the Lythrankomi figure is far removed from that conveyed by the infant heads of Christ on the Berlin ivory and the Sinai icon.[345] Closest in this respect to our mosaic is the Christ Child in the nave of S. Apollinare Nuovo.[346] Earlier monuments, such as the ambo relief and the St. Demetrius mosaic, are not well enough preserved or recorded to establish that this mature type was adopted in autonomous Theotokos images from the outset, though the formal nature of official portraiture on which the iconographers drew makes this most likely. The contradiction implicit in portraying a grown child rather than an infant in his mother's lap can hardly have been accidental. Rather, we are faced with another reminder of the concept of the Theanthropos, comparable with the device of transposing the essentially human scene of mother and child to a transcendental plane by enveloping it in a mandorla. By such devices the mosaicist sought to underline the basic message of his composition: the birth to Mary of the Son of God.[347]

In this context, to seat the Theotokos on the ivory lyre-back throne of the Almighty is not necessarily an oversight. It is true that in the S. Apollinare Nuovo mosaics the straight-back throne of the Theotokos is contrasted with the lyre-back throne of Christ; also that on the Grado reliquary lid where the Theotokos is seated on the latter type, this could be counted another

---

[344a] Dodd, *Silver Treasures*, 40 ff.

[345] The same type of infant head is clearly represented on some of the ampullae, e.g., Monza 3 (Grabar, *Ampoules*, pl. 8).

[346] Deichmann, *Bauten und Mosaiken*, pl. 115. If the infant figure was characteristic of the later sixth and the seventh centuries, the reappearance of the mature Child in the S. Maria in Trastevere icon indicates its dependence on an earlier Byzantine iconography (see *supra*, note 210).

[347] Cf. Wellen, *Theotokos*, 154.

iconographic blunder by a North Italian silversmith, like the long-shafted cross in her right hand and her christogram nimbus.[348] But the same lyre type was featured in the St. Demetrius aisle mosaic and reappears on the Dumbarton Oaks medallion, a product of the imperial mint, as well as in the Adoration miniature of the Etchmiadzin Gospels and the *Maria Regina* fresco. It may then have been part of the official Theotokos formula, introduced as one more evocation of the Incarnation.

This is to some extent confirmed by the lack of consistency in the type of throne represented where the lyre-back form is not adopted. In the ambon relief it is evidently the basketwork chair of which side views appear in the Adoration and Annunciation on the Etchmiadzin diptych.[349] The ampullae favor a high-back throne with a drooping toprail; in the Sinai icon and the Turtura fresco the back has a reverse, upward curvature; while in the Poreč mosaic the throne has no back at all. Only in some of the Bawit niche frescoes does the throne of the Theotokos approximate that of the S. Apollinare Nuovo mosaic. Certainly, in the late fifth and early sixth century it was more usual to represent the Virgin and Child seated on the lyre-back throne than on any other single type.

As to the cushion, we have seen that in the Lythrankomi mosaic the color of its central section was originally red. In this it matched the red cushions on which the Virgin sits in the St. Demetrius and S. Apollinare Nuovo mosaics and in the Turtura fresco. But the rich embroidery of the preserved end section is found in none of these nor in any other comparable Theotokos representation, though horizontal seams are occasionally shown.[350] The source of the encircling bands and terminal medallions (fig. 81) is undoubtedly official portraiture, for they appear on the consular diptych of Anastasius and can perhaps be traced back to the fourth century through a Carolingian miniature representing Constantine the Great.[351]

The triangular area by the Virgin's left knee, extending from the cushion to the footstool (fig. 79), which was originally red in color, represents a drape hanging down vertically from the seat of the throne, a feature which appears in several representations of the empty Throne of God.[352] In comparable

[348] Grabar, *Byzantium*, fig. 358. For a recent discussion see Wellen, *op. cit.*, 155f. [The derivation of the lyre-back throne from the imperial iconography of Constantinople, first suggested by C.-O. Nordström (*Ravennastudien* [*supra*, note 204], 81), is supported by M. Sacopoulo (*op. cit.*, 17–20), who employs this feature primarily as a chronological criterion. Regarded as an attribute of dominion (it appears in imperial portraits on coinage from the fifth to the ninth century), in a figuration of the Incarnation it could well proclaim Christ's sovereignty, as the mandorla proclaims His divinity. See also Cutler, *Transfigurations* (*supra*, note 311), 10ff.]

[349] Grabar, *Iconography*, fig. 205. Also, in oblique view, in the Annunciation on the Berlin gold medallion (*ibid.*, fig. 247).

[350] E.g., Bawit chapel 6: blue seam on faded red (Grabar, *Byzantium*, fig. 186).

[351] The Pseudo-Apuleius in Kassel: Weitzmann, *Akten des VII. intern. Kongr. für Chr. Arch.* (*supra*, note 336), pl. 150, fig. 30A. The encircling bands reappear on what is probably a derivative of Byzantine sixth-century iconography: Pope John VII's icon in S. Maria in Trastevere (see *supra*, note 210).

[352] In the fifth century in S. Prisca at S. Maria Capua Vetere (Grabar, *Iconography*, fig. 278), at the beginning of the sixth in Ravenna in the dome of the Arian Baptistery (Volbach-Hirmer, *E. C. Art*, pl. 149). The drape also appears on the marble relief in Berlin representing the Throne of God: H. Brandenburg, in *RM*, 79 (1972), 123ff. and pls. 66–80.

Incarnation images the throne was draped in this way only in the St. Demetrius aisle mosaic. The drawings made before its destruction show a red fabric hanging behind the Virgin's right leg.[353]

In all the comparable examples the feet of the Virgin rest on a footstool placed before the throne. Enough is preserved to prove its presence in the Lythrankomi mosaic also (fig. 84). There is no warrant for the restoration in its stead of a Globe of the World on which the throne is set.[354] What is unusual is the setting of the footstool with an angle, and not a side, to the front; but this was entirely determined by the need to accommodate it within the lower point of the mandorla (fig. M). Comparable is the curious form of the throne on one of the smaller ampullae, where both sides are seen receding obliquely to conform with the curvature of the circular border.[355]

The most remarkable feature of the mandorla itself is its pointed almond shape. For seated figures the circular form has been regarded as normal;[356] this was used in the late fifth century in the apse of Hosios David in Salonica for the Redeemer seated on the Arc of Heaven, in the sixth century and later for the enthroned Christ in the Bawit chapels. The same circular form was retained in the ninth century for the mandorla of the enthroned Theotokos in St. Lawrence at the source of the Volturno.[357] But the Lythrankomi Theotokos is not unique among seated figures in its enclosure in a mandorla of an elongated form. For the mandorla of the enthroned Christ in the ampulla Ascensions is normally oval. Oval also is the clipeus-mandorla containing a seated Christ Child which the Virgin holds in the niche fresco of Bawit chapel 28. This oval form was naturally preferred for a standing figure. Such, but somewhat pear-shaped, is the mandorla of the Sinai Transfiguration; such also is that of the standing Christ of the Ascension miniature in the Rabbula Gospels. What is curious about the Lythrankomi mandorla is that it conforms with neither of the types favored in the sixth century, but instead matches the vesica form which was to prevail at a much later date. However, it is not unique in this respect, for the vesica is used in one of the eight versions of the Ascension on the ampullae;[358] and this version is one which, through the cross-scepter carried by Andrew, has specific iconographic connection with Constantinople.[359] A second example is provided by one of the early encaustic icons in the Sinai monastery, where it encloses an unusual "Emmanuel,"

---

[353] Kluge, in *IRAIK*, 14, pl. 3 (with white patterning); Cormack, "S. Demetrios," pl. 7.

[354] See *supra*, note 198.

[355] Monza 4: Grabar, *Ampoules*, pl. 10.

[356] Van der Meer, *Maiestas Domini* (*supra*, note 251), 264 ff.

[357] See *supra*, note 254.

[358] Represented by three examples from a single set of molds: Monza 14, 15, and 16 (Grabar, *Ampoules*, pls. 27, 29, 30). Comparable, but lacking the sharp points, is the clipeus-mandorla isolating the cross from the adoring angels on Bobbio 1 (*ibid.*, pl. 32).

[359] *Ibid.*, 30 and 59. See also note 457 *infra*.

[360] M. and G. Soteriou, Εἰκόνες τῆς Μονῆς Σινᾶ, II (Athens, 1958), 23–25 and figs. 8–9. Compare the vesica-mandorla of the Pantocrator on the ivory panel in the Walters Art Gallery, Baltimore, tentatively dated to the sixth century: Beckwith, *Coptic Sculpture* (*supra*, note 229), pl. 109. The vesica enclosing the cross painted in the apse of the rock-cut basilica at Midye is assigned by Nicole Thierry not to the initial sixth-century decoration but to the ninth century (*CahArch*, 20 [1970], 76).

represented as the Ancient of Days seated on the arc of a starry heaven.[360] Consequently, although the vesica form used in our mosaic is a *hapax* among surviving apse decorations of early date, it is not to be regarded as a local innovation.

In its color also, and in the presence of a well defined border, the mandorla in the Panagia Kanakaria is noteworthy. That in the Hosios David apse is rendered in white and pale green tesserae forming radial bands which leave no doubt that it was conceived as a source of light. In the Sinai apse the rays of light are even more in evidence, although at the center this mandorla approaches the dark blue-green tones used in our mosaic. In neither the Salonica nor the Sinai apse is the outer limit of the mandorla strongly defined. At Lythrankomi, the bold border and the suggestion of a reflecting surface within it, rather than a source of light, give this mandorla the character of what Van der Meer aptly called an ethereal clipeus. In this guise the choice of a rainbow pattern for the border is no accident, recalling as it does the Arc of Heaven on which Christ is seated in such representations as the Hosios David mosaic. As an ethereal clipeus our mandorla is close to that of the ascending Christ in the Rabbula Gospels: oval in form, dark blue-green in color, edged with a simplified border, and grasped by the flying angels. These ornamented rims give substance to the mandorla, as does the jeweled border encircling the star-filled firmament in which the great cross appears in the apse of S. Apollinare in Classe.[361]

As to the irisated character of the border, which it will be remembered recurs as a frame to the whole apse decoration (see *supra*, p. 39), rainbow effects had an early development in floor mosaics, notably in the fourth and fifth centuries at Antioch,[362] where comparable borders remained in favor around the year 500.[363] When such borders appear in the Vienna Dioscorides[364] and *ca.* 586 in the Rabbula Gospels,[365] the small square facets in which they are rendered leave no doubt that the illuminator was following the mosaicist. In mural mosaics, a border similar in all respects to that of the Lythrankomi mandorla appears, already in the fifth century, round the ornate clipeus of Christ in the dome of the Salonica Rotunda, grading from red (on the inside) to dark green with a line of gold tesserae between them.[366] In the sixth century, S. Vitale offers further examples: ringing the clipeus of Christ at the summit of the apostle arch and a cross-clipeus held by flying angels;[367] while on the arch bordering the apse composition there is a more elaborate version,

[361] Grabar, *Byzantium*, fig. 153. Solid also is the ethereal clipeus in the dome of the Salonica Rotunda, with three concentric borders around the rim: Torp, *Mosaikkene*, figs. on pp. 11 and 30.

[362] Levi, *Antioch Pavements*, I, 405 ff.

[363] E.g., in the House of the Ram's Heads (*ibid.*, II, pl. 133, c).

[364] E.g., the frame round the miniature of Dioscorides receiving the mandrake root (Grabar, *Byzantium*, fig. 215), discussed by C. R. Morey, *ArtB*, 11 (1929), 32, and Frantz, "Byz. Illum. Ornament," 46.

[365] Elaborated with a counterchange of triangles on the arches of the canon tables on fol. 3ᵛ: Grabar, *Byzantium*, fig. 234.

[366] Torp, *Mosaikkene*, figs. on pp. 11 and 30.

[367] Clipeus of Christ: Volbach-Hirmer, *E. C. Art*, pl. 161; cross-clipeus: Lazarev, *Storia*, fig. 57.

counterchanged with reverse coloring in oblique bands.[368] Another parallel is provided by the Casaranello church, where an irisated border edges the ethereal clipeus containing a cross in the domical vault.[369] Consequently in its form, in its character of a clipeus with an ornate rim, and in the rainbow decoration used on that rim, the Lythrankomi mandorla is paralleled in sixth-century monuments, but without these providing evidence for close dating.

The fragments of the two archangels suffice to leave no doubt of the iconographic type portrayed. Nimbed in silver, as in virtually all monumental examples of the sixth century (color fig. 134),[370] they wear the philosopher's robes, which gradually gave way to military dress.[371] The chiton, like that of Christ, had wide three-quarter sleeves which exposed the forearm (fig. 77). This type remained common in the East,[372] where the tight-sleeved tunic worn by the archangels in the St. Demetrius aisle mosaic and the Cleveland tapestry[373] was never adopted so exclusively as at Ravenna and elsewhere in the West.[374]

To denote their rank and their function as guards, the archangels carried in their left hands a ceremonial staff, such as those of the ἔκδικοι who policed Byzantine religious processions,[375] and with their free right hands acclaimed the vision of which they were witnesses. This, with the left hand covered by the himation and some variation in the position of the right hand, was the

---

[368] Volbach-Hirmer, *E. C. Art*, pl. 158.

[369] Bovini, "Mosaici di Casaranello" (*supra*, note 186), fig. 3.

[370] Silver also in the Sinai Theotokos icon; blue for silver in the Cleveland tapestry and in the niche frescoes of the Coptic monasteries, cell 1719 at Saqqara alone excepted if the published drawing can be relied on (*Saqqara*, IV, pl. 23, bottom).

[371] The earliest surviving representations of archangels in military dress are probably the worn reliefs of Michael and Gabriel on the jambs of the main entrance to the west church at Alahan. The chlamys, fastened by a fibula on the right shoulder, appears hanging down behind the ornamented tunics, a detail which is clearer in Gough's sketches, in *AnatSt*, 12 (1962), 181, fig. 6, than in published photographs, e.g., *CahArch*, 9 (1957), 95, fig. 6. Gough maintained that the monastery with the west church was a foundation of the time of Leo I (*AnatSt*, 22 [1972], 210). Similar tunics, without the chlamys, were represented in the sixth century in the niche fresco of Bawit chapel 28 (Clédat, *Baouît*, pls. 96, B and 98). More commonly, the front of the tunic is largely covered by the chlamys, as in the little figures at the extremities of the top panel of the Murano diptych leaf in Ravenna (Volbach-Hirmer, *E. C. Art*, pl. 223); also in the Berlin Theotokos ivory and Saqqara chapel A (*Saqqara*, II, pl. 42). For a recent discussion, see T. Klauser, *RAC*, V (1962), s.v. "Engel X (in der Kunst)," 258 ff. See also the two archangels in one of the votive mosaic panels in the amphitheater chapel at Durrës: N. Thierry, in *CahArch*, 18 (1968), 228, fig. 1; Anon., *Architectural Monuments in Albania* (Tirana, 1973), color pl. 42. These may well be dated as early as the sixth century, for in the adjoining panel the two archangels flanking the standing Virgin (largely destroyed) are clad in the earlier fashion, in philosopher's robes (unpublished, examined by Hawkins). Already before 538, Severus, the Monophysite patriarch of Antioch, inveighed against the portrayal of archangels "like princes or kings" (Severus, *Homily* 72, PO, 12, p. 365 f.).

Our view that the Lythrankomi figures represent archangels, despite their simple garments, was considered a possibility by Matthiae (*CorsiRav*, 19 [1972], 260).

[372] E.g., the Rabbula Ascension (Grabar, *Byzantium*, pl. 1), the Hermitage silver plate with the cross and guardian angels (Volbach-Hirmer, *E. C. Art*, pl. 245), and the mosaic at Kiti in Cyprus (Ihm, *Programme*, pl. 18, 2).

[373] Also by Michael on the British Museum diptych leaf (Grabar, *Byzantium*, fig. 321).

[374] Among the few exceptions there are the caryatids supporting the "ethereal clipeus" of the Lamb in the presbytery vault of S. Vitale.

[375] D. Th. Běljaev, *Byzantina*, II (St. Petersburg, 1893), 165 note 1, quoted in Grabar, *Martyrium*, II, 97.

original Byzantine iconography,[376] and it was used whether the archangels flanked an image of the Theotokos or one of Christ.[377] In two Theotokos groups of narrow format, where the presence of saints and votaries necessitated the posting of the archangels behind the throne, their free hands either clasp the knobs of the back of the throne, as in the St. Demetrius aisle mosaic, or do not appear at all, as in the Sinai icon. In both these cases the demands of a rigid symmetry place the staff in the right hand of one archangel and in the left hand of the other.

By the sixth century some archangels were portrayed carrying the globe, symbol of Christ's dominion on earth, as does Michael on the diptych leaf in the British Museum and in the mosaic panel between the apse windows of the Poreč basilica, which is in the nature of an "autonomous" image.[378] The globes gradually appeared in the hands of archangels included in Incarnation compositions, such as the Berlin Theotokos ivory panel, the ampulla Monza 4, and the Cleveland tapestry.[379] In another departure from the original iconography the archangels carry censers in addition to the globes, and the staffs necessarily disappear;[380] while in the *Maria Regina* fresco the archangels offer not globes but crowns, and the staffs are retained, though with some awkwardness. No suggestion of any of these developments appears in the Lythrankomi mosaic, and its retention of the original iconography weighs in favor of a relatively early date in the sixth century.

Too little is preserved of the Paradise landscape in which the Theophany is set to allow much comparison with other representations of the heavenly scene. The species of palm tree represented is exceptional. When palm trees appear in other early mural mosaics, and the examples are all in Western monuments, they are almost invariably represented with the feather-shaped leaves of the common date palm (*phoenix dactylifera*). Our mosaicist, by his bunches of drooping fan-shaped leaves springing from the crown of the trunk (fig. 74) and from suckers at the base (fig. 77), was clearly representing a different tree, evidently the Palmyra palm (*borassus flabellifer*). It is possibly the same fan palm that is represented by the two trees in the apse mosaic of the Giving of the Law in S. Costanza; certainly with their drooping fronds they are distinct from the heavily pruned date palms in the companion mosaic

---

[376] Seen in the Ostrogothic mosaics of S. Apollinare Nuovo as well as in the Poreč apse; also in the Dumbarton Oaks medallion.

[377] In Ravenna with both Christ and the Theotokos in S. Apollinare Nuovo, and with Christ in the apses of S. Michele in Affricisco (in Berlin), S. Agata (lost), and S. Vitale, though in this last the representation of the patron and founder has necessitated minor changes of pose.

[378] In the Poreč mosaic he carries the globe in both hands (van Berchem-Clouzot, *Mosaïques*, fig. 226; Prelog, *Mosaïques de Poreč*, fig. on p. 15). Where the archangels wear military dress in such autonomous representations, they almost invariably carry the globe: e.g., in the Alahan reliefs, on the Murano diptych leaf (see *supra*, note 327), and in the damaged marble relief of Gabriel in Antalya (Peirce-Tyler, *L'art byzantin*, II, pl. 32).

[379] Also in some Coptic niche frescoes: globes as well as staffs in Saqqara cell 1727 (*Saqqara*, IV, pl. 24), globes and cross scepters in Saqqara chapel A (*ibid.*, II, pl. 42).

The globes feature also in other themes, e.g., in the Sinai basilica on the wall above the Transfiguration mosaic, where flying archangels offer their globes to the Lamb (Forsyth-Weitzmann, *St. Catherine*, pls. CXXII,B, CXXIII,B).

[380] Bawit chapel 28: Ihm, *Programme*, pl. XVIII, 1.

representing Christ enthroned on the globe.[381] Elsewhere we have been able
to find no other early representations of fan-leaved palms. Even the considerable repertories of the Antioch mosaics and the Great Palace floor include
only date palms.[382] In Early Byzantine iconography as in that of the Early
Christian West, it was this feather-leaved palm that was normally used to
denote a celestial environment.[383] The choice of the fan-leaved tree by those
who set the Lythrankomi mosaic is perhaps explicable because it is known
that in antiquity, among several other varieties, one "with a broader leaf"
flourished in Cyprus.[383a]

The foliage of one of the other trees, of which only a small area survives,
is less easy to identify (fig. L). In such a landscape the pomegranate is the
first to be considered, since this tree figures in more than one sixth-century
representation of Paradise, notably the Cotton Genesis miniature of the Third
Day of the Creation.[384] There are numerous pomegranate trees in mosaic
in the Antioch floors, which range, on Doro Levi's datings, from the third
quarter of the fifth century to the early sixth, but a comparison of the
Lythrankomi foliage with these produces negative results. The leaves are more
rounded in the Worcester Hunt,[385] and trilobed in the floor of the House of
Ktisis.[386] Where, in the Hall of Philia, the leaves are more pointed, they are
on well separated branches which do not form the solid outline of the Lythrankomi tree.[387] The leaves of a pomegranate in the peristyle mosaic of the
Great Palace are indeed pointed,[388] but, as we shall see, it is another tree in
that floor that offers the closest parallel to our fragment of foliage.

The tentative identification of these dark leaves as part of a citron tree
(*supra*, p. 54) requires a comparison with those behind the Virgin in the
niche of chapel 17 at Bawit, but it is not helpful owing to the summary execution of this fresco.[389] The fragment of a citrus tree, surely a citron, preserved
in the Great Palace floor is much more sophisticated.[390] Here, the sharply
pointed leaves and the manner in which those of lighter color overlie others
of dark tone seem not only to seal the identification of the Lythrankomi
foliage, but to reveal a rather close relationship in execution. This is significant
in view of the sixth-century date now widely accepted for the Great Palace
floor.[391]

[381] Together in Volbach-Hirmer, *E. C. Art*, pl. 53.

[382] *Great Palace*, I, pl. 29; Martyrium at Seleucia: *Antioch-on-the-Orontes*, III (Princeton, 1941),
pl. 91. For other representations of date palms, see Levi, *Antioch Pavements*, I, 362, note 4.

[383] E.g., a relief in the Istanbul museum (Peirce-Tyler, *L'art byzantin*, I, pl. 165) and the Vatican
situla (Burke, "A Bronze Situla," figs. 1–3).

[383a] Theophrastus, Περὶ φυτῶν ἱστορίας, II, vi, 8.

[384] Grabar, *Byzantium*, fig. 224. Compare the pomegranate trees beside the four rivers of Paradise
in the miniature of the Wise and Foolish Virgins in the Rossano Gospels (*ibid.*, fig. 231).

[385] Levi, *Antioch Pavements*, I, 364; II, pl. 170.

[386] *Ibid.*, I, 357; II, pl. 174, b.

[387] *Ibid.*, I, 317; II, pl. 72, a. Other representations of pomegranate trees in mosaic floors (listed
ibid., I, 337 and note 10) include no close parallel to the Lythrankomi foliage.

[388] *Great Palace*, II, pl. 43.

[389] Grabar, *Byzantium*, fig. 189.

[390] *Great Palace*, II, pl. 45.

[391] D. Talbot Rice, "On the Date of the Mosaic Floor of the Great Palace," Χαριστήριον εἰς ᾽Αναστά-
σιον Κ. ᾽Ορλάνδον, I (Athens, 1964), 1–5.

The Intermediate Border (figs. 46, 47, and color fig. 138)

The same feature of an intermediate border recurs in two other apse mosaics which combine a main figural composition in the conch with a quite distinct decoration of the soffit of the apse arch. Both are Justinianic. In all three cases the function of this border was the same: to isolate the area designed to be viewed from the body of the church from those areas designed to be viewed from either side. In the apse of S. Vitale this purpose is served by a bold irisated border, sliced into oblique bands of counterchanged coloring.[392] In that of the Poreč basilica, loosely entwined red and green ribbons with blue reverses encircle rosettes and stars in the brown ground of this dividing band.[393] The more austere and somewhat later Sinai mosaic lacks this feature.

Jeweled borders are among the commonest in Early Byzantine mural mosaics, but this one is unusually elaborate, surpassed only in S. Vitale.[394] The alternating circular and square cabochons (fig. I, a), red and green, are normal, but the decoration between them, possibly modeled on enamelwork, is not. Nor, as an ornamental motif, can the iris flowers be matched,[395] though the meander-like tendrils on either side of their stems recall floor mosaic borders including more elaborate meander elements.[396] An abbreviated version of our border occurs on a fragment of marble relief decoration found during excavation of the remains of the church of St. Polyeuktos at Saraçhane in Istanbul (fig. I, b).[397] Here the flowers are omitted, but not their meander tendrils, and their stems are also retained to link the frame of one jewel to that of its neighbor. The deep undercutting of this fragment leaves no doubt that it formed part of the original decoration of the church, which was built in the third decade of the sixth century. A comparable border, in which a normal meander motif alternates with square "jewels" set at an angle, surrounds the cross on a pierced closure panel from S. Apollinare Nuovo (fig. I, c).[398]

---

[392] Deichmann, *Bauten und Mosaiken*, pls. 333, 347; Volbach-Hirmer, *E. C. Art*, pl. 158. In S. Apollinare in Classe, consecrated 549, there is no separate intermediate border but the soffit decoration is well isolated by a substantial edging on either side (Deichmann, *op. cit.*, pl. 385).

[393] Prelog, *Mosaïques de Poreč*, color illus. on p. 26.

[394] Here the jewels (or are they cymbals?), all circular, are themselves decorated and interspersed with intricate designs: forming the outer edging of the band of cornucopias on the soffit of the apse arch (Deichmann, *op. cit.*, pl. 347) and framing the apostle border on the arch at the entrance to the presbytery (*ibid.*, pl. 334 ff.; Volbach-Hirmer, *E. C. Art*, pl. 161).

[395] Representations of lilies are closely similar, lacking only the two falls of the iris; e.g., those accompanying the figure of Spring in a floor of the Constantinian Villa at Antioch (Levi, *Antioch Pavements*, II, pl. LIV, a) and others in the sixth-century Ravenna mosaics (Grabar, *Byzantium*, fig. 151).

[396] E.g., in the fifth-century Antioch mosaic of the Beribboned Lion (Levi, *op. cit.*, II, pl. CXXVI), and in the border of the hunting mosaic at Apamea, now dated to the late fourth century (J. Balty, *La grande mosaïque de chasse du Triclinos* [Brussels, 1969], 34 and pl. XV). The "double fret" or "keyhole" border in a floor at Gerasa, datable around 500, is also comparable (*Gerasa*, 314 and pl. LXI, b), and meander motifs were still used in the second quarter of the sixth century in Basilica A (St. Demetrius) at Nicopolis (E. Kitzinger, "Studies on Late Antique and Early Byzantine Floor Mosaics. I. Mosaics at Nikopolis," *DOP*, 6 [1951], fig. 21 and, for the date, p. 91 ff.).

[397] We are obliged to Professor M. Harrison for the photograph on which this drawing was based.

[398] Deichmann, *Geschichte und Monumente*, fig. 62; Volbach-Hirmer, *E. C. Art*, pl. 181, top left.

In the development of ornamental sculpture in sixth-century Constantinople, it was a short-lived phase that is represented by the eclectic and highly imaginative marble decoration of St. Polyeuktos. Its orientalizing character has been related to the influence of the pro-Monophysite emperors and especially Anastasius (491–518).[399] Already only a few years after the building of St. Polyeuktos it gave place in St. Sophia (532–37) to a more conventionalized manner, including, it is true, some motifs derived from the earlier style. The Lythrankomi border cannot, however, be classed as a Justinianic derivative; for in the relationship between it and the corresponding St. Polyeuktos border the unabbreviated design of the former is primary. Our intermediate border is therefore to be linked with the sources of the St. Polyeuktos repertory rather than with its derivatives. On this evidence, viewed in isolation, a Justinianic date for the setting of the Lythrankomi mosaic would seem rather late.

The Apostle Border

By the sixth century the portrait bust in a medallion, the *imago clipeata*, already had a long history in church decoration.[400] Taken over from pagan to Christian portraiture, initially of a funerary character, this format was used in the second quarter of the fifth century for a set of the twelve apostles with Christ on the face of the apse arch in S. Sabina, known from a seventeenth-century drawing.[401] Such galleries of the Twelve, matching that of the popes painted in fresco in S. Paolo fuori le mura[402] and that of the Christian emperors in mosaic once to be seen in Ravenna on the apse arch of S. Giovanni Evangelista,[403] may have been current even earlier. There is a set of apostle busts on the fourth-century ivory reliquary in Breccia,[404] though in this case the medallions, through their skyphate form, evidently derive from reliefs such as the survivor of a set of four evangelists in the Istanbul museum.[405]

It was not, however, until the turn of the fifth to the sixth century that the earliest surviving medallion portraits of the Twelve in mosaic were set: in the Archiepiscopal Chapel in Ravenna erected by Peter II (494–519). On account of the small size of the building, the apostles occupy both transverse arches of the central vault, arranged in each case in three medallions on either side of a central one containing a bust of Christ.[406]

---

[399] Grabar, *Sculptures*, 65.

[400] See J. Bolten, *Die Imago Clipeata. Ein Beitrag zur Portrait- und Typengeschichte* (Paderborn, 1937); A. Grabar, "L'*Imago clipeata* chrétienne," *CRAI*, 1957, pp. 209–13.

[401] Ciampini, *Vetera Monumenta*, I, pl. 47, on which the modern restoration in fresco is based. The church was consecrated under Sixtus III (432–40). See also Ihm, *Programme*, 151–53 with bibliography.

[402] Wilpert, *MM*, IV, pl. 219, and II (text), 560ff. The series is thought to have been started under Leo I (440–61).

[403] Datable between 424 and 434. See Bovini, in *FelRav*, 17/18 (1955), 60. His reconstruction of the program is reproduced in Ihm, *Programme*, 17, fig. 2; cf. 169–71 with bibliography.

[404] Volbach-Hirmer, *E. C. Art*, figs. 85–87, where the reliquary is assigned to the second half of the fourth century.   [405] Grabar, *Sculptures*, 9ff. and pl. II, 2.

[406] Deichmann, *Bauten und Mosaiken*, pls. 220, 226–37. The medallion of Christ at the summit of the west arch is modern. These mosaics are commonly assigned to the years around 510. Cf. L. Ottolenghi, "La Cappella Arcivescovile in Ravenna," *FelRav*, 3rd. ser. 22 (1957), 5ff.

Two other apostle borders in mosaic compare better with that of the Panagia Kanakaria in that the Twelve are figured in the medallions of a single arch: that on the arch across the entrance to the presbytery of S. Vitale,[407] and that on the soffit of the apse arch in Justinian's basilica in the Sinai monastery.[408] In the same position, thus corresponding with our Lythrankomi border, there is a similar series of medallions in the Poreč basilica, but here, since the apostles are figured full-length on either side of Christ on the wall above the apse, the *imagines clipeatae* are of female martyrs.[409]

On some points of iconographic detail it is useful to compare also those rings of medallions containing diminutive representations of the apostles which border some of the ampullae.[410] These have sometimes been thought to have derived from monumental apostle borders in hypothetical mosaics at the Holy Places, but this derivation cannot be pressed now that Grabar has established the Constantinopolitan background of ampulla iconography. Grabar's juxtaposition of one of these ampullae with a Roman gold plate ringed with imperial medallions is very telling;[411] but the possibility of a connection with monumental iconography is particularly strong in the case of the gold phylactery medallions from Adana.[412]

The acanthus foliage in the Lythrankomi Apostle Border, linking and framing the medallions against a dark blue to purple ground (figs. 48, 49, 53, 54, and color fig. 137), cannot be matched among the comparable borders. In those of the Archiepiscopal Chapel in Ravenna the medallions are set on a plain gold ground. Those of S. Vitale, of the Poreč basilica, and of the Sinai apse do indeed have dark blue grounds, but there the likeness ends. In the Poreč apse, the names of the saints written in large letters above each medallion leave no scope for ornamentation beyond a small acanthus plant under the lowest medallion on each side.[413] The small foliate motifs isolated in the spandrels between the Sinai medallions, which are reduced to single florets in the lower border,[414] are an exiguous substitute for the luxuriant acanthus at Lythrankomi. In its abundance the Lythrankomi foliage has something in common with the opulent setting of the S. Vitale medallions, each resting on a pair of dolphins with knotted tails,[415] and also with the rich garland

---

[407] Deichmann, *Bauten und Mosaiken*, pls. 334–39; Volbach-Hirmer, *E. C. Art*, pls. 160–61; Lazarev, *Storia*, fig. 58.

[408] Forsyth-Weitzmann, *St. Catherine*, pl. CIII. For the date, see *supra*, note 200.

[409] Prelog, *Mosaïques de Poreč*, fig. on p. 17.

[410] Monza 3, 12, and 13; Bobbio 2 and 8 (Grabar, *Ampoules*, pls. 9, 23, 25, 33, and 41). Compare a pottery lamp (Garrucci, *Storia*, VI, pl. 473, 1, 2, and 5) and a gold glass disk in the Parma museum (*ibid.*, IV, pl. 188, 4).

[411] Grabar, *Iconography*, figs. 176–77.

[412] See *supra*, note 288.

[413] Barely visible on van Berchem-Clouzot, *Mosaïques*, fig. 221.

[414] Forsyth-Weitzmann, *St. Catherine*, pls. CXVI, CXVII, CLXIIff. Comparable are the simple motifs isolated in the spandrels between the medallions on the niche wall of chapel B at Saqqara, yellow on a green ground (*Saqqara*, II, pls. 46–47).

[415] Deichmann, *Bauten und Mosaiken*, pls. 336–39. Comparable in elaboration, though not in detail, is the cornucopia and acanthus decoration of the non-figural soffits of the apse arches of the same church and of S. Apollinare in Classe (*ibid.*, pls. 347, 385).

carrying those of the Cleveland tapestry, which is reasonably derived from an apse decoration.[416]

The stark backgrounds of the medallions in the Ravenna Archiepiscopal Chapel borders were matched by the plain grounds of most of those in the lost mosaics in St. Demetrius.[417] The Lythrankomi border suggests that the more opulent treatment to which this austerity gave place in Ravenna had its counterpart, if not its inspiration, in the East. There, its derivatives may be seen in the foliage linking the medallions on the silver censer from Cyprus in the British Museum[418] and the garland of the Cleveland tapestry border.[419]

In the Lythrankomi border the medallions themselves are smaller than those of the other apostle series and they lack the wide and ornate frames of S. Vitale; but they have a subtlety not found elsewhere. Though blue like those in the Ravenna chapel and S. Vitale, they are of a much paler tone, and this pale blue is graded to suggest the skyphate form of the clipeus (e.g., figs. 55, 59, 63, and color figs. 139–43). A slight radiance is contrived round the heads in the Archiepiscopal Chapel, in the absence of nimbi; but the dark blue grounds are otherwise uniform. In S. Vitale the grounds of the medallions are quite homogeneous and those of the martyr medallions in the Poreč basilica are the same, though here they are alternately dark blue and light blue. The Sinai medallions are rendered altogether differently, as flat disks of gold, found also (in yellow) on the Cleveland tapestry, alternating with plain blue disks.

Earlier in the sixth century, as in the fifth, the blue-ground medallion was usual,[420] but it is only among the *imagines clipeatae* of the lost St. Demetrius mosaics that something akin to the Lythrankomi treatment is recorded. As is to be expected in a piecemeal series of votive panels, the treatment was not uniform. The grounds of the five medallions included in the panel centered

---

[416] Shepherd, "Tapestry Panel," 105. Miss Shepherd (*ibid.*, 100) compares the fifth-century garland interrupted by busts of the Seasons around the centerpiece of the Antioch Ananeosis floor (Levi, *Antioch Pavements*, II, pl. LXXIII, b). The garland itself is matched by those in the presbytery vault at S. Vitale (Deichmann, *Bauten und Mosaiken*, pls. 342–45; Volbach-Hirmer, *E. C. Art*, fig. 161). [No floor mosaic makes use of acanthus leaves in the same manner as does the Lythrankomi border, but among their acanthus scrolls M. Sacopoulo (*La Théotokos à la mandorle*, 59f.) finds the closest parallel to the Lythrankomi type of leaf in the church of Procopius at Gerasa (526). Here, in the nave border, the leaves are flattened and there are comparable florets in the field (*Gerasa*, pl. LXXIX, b–c).]

[417] In the earlier series in S. Sabina (see *supra*, note 401) Ciampini's drawing shows only simple foliate motifs in the interspaces.

The mosaic clipei decorating the ambon of Basilica B at Nikopolis are also displayed on an unornamented ground of turquoise tesserae. These doubtless belong to the original decoration of the basilica, probably constructed before the close of the fifth century, since the mosaic floor of an addition to it was the work of Bishop Alkison, who died in 516 (cf. Kitzinger, "Mosaics at Nikopolis" [*supra*, note 396], 89). These mosaic clipei, first published by G. Soteriou, have lately been reexamined by A. Xyngopoulos (see *infra*, note 512).

[418] O. M. Dalton, *Catalogue of Early Christian Antiquities, British Museum* (London, 1901), 87 ff., no. 399. It bears a stamp with the monogram of the Emperor Phocas (602–10); see E. Cruikshank Dodd, *Byzantine Silver Stamps* (Washington, D.C., 1961), 130, no. 35.

[419] The rich ornament of some of the humble Coptic frescoes would then reflect this widespread phase of luxuriance in sixth-century church decoration: e.g., at Bawit around a niche in chapel 32 (Clédat, *Baouît*, 39, pl. 7) and under the saints on the north wall of room 40 (Maspéro, in MémInstCaire, 59 [*supra*, note 221], pls. 48–50); at Saqqara around the niche of cell 1725 (Grabar, *Byzantium*, fig 194).

[420] Such are the mosaic clipei on the Nikopolis ambon (see *supra*, note 417).

on the enthroned Theotokos were plain white. The eight others are all a uniform light blue on Walter George's drawings,[421] with one exception. This is the clipeus of Christ with a chi-rho nimbus over arch 7, where three shades of light blue, the lightest next to the rim, were used to suggest the skyphate form.[422] At Lythrankomi the same three-dimensional effect is produced by a realistic use of highlight and shade (see *supra*, p. 40f.). Such subtleties seem far removed from the stark and forceful treatment in the Sinai border.

The manner in which the name of each apostle is included within his clipeus is repeated in the Sinai mosaic, with the first part of the name on one side of the head and the remainder on the other. In the S. Vitale apostle border the arrangement is similar but the writing is strictly horizontal. Elsewhere, the name is written horizontally above the clipeus in each case, as in the Ravenna chapel and the Poreč martyr border. The vertical arrangement of the letters in the Lythrankomi inscriptions and the letter-forms used are discussed separately (see *infra*, p. 121 ff.).

A feature which links the Lythrankomi and Sinai borders is the absence of the designation ἅγιος before the names of the apostles. Weigand, writing over forty years ago, judged that its use did not become general until the second half of the sixth century.[423] Its appearance before the names of Michael and Gabriel on the Cleveland tapestry in conjunction with its absence in the case of the apostles suggests that it appeared spasmodically somewhat earlier. This indication would have confirmation from the Theodosia lunette fresco at Antinoë if it is to be dated in the first half of the sixth century;[424] for here the attendant figures are named ΑΓΙΟ(C) ΚΟΛΛΟΥΘΟC and ΑΓΙΑ ΜΑΡΙΑ. The examples recorded in the St. Demetrius aisle mosaics, in inscriptions identifying three saints in clipei, are discussed below (p. 131). It is there argued that, on epigraphic grounds, these inscriptions are anterior to those naming the Lythrankomi apostles. They would in any case suggest that the designation was current in the East somewhat earlier than Weigand indicated. In the West, the equivalent *sanctus* was normal before the middle of the sixth century. It was used in Ravenna for the patron saints in the apses of S. Vitale and S. Apollinare in Classe, for Cosmas and Damian in S. Michele in Affricisco, and in the nave processions in S. Apollinare Nuovo; also in the Poreč mosaics, *passim*; but not in the S. Vitale apostle medallions. The fact that the Lythrankomi apostles are named *simpliciter* does not necessarily mean that the mosaic

---

[421] The last two in spandrel H appear blue in the reproduction (Cormack, "S. Demetrios," pl. 9), though they are described by Cormack as gold (*ibid.*, 31). The darker tone of blue at the top of the clipeus of Zacharias (*ibid.*, pl. 6) was evidently due to the seventh-century restoration.

[422] *Ibid.*, pl. 9. The strange treatments in the three clipei introduced in the seventh-century restoration (*ibid.*, pl. 8) are not relevant.

[423] *BZ*, 39 (1939), 137.

[424] M. Salmi, "I diplinti paleocristiani di Antinoe," *Scritti dedicati alla memoria di Ippolito Rosellini* (Florence, 1945), pl. XXVIII and p. 166 (first half of the sixth century); A. Grabar, in *Synthronon* (1968), 5 (first half of the sixth century); *idem, Byzantium*, fig. 185 (sixth-seventh century). A date in the sixth century has also been suggested for the Durrës mosaic panels, in one of which St. Stephen's name is preceded by +ΟΑ|ΓϞ (see note 371 *supra*). The relief of St. Symeon Stylites in the Louvre, on which ἅγιος is used, has been dated to 492, but erroneously (see note 573 *infra*), though the "square" letter-forms used would be normal at that date as well as somewhat later (see note 575 *infra*).

was set before the use of the designation ἅγιος became general. The exiguous space available for the inscription within the clipeus would have made the addition of an extra word impossible, unless the letters had been reduced in size below what easy legibility required. This applies equally in the S. Vitale and Sinai borders; whereas in the martyr border of the Poreč mosaic in the greater space available outside the clipei the abbreviation S̄C̄S̄ could be included. Despite the absence of the corresponding designation in our mosaic, it can then properly be assigned to a relatively early date in the sixth century when the prefix was becoming usual wherever space permitted. The Sinai mosaic provides some confirmation because, although the border apostles lack the ἅγιος, the names of those in the Transfiguration are prefixed by an equivalent, a cross.

Apart from the substitution of a flat disk for a spatially treated clipeus, it is the lack of nimbi in the Sinai medallions that make them so different. As a result the heads are proportionately as well as actually much larger. It is certain that if the Lythrankomi treatment had been followed in these medallions, which are only slightly larger, the heads would have been scarcely recognizable at the much greater height of the Sinai conch; nor in the reduced area of the clipeus outside the nimbus could the name have been made large enough to be legible. But it is not only for such functional reasons that the nimbi were discarded, for they are lacking also in the main composition of the Transfiguration (save in the case of Christ). There is ample room for them here, and room could have been made for them in the border also by increasing its width.

Generally speaking, in fifth-century mural art nimbed saints and martyrs were exceptional while in the Justinianic period they were normal. Weigand put the changeover as late as *ca.* 530 and evidently regarded the Sinai mosaic as backward in this respect.[425] That date may still hold good for Rome, and if so its virtual coincidence with the Byzantine occupation of the city in 536 seems significant. But if a date not later than the early sixth century is to stand for the aisle mosaics of St. Demetrius, the general adoption of the nimbus in the East must be placed somewhat earlier.[426] This is indirectly attested by the appearance of the nimbus in Ravenna in the mosaics of the time of Theodoric: in the Arian baptistery where the apostles have nimbi graded from white round the head to blue at the rim, perhaps imitating the silver nimbi of the prophets and saints in the clerestory of S. Apollinare Nuovo. In that church the gold nimbus was reserved for Christ and the Virgin, whereas in St. Demetrius it was normal for saints also.[427] The apostles in the

---

[425] *BZ*, 39 (1939), 139.

[426] Even so, it seems somewhat hazardous to assign to the beginning of the fifth century the ivory panel in the Louvre portraying a nimbed apostle: Volbach-Hirmer, *E. C. Art*, 330 and pl. 99.

If the two mosaic busts without nimbi on the Nikopolis ambon (see *infra*, note 512) are those of saints, as Xyngopoulos reasonably suggests, they show that the nimbus was optional for saints at an advanced date in the fifth century.

[427] At Salonica gold was already used in the Rotunda mosaics for the nimbi of the angels supporting the great mandorla in the dome (Torp, *Mosaikkene*, facing p. 32), and for that of the angel of St. Matthew at Hosios David (Volbach-Hirmer, *E. C. Art*, pl. 135).

borders of the Archiepiscopal Chapel lack the nimbus, as did the lost series in S. Sabina in Rome, and though the chapel decoration may be a few years earlier than the clerestory it is evident that Archbishop Peter's mosaicist held closer to the Western tradition than did Theodoric's.

In panel painting and in representations on a smaller scale the exigencies of space could be overriding, although even in some crowded compositions like the early Theotokos icon in the Sinai monastery all the figures were nimbed. In sixth-century manuscript illumination the nimbus was optional for the apostles, if we may judge by the Rabbula Gospels, [428] and the same is true of silverwork under Justin II.[429] Irrespective of the figure represented, diminutive size evidently excluded the nimbus in some very small clipei, such as the two smallest of those in the St. Demetrius mosaics[430] and those at the top of the early icon of Peter in the Sinai monastery, where even Christ has no nimbus other than the gold clipeus itself.[431] The diminutive apostle busts or heads in clipei encircling some of the ampullae are likewise without nimbi.[432] On the other hand, the apostles' busts in the comparable borders of the pair of gold phylactery medallions from Adana are represented with nimbi, but this was possible only because the busts were not set in constricting clipei.[433]

However, the treatment without nimbi in the Sinai border cannot be explained simply by lack of space. Rather does it suggest, together with the lack of nimbi in the Transfiguration, a conscious reaction against the use of this symbol of holiness in representations of mortals, by rejecting which the divinity of the nimbed Christ was thrown into relief. For whatever reason, the nimbus does seem to have been out of favor in the mid-sixth century, if only temporarily. The S. Michele in Affricisco mosaic provides examples in the unnimbed figures of Cosmas and Damian,[434] and there are many in the ivory carvings of the period: among others,[435] the Berlin Theotokos diptych leaf, where even the Christ Child is denied a nimbus, and the throne of Maximian in Ravenna, where Christ alone is nimbed though not invariably.[436] Certainly there is no such inhibition at Lythrankomi. There the nimbi of the border link it with an earlier sixth-century Byzantine iconography which is reflected in the S. Vitale apostle border and at Poreč in the nimbi of the standing apostles and of the martyrs in the apse border.

[428] Present in Pentecost (Grabar, *Byzantium*, fig. 233), lacking in the Ascension (Grabar, *Iconography*, pl. 1); lacking also in the Rossano Gospels, *passim*, and on the ampullae.

[429] The Stuma paten, nimbed with three exceptions (Grabar, *Byzantium*, fig. 365); the Riha paten, no nimbi (Cruikshank Dodd, *Byz. Silver Stamps*, no. 20).

[430] Cormack, "S. Demetrios," pls. 5 and 9.

[431] Soteriou, Εἰκόνες τῆς Μονῆς Σινᾶ, I, pl. 1, II, 19ff.

[432] Monza 3 (Grabar, *Ampoules*, pl. 9), Monza 12 (*ibid.*, pl. 23), Bobbio 2 (*ibid.*, pl. 33).

[433] Grabar, *Iconography*, fig. 248.

[434] Wulff, *Altchristl. und byz. Kunst* (*supra*, note 4), II, 427, fig. 367, from a drawing made before removal; cf. Deichmann, *Geschichte und Monumente*, figs. 210, 212.

[435] E.g., the Adoration panels in the British Museum (Volbach-Hirmer, *E. C. Art*, pl. 222) and Manchester (see *supra*, note 326), and the Murano diptych leaf in Ravenna (Volbach-Hirmer, *op. cit.*, pl. 223), in all of which not even Christ is nimbed.

[436] Christ nimbed: Multiplication of the Loaves (Volbach-Hirmer, *E. C. Art*, pl. 233). Christ without nimbus: Baptism (*ibid.*, pl. 232) and Healing of the Blind Man (Grabar, *Iconography*, fig. 65).

In the treatment of the robes also the Sinai apostles stand apart. In all except three cases the himation passes from the right shoulder under the bearded chin and over the other shoulder, so that the chiton is not seen at all. In the cases of Thomas (beardless), Luke, and Mark (short beards), where something of the undergarment is seen, the himation covers much more of the right shoulder than at Lythrankomi, where only a small segment is visible (figs. 67, 71). In the S. Vitale apostle border, where more of each figure is seen, the garments are worn in a variety of ways; but where only a little of the himation appears on the right shoulder (e.g., Peter and Jude) it is misunderstood and the clavus of the chiton is carried across it.[437] In this respect the treatment of the robes at Lythrankomi is superior and closer to that in the earlier borders in the Archiepiscopal Chapel and in the figures of the apostles in the Arian Baptistery. Here the garments are more correctly rendered, often with the optional detail of a fold in the neckline of the chiton, which is common at Lythrankomi but lacking in the three represented in the Sinai border.

In another respect, however, the Cyprus and Sinai borders are linked together: by the presence of all four evangelists, each carrying his Gospel book. In the Ravenna mosaics Mark and Luke are not included among the Twelve, in conformity with the lists in the New Testament;[438] nor are Matthew and John distinguished as evangelists. Yet, curiously enough, it is in Ravenna that we find what was thought to be the earliest evidence of the inclusion of Mark and Luke. Their names are inscribed on the projecting "ears" of the monolithic cap of Theodoric's tomb, but the letter-forms will hardly allow that they were cut at the time of its construction.[439] The inclusion of all four evangelists as well as Paul constituted a popular version of the symbolic college which prevailed in the East over the biblical lists. But it is clear that at one time the list in the Acts was followed in the East also, revised only to include Paul. For, although there is no list of the Twelve in the Greek liturgy corresponding to that in the canon of the Latin mass,[440] the same scriptural

[437] Deichmann, *Bauten und Mosaiken*, pls. 337, 338.

[438] Save only that Paul is included instead of Matthias, Judas Iscariot's elected replacement (Acts 1:26).

[439] R. Heidenreich and H. Johannes, *Das Grabmal Theodorichs zu Ravenna* (Wiesbaden, 1971), 80ff. Cf. G. de Jerphanion, "Quels sont les douze apôtres," *La voix des monuments* (Paris, 1930), 194.

It is also questionable whether the carving of the sarcophagus with the Mission of the Apostles in Arles and the inscriptions which identify four of them as the evangelists are in fact contemporary (J. Wilpert, *I sarcofaghi cristiani antichi* [Rome, 1929–32], II [Text], 337, and I [Plates], pl. 34, 3). Separate representation of the evangelists is found on the sarcophagi, notably on the sides of that in Apt cathedral (*ibid.*, I, pl. 37, 2–3), but on the Arles sarcophagus the appearance of the figure named Matthew in the fourth place and of that named John in the ninth is hard to explain unless the names were added later wherever the features seemed to fit.

Definitely to be excluded is the fifth-century Barletta relief in the form of a sarcophagus front, identified as Christ and the Haemorrhoissa with the Twelve in attendance (P. Testini, "Un rilievo cristiano poco noto del Museo di Barletta," *Vetera Christianorum*, I [Bari, 1964], 129–63). The paleography of the Greek names of the apostles shows that these were added in the post-iconoclastic period. The names of Mark and Luke are included, with that of Andrew incongruously between them, but there is no reason to suppose that the sculptor consciously portrayed them.

[440] This list adds Paul to the eleven present at the Ascension and thus omits Matthias; cf. A. Baumstark, "Das *Communicantes* und seine Heiligenliste," *JbLw*, 1 (1921), 12f. Such were the Twelve (but

list recurs in the Greek version of the Syrian liturgy[441] and is followed in the accepted version of the Greek Synaxarion for June 30.[442] Visual evidence of this is not lacking, for the apostles on the bronze situla in the Museo Cristiano, where they are named in Greek, include Paul but omit Mark and Luke.[443] Likewise in the Rabbula Gospels, though there are no names in either the Pentecost or Ascension miniatures, there is an unmistakable Paul in each case and no suggestion of four evangelists.[444] Finally, one of the ampullae provides an example of the apostles at the Ascension without Mark and Luke, for the two who carry books are certainly Matthew and John.[445]

The inclusion of all four evangelists in the symbolic Twelve avoided, and may have been designed to avoid, the sort of tautology that arose when both the Twelve and the Four were separately represented in a single scheme of decoration. In the Orthodox Baptistery at Ravenna, for example, Matthew and John were represented first by their Gospel books, open and inscribed with their names in the lower register of the mosaics, and again among the Twelve in the dome.[446] The practice of telescoping the two series into one was current in Byzantium in the mid-sixth century and probably earlier. Four evangelists appear with their Gospels at the Ascension on two of the ampullae,[447] and again in a scene of the Incredulity of Thomas on another.[448] Where names are given, it is normally James Alphaeus and Jude who are dropped to make room for Mark and Luke and this selection has the sanction of the Patmos manuscript of the Synaxarion.[449] The names on the tomb of Theodoric conform, but if these are later additions there is no surviving example to prove that the inclusion of Mark and Luke was normal before the time of Justinian. On the other hand, if the Cleveland tapestry, on which Mark and Luke are figured, was woven in Egypt "not long after the middle of the sixth cen-

---

not in the same order) in the lost mosaics of S. Agata dei Goti (460–70), as well as in the Ravenna monuments, starting with the Orthodox Baptistery, in the Poreč basilica, and already in the fourth century on the Brescia reliquary, if Delbrueck's identifications of the unnamed apostles are accepted (G. Delbrueck, *Probleme der Lipsanothek in Brescia* [Bonn, 1952], 38f.).

[441] Baumstark, *loc. cit.*; also in the diptychs of Jerusalem written for use at Sinai (F. E. Brightman, *Liturgies Eastern and Western* [Oxford, 1896], 501). The liturgy of the Abyssinian Jacobites follows the scriptural list scrupulously, including Matthias in the Twelve but not Paul (*ibid.*, 228).

[442] *Synaxarium CP*, col. 779ff.

[443] Burke, "A Bronze Situla," 163ff. The missing name of Simon is surely that obscured by the handle attachment, the ΖΗ which is visible being part of an abbreviation of Σίμων ὁ ΖΗλωτής.

[444] *Rabbula Gospels*, fols. 13ᵇ and 14ᵇ. The Election of Matthias (fol. 1ᵃ), where there are remains of legends, is treated historically with eleven apostles, and Paul is excluded. It is this assembly, plus Matthias, that is represented in Bawit chapel 6 (Maspéro, in MémInstCaire, 59 [*supra*, note 221], VII) with, as thirteenth, Holy Apa Paul of Psilikous.

[445] Grabar, *Ampoules*, pl. 3 (Monza 1).

[446] Nor was tautology avoided in S. Vitale, where Matthew and John are represented both in the apostle border and, as evangelists, on the sanctuary walls. Similarly, the two evangelist members of the original Twelve are figured twice in the clerestory of S. Apollinare Nuovo, if the 32 original figures comprise 16 prophets, 12 apostles, and 4 evangelists. If the feet surviving in the zone below the flying angels in the Salonica Rotunda mosaic belong not to angels but to a similar 32-figure assembly (see *supra*, note 197), here also Matthew and John would have appeared twice.

[447] Monza 10 (Grabar, *Ampoules*, pl. 17, with an identifiable Paul); Monza 11 (*ibid.*, pls. 19–21).

[448] Monza 9 (*ibid.*, pl. 15).

[449] Cod. 266, end of the ninth or beginning of the tenth century, published by A. Dmitrievskij, *Opisanie liturgičeskih rukopisej*, I (Kiev, 1895), 1–152. Cf. J. Mateos, *Le typicon de la Grande Eglise*, I (Rome, 1962) (= OCA, 165), 327.

tury,"[450] the local monumental model for its border might have been executed substantially earlier. Such indications of the date from which Mark and Luke were regularly figured in the Byzantine Twelve are compatible with the setting of the Lythrankomi mosaic at the beginning of Justinian's reign, which other considerations suggest.

In the Sinai mosaic the appearance of three of the apostles in the main composition left room in the border not only for James Alphaeus and Jude, as well as Mark and Luke, but also for Matthias, who was demoted to make room for Paul both in Constantinople and in Rome. The Cleveland tapestry also is exceptional since, in addition to suppressing James Alphaeus and Jude to make room for Mark and Luke, it excludes Simon also to admit Matthias. In Egypt some special consideration for the Apostle of Ethiopia is not surprising.[451] As in the tapestry, so in the Lythrankomi border Simon is omitted, but here in his place not Matthias but Jude is included. This makes the Twelve in our mosaic a unique selection which could be explained by some local, or perhaps wider but transient, preference for Jude over both James Alphaeus and Simon. However that may be, it does seem permissible to conclude that our mosaic was set, and perhaps the model for the Cleveland tapestry border also, before the sacrifice of James Alphaeus and Jude in favor of Mark and Luke was generally accepted.

The order in which the apostles are represented at Lythrankomi is exceptional in several respects. There was indeed little uniformity in the order of seniority in the sixth-century monuments;[452] in the S. Vitale border the list in Matthew 10:2ff. is followed, in the Poreč Twelve that in Luke 6:14ff., but elsewhere neither scriptural nor other lists were strictly adhered to. Neither version of the Synaxarion is followed in any surviving Eastern monument of early date, and in the West the order in the Roman mass is not represented anywhere before the seventh century.[453] Yet there was a measure of agreement with the indications of seniority given in the four lists in the New Testament, no two of which are exactly the same.[454] Paul, upon his inclusion, almost invariably takes second place after Peter, as at Lythrankomi. But when Mark and Luke are added, there is no agreement where they should go. At Lythrankomi they are not adjacent, but reasonably they follow John and Matthew taking seventh and tenth places. On the tomb of Theodoric they are together and immediately follow Matthew. In the Sinai border, however, Mark precedes Matthew and Luke comes last, after Matthias, in which position it cannot be claimed that he was included among the Twelve at

[450] Shepherd, "Tapestry Panel," 115.

[451] Matthias also replaces Simon in the liturgy of the Abyssinian Jacobites (Brightman, *Liturgies* [*supra*, note 441], 228).

[452] Earlier, the list in Matthew 10:2–4 was followed for the last seven apostles (the names of the others are not preserved) on the Puebla Nueva sarcophagus (H. Schlunk, *Madrider Mitteilungen*, 7 [1966], 210ff., pls. 59–65). But Delbrueck's identifications of the heads on the Brescia reliquary (Delbrueck, *Lipsanothek* [*supra*, note 440], 38f.) follow the list in Mark 3:16–19.

[453] E.g., on the coffin of St. Cuthbert, see E. Kitzinger, in *The Relics of St. Cuthbert*, ed. C. F. Battiscombe (Oxford, 1956), 269.

[454] Matthew 10:2–4; Mark 3:16–19; Luke 6:14–16; Acts 1:13 and 26.

all. Finally, on the Cleveland tapestry the placing of the two added evangelists, like that of all the apostles, is entirely capricious.[455] In spite of this apparent anarchy, the positions of several of the apostles in the Lythrankomi border call for comment.

John, though he has not survived, clearly occupied the third place, taking precedence over Andrew. This is unusual but has the authority of the lists in Mark 3:16ff. and Acts 1:13ff. In Bawit chapel 6, too, John precedes Andrew.

Andrew's occupation of fourth place at Lythrankomi is not in strict accordance with those lists, for they have James also before Andrew, and in our mosaic James is given a very low place. Andrew is normally third and that is his place in the Synaxarion and in the Sinai mosaic. His demotion in the Panagia Kanakaria is noteworthy, particularly if Andrew's usurping of Paul's place on one of the ampullae[456] is a reflection of the favor the *Protokletos* came to enjoy at Constantinople. In Cyprus, where metropolitan influences increased in the sixth century, Andrew's position would suggest that our mosaic was set before the apostle was claimed as the founder of the Church in Byzantium.[457]

Jude's elevation to the eighth place is in conflict with all the New Testament lists, where he is last or last but one; and we have seen that on admission of Mark and Luke he was usually excluded from the Twelve altogether. Exceptional seniority is also given to Jude on the bronze situla in the Museo Cristiano, where he has fourth place. That this unusual respect for him is an early phenomenon is suggested by his high position in the lost fifth-century mosaic in the apse of S. Agata dei Goti in Rome, where he was sixth.[458] May not this early popularity of the Apostle of Mesopotamia have developed as a result of the sixty years of peace on the Eastern frontier which ended in 502?

James the son of Zebedee, as one of the first four disciples to be called, has a high place in all the New Testament lists and is never lower than fifth in other representations of the apostles in monuments of the sixth century which include Paul. Like that of Jude, his treatment at Lythrankomi, where he drops to ninth place, can be matched only in S. Agata dei Goti, where he was eighth.

Simon, finally, is conspicuous by his absence. As we have said before, he is excluded from the Twelve in only one other comparable example, the Cleveland tapestry.[459] Elsewhere he normally appears among the last of the

---

[455] Capricious also is the order on a textile fragment in London (A. F. Kendrick, *Catalogue of Textiles from Burial Grounds in Egypt* [Victoria and Albert Museum, 1922], III, p. 67, no. 789 and pl. 20) and on a lintel from Saqqara (*Saqqara*, III, pl. 31, 6).

[456] Monza 3 (Grabar, *Ampoules*, 20 and pl. 9).

[457] In Dvornik's view the terminus a quo for the formation of the tradition concerning Andrew's legendary foundation of the Church in Byzantium may not be before the end of the sixth century (F. Dvornik, *The Idea of Apostolicity in Byzantium* [Cambridge, Mass., 1958], 160f.).

[458] Ciampini, *Vetera Monumenta*, I, pl. 77, whence Ihm, *Programme*, pl. 4, 1. Later Jude falls to tenth place in the Archiepiscopal Chapel in Ravenna, to eleventh at S. Vitale, and to twelfth in the Poreč basilica.

[459] Simon is excluded also in the Abyssinian Jacobite liturgy (Brightman, *Liturgies*, 228).

apostles, conforming with the New Testament order; but in Bawit chapel 6 he is ninth and on the bronze situla sixth.[460] His omission at Lythrankomi was a consequence of the special favor shown to Jude, and may have been excused by an aura of remoteness surrounding the Apostle of North Africa who, according to the Synaxarion, was crucified in Britain.

If any conclusion can be drawn from the order in which the apostles appear in our mosaic, it is from the treatment of Andrew and Jude. Neither the relegation of Andrew to the fourth place nor the favor shown to Jude conform with mid-sixth-century practice (in the Sinai mosaic Andrew comes next after Paul and Jude twelfth, if the three apostles in the Transfiguration are counted above him). On the other hand, they would be less surprising in a mosaic set about 520–30, the date for the decoration of the Lythrankomi apse to which other features of the iconography point.

The differentiation of the individual apostles in the Lythrankomi border remains to be considered. The heads are posed frontally without exception, unlike those of the Sinai and S. Vitale borders, some of which are set slightly obliquely. There is uniformity in other respects also: in the shape of the heads, where there are only minor differences (Luke's is narrower than the others, Bartholomew's more pear-shaped); in a standard cast of feature with almond eyes and raised eyebrows; and in the ears, all rendered by a simple outline without interior drawing. A certain sameness results, which is not wholly dispelled by variations in the form and coloring of the hair and beard. Such variations are used to represent those characteristics of individual apostles which became increasingly standardized in sixth-century iconography.[461]

In early representations, Peter and Paul were the first to be well differentiated, usually by white curly hair and beard for Peter and by dark receding hair and pointed beard for Paul, though Epiphanius could complain that two versions of Paul were still current in his time.[462] Paul at Lythrankomi (figs. 53, 57), with high brow and long, pointed purple-black beard, is of the type that was universal by the sixth century. By then, increasing conformity with standardized conceptions had replaced both the diverse characterizations of individual apostles (sometimes as an elder and sometimes as a youth) which had offended Epiphanius,[463] and also the equally unsatisfactory practice of using a single generalized type for all.[464] Most distinctive was the long, unkempt gray hair and beard adopted for Andrew, of which the Lythran-

---

[460] Quite exceptionally, he is fourth in the Patmos manuscript of the Synaxarion (see *supra*, note 449).

[461] Cf. J. Ficker, *Die Darstellung der Apostel in der altchristlichen Kunst* (Leipzig, 1887); J. E. Weis-Liebersdorf, *Christus- und Apostelbilder* (Freiburg im Breisgau, 1902); K. Künstle, *Ikonographie der Heiligen* (Freiburg im Breisgau, 1926).

[462] K. Holl, *Gesammelte Aufsätze zur Kirchengeschichte*, II (Tübingen, 1928), 362, reconstructing Epiphanius (frag. 26) from Nicephorus, *Adv. Epiph.*, xix, 86 (J. B. Pitra, *Spicilegium Solemniense*, IV [Paris, 1891], 292 ff.).

[463] *Ibid.*, 361 (frag. 24). This refers to saints generally, but the preceding fragment 23 refers specifically to "Peter, or Andrew, or James, or John, or the other apostles." Portrayals in mosaic are the subject of fragment 30 (*ibid.*, 362).

[464] E.g., on the Vatican situla, where only Peter and Paul are differentiated (see *supra*, note 276).

komi head provides an excellent example (figs. 55–56, and color fig. 141).[465] If we may judge by the portrayal of Andrew in the earlier Ravenna mosaics, this hirsute formula was not universally accepted before the sixth century; for in the Orthodox Baptistery Andrew has short hair and beard,[466] and in the Archiepiscopal Chapel though the hair is long the beard is still short.[467]

Philip at Lythrankomi, with high brow, dark hair, and pointed beard (figs. 54, 58), is normal for the sixth century, matching the Sinai head and that in S. Vitale.[468] Exceptionally, a more youthful Philip is portrayed in the Rabbula Gospels,[469] following an earlier convention represented by the short-bearded head in the Orthodox Baptistery in Ravenna.[470] Since the youthful type was still current in the time of Theodoric,[471] its rejection at Lythrankomi in favor of the older Philip suggests that our mosaicist was familiar with a more advanced iconography.

For Matthew also there were two conventions and in this case both were followed well into the sixth century. The elderly Matthew of the Orthodox Baptistery, with white hair and beard,[472] is retained in S. Vitale, both among the evangelist figures on the bema walls and among the Twelve in the apostle border, and in the Poreč basilica also. This first type recurs in the Sinai border and some other sixth-century representations in the East.[473] A second type for Matthew, dark-haired and beardless, is used in the Archiepiscopal Chapel at Ravenna[474] and is matched by a youthful Matthew with incipient beard in the Rabbula Gospels.[475] The Lythrankomi head with dark hair and trim beard (color fig. 139) represents a compromise between the two types which could well be specifically a Byzantine one, for the dark-bearded Matthew is represented in the series of small bust portraits of the evangelists in the Rossano Gospels.[476]

[465] Such also is Andrew in S. Vitale, but with curly beard (Deichmann, *Bauten und Mosaiken* pl. 237), in the Election of Matthias miniature in the Rabbula Gospels (fol. 1ʳ), in the Bawit chapel 6 fresco, and in the Cleveland tapestry. Even where the apostles are not named, Andrew is easily recognizable by his unkempt hair: in the Rossano Gospels (Washing of the Feet, Last Supper, Communion) and on the ampullae Monza nos. 3, 9, 11, and 12, Bobbio nos. 2 and 10 (Grabar, *Ampoules*, pls. IX, XV, XXI, XXIII, XXXIII, XLII).

[466] Deichmann, *Bauten und Mosaiken*, pl. 59.

[467] *Ibid.*, pl. 234.

[468] Though there the beard is less pointed (*ibid.*, pl. 335). The same type recurs on the Cleveland tapestry.   [469] In the miniature of the Election of Matthias.

[470] Deichmann, *Bauten und Mosaiken*, pl. 46.

[471] In the Archiepiscopal Chapel (*ibid.*, pl. 231) and, unnamed, in the Arian Baptistery (*ibid.*, pl. 261).

[472] *Ibid.*, pl. 56; repeated in the Arian Baptistery (*ibid.*, pl. 266).

[473] Bald at Sinai (Forsyth-Weitzmann, *St. Catherine*, pl. CXVII), white-bearded in the canon table miniature of the Rabbula Gospels (fol. 9ʳ) and in the niche fresco from Bawit chapel 6. Matthew is also heavily bearded on Maximian's throne at Ravenna (Volbach-Hirmer, *E. C. Art*, pl. 228, right); for although the evangelists are not named, by process of elimination this must be Matthew. The youthful John is unmistakable (*ibid.*, pl. 229, left), the narrow pointed head of his neighbor conforms with the normal type of Luke (*ibid.*, pl. 229, right), and the broad-headed, somewhat uncouth figure at the extreme left (*ibid.*, pl. 228, left) is surely Mark, the *servus servorum dei*.

[474] Deichmann, *Bauten und Mosaiken*, pl. 228.

[475] In the Election miniature (fol. 1ʳ).

[476] The miniature portraits are on fol. 1ʳ, a decorative frontispiece to the Eusebian Canons: A. Haseloff, *Codex purpureus Rossanensis* (Berlin-Leipzig, 1898), pl. IX. On the connection of the codex with undoubtedly metropolitan manuscripts, see Volbach-Hirmer, *E. C. Art*, 357. The bust of Matthew in the Cleveland tapestry is comparable: Shepherd, "Tapestry Panel," fig. 11, a, above.

For Luke and Mark there are few *comparanda* in the West, since there they were not included among the Twelve, and the evangelists on the sanctuary walls of S. Vitale are unhelpful, for all four are generalized white-bearded elders. In the East Mark and Luke are usually more youthful with dark hair and rather short beards, as they both are at Lythrankomi, though here they are well differentiated in other respects. Luke is given an exceptionally long and narrow head (figs. 54, 61, 62) and Mark a rather broad one (figs. 67 and 68). In these respects, they correspond with the two outer evangelists on Archbishop Maximian's throne in Ravenna.[477] Wherever the throne was made, the connection of the evangelist panels with Byzantine court art is not in dispute.[478] Comparable also with the Lythrankomi Mark is the dark-haired and short-bearded head in the author portrait of this Evangelist in the purple codex at Rossano, which likewise has metropolitan affiliations.[479] An acquaintance with Constantinopolitan iconography is thus tenuously indicated for the Lythrankomi mosaicist. In the Sinai border, however, Luke and Mark have elderly heads, and although Mark's has the characteristic broad proportion his full gray beard gives him an entirely different appearance.

Some sixth-century representations of Jude follow very closely the earliest surviving example in mosaic, the youthful "Judas Zelotes" in the Orthodox Baptistery in Ravenna, with dark hair and slight beard ending in twin points.[480] Such, and perhaps even younger looking, is "Thaddeos" at Lythrankomi (color fig. 143). He has the same incipient brown beard in the Poreč basilica, where he appears as "Judas Iacobi" among the Twelve above the apse; also in the Election miniature of the Rabbula Gospels. In the Sinai border the beard is longer, but here again it ends in twin points. Two of the exceptions are in Ravenna: graying hair and beard in the Archiepiscopal Chapel,[481] and an ample dark beard rounded at the point in the S. Vitale border.[482] The Cypriot mosaicist was evidently following a long-established Byzantine characterization.

James at Lythrankomi (color fig. 142) is exceptional in that the mosaicist has adopted a specifically fifth-century convention, to judge by the short gray hair and beard with which he is portrayed at Ravenna in the Orthodox Baptistery.[483] In sixth-century monuments, including the Sinai apse, James

---

[477] Presumably Luke on the right and Mark on the left (see *supra*, note 473): Volbach-Hirmer, *E. C. Art*, pls. 229 and 228 respectively.

[478] *Ibid.*, 40.

[479] Fol. 125ʳ: Morey, *Early Christian Art* (*supra*, note 191), fig. 112. Mark is similarly represented with a short beard (Luke also) in the frame of the canon table frontispiece in the same manuscript (see *supra*, note 476); likewise flanking the canon tables of the Rabbula Gospels (fol. 10).

[480] Deichmann, *Bauten und Mosaiken*, pl. 61.

[481] *Ibid.*, pl. 229. The pointed white beard of Thaddeus in the fresco from Bawit chapel 6 may not, therefore, be capricious.

[482] *Ibid.*, pl. 338.

[483] *Ibid.*, pl. 44. Such also is the unnamed elderly figure paired with a recognizable Andrew (*ibid.*, pl. 29) in the north lunette of the Mausoleum of Galla Placidia (*ibid.*, pl. 27, right). That this is James, in what is apparently fourth place since Peter and Paul are unmistakable in the adjoining east lunette (*ibid.*, pl. 28), is suggested by the seniority given him elsewhere in Ravenna: fifth in the Orthodox Baptistery, fourth in the Archiepiscopal Chapel.

is almost always a younger man with dark hair and beard, incipient at Poreč and in S. Vitale.[484] That our mosaicist followed the earlier type suggests that he was working before the full impact of Justinianic iconography was felt.

Contrasting with the early representation of Bartholomew in the Orthodox Baptistery, with receding gray hair and a gray beard,[485] our dark-haired type (figs. 69, 70) is normal in the sixth century and conforms with the description of the Apostle in the Μαρτύριον Βαρθολομαίου.[486] The twin points to his beard in the Lythrankomi head reappear in S. Vitale and as two curly locks in the longer beard worn by Bartholomew in the Sinai mosaic.

In representations of Thomas (figs. 71, 72), almost always a beardless or lightly bearded youth, there is very little variation. At Lythrankomi, the row of dark purple tesserae below the chin (frontispiece) is not an outline, but represents an incipient beard such as Thomas wears both in the Orthodox Baptistery and in S. Vitale at Ravenna.[487] Quite unlike these, and the apparently beardless heads in the Arian Baptistery[488] and the Sinai mosaic, are two full-bearded Western variants: with dark hair in the Archiepiscopal Chapel at Ravenna,[489] gray hair in the Poreč basilica.

To sum up, in three cases where conventional characteristics favored in the fifth century were superseded in the sixth (Andrew, Philip, and Bartholomew), the Lythrankomi apostles conform with the later types. Only in the fourth case, that of James, does the mosaicist hold to the earlier iconography. Such conservatism would be surprising at a date at all far advanced in the sixth century, particularly since the later characterization for this Apostle is followed in the Sinai mosaic.

The Outer Borders

The Irisated Border which enclosed the entire decoration of the conch, both the main composition and the Apostle Border, is essentially the same as that framing the mandorla, which has been discussed above (p. 95).

The narrow Crowstep Border, which passed below it along the cornice (fig. 52), is as common as it is rudimentary. It is found in precisely the same position at the bottom of the Sinai apse mosaic.[490] But it was also used in pre-Justinianic contexts, notably around one of the surviving fragments of the

---

[484] *Ibid.*, pl. 336. This type appears earlier in the Archiepiscopal Chapel (*ibid.*, pl. 236) and for the unnamed James in the Arian Baptistery (*ibid.*, pl. 260), where the beard ends in twin points, a detail repeated in the Sinai apse: Forsyth-Weitzmann, *St. Catherine*, pl. CXIII.

[485] Deichmann, *Bauten und Mosaiken*, pl. 60. Bartholomew has white hair and beard also in the fresco from Bawit chapel 6.

[486] Quoted in Weis-Liebersdorf, *Christus- und Apostelbilder* (*supra*, note 461), 116, and Ficker, *Darstellungen* (*supra*, note 461), 30, from R. A. Lipsius, *Die Apokryphen Apostelgeschichten und Apostellegenden*, I (Braunschweig, 1883), 577, 582.

[487] Deichmann, *Bauten und Mosaiken*, pls. 57 and 335.

[488] *Ibid.*, pl. 267. Beardless also in the Election miniature of the Rabbula Gospels.

[489] *Ibid.*, pl. 230. The red-headed Thomas on the Cleveland tapestry is scarcely to be taken into account, for here normal conventions are often disregarded; cf. Shepherd, "Tapestry Panel," 103.

[490] Forsyth-Weitzmann, *St. Catherine*, pls. CXX, CLXff.; Weitzmann, "The Mosaic" (*supra*, note 200), figs. 13, 18, 21.

initial decoration of St. Demetrius' basilica in Salonica, that on the west wall of the inner north aisle.[491]

The outer border proper, that which decorated the rounded edge of the conch (fig. K), is an unusually elaborate version of another stereotyped border design, a representation in schematic perspective of the ends of a series of timber joists, normally all pointing in the same direction.[492] A common form of the basic motif gives an oblique view of the dentils or γεισήποδες of the classical cornice, themselves derivatives of the joists which carried an upper floor in timber construction. The dentils are set obliquely in their proper architectural context in the mosaic representation of a complete classical entablature at the head of the martyr zone in the Salonica Rotunda.[493] Divorced from its context this row of dentils was a popular border motif, which was used even in floor decoration.[494] More congruously, and at a date not far removed from the setting of the Lythrankomi mosaic, the motif appears in its simplest form as a framing border to the purely decorative mosaic in the east vault of S. Maria della Croce at Casaranello.[495] The use of an elaboration of the motif around the opening of the apse at Lythrankomi suggests appreciation of its origin, and an attempt by a trompe l'œil effect to simulate a structural cornice appropriate for such a position.[496] In its basic form the motif is used to suggest such an arching cornice in the mosaic decoration of the Dome of the Rock.[497] Our border is more subtly conceived with the joist ends alternating in direction to give the pattern a balanced rhythm.[497a] This elaboration is in step with the opulent and imaginative style of ornament attested for the third decade of the sixth century by the marble sculpture from the church of St. Polyeuktos, with which we have already observed a link in the Intermediate Border of our mosaic.

[491] M. and G. Soteriou, Ἡ βασιλικὴ τοῦ ἁγ. Δημητρίου Θεσσαλονίκης (supra, note 179), pls. 60–61.

[492] Recently discussed, with reference to examples as early as the Hellenistic period, by M. Restle, "Das Dekorationssystem im Westteil des Baptisteriums in San Marco zu Venedig," JÖBG, 21 (1972), 235. For the example in a fourth-century hypogeum near Iznik there cited, see now N. Fıratlı, "An Early Byzantine Hypogeum Discovered at İznik," Mansel'e Armağan (Mélanges Mansel), II (Ankara, 1974), 925 f. and pl. 334, b.

[493] Torp, Mosaikkene, fig. on p. 20. Compare the example in opus sectile, limited to the dentils, which was formerly to be seen at the top of the revetment of the main nave arcades of St. Demetrius, illustrated in color by Papageorghiou, in BZ, 17 (1908), pl. VI.

[494] E.g., at Antioch in Room 2 of the House of the Mysteries of Isis (Levi, Antioch Pavements, II, pl. CII, g). Panels made up of multiple rows of dentils also occur (ibid., pls. XV, a, XCIII, c, XCIV, e, and XLIV, e).

[495] Bovini, in CorsiRav, 11 (1964), 38, fig. 2. The character of the ornament fits the sixth-century date proposed by Wilpert. A related sixth-century representation of modillions in a context clearly revealing their architectural origin is provided by the Cleveland tapestry, on the lintel of the ciborium (Shepherd, "Tapestry Panel," back cover).

[496] Visually it would have performed the same function as the projecting arch which there is good reason to believe spanned the opening before the mosaic was set. See supra, p. 30.

[497] M. Gautier-van Berchem, in K. A. C. Creswell, Early Muslim Architecture, 2nd ed., I (Oxford, 1969), fig. 348 and pls. 15, a, 16, 17, a. References to further examples in pavement mosaics are given in notes 2 and 3 on p. 296.

[497a] Mr. Charalambos Bakirtzis has brought to our notice examples of dentils alternating in straight and oblique directions in classical architecture, in the cornices of the exedrae in the altar court of the Temple of Jupiter at Baalbek, where every fourth dentil is set obliquely, alternately to the right and left (Baalbek, I [Berlin-Leipzig, 1921], pl. 33). These are explained by the slightly forward projection of the entablature above each pilaster, the oblique dentils carrying the cornice at the angles. We can find no such rationale for the Lythrankomi border.

STYLE

Conformity with the demands of approved iconography, which in the sixth century seem to have become increasingly rigid, still left the mosaicist some latitude for the expression of his individual style. The areas where this is most in evidence are the rendering of faces and other exposed parts of the anatomy, the drapery treatment, and the range and balance of color.

In the faces preserved in the Panagia Kanakaria, the small size of the heads and the relatively large size of the tesserae used have forced the mosaicist to reduce the features to a very simple formula, well represented in the head of the Christ Child (fig. 89, color fig. 136). Secondly, with the sole exception of the one preserved archangel's head (fig. 76, color fig. 134), all are represented frontally. The most characteristic detail of this formula is the use of only two rows of tesserae, both of flesh color, between the eyelashes and the eyebrows. This gives all the faces a raised-eyebrow expression, which is usually avoided in heads of larger size by introducing an intermediate row of darker tesserae to define the upper outline of the eyelid. Exceptionally, in the head of Christ in the Sinai Transfiguration this outline is absent, as at Lythrankomi, but the eyelid is defined by using tesserae of a lighter tone in the row next to the eyelashes.[498] This device is also used in several of the Lythrankomi apostle heads, including Andrew (fig. 56, color fig. 141) and Matthew (fig. 60, color fig. 139). This imprecise rendering of the eyelid is seen again in the head of the Christ Child in the Poreč apse,[499] and here also by reason of the small scale. The appearance of this detail in these three mosaics does not denote any general community of style; for the other heads in the Sinai apse, both in the Transfiguration and in the apostle border, are far removed in style from those at Lythrankomi, while the rather wooden and malproportioned Poreč Christ Child offers a poor comparison to the Theanthropos in our mosaic.

The treatment of the slightly oblique head of the Lythrankomi archangel (fig. 76, color fig. 134) puts it in an intermediate position in the development of the increasingly formal Byzantine style. Fifth-century heads in comparable poses are usually drawn in true three-quarter view, with pear-shaped eyes.[500] The resulting "Hellenistic" quality was repeated in the archangel's head in the lost Theotokos panel of the St. Demetrius aisle mosaics, which Kluge recorded.[501] The Lythrankomi head is much closer to a frontal view: the nose is nearer to the center, the two ears are given equal prominence, and it is mainly by setting the iris of each eye to the side that the oblique pose is established. Already in the time of Theodoric the two innermost angels attending the Theotokos in the nave of S. Apollinare Nuovo accord her only a passing glance,[502] while in the later Turtura fresco the head of St. Audactus is only slightly turned and that of the Theotokos' other attendant is strictly

[498] Forsyth-Weitzmann, *St. Catherine*, pl. cv.
[499] Peirce-Tyler, *L'art byzantin*, II, pl. 60, b.
[500] E.g., the head of Ktisis in a fifth-century floor mosaic at Kourion: V. Karageorghis, *Cyprus* (London, 1969), pl. 180.
[501] N. K. Kluge, in *IRAIK*, 14 (1909), pl. 5.
[502] Deichmann, *Bauten und Mosaiken*, pl. 117.

frontal.[503] The archangels in the S. Vitale and Poreč apses are not altogether comparable since their attention is divided between the central image and the approaching patrons; but the advance of the frontal style is well enough illustrated by the panels in the Ravenna church representing Justinian and Theodora with their suites. At Lythrankomi, as much as anything about the archangel, it is the set of his wings, extended obliquely behind him to suggest arrested motion, that attach the figure to the less formal pre-Justinianic style.[504] No less evocative of that stylistic phase are the treatment of the other archangel's bare forearm and hand, in a rather sharply lit chiaroscuro, and the effective foreshortening of Christ's right foot (fig. 87).

Many tesserae in the archangel's face are in an advanced stage of decay and those in that of Christ have also suffered, but, thanks to the masonry that had covered them (probably since the twelfth century), most of the faces of the apostles surviving in the border are in good condition. In spite of the stereotyped treatment of the features, the execution of the flesh areas is sensitive: pink and white marble tesserae are broken with yellow or blue glass and grade to light purple and other shadow tones enriched with occasional red accents. This has given the apostles' heads a plasticity and a humanity not easily matched in the sixth century. They stand apart both from the awesome heads in the Sinai border and from their counterparts in S. Vitale; for the latter, by enlargement and elaboration of the eyes, foreshadow the more iconic type of image which was to predominate in Byzantine mosaic.[505] The softer quality in the Lythrankomi Matthew (fig. 60, color fig. 139), or even Andrew (fig. 56, color fig. 141), suggests connections with a tradition of more lifelike secular portraiture.

So far as we can judge from their inferior preservation, the heads of Christ and the archangel were of similar quality, though in the former the smaller scale in conjunction with the use of standard-size tesserae has made the eyes overlarge (fig. 89, color fig. 136). Indeed, in these two heads the same sensitive treatment of the flesh areas is apparent, notably in the attempt to give some form to the ears by varying the colors inside the outline. Also noteworthy is the mosaicist's attention to anatomical details, such as the ulna indicated on Christ's right wrist (fig. 86), a detail which is overlooked in Ravenna even in figures on a substantially larger scale.[506] The forearm of the archangel to the south is a no less telling example of our mosaicist's familiarity with realistic, three-dimensional figure style.

[503] Grabar, *Byzantium*, fig. 176. A similar phase in the growing predominance of the frontal style is represented by the archangels flanking the Theotokos in the niche fresco of Bawit chapel 28 (*ibid.*, fig. 193).

[504] Contrast the fully frontal poses of the corresponding figures in S. Vitale, in the mosaic from S. Michele in Affricisco, and in the Poreč apse. Fully frontal also are all four archangels in the Durrës mosaics (see note 371 *supra*).

[505] E.g., James and Andrew (Deichmann, *Bauten und Mosaiken*, pls. 336–37). On the other hand, Peter and Paul in S. Vitale (*ibid.*), more strongly colored and with heads set obliquely but eyes turned to the front, are more reminiscent of the style of the Ostrogothic period.

[506] Compare the right forearm of Abel in S. Vitale: G. Bovini, *San Vitale di Ravenna* (Milan, 1955), pl. 22; Deichmann, *Bauten und Mosaiken*, pl. 324.

The Lythrankomi mosaic has been pronounced archaic when considered in the framework of the Ravenna monuments and closest to the latest Ostrogothic examples.[507] That in style it is distinct from the decoration of the S. Vitale presbytery walls and vault, set probably in the fifth decade of the sixth century, comparison of the two apostle borders now permits us to confirm. On the other hand, while our mosaic may well have been set before the death of Theodoric in 526, the stark apostle busts set before 519/20 in the Archiepiscopal Chapel have too little in common with ours to allow an association with them on grounds of style.[508] The heads in the Chapel are much closer to those of the apostles in the Arian Baptistery. There, the somewhat extravagant use of strident red tesserae among the flesh tones, which is found also in Rome in the apse of SS. Cosmas and Damian,[509] reveals by contrast a quality in the Lythrankomi heads verging on the effeminate. Where the stark manner of Theodoric's mosaicists is modified in S. Apollinare Nuovo, notably in the Theotokos group in the nave, it is precisely there that the impact of Byzantine style is most in evidence. But even there, despite some iconographic links such as the mature Child, little affinity of style with the Lythrankomi mosaic can be claimed. And if a softer, more sophisticated style appears in mid-sixth-century Ravenna in the conch of S. Vitale, particularly in the heads of Christ and the archangel who presents the patron saint,[510] and if the figure of St. Apollinare in the conch of his basilica in Classe (consecrated 549)[511] comes rather close to the style of the Lythrankomi apostles, it does not follow that the Cypriot mosaic is the contemporary of these two Ravenna apses. Rather must we envisage in Byzantine mosaic figure style a continuing tradition of Hellenistic descent, the full impact of which was not felt in the West before the campaigns of Belisarius. Of this tradition the Lythrankomi apse is an earlier, and also probably a closer, reflection.

In the absence of surviving examples in the capital, the continuity of this Byzantine tradition can be traced to some extent in Salonica. Here, despite changes of conception and iconography in a space of nearly two centuries, the painterly figure style of the seventh-century pier mosaics in St. Demetrius is still basically that of the fifth-century martyrs in the Rotunda. Most of the intervening examples of this style cover only a limited period in the late fifth and the beginning of the sixth century. It is well illustrated in the Hosios David conch and by the two heads on the ambon of Basilica B at Nikopolis.[512] Those of Christ and Peter in the fragmentary *Traditio legis* mosaic

---

[507] Bettini, *La pittura bizantina* (*supra*, note 4), 43 f.

[508] For the view that our mosaic is later than those in the Ravenna Chapel, see Galassi, "Musaici di Cipro," 7; also Ottolenghi, "La cappella arcivescovile in Ravenna" (*supra*, note 406), 27.

[509] Under Felix IV (526–30); Oakeshott, *Mosaics of Rome* (*supra*, note 277), pls. XI–XIII.

[510] Deichmann, *Bauten und Mosaiken*, pls. VIII, 351, and 354. We assume that the conch was set at the same time as the imperial panels below it, between 540 and 548.

[511] *Ibid.*, pls. XII and 389. Compare also the head of Melchisedek in the seventh-century panel (*ibid.*, pl. 400) with Andrew at Lythrankomi.

[512] G. Soteriou, Ψηφιδοταὶ προσωπογραφίαι ἐκ Νικοπόλεως, in 'Επ.'Ετ.Βυζ.Σπ., 23 (1953), 519ff. Xyngopoulos regards them as heads of saints and places them around 500: Αἱ δύο ψηφιδωταὶ προσωπογραφίαι τῆς Νικοπόλεως, in 'Αρχ.Δελτ., 22 (1967), 15–20. See also note 417 *supra*.

at Pola, for which a date in the sixth century is preferred,[513] appear to belong
to the same tradition. What survives of the original mosaic decoration in
St. Demetrius reveals a more popular interpretation with a well-molded, fleshy
quality in the faces, particularly in those of St. Demetrius and the flying
angel on the west wall of the north aisle.[514] This quality recurs in early encaustic
icons attributable to Constantinople, for example, in the faces of the angels
behind the enthroned Theotokos and in the Christ Child on the panel in the
Sinai monastery, though here associated with the more disembodied, glyptic
aspect of the other faces.[514a] The realistic handling of the forms and flesh
tones at Lythrankomi is then part and parcel of Early Byzantine figure style.
The question how far this is indicative of a relatively early date in the sixth
century for our mosaic is less easily answered.

The development of Byzantine pictorial style cannot be regarded as a
gradual rejection of its Hellenistic ancestry in favor of an increasingly hieratic
mode; rather, as Kitzinger has stressed, was the classical tradition an ever-
present source of inspiration which could be tapped or ignored as changes in
official policy and popular taste required. Nor can there have been any simple
choice between current formalizing trends and the greater freedom and
impressionism of a single alternative earlier style. The antique statuary,
manuscript illustrations, and figural representations on minor works of art
of diverse origins and dates surviving in Constantinople in the sixth century
must have offered the Byzantine painters a wide variety of styles on which
to draw if they wished.[515] It is doubtless this factor rather than any great
disparity in date that explains the difference between the heads of the
Lythrankomi apostles and those of the figures in the Sinai mosaic, particularly
if Weitzmann is correct in attributing the latter to craftsmen from Constantinople. He has compared the gaunt head of the Baptist to an antique tragic
mask.[516] This head, with the two prophets in the Transfiguration and Andrew,
among others, in the border—their heads set obliquely with heavily shaded
eye sockets below beetling brows—all evoke the Scopaic phase of later Greek
sculpture. This is reflected also in a floor mosaic of the third century near
Baalbek, in the busts of the seven philosophers encircling Calliope,[517] and in

---

[513] A. Morassi, "La chiesa di Santa Maria Formosa del Canneto in Pola," *BA*, 4 (1924–25), 23;
Bettini, *La pittura bizantina* (*supra*, note 4), 50.

[514] M. and G. Soteriou, Ἡ βασιλικὴ τοῦ ἁγ. Δημητρίου Θεσσαλονίκης (*supra*, note 179), pls. 60–61.

[514a] Grabar, *Iconography*, pl. III. Insofar as this icon can take its place with the Sinai panel of St. Peter
(G. and M. Soteriou, *Icônes du Mont Sinaï*, I [Athens, 1956], pls. 1–3 and color pl.) as a product of
the "Justinianic revival" in the late seventh century, this "Pompeiian" facial treatment could derive
from some much earlier prototype (cf. Kitzinger, "Between Justinian and Iconoclasm," 30 and 32 f.).

[515] Even under Justinian the adornment of the city with antique sculptures from pagan shrines
continued. Nor was paganism entirely eradicated in his time. Cf. C. Mango, "Antique Statuary and
the Byzantine Beholder," *DOP*, 17 (1963), 58. On the dichotomy of sixth-century Constantinopolitan
art as between "perennial Hellenism" and increasingly abstract sytle, see Kitzinger, "Between Justinian and Iconoclasm," 18 ff.

[516] Forsyth-Weitzmann, *St. Catherine*, pl. CXXIV; K. Weitzmann, in *ProcAmPhS*, III (1966), 392 ff.
and reference quoted in note 23. For the view that the mosaicists who worked in the Sinai monastery
came from Constantinople, see Forsyth-Weitzmann, *St. Catherine*, 12, 16.

[517] M. Chéhab, *Mosaïques du Liban* = *Bull. du Musée de Beyrouth*, 14 (1957), Texte, 43, and 15
(1959), Planches, pl. XV ff. For the comparable head of St. Andrew in the Sinai mosaic, see Forsyth-
Weitzmann, *St. Catherine*, pl. CXVI, A.

some Christian products of "Syrian expressionism," which, however, by the late sixth century had been naturalized in metropolitan art.[518] Wherever they came from, the Sinai mosaicists did not invent this dramatic style but drew on a living tradition of long standing. Those working at Lythrankomi sought to offset the rigid framework of their composition and the stereotyped features of their apostle heads by recourse to a more naturalistic tradition which had derived, through Graeco-Roman art, from a different strain in late classical style. It is worth remembering that it was Apelles, contemporary of Alexander and master of realism, whom the writers of Byzantine *ekphraseis* were wont extravagantly to claim their contemporaries had surpassed. In Cyprus, as elsewhere, examples of the realistic late classical figure style were not lacking: a wealth of Antonine marble statuary after Greek originals has been recovered during excavation of the Salamis gymnasium[519] and, apart from mythological representations surviving in both floor[520] and wall mosaics of the Graeco-Roman period,[521] the currency of the style in fifth-century Christian contexts is attested by the Kourion Ktisis.[522] The Lythrankomi mosaicists did not depend directly on such local models, but their work does reflect the continued currency, in the early sixth century, of a naturalistic, organic figure style of Hellenic descent.[523]

Turning to drapery treatment, we find quite as startling a contrast between the soft, flowing robes of the Christ Child and the Theotokos at Lythrankomi and the angular folds of that worn by Christ in the Sinai apse. Even allowing for the conscious adoption of a more abstract mode for the transfigured Christ, the linearism of this striking figure marks a great advance on the Justinianic norm. The drapery in our mosaic, on the other hand, is considerably less stylized than that in the apses of S. Vitale and the Poreč basilica, and repeats much of the organic, flowing quality of the robes of Christ in the conch of Hosios David in Salonica. The modeling of folds is achieved by a realistic use of light and shade and, at some points, by the casting of shadows from one fold onto its neighbor, or from the sleeve of the south archangel's chiton onto the forearm. Niceties of this sort are, however, often subordinated to the principle of what may be called stereoscopic projection. This demands

---

[518] See Kitzinger, "Between Justinian and Iconoclasm," 35–38.

[519] V. Karageorghis, *Sculptures from Salamis*, I (Nicosia, 1964), *passim*. Some of this classical statuary was still displayed in the seventh century in the Gymnasium Baths after their reconstruction, probably under Justinian.

[520] At Paphos: K. Nicolaou, "The Mosaics at Kato Paphos—The House of Dionysos," *RDAC*, 1963, p. 56 ff. and pl. x; W. A. Daszewski, "Polish Excavations at Kato (Nea) Paphos in 1968–1969," *RDAC*, 1970, pl. xxiii, 1. At Kourion: V. Karageorghis, in *BCH*, 92 (1968), 346–48 (gladiator mosaics).

[521] At Salamis: V. Karageorghis, *Salamis in Cyprus* (London, 1969), pls. xvii, 123, 124.

[522] See *supra*, note 500.

[523] That this style was still alive, though in decline, in the secular art of Antioch is attested by some of its early sixth-century floor mosaics such as the Worcester Hunt, where a statuesque huntsman poses as its centerpiece (Levi, *Antioch Pavements*, II, pl. lxxxvi, b). A certain kinship with the heads of Christ and of the archangel at Lythrankomi is seen in the treatment of the personification of Ge from the House of Aion and in that of the bust which gave its name to the House of Ktisis (*ibid.*, pls. lxxxiv, d, and lxxxv, a), both assigned by Levi to the early sixth century. Cf. Soteriou, Τοιχογ-ραφίαι μοναστικῆς τέχνης (*supra*, note 7), 246. The question whether our mosaic should be attached to an Antiochene school is one which we consider *infra*.

that highlighted forms and forward planes should be given maximum relief by offsetting them against darker tones, while shaded forms are given greater depth by illuminating whatever adjoins them. Thus the shaded folds passing around Christ's left leg, below the Virgin's hand, end incongruously in a highlight to accentuate the deep shadow and recession of the adjoining area of the maphorion (fig. 79). And while the varying blue grounds of the apostles' medallions may consciously represent the concave form of clipei, the darker tones also serve to set off the highlighted right shoulders, while the shadows on the other shoulders are intensified by the lighter blues used above them (e.g., frontispiece, color figs. 140–43). We shall return to these devices in the discussion of technique; here it should be noted that stereoscopic projection was used in other sixth-century mosaics.[524]

It remains to consider the color element in the style of the Lythrankomi mosaic. As is to be expected in a small provincial church the palette used is not particularly rich.[525] What is impressive is the restraint with which it is used, resulting in a somewhat subdued spectrum of color which contrasts with the more garish quality of most mosaics in the West. Nor should it be forgotten that the startling effect of the whitened zone comprising the back of the throne and the cushion, now sharply dividing the dark turquoise of the mandorla from the dark blue of the maphorion, is entirely adventitious. Originally this would have been a zone of muted red, composed of white marble tesserae dipped in an earth color. The same is true of the seemingly brilliant highlight on the inner side of the irisated frame of the mandorla.

The temperate quality of the overall color scheme serves as a foil to the occasional accents of brilliance, such as the nimbus of Christ and the footstool, where both silver and gold are used. Equally telling though less extensive must have been the glitter of gold and silver embroidery on the cushion. Gold highlights still catch the eye on the archangel's staff, on Christ's sandals, and on the clavus of His chiton, here, as on that of the archangel's garment, representing gold thread embroidery. The silver highlights on the blue chitons of Christ and the archangel are not repeated on the apostles' garments; and elsewhere silver is used only for the arms of the nimbus cross, for pearls on the footstool, and for the archangel's nimbus. No silver tesserae are used to add sparkle to the borders as in Hosios David in Salonica, though gold serves not only for the settings of the jewels of the intermediate border, but also to outline the "joist ends" in the outer border. These are relatively few accents of brilliance in what the preserved areas indicate was a color scheme of admirable restraint. Coupled with it was a certain sophistication in the avoidance of monotonous repetitions of color associations. In the figures, the color of the outer and inner garments is never the same,[526] though

[524] The Poreč apse provides a striking example in the unnatural illumination of the cushion at the point where the Virgin is seated on it (see note 187 *supra*).

[525] See list *infra*, p. 136.

[526] Contrast the curious monochrome figures in some of the scenes of the Life of Christ in S. Apollinare Nuovo (e.g., Grabar, *Byzantium*, fig. 165).

different tones of the same color are occasionally found together; and in the surviving apostle busts no combination of garment colors is ever repeated.

The style of the Lythrankomi mosaic, we may conclude, is not closely matched in any other surviving monument. Where there are links with the Ravenna mosaics they are with the later Ostrogothic monuments, rather than with those set following the establishment of Byzantine rule in 540. On the other hand, while sharing with the pre-Justinianic mosaics of Salonica their attachment to an organic figure style of Hellenic descent, our mosaic displays a more rigidly decorative manner which matches what we know of the art of Constantinople when Justinian came to the throne. In style it is far removed from the austere representation of the Transfiguration in the monastery of St. Catherine, and nowhere does it reveal the anticlassical, abstract tendencies of which that representation, if it was indeed set in 565, offers some of the earliest surviving evidence. There is thus no conflict on grounds of style with the indications already noted that our mosaic was set in or about the third decade of the sixth century.

THE PALEOGRAPHY OF THE INSCRIPTIONS

Letter-forms

The notorious lack of consistency in the lettering of late antique inscriptions, even in a single technique and in restricted areas, makes it doubtful if much can be learned from the choice of letter-forms in the names of the apostles in the Lythrankomi mosaic. But as some rather distinctive forms are used (fig. N) a comparison with those of approximately contemporary inscriptions is not out of place.

The only other wall mosaic inscriptions surviving in Cyprus are those in the apse of the Kiti church; and there the labels of the three figures offer little scope for comparison, since they do not include several of the most significant letters, such as *upsilon* and *omega*.[527] One of the two *rho*s, that of ΓΑΒΡΙΗΛ, has a tail made of a single tessera as in both examples of the letter in the names of the Lythrankomi apostles (figs. N, 41, 42). But the *beta*s in the two churches are quite distinct; that used at Kiti is angular at the top and has a straight bar at the bottom extending beyond the limits of the letter in both directions. In addition the whole character of the Kiti letters differs through the use of contrasting thick and thin lines. Double rows of tesserae are used for the former; in the Lythrankomi church the letters are rendered throughout with a single row. These are indications that the inscriptions in the Kiti church are the more developed, as are the style and iconography of its mosaic, which suggest a date for its setting in the late sixth century at the earliest.[528]

---

[527] Šmit, Παναγία 'Αγγελόκτιστος (*supra*, note 4), color plate supplement; Megaw-Stylianou, *Mosaics and Frescoes*, pl. III.

[528] Megaw-Stylianou, *op. cit.*, 14. For points favoring a date within the sixth century, see Megaw, "Metropolitan or Provincial?", 75f.

The floor mosaics which have been exposed in Cyprus offer a few inscriptions for comparison. That found under the church of St. Spyridon at Tremetousha in a pavement datable to the late fourth century[529] is too early to be relevant; nor are its wide forms, its angle-bar *alpha*s, and its very open *omega*s at all comparable.[530] The most extensive are those in the buildings annexed to the baths by the theater at Kourion.[531] Coins discovered under the *Ktisis* panel in the bath proper provide a terminus post quem in the early fifth century,[532] both for this panel and for those of similar quality in the annex containing the only substantial inscriptions. The use here of the "square" alphabet as well as the angle-bar *alpha* puts the names of the apostles in the Panagia Kanakaria far apart from these fifth-century inscriptions, despite the appearance in both of the tailed *rho* and the barred *upsilon* and the use, exceptionally, of two lunate *sigma*s in the name of the Kourion *Ktisis*. The apostle names are clearly closer to an inscription in the "oval" alphabet in the Paphos Museum, from a floor of sixth/seventh-century style.[533]

Monumental and funerary inscriptions on stone and marble are more numerous, but only to a limited extent are these comparable with our mosaicist's lettering, which followed the more cursive forms painted rapidly on the fresh plaster. Mitford has indicated the main lines of development in the lapicide's letter-forms in Cyprus from the fifth to the seventh century.[534] The narrow "oval" alphabet of the fragment of a rescript of Justinian from Kythraea, possibly of the year 554,[535] offers the closest similarity to the Lythrankomi mosaic inscriptions among the few dated specimens on which Mitford's sequence is based. The *alpha*s are similar, as are the pear-shaped *theta*s and *omicron*s, and the *mu* has an incipient *gutta* below the point of the angle-bar. But here the distinctive forms of the ρ, υ, and ω in our mosaic are not repeated. Nor are they found in the fragment of an earlier imperial ordinance in the Cyprus Museum,[536] which Mitford connects with an edict of Anastasius using the same letter-forms from the southern Hauran.[537] They were again out of fashion by the second quarter of the seventh century, to judge by the long series of inscriptions recording work on the Salamis aque-

---

[529] A. Papageorghiou, in Κυπρ.Σπουδ., 30 (1966), 25 and pl. VIII, 2; V. Karageorghis, in *BCH*, 91 (1967), 366, fig. 174.

[530] The same can be said of the shorter and inferior, but approximately contemporary, inscription in the Soli basilica: *BCH*, 91 (1967), 362, fig. 170. Those in the floor of the Ayia Trias basilica near Yialousa are associated with patterns suggestive of a renovation not before the late fifth century (*ILN* [March 1975], 79); but the square alphabet they employ is entirely different from that used in the Lythrankomi mosaic. [See Megaw, "Interior Decoration," 13 and fig. 18.]

[531] *Pennsylvania University Museum Bulletin*, 7 (1938), no. 2, 4 ff.; *ibid.*, 14 (1950), no. 4, 27 ff. and pls. VII–VIII; T. B. Mitford, *The Inscriptions of Kourion* (Philadelphia, 1971), 352ff., nos 201–6.

[532] *JHS*, 71 (1951), 259; Megaw, "Metropolitan or Provincial?," 60 and note 5.

[533] *BCH*, 88 (1964), 374 and fig. 109, from Ktima.

[534] T. B. Mitford, "Some New Inscriptions from Early Christian Cyprus," *Byzantion*, 20 (1950), 105–75, table on p. 172.

[535] *Ibid.*, 132, no. 7 and note 3.

[536] *Ibid.*, 162, no. 22. Nor yet in the Philoxenos inscription, not before 533 if it refers to Philoxenos the Younger, though this repeats the "oval" *omicron*, *epsilon*, and *sigma* (see note 262 *supra*).

[537] *Syria: Princeton Univ. Arch. Exped., 1904–5 and 1909*, III, A (Leyden, 1921), 24ff., no. 20.

duct.[538] On the other hand, the undated Soli text recording the restoration of an *apantiterion*, which Mitford would not place before the late sixth century, has not only *rho*s with tails, *upsilon*s with crossbars, and divided *omega*s,[539] but has also a *mu* approximating those in the names of Bartholomew and Thomas in the Panagia Kanakaria (figs. N, 29, 30). But the same forms of *upsilon* and *omega* are found, though not together, on inscriptions for which an early sixth-century date is more suitable,[540] and the tailed *rho* occurs in the painted inscriptions of the *hagiasma* at Salamis-Constantia, which have been assigned to the reign of Justinian.[541] Taken as a whole, and in isolation, the paleography of Cypriot inscriptions on marble would indicate a date for the labels in the Panagia Kanakaria mosaic in the reign of Justinian, or a little before or after.

Outside Cyprus there are two important series of inscriptions in wall mosaics for comparison: those in Salonica and those in the monastery of St. Catherine in Sinai. The former begins with the labels of the martyrs in the calendar mosaic in the Rotunda of St. George.[542] These display a strikingly narrow alphabet, giving *theta*s, *omicron*s, and *sigma*s the forms which became prevalent in the sixth century and were used in the Panagia Kanakaria. Two of the distinctive letter-forms found in the Cyprus mosaic also occur: the *mu* with *gutta* and the barred *upsilon*. Nevertheless, the Rotunda inscriptions have a monumental quality which, together with their angle-bar *alpha*s and their *omega*s in the form of an inverted M, puts them in a different and evidently earlier class than the names of the Kanakaria apostles.

The published photographs and drawings of the mosaics in the north aisle of the basilica of St. Demetrius, which were destroyed in the fire of 1917, give further indications of the letter-forms current in Salonica in the late fifth century.[543] The short inscription beside the orant figure of St. Demetrius of the westernmost panel,[544] already damaged in the seventh-century fire, had much in common with the Rotunda inscriptions but not their elongated letter-forms. It included three examples of the barred *upsilon* but no other significant links with our apostle medallions. Not all the saints portrayed in comparable medallions in the Salonica church are named, but where they are the inscriptions differ both in the way they were written, circumscript,

---

[538] Mitford, *op. cit.*, 125 and table at p. 172, nos. 4–5, *LBW*, 2763, 2764, and 2766.

[539] *Ibid.*, 151, no. 17 and table at p. 172. However, the presence here of the later form of *theta* with crossbar extending on either side speaks against a very close association of the Lythrankomi alphabet with this late sixth-century inscription. One of the earliest dated examples of this later form of *theta* in mosaic is in the predominantly "square" alphabet of the *ananeosis* inscription of 539 adjoining the hunting mosaic at Apamea: Balty, *La grande mosaïque de chasse du Triclinos* (*supra*, note 396), pl. XVIII.

[540] The *upsilon*, Mitford, *op. cit.*, 160, no. 21; the *omega*, *ibid.*, 139, no. 11.

[541] *AntJ*, 13 (1933), 105, fig. 3; for the date, *AntJ*, 19 (1939), 443 ff. For a more complete study, see M. A. Sacopoulo, in *CahArch*, 13 (1962), 61 ff.

[542] On the date, see note 197 *supra*, and on the inscriptions, see the recent article by G. Gounaris there cited. He concludes that the letter-forms and the abbreviations are admissible both for the mid-fifth century and for the close of the fourth, the dating which he, among others, still prefers.

[543] On this dating, see note 179 *supra*.

[544] Cormack, "S. Demetrios," pl. 11, b.

not vertically, and in the use of the *alpha* with angle-bar.[545] Only one of the early mosaics found during Soteriou's investigations is inscribed: a fragmentary bust of St. Demetrius in a niche on the south side of the apse, in which position it probably belongs to the earliest phase of the decoration. The inscription does employ the cursive *alpha*, but in conjunction with a square *sigma* quite alien to the Panagia Kanakaria alphabet.[546] Approximately contemporary with the inscriptions of the original decoration in St. Demetrius is the apse mosaic in Hosios David.[547] Here both types of *alpha* appear as well as the *upsilon* with crossbar and a *mu* with a prolonged *gutta*; and the *omega*s, unlike those used in the Rotunda, are close to the form used in the Cyprus mosaic (figs. N, 53, 54).

Such links as these with the pre-Justinianic mosaics of Salonica are not decisive because they are balanced by others with the inscriptions set in St. Demetrius during the restoration in the second quarter of the seventh century.[548] Here the *alpha* type of the Panagia Kanakaria is used, the *omega*s are virtually identical, and the *upsilon* with crossbar recurs. On the other hand there are new developments, such as the *theta* with crossbar extending on either side.[549] Consequently, all that can be said is that the letter-forms used in the Salonica mosaics, taken as a whole, reveal no paleographical anomaly in placing those used in the Panagia Kanakaria within, or close to, the reign of Justinian.

The inscriptions in the Sinai mosaic are of importance for checking this conclusion, since its completion cannot be dated before the autumn of 565.[550] Making allowance for the rather large size of the letters (eight to ten tesserae high against five to seven in the Cyprus church), those used in the medallions of the Sinai mosaic are very similar. An "oval" alphabet is employed with *theta*s and *omicron*s frequently of the pear-shaped form, similar *alpha*s, and, in addition, almost all the special forms found in the Panagia Kanakaria: the *mu* with a *gutta* below the angle-bar (Matthew and Mark), the *rho* with tail (Andrew), and the *upsilon* with crossbar. The only apparent conflict is in the use of the "square" *omega* of inverted M form, both in the medallions (Thomas and Simon) and in the Transfiguration (James and John).[551] But to

---

[545] *Ibid.*, pls. 3 (Pelagia and Matrona) and 14, a (name illegible). Cf. Uspenskij, *IRAIK*, 14 (1909), pl. x; Grabar, *Martyrium*, II, p. 365, fig. 145.

[546] M. and G. Soteriou, Ἡ βασιλικὴ τοῦ ἀγ. Δημητρίου Θεσσαλονίκης (*supra*, note 179), 198 and pl. 71, b. The Soterious related this fragment to the mosaics with which the piers of the bema were decorated after the seventh-century reconstruction. But the St. Demetrius fragment is on a part of the structure unaffected by the fire, and in all the pier inscriptions the "oval" *sigma* is used.

[547] See note 199 *supra*.

[548] Uspenskij, *IRAIK*, 14 (1909), pls. xiv–xv; M. and G. Soteriou, *op. cit.*, pls. 63, 66, 67, and 71, a. On the date of the restoration, see P. Lemerle, in *BZ*, 46 (1953), 356. It must have been undertaken without delay following the fire, which occurred soon after the death of Archbishop John (about 620 or 630). An inscription on a related patch in the aisle mosaics referred to the restoration, so the pier mosaics are unlikely to have been later than the mid-seventh century (Kitzinger, "Between Justinian and Iconoclasm," 26).   [549] On the appearance of this type of *theta*, see *supra*, note 539.

[550] See *supra*, note 200.

[551] Forsyth-Weitzmann, *St. Catherine*, pls. cx, cxi, cliii, A, and clvi, B. Rare after the fifth century, the inverted M form is used in an inscription of 533 at Gerasa (*Gerasa*, p. 470, no. 278, pl. cxxx, b, and p. 367, fig. 16); in the church at Zahrani, in the diaconicon floor inscription dated 535 (Chéhab, in *Bull. du Musée de Beyrouth*, 14 [*supra*, note 517], p. 105, no. 10, and pl. lviii, 3); in the Qabr Hiram

provide one more link with the Cyprus mosaic, the type of *omega* used there reappears in the dedicatory inscription below the Transfiguration, though here with interior decorative elements.[552] These similarities would weigh against assigning the Lythrankomi inscriptions to the very early sixth century, unless those in the Sinai apse can be regarded as in some degree *retardataires*.

Although floor mosaic inscriptions are not equally comparable, there is such a large series of them in the Syro-Palestinian area, and so many of them are dated, that they do provide some indication of the period when the distinctive letter-forms used in the Panagia Kanakaria were in vogue there. Two of them, the *mu* with *gutta* and the tailed *rho*, appear at Antioch only in the two series laid after the earthquake of 526: Bath F, the upper level, and the Machouka church.[553] Others, the barred *upsilon* and the divided *omega*, are not found there, though they occur in earlier Antioch floors.[554] And where these four distinctive forms are used they are not associated with the cursive *alpha* of our apostle labels. While there is no single inscription at Antioch displaying all or even the majority of their characteristics their closest connections are with some of the latest of the Antiochene series. This is borne out to some extent by examination of the numerous inscriptions at Gerasa associated with Bishop Paul, who was active in the fourth decade of the sixth century. For there the cursive *alpha* is almost always used, the divided *omega* reappears,[555] as does the barred *upsilon*.[556] The *mu* with *gutta* and the tailed *rho* do not occur in sixth-century Gerasa, though this form of *rho* was used in 539 at Qasr el-Lebia in Cyrenaica[557] and the distinctive *mu* in 555 in the floor at Sumātā south of Tyre.[558]

---

mosaic floor in the Louvre dated 575/76 (E. Renan, *Mission en Phoenicie* [Paris, 1864–74], p. 615 and pl. XLIX); and in the inscriptions of the upper floor at Ain es-Samaké (Chéhab, *op. cit.*, p. 176 and pl. CXV). These last are dated to the years 661 and 685, but the era used is uncertain. That of Berytus yields 580/81 and 604/5, which do not correspond with the indiction years recorded.

[552] Forsyth-Weitzmann, *St. Catherine*, pl. CXIV. These are not rare in the sixth century: Gerasa, dated 531, church of St. John the Baptist (*Gerasa*, p. 479, no. 306, and pls. LXVI, b, LXVII, a); Gerasa, dated 533, church of SS. Cosmas and Damian (*ibid.*, p. 482, no. 314, and pl. LXXIII; also p. 367, fig. 16, nos. 311–16); Madaba, dated 596, Sergius inscription in the crypt of the church of the Prophet Elias (*IRAIK*, 8 [1903], 98); also the rather later dedication of Leontios dated 604 (C. M. Kaufmann, *Handbuch der altchristlichen Epigraphik* [Freiburg im Breisgau, 1917], p. 406, fig. 237). On wall mosaics, similarly decorated *omegas* are used in the apse of Hosios David in Salonica on the roll held by Christ (Xyngopoulos, Καθολικὸν, pls. 6 and 8).

[553] *Antioch-on-the-Orontes*, III (*supra*, note 382), p. 84, no. 112, and pl. 47, no. 104 (Bath F); Levi, *Antioch Pavements*, I, 369, and II, pl. CXLI, b (Machouka church). See also *ibid.*, 626 (chronological table) and 629 (table of letter-forms).

[554] The *upsilon* and *omega* in the mosaic of Megalopsychia, ca. 450 (Levi, *Antioch Pavements*, I, 323, and II, pls. LXXVI–LXXX); the *omega* in the Mosaic of the Biblical Inscription of somewhat later date (*ibid.*, I, 320, and II, pl. CXXXI, a). The *upsilon* also occurs at Serdjilla in central Syria in a floor inscription dated 473 (*RA*, 39 [1901], pt. 2, 62–67 and pl. XII).

[555] Unassociated dedication of 533: *Gerasa*, p. 469, no. 277, pl. CXXX, a, and p. 367, fig. 16 (table of alphabets).

[556] Painted on a building block of the church of SS. Cosmas and Damian where the floors are dated 533: *ibid.*, p. 483, no. 318, pl. CXXXIII, f, and p. 367, fig. 16. Also used in 535 at Zahrani: Chéhab, *Bull. du Musée de Beyrouth*, 14, p. 105, no. 10, and pl. LVIII, 3.

[557] R. Goodchild, "Christian Mosaics at Qaṣr el-Labia," *ILN*, December 14, 1957, Suppl. following p. 1034; H. Sichtermann, in *AA*, 1959, col. 346, fig. 107 ff.

[558] *QDAP*, 3 (1933), 99 ff. and pls. XXX–XXXI. Compare at Gerasa the *gutta* of an angle-bar *alpha* in the dedicatory inscription in the church of St. John the Baptist naming Bishop Paul: *Gerasa*, p. 479, no. 306, pl. LXVI, b, and p. 367, fig. 16.

Another indication that the inscriptions in the Cyprus mosaic should not be placed much before the close of the Antioch floor series (*ca.* 530) is provided by the letter-forms used on the Phela cross in the Dumbarton Oaks Collection, said to have been found near Latakia.[559] This bears no date or control stamps, but it formed part of a silver treasure which was not buried before the third quarter of the sixth century, for it included a paten with stamps of Justin II.[560] The cross, which is not necessarily contemporary with the paten, is of the type with tear-drop serifs at the ends of the arms, a type at least as old as the time of Justinian.[561] Like a second paten in the find, which bears an inscription employing similar letter-forms and likewise ending with the name of the *kome* Phela, but no stamps,[562] the Dumbarton Oaks cross was evidently inscribed locally. The two objects provide evidence of the letter-forms favored on the Syrian coast, possibly as early as the mid-sixth century, and these have much in common with those used in the Panagia Kanakaria, despite the presence of "square" *epsilon*s and *sigma*s, for these long survived in Syria. The *mu* with *gutta*, the tailed *rho*, the barred *upsilon*, and the divided *omega* all appear. Such close correspondence weighs against placing our mosaic much before the time of Justinian. Furthermore, this affinity with the Phela silver suggests continuing close relations between Cyprus and the Syrian coast at the time the mosaic was set.[563]

To compare the rapidly executed lettering of a mosaicist working in Cyprus with the monumental inscriptions of Constantinople is, to say the least, unpromising. Yet even there some confirmatory links exist. The *mu* with the *gutta* is used in the large and elegant inscription on the architectural blocks sound at Saraçhane in Istanbul in 1960, which led to the identification of the ifte of the church of St. Polyeuktos, erected *ca.* 524–27.[564] The same form is used in the very similar inscription of the Empress Theodora encircling the interior entablature of the church of SS. Sergius and Bacchus, on which work started in 527. And here too the *upsilon* with crossbar is normal.[565] Whatever

[559] M. C. Ross, *Catalogue of the Byzantine and Early Mediaeval Antiquities in the Dumbarton Oaks Collection*, I (Washington, D.C., 1962), 14 f., and pl. XVIII.

[560] Abegg Stiftung, Bern, inv. no. 8.37.63; cf. Cruikshank Dodd, *Silver Treasures*, p. 24 ff., no. 6, and pls. XI–XII.

[561] Compare the cross in the *opus sectile* panel forming part of the revetment of the west wall of the nave of Hagia Sophia: P. A. Underwood, "Notes on the Work of the Byzantine Institute in Istanbul: 1957–59," *DOP*, 14 (1960), p. 206 ff. and fig. 3. Though possibly not in its original position, it presumably formed part of the Justinianic revetment. Crosses with similar teardrop serifs appear in the original mosaic decoration (*ibid.*, fig. 6).

[562] Abegg Stiftung, Bern, inv. no. 8.36.63; cf. Cruikshank Dodd, *Silver Treasures*, p. 26, no. 7, and pl. XIII. The letter-forms of the dedication of Sabiniana, Martha, and Maria to the Theotokos are similar to those on the cross, except that narrow "oval" *epsilon*s and *sigma*s appear side by side with the "square" forms used exclusively on the cross.

[563] None of the inscriptions on the stamped silver imported to Syria in the sixth century (including the stamped paten from the Phela find) offer the same close parallels.

[564] *DOP*, 15 (1961), p. 243 ff. and figs. 1–3. The same form is repeated on the further sections of the inscriptions found in the subsequent excavations: *DOP*, 20 (1966), p. 228 and figs. 6–7; *DOP*, 21 (1967), p. 276 and fig. 10.

[565] A. van Millingen, *Byzantine Churches in Constantinople* (London, 1912), fig. 20, and, for the M, pl. XIV. Grabar has observed a relationship between the lettering of this inscription and of those encircling the Monza and Bobbio ampullae: Grabar, *Ampoules*, 14. On these the *mu* with *gutta* is used consistently.

weight these correspondences are given, they do support the conclusion that, despite affinities with the inscriptions of the Sinai mosaic, the paleographical evidence as a whole does allow, though it does not impose, a date for the Cyprus mosaic near the beginning of the reign of Justinian.

Column Writing

It is at first sight surprising that, while many of the letter-forms used in the Panagia Kanakaria appear in the labels of the apostles and prophets in the Sinai mosaic, the manner of composing the names in the two mosaics is so different. Instead of writing *kionedon* in the manner of the Lythrankomi mosaicist,[566] the Sinai mosaicist used a compromise between that system and normal horizontal writing. He divided the names into units of one, two, or three letters and set these units one below the other so that, as in the Cyprus medallions, the first part of the name is on the left of the head and the remainder on the right: e.g., A|N‖ΔP|EAC, ΦI|ΛIΠ‖ΠOC.[567] The shape of the areas available for the names was the determining factor. The absence of nimbi in the Sinai medallions provided a format which made fully vertical writing unnecessary, but its influence is felt, particularly when single letters do occasionally appear one below the other.[568] On the other hand, in the Panagia Kanakaria two letters are occasionally set side by side where the length of the name required it: e.g., B|A|P|ΘO‖Λ|O|ME|OC. Both sets of labels clearly belong to the period when to write *kionedon* was regarded as an acceptable device where the space available was unsuitable for a horizontal inscription.[569] Later, by the seventh century, the practice became general and was often applied where there were no restrictions of space to justify it. Consequently, because of the absence of nimbi in the Sinai mosaic, the more fully vertical labels in the Panagia Kanakaria cannot be used as a criterion in support of a later date for our mosaic. On the other hand, to establish when this form of writing first gained acceptance would provide a useful terminus a quo.

In the Greek inscriptions of Northern Syria, vertical writing, when suited to the space available, was current quite early in the sixth century. It appears

---

[566] Γράφεται κιονηδὸν δίκην κίονος ἤτοι παραλλήλως κατὰ γραμμήν. Thus, *Scholia in Dionysii Thracis Artem grammaticam*, ed. A. Hilgard, in *Grammatici Graeci*, pt. I, vol. 3 (Leipzig, 1901), p. 191, line 18.

[567] The division of the names is conveniently indicated in van Berchem-Clouzot, *Mosaïques*, 185. For some of the names in the lower border pure vertical writing is used: I|W‖N|A|C, I|W‖H|Λ (*ibid.*, pl. CLXVIII, A). Cf. Forsyth-Weitzmann, *St. Catherine*, pls. CLIV, A (Andrew), CLV, B (Philip).

[568] The same compromise between horizontal and vertical writing is used for the names of the personifications of the months in the floor dated 575/76 from Qabr Hiram near Tyre: e.g., ΠE|PI|TI|OC (Renan, *Mission en Phoenicie* [*supra*, note 551] pl. XLIX).

[569] Outside and below the mosaic medallions of saints with which the tympana of the room over the southwest ramp of St. Sophia were decorated (probably under Justin II), their names were written horizontally (P. A. Underwood, in *DOP*, 9–10 (1956), p. 292f. and figs 107–9), as were those of the apostles in the Archiepiscopal Chapel in Ravenna and those of the martyrs in the Poreč basilica. In S. Vitale, horizontal labels could be retained in the apostle border even within the medallions, since these were of larger size. But in one of the Durrës panels (see note 371 *supra*) the mosaicist was obliged to write CTE|ΦA|NOC.

on two lintel inscriptions dated 517[570] and 523.[571] In similar circumstances
in the late fifth century it was not used,[572] and contrary to Perdrizet's belief,
the date 492 does not in fact appear on the crude relief in the Louvre portraying the elder Symeon Stylites, which is labeled in two columns on either
side of his pillar.[573] For a relief of this kind[574] and for its exclusive use of the
"square" alphabet that date is not impossibly early,[575] but as proof of the
currency of vertical writing before the sixth century it is unreliable. Dated
examples in monumental painting from the reign of Justinian are lacking,
but the currency of the *kionedon* system at that time can be inferred from its
use in other media. In the key panel of the Qasr el-Lebia floor mosaic the
town is labeled in two columns Π|O|Λ|Ι|C|N|E|A||Θ|E|O|Δ|ω|P|I|A|C, indi-
cating a rededication in honor of the Empress Theodora. Taken in conjunction
with the indiction year 3 recorded elsewhere in the floor, this fixes the date
as 539.[576]

The use of *kionedon* labels in mid-sixth-century Egypt is indicated by
those beside the apostle medallions in the Cleveland tapestry icon.[577] Though
written downward, the names here have to be read sideways, as the weavers
saw them, sitting along what became the left side of the finished picture;
but it can hardly be doubted that the models they used for the medallions
bore *kionedon* labels, since here and there a letter was woven to read correctly
when the tapestry was hung.[578] The earliest of the examples at Bawit and Saqqara, though not dated, probably belong to the original decoration of the two
monasteries, which were constructed or reconstructed in the mid-sixth century.[579] At Bawit the medallions of nimbed saints in chapel 1 have labels
as vertical as the meager areas available for them would allow.[580] In the David
cycle in chapel 3, while others are written horizontally, David's name is
invariably *kionedon*,[581] and the label of Menas the Young is only partly

---

[570] W. K. Prentice, *Syria: Princeton Univ. Arch. Exped., 1904–5 and 1909*, III, B (Leyden, 1908),
p. 140, no. 1109. The practice is as old as the fourth century if the dates in the Deir Salîh dedicatory
inscription (*IGLSyr*, II [Paris, 1939], no. 322) are given in the Seleucid era, as the editors suppose.

[571] Prentice, *op. cit.*, p. 203 ff., no. 1202. For contemporary examples on the Kefr Antin lintel, see
IGLSyr, II, no. 393.

[572] E.g., Prentice, *op. cit.*, p. 190, no. 1177, dated 496.

[573] P. Perdrizet, *Le calendrier parisien* (Strasburg, 1933), 287 ff. and fig. 28. Cf. *IGLSyr*, I (Paris,
1929), p. 135, no. 256, and V. H. Elbern, "Frühbyzantinische Reliefdarstellung des älteren Symeon
Stylites," *JdI*, 80 (1965), 283, fig. 3. The last two letters of the inscription are not a date, but part of
the name, of which *Symeones* was a popular spelling (Prentice, *op. cit.*, 165 and index, p. 220).

[574] Cf. the report in Theodoretus, *ca.* 440, on images of Symeon used as apotropaia in Rome:
Religiosa historia, XXVI, PG, 82, col. 1473A.

[575] Analysis of sixty-five inscriptions from Northern Syria published by Prentice and dated between
470 and 569 indicates a maximum use of "square" letter-forms in the twenty years beginning 490:
in 75% of all dated inscriptions and in 25% of them exclusively. In the preceding twenty years the
corresponding percentages are 40% and 13%; in the next twenty years beginning 510, 46% and nil.
The "square" forms continued to be used in a minority of cases throughout the sixth century and even
later, but rarely to the exclusion of "round" and "oval" forms, as in the Stylite stele.

[576] Goodchild, "Christian Mosaics at Qasr el-Labia" (note 557 *supra*); H. Sichtermann, in *AA*,
1959, col. 346, fig. 108.

[577] Shepherd, "Tapestry Panel," 112, fig. 11, a.

[578] The A of *Andreas* and the C of *Bartholomaios*. Nevertheless, the weavers may also have been
influenced by Syriac sideways writing (see *infra*).

[579] For this dating, see references in note 219 *supra*.

[580] Clédat, *Baouît*, pl. x.   [581] *Ibid.*, pls. XVI, XVII, XIX.

horizontal: Π|ⲀⲤⲞ(Ⲛ)|ⲘⲎ|ⲚⲀ|Ⲕ|Ⲟ|Ⲩ|Ⲓ.[582] By the late sixth century the practice was evidently general in Bawit.[583] A carved example at Saqqara, running down the margin of a chancel post, could be as early as the construction of the mid-sixth-century monastery.[584] Among those in fresco a damaged medallion containing a bust with nimbus and vertical label is of good enough quality to date from the initial decoration.[585] Relatively early also seems the figure of Apa Apollo with *kionedon* label on one of the columns of the church,[586] but other examples on frescoes of inferior quality can hardly belong to the mid-sixth-century decoration.[587]

In monumental painting in Syria also, a recourse to vertical writing by the time of Justinian could be presumed from its appearance in the Greek inscriptions on stone already mentioned. The possible genesis of the practice in imitation of Syriac sideways writing has to be considered. At first sight some examples in the Rabbula Gospels seem close to Greek column-writing; but in fact they were written, and are to be read, with the book turned sideways in what might be called "vertical (sideways) writing." Such are the names of the apostles in the Election of Matthias (fol. 1r), those of Moses and Aaron (fol. 3v), and of Luke (fol. 10r), and the texts above the angel and the Virgin of the Annunciation (fol. 4r). There can hardly be any question of the scribe following κιονηδόν labels in the Greek model for the miniatures; for similar vertical (sideways) writing goes back to the earliest period of written Syriac (and before that to Palmyrene), and it continues in later Syriac manuscripts, even in bilingual titles with Greek *kionedon*.[588] True column writing, with one letter erect below the other, is extremely rare in Syriac; and when it is used in some sixth-century inscriptions from Northern Syria, more often than not, as in the Zebed trilingual of 511, the columns lay horizontally when the texts were in position. Such examples can hardly have been models for Greek κιονηδόν. It is more probable that this developed under the influence of normal Syriac vertical (sideways) writing, and conceivable that the few Syriac inscriptions in true vertical column writing imitated by Greek vertical

---

[582] *Ibid.*, pl. XIII.

[583] Chapel 17, *ibid.*, pl. XLV; chapel 28, *ibid.*, pls. XCVIII, CI, and CIV. Chapel 17 has been placed at the end of the sixth century: M. Salmi, "I dipinti paleocristiani di Antinoe," *Scritti dedicati alla memoria di Ippolito Rosellini* (Florence, 1945), 168.

[584] *Saqqara*, IV, pl. XXXVIII, 1, and p. 85, no. 272.

[585] From a room opening onto the octagon court: *ibid.*, pl. VII, 2, whence Dalton, *Byz. Art and Archeology* (*supra*, note 4), 283, fig. 172, wrongly attributed in the caption to El Khargeh.

[586] *Saqqara*, III (1907–8), 6, fig. 2. The varying materials and condition of the columns would have necessitated plastering (and painting?) *ab initio*.

[587] *Ibid.*, II (1906–7), pl. XLIV, 4, labels of saints on north wall of cell A; *ibid.*, III, pl. IX, labels of Faith, Hope, and Charity in cell 709 (= Dalton, *op. cit.*, 283, fig. 176); *ibid.*, IV, pls. XXII and XXIII, 1, labels of heads in medallions above the niche in cell 1725.

[588] See facsimiles in *Rabbula Gospels*. For vertical (sideways) inscriptions of the second and third centuries, see J. B. Segal, *Edessa the Blessed City* (Oxford, 1970), pls. 3, 16b, 17a, 28b, and 41; R. du Mesnil du Buisson, *Inventaire des inscriptions palmyréniennes de Doura Europos* (Paris, 1939), 43–44; J. Cantineau, "Textes palmyréniens," *Syria*, 12 (1931), 125 no. 26 *bis*. For the bilingual Syriac and Greek titles in later codices, see J. Leroy, *Les manuscrits syriaques à peintures* (Paris, 1964), pls. 52, 1, 53, 1 (A.D. 1054), and 138, 1 (13th cent.). For the references in this and the following note, and for his comments and suggestions, we are indebted to Dr. Sebastian Brock.

texts, themselves inspired by normal Syriac writing.[589] If Syria was indeed the area where Greek column writing was first practiced, it is not surprising to find examples in Cyprus rather earlier than further west.

A custom which must have had much to do with the spread of Greek column writing was the inscribing of dedications on crosses, particularly those of silver of the processional type. Though not of this class, the Moses cross at Sinai is significant in that it attests the prevalence of the custom already in the time of Justinian; that is, if this great bronze cross surmounted the original iconostasis of his basilica, as Weitzmann reasonably suggested.[590] Since this cross is so large, the text on the vertical arms could be written normally, in short lines of six to nine letters each, not unlike the labels in the mosaic medallions, where the format imposed a maximum of only three letters per line. The vertical arms of the processional crosses, on the other hand, are so much narrower that they can accommodate only one letter, and so the first part of the dedication is written *kionedon*, down the vertical arms, and the remainder, normally, across the horizontal arms. None of these silver crosses bears a control stamp, but Ševčenko found in the letter-forms on one of them from the "Hama" treasure, now in Baltimore, the closest parallels to those of the probably Justinianic Moses cross.[591] The similar Phela cross in the Dumbarton Oaks Collection bears an inscription in which several of the letter-forms repeat those of the labels of the Cyprus mosaic;[592] this cross also could be Justinianic.[593] The cross of the same type from the Luxor treasure in the Cairo Museum is similarly inscribed, but with a different type of lettering,[594] and like the Phela cross has the tear-drop serifs which were current at least from the time of Justinian. It seems safe to conclude that the inscribed crosses of this class were effective from the mid-sixth century in popularizing vertical writing of the type used in the Lythrankomi mosaic.

As early examples of vertical labels, we must reject the names of the apostles beautifully cut in Greek on the damaged relief in the Barletta museum,[595] for these must have been added in Constantinople itself, to judge

---

[589] The four columns of letters one below the other on the undated inscription from Ir. Ruḥaiyeh (E. Littmann, *Syria: Princeton Univ. Arch. Exped., 1904–5 and 1909*, IV, B [Leyden, 1934], no. 3) would also have lain horizontally if this was a lintel, as seems most probable. For the Zebed trilingual, see *IGLSyr*, II, no. 310; for other Syriac examples in columns set horizontally, compare the lintel inscription of the Deḥḥes baptistery (H. Pognon, *Inscriptions sémitiques* [Paris, 1907], no. 85) and that on the Bennaoui ambon in the Damascus Museum (J. B. Chabot, *Syria*, 10 [1929], 252f.).

The appearance side by side on other Zebed inscriptions of Syriac vertical (sideways) writing and Greek κιονηδόν (in some cases transcribing Syriac words) is very indicative (Littmann, *American Arch. Expedition to Syria, 1899–1900*, IV, 46–50, nos. 22–24; *IGLSyr*, II, nos. 312–14).

[590] K. Weitzmann and I. Ševčenko, "The Moses Cross at Sinai," *DOP*, 17 (1963), 390.

[591] Walters Art Gallery, inv. no. 57.632; cf. Ševčenko, in *DOP*, 17, p. 397, and fig. 15.

[592] See *supra*, note 559.

[593] It is not necessarily contemporary with the paten of the time of Justin II with which it was found.

[594] J. Strzygowski, *Catalogue général des antiquités égyptiennes du Musée du Caire*. II, *Koptische Kunst*, 340f., no. 7201 and pl. XXXIX.

[595] This relief (see *supra*, note 439) is dated by Testini *ca.* 400. Similarly we must pass over the *kionedon* label on an early relief in Istanbul, immured in a *hagiasma* of the Armenian Taxiarches church, for this must have been added when the relief was reworked, *ca.* 1000, to serve as an image

by their style and quality, in some post-iconoclastic rehabilitation of the relief. The name of S(an)C(tu)S|YPOL|LI|TV|S among horizontal labels in the mosaics of Pelagius II (578–90) in S. Lorenzo fuori le Mura is perhaps still the earliest datable approximation to vertical writing in Italy.[596] There are several good examples in catacomb frescoes which Wilpert assigned to earlier pontificates,[597] but his datings are now considered too early.[598]

Some labeled representations of saints in which vertical writing could with advantage have been used, but was not used, are helpful in establishing when it began to be popular. In Salonica the labels of the martyrs in the Rotunda of St. George, set in narrow panels of five- or six-letter lines and employing exceptionally narrow letters, are still a long way from fully vertical writing.[599] Among the north aisle mosaics of the basilica of St. Demetrius there was a series of *imagines clipeatae* of nimbed martyrs, quite comparable with the apostle medallions of the Panagia Kanakaria. But here the names, where given, were inscribed around the border in the manner of coin legends.[600] Convenient on a coin or an ampulla which can be rotated in the hand, this system, though amenable to the format of this particular type of representation, does not make for legibility when used on a wall. But on the evidence of these examples the more legible labels of the *kionedon* system were not in use among Byzantine mosaicists around the turn of the fifth century, if that is indeed the date of the aisle mosaics of the first decoration of St. Demetrius.[601]

It follows from this survey that, wherever the exigencies of spacing made its use appropriate, vertical writing, probably under the influence of Syriac vertical (sideways) writing, became the generally accepted solution in the

---

of St. Artemios: K. Lehmann, *BNJbb*, 1 (1920), 381 f.; R. Lange, *Die byzantinische Reliefikone* (Recklinghausen, 1964), 16.

[596] Cf. C. R. Morey, in *ArtB*, 11 (1929), 48 note 34.

[597] Semi-vertical, MAR|CEL|LI|NVS and SCS|PE|TR|VS in the tomb of St. Polion in the catacomb of Ponziano: J. Wilpert, *Die Malereien der Katakomben Roms* (Freiburg im Breisgau, 1903), pl. 255, 2, and p. 565 ("end of the fifth century"). Vertical, the names of Simplicius, Faustinus, and Viatrix in their burial place in the catacomb of Generosa: *ibid.*, pl. 262–64 and pp. 498 ff. and 566 ("first half of the sixth century"); the names of Cornelius and three others in the catacomb named after him in the cemetery of Callisto: *ibid.*, pl. 256 and p. 501 ("restored under John III, 560–573").

[598] Polion in Ponziano: even the sixth-century dating favored by other authorities is considered too early (R. Farioli, *Pitture di epoca tarda nelle catacombe romane* [Ravenna, 1963], 19; Matthiae, *Pittura romana del medioevo*, I [*supra*, note 329], 145), Simplicius and others in Generosa: seventh century (Farioli, *op. cit.*, 12; Matthiae, *op. cit.*, 149); Cornelius and others in Callisto: end of the sixth or beginning of the seventh century (Farioli, *op. cit.*, 39) or even the beginning of the ninth (Matthiae, *op. cit.*, 219).

[599] Torp, *Mosaikkene*, fig. on p. 28. For the date, see *supra*, note 197.

[600] Labels of SS. Pelagia and Matrona: Uspenskij, in *IRAIK*, 14 (1909), pl. x; Grabar, *Martyrium*, II, 365, fig. 145; Cormack, "S. Demetrios," pl. 3. It is noteworthy that in the two medallions in the upper corners of the easternmost panel with St. Demetrius orant the heads are not nimbed, leaving more room on the ground of the clipei for labels. Yet, the one which was labeled has the name circumscribed on the frame of the clipeus (*ibid.*, pl. 14, a). This probably represents the original practice for labeling such medallions, whose illegibility would explain its replacement by κιονηδόν.

[601] See *supra*, note 179. It speaks in favor of the Eastern inspiration of Byzantine column writing that coins of the Edessene dynasty bore vertical (sideways) labels as early as the third century: e.g., Segal, *Edessa the Blessed City* (*supra*, note 588), pl. 28 b.

course of the sixth century, the earliest dated examples being on the Syrian lintels of 517 and 523. Its employment in the Panagia Kanakaria mosaic is not consequently an impediment to assigning this to a period a good deal earlier than the decoration of the Sinai apse.

TECHNIQUE

The mosaic was set in the usual manner on a thick bed of lime plaster laid in three renderings totaling about 0.05 m. in depth. The under layers contained a quantity of chopped straw. The porous nature of the soft stone masonry necessitated this thick pad to avoid too rapid drying of the top layer, in which the tesserae were to be inserted.

On this setting-bed the design was set out in color; earth red, green, and black can be seen in places where the tesserae have fallen, and other colors may have been used in the robes and faces where more detail and lighter tones would have been desirable. Red was used for the gold of the background, a common practice, giving reinforcement and warmth to the color of the gold tesserae where the paint showed in the interstices between them. The sketch was painted rapidly in a broad manner, with which the final drawing and coloring worked out in the mosaic did not always conform. For example, the white marble line between the blue ground and the frame of the mandorla was not indicated in the sketch, but was set in the band of red color defining the inner half of the frame. Elsewhere, in various places where black paint was used, tesserae of another color were set. In short, the underpainting was a layout and rough sketch, not a detailed painting in the precise colors which were to be employed in the mosaic.

The tesserae vary considerably in size. The largest are those in the gold ground, where they are often of elongated form, measuring about 0.010 by 0.008 m. Those in the nimbi of the apostles are only a little smaller, often 0.009 m. square. This size is normal in the robes also, but elsewhere the tesserae are not so large. The smallest are those in the faces of Christ and of the apostles, often as small as 0.004 m. square.[602] In the face of the north archangel, which is only a little under life size, somewhat larger tesserae are used, none of them smaller than 0.005 m. square; of similar size are those in the south archangel's forearm.

The range of colors used in this mosaic and the materials—glass, marble, and stone—are not unusual in Early Byzantine mosaics, though mother-of-pearl and ceramic tesserae, which are used elsewhere, do not occur at Lythrankomi. More than forty variations were selected for use as individual colors or tones; these are listed below. With the exception of one color, all the glass tesserae other than those capped with gold or silver are opaque; only those used for clear brown are of translucent glass. Almost certainly these were formed from the disks of clear amber glass which were the basis for the

---

[602] Such also were the tesserae used in the faces in the Theotokos panel of the St. Demetrius aisle mosaics: 0.004 m. (Diehl, *Le Tourneau*, and Saladin, *Monuments chrétiens* [*supra*, note 300], 112).

production of gold and silver tesserae. This material, though quite light in color when held to the light, acquires a deeper but variable translucent tone when embedded in the plaster. It is employed with particular effect in outlines where a dark value of an opaque color would be too emphatic. It is used to outline the head, forearm, and hand of Christ as well as for the outlines of the Virgin's hand.[603] The only extensive use of these translucent amber tesserae to give a specific brown color is in the band three rows wide which borders the main composition (fig. 44, color fig. 138).

Supplementing the glass tesserae and those of marble and stone in their natural colors, white marble tesserae are also found coated with earth colors, which had been applied before insertion in the plaster. These were used quite extensively, but by now the color on their exposed faces has almost invariably been lost. This expedient was employed only in red areas, but probably for more than one tone of that color.[604]

It was the need for a lighter tone of red than could be procured in glass that probably determined this use of tesserae dipped in earth red paint, rather than a shortage of the deep red glass normally used at Lythrankomi. This explanation seems unavoidable in the case of the outer border, in which the lighter sides of the red rafters are made mainly with pigmented tesserae and the dark sides mainly with purple-brown glass, while the deep red glass is used to accentuate the edges of both.

The red glass was opaque and could not be produced in a gradation of tones, as were most of the other colored glasses. It was confined to the familiar deep red and two variations of it, which occasionally occurred in the manufacture of disks of this color, in the form of streaks of the darker purple-brown or, more rarely, of the bright orange-vermilion, which was clearly very scarce.[605] The purple-brown was sometimes used at Lythrankomi as an independent color, notably to give the darker sides of the red rafters in the outer border. Elsewhere the purple-brown was used indiscriminately with the normal deep red glass.

The pigmented tesserae are much in evidence in the intermediate border where it is preserved on the north side: they predominate in the background, where they are used to outline the motifs of the design leaving only comparatively small areas of the background to be filled with red glass tesserae (figs. 46, 47, and color fig. 138). At the apex of the conch this treatment is reversed, with red glass for the outlines, and it is probable that this arrangement

---

[603] Also to outline the segment of Christ's himation on his right shoulder, for the outlines of the north archangel's himation and Jude's chiton, and to delineate Bartholomew's pale blue himation against the light blue ground of his clipeus.

[604] In the mosaic in the Kiti church, stone or marble tesserae artifically colored black and yellow, as well as red, are extensively used. For a probably pre-Justinianic example of the use of red pigment, see reference in note 614 *infra*. For the same expedient in later Byzantine mosaics elsewhere, see Mango and Hawkins, "The Apse Mosaics of St. Sophia" (*supra*, note 177), 138, note 31. In the late-seventh-century mosaics of the Dome of the Rock, "rose-colored" pigmented tesserae have been identified (Gautier-van Berchem, in Creswell, *Early Muslim Architecture* [*supra*, note 497], 310).

[605] See E. J. W. Hawkins, "Further Observations on the Narthex Mosaic in St. Sophia at Istanbul," *DOP*, 22 (1968), 165 note 16.

continued on the south side. Taking into account that the pigmented marble tesserae would have been lighter in tone than those of glass and non-reflecting, it seems possible that the mosaicist was consciously seeking contrasting effects on the two sides of the conch.[606]

In the heads, the warmer flesh tones are given by the small pink marble tesserae which were generally used for this purpose. The darker reds are obtained by the deep red and purple-brown glasses, while the brighter touches are supplied by the orange-vermilion, except in the heads of the archangel and Bartholomew; there this rare glass is replaced by white marble tesserae which must originally have been artificially colored red. Although no trace of the pigment has been found in these cases, there is little doubt that these marble tesserae were dipped in red lead paint to give an approximation to the color of the orange-vermilion glass. Red lead is subject to disintegration in the atmosphere and it is not surprising that it has perished completely under conditions in which most of the much more stable earth red paint has been eroded. It may be supposed that the meager supply of the rare orange-vermilion glass was depleted by the time the setting of the medallions was nearly finished, the work having proceeded downward from the top, and that the substitution of pigmented marble was necessary to complete Bartholomew in the lowest medallion on the south side. Similarly, in the central composition, while there was doubtless sufficient of the rare glass to furnish what was required for the heads of the Virgin and Christ (the latter in fact retains several tesserae of this material and there are others in the bare forearm), for the archangel it was again necessary to fall back on painted marble.[607]

It seems probable that the red tinted tesserae were prepared in a considerable range of tones, for only in this way could the diminishing redness required for the irisated borders have been procured. Variations of tone could easily have been achieved by using earth red and lime white in varying proportions in the color mixtures in which the tesserae were dipped.

In this mosaic two colors sometimes alternate in a single row of tesserae to effect a gradation of tone, usually in order to represent the transition from one plane to another. This technique is employed in the head of the archangel and also in that of Luke, at the sides of their noses (figs. 62, 76, and color fig. 134); also on the cuff of the south archangel's chiton. A similar

[606] Other areas in which the pigmented red tesserae were used are: on both north and south sections of the Irisated Border, at the bottom (*supra*, p. 39, figs. 43, 48, and 52); for one pyramid in the Crowstep Border next to the cornice (p. 40); in the stars on the ground of the Apostle Border (p. 40); in Luke's himation (p. 44); on Mark's Gospel book (color fig. 139); on the edge of Matthew's Gospel book (fig. 138); on the neckline of Andrew's chiton among red glass (frontispiece); on Bartholomew's upper lip (fig. 70); in the archangel's face (fig. 76, color fig. 133); for the inner edge of the mandorla frame (p. 54); for the back of the throne (p. 56); for the drape on which the Theotokos sits (p. 56); for her slippers (p. 59); and for the center section of the cushion (p. 57). There were also a few tinted red tesserae among those fallen from the face of the wall above the apse.

[607] We suppose that the setting of the mosaic started with the central figures of the Virgin and Child and proceeded outward. Between the Apostle Border and the Intermediate Border separating it from the main composition there is a vertical suture on the preserved north side; this marks the limit of the decoration of the conch, which was completed first.

alternation of colors in a single row is used to blur the transition from gold to marble tesserae at the edge of the gold ground. First, gold and yellow glass tesserae alternate in a single row between rows of gold and of yellow glass alone; then, after two rows of yellow marble, comes a row in which yellow and white marble alternate; finally, a row of white marble alone (fig. 44). In only one area is this type of alternation used in bands two or more tesserae wide at the meeting of two colors: on the footstool, toward the missing south corner, where gold and yellow merge in interlocking "fingers."[608]

More usually, changes of plane and deepening of shadows are suggested by changing the tone of whole adjacent rows of tesserae, as in the main area of the mandorla. In some cases a special effect is achieved by alternating entire gradations of color in successive rows, as in the trunk of the palm tree on the south side, where both its texture and its rotundity are thus suggested (fig. 77).

Forms are emphasized and an illusion of projection obtained not only by shading but also by the juxtaposition of lighter and darker tones, sometimes regardless of where shadows would fall in actuality. Thus, the right forearm of Christ and the scroll are logically defined on the upper contour with highlights which are reinforced by the shadowed robe behind them (fig. 86, color fig. 135); however, below, where these forms are shaded as they should be, the light on the robe is maintained to give them relief, whereas at this point they would, in reality, themselves cast shadows on the robe. We may contrast the gathered folds of the north archangel's himation where they pass obliquely to his left shoulder (fig. 75, color fig. 134); the lower limit is shaded, and they are given further volume by highlighting what is visible of the underlying section of the garment covering the upper part of the left arm, but not without correctly representing, by an additional row of dark tesserae, the shadow cast by the voluminous oblique folds. More usually, niceties of this sort are lost in the application of what we have called stereoscopic projection. In its simplest form this is illustrated by the forearm of the south archangel; where the trunk of the tree appears behind the forearm it is unnaturally darkened to set off the light flesh tone of the upper contour; while below, where the forearm is shaded to dark purple-brown, the tree is brightened with an alien row of yellow-green tesserae.

---

[608] The merging of two colors by means of interpenetrating "fingers" has no precise chronological or geographical significance. In Cyprus, in the fifth century, this technique was used in Eustolios' baths at Kourion, e.g., on the hand of the bust of Ktisis (Karageorghis, Cyprus [supra, note 500], pl. 180); in Ravenna, in the "Mausoleum of Galla Placidia," where the ground colors change (Deichmann, Bauten und Mosaiken, pl. 11); and in the Arian Baptistery on the robes of one of the apostles (ibid., pl. 262) and between Peter and Paul and the throne toward which they advance, in the yellow transition between the green ground and the gold sky (ibid., pls. 256–57). The technique was also current in Salonica. Its use to soften shadows on drapery in the lost mosaics of St. Demetrius is well documented by Kluge's drawing of the central figures of the Theotokos panel (IRAIK, 14 [1909], pl. 3).

As a device to effect transitions in facial modeling, alternation of colors in a single row, sometimes arranged to give a checkerboard pattern, appears already in the martyr figures of the Salonica Rotunda, e.g., St. Priscus (Torp, Mosaikkene, 79) and St. Ananias (Greece: Byzantine Mosaics [UNESCO, 1959], pl. II). Among examples of this technique, Kleinbauer cites occurrences in late fifth- and early sixth-century floor mosaics in Yugoslavia and in the apse mosaic from S. Michele in Affricisco (Kleinbauer, "Mosaics of the Rotunda," 79 note 196, 107 note 293).

List of Colors Used

In many of the colors for which glass was used there is a wide gradation from the basic color to paler shades. In this list we include only those three or four values in each case (five in the case of green) into which the tesserae appear to have been sorted to meet the requirements of the mosaicist's "palette."[609]

Metallic

1. Gold (gold-leaf cap on translucent glass, usually of amber color)
2. Silver (silver-leaf cap on similar glass)

Glass

3. Deep red
4. Purple-brown
5. Orange-vermilion
6. Clear brown (the translucent glass used for the gold tesserae)[610]
7. Dark brown
8–11. Opaque brown, used in four values (of coarse texture)
12–15. Purple, used in four values
16. Purple-black
17–20. Deep blue, close to ultramarine, used in four values
21–23. Blue, close to cerulean, used in three values[611]
24–27. Turquoise blue, used in four values
28–31. Olive, used in four values
32–36. Green, ranging from viridian to yellow-green, used in five values
37. Yellow
38–39. White and blue-white

Natural materials

40. White Proconnesian marble
41. Gray Proconnesian marble (only observed among the fragments from the wall face above the conch)
42. Yellow marble
43–45. Fine grained marble, pink, cream, and white
46. Dull yellow stone

Tesserae dipped in paint

47. Earth red (red iron oxide with lime white), probably in more than one value
48. Bright red (orange tetroxide of lead), presumed but not actually identified

[609] Cf. Mango and Hawkins, "The Apse Mosaics of St. Sophia," 132 note 18.

[610] This is essentially the same material as that designated "bottle glass" by Mango and Hawkins describing the ninth-century tympanum mosaics of St. Sophia (*DOP*, 26 [1972], 17). That designation is retained for similar tesserae by Hawkins and Mundell in their account of the early sixth-century Kartmin mosaic referred to in note 614 *infra*, p. 268 and note 57. Cf. Hawkins, "Further Observations on the Narthex Mosaic in St. Sophia at Istanbul," 154, nos. 25–26 and note 5.

[611] Some blue tesserae have accidental streaks of deep red; for an explanation, see R. H. Brill's note on the chemical composition of ancient glass (Hawkins, *op. cit.*, 165 note 16).

CONCLUSIONS

This fragmentary composition presents two related problems: to locate its position in the history of Early Byzantine apse decoration, and, with that position fixed as far as possible, to establish whether it represents the art of Constantinople or of some provincial center.

The Date of the Mosaic

This first problem is aggravated by the lack of comparable monuments and our consequent dependence to a large extent on deductions from examples sometimes only remotely relevant. But we have seen that in its main subject the Lythrankomi mosaic may have belonged to a relatively early phase in the gradual exclusion of commemorative elements from the apse, the focal point of the decoration of a basilical church, a process that had begun before the end of the fifth century. Secondly, its relatively early position among representations of the Incarnation is also indicated, particularly if such features as the lyre-back throne and the mandorla are explained by dependence on earlier themes of which Christ was the centerpiece. If, on the other hand, this unique use of the mandorla arose from a desire to isolate the archangels from the ἀνωτέρα ἀγγέλων, it stands at the beginning of a process which led ultimately to the exclusion of the archangels from the conch altogether. It has been suggested, however, that the use of the mandorla here constitutes an assertion of Chalcedonian doctrine arising from the new disputes about the Dual Nature when Justinian came to the throne. In that case, the theological error in the divinity it accords to Mary was corrected in those Theotokos groups where the mandorla encloses the Child alone, a solution which appeared in the course of the sixth century. All these considerations indicate a relatively early date in that century for the setting of the Lythrankomi mosaic. This conclusion is supported by the retention of the trees of the Paradise landscape, which Justinianic practice normally reduced to an exiguous band representing a flower-sprinkled meadow; while the Sinai mosaic carried the suppression of landscape even further, to the complete exclusion of any indication of Mt. Tabor, so that the three prostrate apostles appear to be levitating in space.

Several iconographic pointers to an early Justinianic, if not a pre-Justinianic, dating have been identified. Although standing types of the Theotokos, with the Child either on one arm or held by both hands before her, are attested in the sixth century, at Lythrankomi the Theotokos not only follows the original enthroned and frontal formula adopted in the fifth century but adheres to its most elementary form: the kerchief and girdle do not appear and both the Virgin's arms extended downward, in strict symmetry, to hold the Child. Further, the position of Christ's right hand clasping the top of the roll, not raising it in a gesture of speech, conforms with the earliest surviving monumental example, on the fifth-century ambon from the Salonica Rotunda. Enough remains of the archangels to show that here, too, the mosaicist held to the earlier iconography; they neither offered globes nor wore military garb and, since they are nimbed like both figures of the central image and the apostles in the border, there is no suggestion here of the bias against the nimbus which seems to have developed by the mid-sixth century.

We have seen that the inclusion of Mark and Luke among the Twelve Apostles is less remarkable than the manner in which they were accommodated: Simon, normally retained, was dropped; Jude, who was later excluded but seems to have enjoyed early favor, was retained and in a position of exceptional seniority, contrasting with his demotion in the Sinai border. Our mosaic should then belong close to the time when all four Evangelists were first included in the symbolic college, but before its final composition had crystalized. A relatively early date is also indicated by the characterization of two of the apostles: for Matthew the youthful type is retained, in contrast to the bearded elder in the Sinai mosaic, while James remains white-haired unlike the younger James normal in the sixth century. Some significant letter-forms used in the apostles' names are matched by those in the Sinai border, but we have found no paleographic obstacle to the suggestion that these were employed around the first years of Justinian's reign as well as in the last. The vertical writing used in the apostles' names does not conflict with a date early in the second quarter of the sixth century, for we have noted that it was used in Syria to meet exigencies of space as early as the year 517.

In strictly formal elements also we have noted features which for the mid-sixth century could be rated archaic. The medallions are not the flat gold disks of the Sinai mosaic, but are pale blue and shaded to simulate the prototype, a skyphate clipeus of shining metal. The classic motif of the joist-end or dentil frieze used in the outer border recurs in Byzantine decoration over a long period, but here it is transformed into a zigzag band (fig. K). This elaboration, coupled with the unusual enrichment of the normal jeweled band (fig. 46) and the luscious quality of the acanthus bed in which the apostle medallions are set, relates the Lythrankomi mosaic to the opulent and imaginative style of decoration in vogue when Justinian came to the throne. A close relationship to that style is confirmed by the reappearance of our intermediate border pattern, in abbreviated form, in the marble relief decoration of St. Polyeuktos (ca. 524–27). The Lythrankomi repertory has little in common with the more austere and stereotyped character of the original mosaic ornament of St. Sophia (not to mention the complete absence there of all figural representation), which in spirit if not in detail is matched in the borders of the Sinai mosaic.

Variations in style in figural representations of the sixth century are not amenable to precise classification by time scale, and not least because, as Kitzinger deduced, both classicizing and formalizing—even anti-classical—models were evidently available to serve the needs of differing modes of expression. We have indeed seen that the Lythrankomi mosaic drew on both traditions: the formalizing in the severe outlines, in the rather stark symmetry of the main composition, and in the frontal pose of the heads, only slightly varied in the case of the archangel; the classicizing, in the rather full-blooded facial style, in the sensitive plasticity of arms and feet, and in the often carefully studied drapery. Characteristically Byzantine, these Hellenistic qualities are rare in the more robust mosaics of sixth-century Ravenna, a deficiency which frustrates comparison of Eastern mosaics with them;[612] but for most scholars our mosaic has greatest affinity with those of the Ostrogothic period and with the decoration of the Archiepiscopal Chapel in particular.[613] Elsewhere, the Lythrankomi figure style has as much kinship with the pre-Justinianic mosaics in Salonica as with any of later date, and since at no point does the drapery stylization approach the abstract patterns which appear at some points in the Sinai apse, there is no stylistic anachronism in assigning our mosaic to the years around the beginning of Justinian's reign, as features of its subject matter and iconography require.

Technical considerations do not provide satisfactory criteria by which to test this conclusion, because so little detailed technical information about most early mosaics is available. The use of white marble tesserae dipped in red pigment, rather extensive at Lythrankomi, has as yet been reported in pre-Justinianic mosaics in the East only at Mār Gabriel,[614] though careful examination may reveal it elsewhere.[615] However, recourse to artificial coloring of marble tesserae in the fourth-century mosaics at Centcelles in Spain[616] coupled with the occurrences of the technique already noted in pre-iconoclastic mosaics in Georgia and Jerusalem as well as in Kiti and Lythrankomi in Cyprus, suggest that the practice may have been normal in Byzantine mosaics from an early date. Its reappearance in the ninth- and tenth-century mosaics of St. Sophia is also suggestive.[617] The other device used at Lythrankomi for obtaining intermediate tones, that of alternating two colors in the same row of tesserae to produce a blend when seen at a distance, is well attested in the pre-Justinianic period, notably in the Salonica Rotunda. In other respects, such as the range of glass colors and the relatively large sizes of tesserae employed, the mosaic presents no technical feature that would inhibit its assignment to the third decade of the sixth century, which we have seen is suggested on other grounds.

---

[612] Cf. Galassi, "Musaici di Cipro," 9, for whom this divergence puts the Lythrankomi mosaic in the middle of the century, after the establishment of Byzantine rule in Ravenna.

[613] Lazarev, *Storia*, 77; Bettini, *La pittura bizantina* (*supra*, note 4), 44.

[614] If the dating of the mosaics there to the reign of Anastasius is accepted. See E. J. Hawkins and M. C. Mundell, "The Mosaics of the Monastery of Mār Samuel, Mār Simeon, and Mār Gabriel near Kartmin," *DOP*, 27 (1973), 284 note 48, and 288.

[615] Some of Torp's color reproductions of the Salonica Rotunda mosaics raise suspicions that tinted marble tesserae featured in the "palette" of the Constantinopolitan workshop which is thought to have set them. On a shaded face of the building in panel IV of the martyr zone there is a strident band of white marble which seems quite out of place (*Mosaikkene*, pl. facing p. 56). These tesserae may well have lost an added tint, probably of light red color; for in the interstices the setting bed is pink, whereas when marble was used for white the setting bed appears to have remained uncolored in the preliminary sketch (*ibid.*, lower illustration opposite p. 32).

[616] T. Hauschild and H. Schlunk, "Vorbericht über die Untersuchungen in Centcelles," *Madrider Mitteilungen*, 2 (1961), 140.

[617] For Jerusalem, see *supra*, note 604; for Zromi in Georgia, see Š. Ja. Amiranašvili, *Istorija gruzinskoj monumental'noj živopisi* (Tbilisi, 1957), 24; for St. Sophia, see *supra*, note 604 and, for the narthex lunette, Hawkins, in *DOP*, 22 (1968), 158 ff., 161, and 163 f.

If, then, so many indications converge on the years around the beginning of Justinian's reign as the most likely time for the setting of the Lythrankomi mosaic, it may reasonably be asked whether it formed part of a general restoration of the basilica which had been built perhaps no more than a generation earlier; and if so, whether this was necessitated by the same circumstances that led to a restoration of the city of Salamis-Constantia by the ἀγαθοὶ βασιλεῖς, who have been identified as Justinian and Theodora.[618] It has been suggested that the restoration of that city was occasioned by local repercussions of the seismic upheavals which virtually destroyed Antioch between 526 and 528.[619] The Carpas peninsula, which geologically is a continuation of the Amanus Range, can hardly have escaped the effects of the first and worst of these earthquakes.[620] If it did not, the Lythrankomi basilica, then some thirty years old, might well have suffered. In that case, assuming that it was repaired and redecorated without delay, the setting of its mosaic could most reasonably be placed between 526 and 530.

Metropolitan or Provincial?

It remains for us to consider to what tradition this decoration belongs. At the outset let it be said that during the two hundred years before the first Arab incursions it is not improbable that Cyprus supported its own workshop of mosaicists; for there is perhaps no area of comparable size and population that has produced as much evidence of wall-mosaic decoration in that period, both in tesserae recovered from church sites and fragments surviving *in situ*.[621] So we are not necessarily seeking to identify the center from which the master employed at Lythrankomi came to Cyprus, but rather are assessing the connections of a local tradition which his work reflects. In the first instance we may dispose of two possible sources of influence which earlier studies have canvased, but which now seem improbable.

The concept of Jerusalem as a creative center of Christian art has been much impaired since Grabar rejected the view that the ampullae acquired there by pilgrims do not reflect archetypal images in the Holy Places but, on the contrary, rather closely follow Constantinopolitan iconography.[622] It no longer speaks for a connection between our mosaicist and Bethlehem that a summary version of the Lythrankomi Incarnation formula appears on an

---

[618] See T. Mitford and I. Nicolaou, *Inscriptions from Salamis, 1952–61* (Nicosia, 1974), 69.

[619] Megaw, "Metropolitan or Provincial?", 71 note 50.

[620] On the simultaneous impact of earthquakes in Cyprus and Syria, see *supra*, note 150.

[621] The substantial iconographic and stylistic differences between the Lythrankomi and Kiti mosaics do not preclude the existence of a local workshop in Cyprus, as has been claimed (Smirnov, "Mozaiki," 89; Galassi, "Musaici di Cipro," 22); for such differences are no more than would be expected in monuments separated by an interval of perhaps half a century.

Remains of thirty-eight basilicas excavated or otherwise identified were listed by A. Papageorghiou, in 'A.B., 27 (1966), 155, and others have been recorded since. In most cases the finding of glass tesserae attests their decoration with wall mosaics. [On fragments of a figured decoration found *in situ* in a chapel of the Kourion basilica, see Megaw, "Interior Decoration," 24f., where they are assigned to the sixth century, with figs. 43, 44.]

[622] Simultaneously, Kitzinger set out other reasons for regarding sixth-century Palestine as increasingly a backwater ("Between Justinian and Iconoclasm," 33–38).

ampulla that was procured there. Nor does the superior version on the gold medallion in Dumbarton Oaks, once thought to be of similar provenance; for this is now regarded as a product of the Imperial mint. And if a mosaic of the Theotokos did once adorn the façade of the church of the Nativity, there is some reason to believe that it was part of a quite different composition. Jerusalem may then be set aside.

Likewise Alexandria. The concept of a still Hellenistic Alexandria as a contributor in the formation of the mosaic style of the Ravenna school seemed to receive some support from the uncovering of the Lythrankomi Apostle Border, offering as it did the possibility of a link in the somewhat tenuous chain Alexandria—Cyprus—Salonica—Ravenna.[623] A distant kinship is perhaps discernible between some of our apostles and the Fayum portraits, but this does no more than relate the Lythrankomi mosaicist with a tradition of antique portraiture that was certainly not exclusively Egyptian. For the rest, the claims of Alexandria receive but scant support from the few Christian frescoes, such as the Theodosia lunette found at Antinoë, which avoid the prevailing Coptic stylization.[624] While against the notion of Alexandria as the guardian of Hellenistic traditions, the view now prevails that those traditions died there with the emergence of the Coptic style.[625] We have indeed cited or postulated sixth-century monuments in Egypt of Byzantine affiliations, but these are to be regarded as reflecting an intrusive metropolitan style; in no way do they establish a specifically Alexandrian inspiration for mosaicists either in Cyprus or elsewhere.

If, then, the concept of a local mosaicist workshop in Cyprus stands, it remains to consider the light our mosaic throws on the respective roles of Constantinople and Antioch in influencing its work in the third decade of the sixth century: Constantinople, whence it was long ago suggested the creators of the mosaic came;[626] Antioch, where approximately contemporary pavements include a few comparable figural representations, links with which might support the suggestion that our mosaic was set by Syrian masters.[627] Against the basic circumstance of the progressive gravitation of Cyprus into the cultural orbit of Constantinople[628] must be set the probability that, until 535, despite its ecclesiastical independence and Orthodox antipathy to Syrian Monophysitism, the Island would have remained in many respects closely linked to Antioch, through which its secular and military administration was channeled.

In the choice of the theme, everything points to the capital as the source of a formula propagating the doctrine of the Incarnation, particularly since at Lythrankomi it avoided the practice, which must at the date in question

---

[623] Galassi, "Musaici di Cipro," 26–33.
[624] See note 424 *supra*. Galassi (*ibid.*, 28) added the Sinai encaustic icon of St. Peter, but this is generally assigned to Constantinople and to the seventh century.
[625] Kitzinger, *op. cit.*, 38 with note 146 citing Morey's earlier critics.
[626] Smirnov, "Mozaiki," 93.
[627] Lazarev, *Storia*, 47 and note 86.
[628] Megaw, "Metropolitan or Provincial?", *passim*.

be regarded as a provincial one, of including commemorative figures, as at Gaza and Poreč. Nor will the distribution of similar apostle borders elsewhere admit of any other origin; and we have seen that the inclusion of Jude, and in a rather senior position, though suggestive of Eastern affiliations, may be no more than a local conservative trait, understandable at a time when there was as yet no final agreement as to which apostles should be dropped when Mark and Luke were included in the Twelve.

The indications of iconographic factors do not so clearly favor the dominance of metropolitan influences. Indeed, the strict symmetry of the Virgin's arms, not found among surviving monuments in the metropolitan area but adopted on the group of ivories commonly attributed to Syria, is at first sight a contrary factor; it might seem decisive but for its reappearance on one of the ampullae, which are now connected iconographically with Constantinople. Instead, this feature and some others, such as the extreme simplicity of the Virgin's costume, the retention of the classical philosopher position for Christ's hands, the natural color of His lamb's wool himation (*vice* gold), are all best explained as features of the archetypal Incarnation image conceived in the capital. If they appear archaic in a sixth-century context, their survival is not surprising in a proverbially conservative milieu such as Cyprus.

Nor can we cite in support of Antiochene inspiration the wide-sleeved chiton exposing the forearm where this is not covered by the outer garment, for in the sixth century it is represented on the Riha paten, a product of the workshops of the city in the time of Justin II. Further, the bare forearms of the Evangelists on the throne of Maximian, for which, if not a metropolitan origin, at least metropolitan influences are now accepted, suggest that this feature of early iconography was equally acceptable at Constantinople under Justinian.

As to the mandorla, if it is to be explained as an intrinsic part of a proclamation of Chalcedonian doctrine in the face of Monophysite heresy, as Marina Sacopoulo has proposed, Syria would be the last place to seek a precedent. We have noted, however, that in its treatment not as a source of light but as a heavily bordered ethereal clipeus it matches the mandorla of Christ in the Ascension miniature of the Rabbula Gospels; but the implication of this similarity is equivocal in view of the probability that the Syrian illuminator used Byzantine models. Furthermore, the appearance of precisely the same treatment of the irisated border round the great medallion in the dome of the Salonica Rotunda links our mosaicist rather closely to Byzantium. Not so the other unique feature, the representation of the fan-leaved Palmyra palm, suggestive of Eastern affiliations though possibly modeled on a local variety. We have also considered whether the appearance of our intermediate border in a simplified form among the marble sculpture from St. Polyeuktos could be the result of independent borrowing by sculptor and mosaicist from Eastern sources; but comparable and approximately contemporary ornament in Ravenna is against this. Among the formal elements, we have also noted, for what it is worth, that some significant letter-forms used in the names of

the apostles recur in the sixth-century inscriptions from the Syrian coast;
and it may be significant that the earliest dated example of the vertical
writing used for these names is on the lintel of a Syrian church (A.D. 517).

Turning to figure style, in considering the Lythrankomi mosaicist's treatment of the heads it should be remembered that they are quite small. In fact,
after the apostles' features had been set, it required only a few dozen tesserae
to render the flesh tones in the exiguous areas that remained, even though
tesserae of reduced size were used. There was thus little scope for the virtuosity
to be expected of a Byzantine mosaicist and to be seen, perhaps at its highest
level, in the heads of the martyrs in the Salonica Rotunda, which are much
larger. There, row after row of well fitted tesserae follow contours carefully
selected to bring out the modeling of the face. This exploitation of the old
vermiculatum manner is reflected in the conch of S. Vitale and is recognized as
a characteristic of Byzantine influence when it appears in later mosaics both
in Ravenna and Rome.[629] It appears in Cyprus in the head of the Theotokos
at Kiti.[630] Even making allowance for the smaller scale of the Lythrankomi
heads, it must be admitted that they were executed differently, with less
systematization of the tesserae into concentric lines and patterns and, particularly in the head of Christ, in a more impressionistic manner. Nevertheless,
especially by comparison with most of the heads of the Ravenna school,
those in the Lythrankomi apse are executed in a sophisticated, painterly
style in which there is a conscious attempt by gradation of tones to give
illusions of relief. These effects were achieved by the use of small fine-grained
marble tesserae, which offers a further contrast to the practice of Italian
mosaicists in the fifth and sixth centuries, who normally used for flesh areas
glass tesserae of the same size as they used elsewhere. However, no such
striking differences of technique are known to distinguish the various Eastern
schools of mosaicists; the use of marble tesserae for faces was probably common
to them all.[631] On the other hand, if the *vermiculatum* manner is the hallmark
of the workshops of Constantinople and only reached Cyprus after the Island,
in 535, passed into the administrative orbit of the capital, we may ask: does
the Lythrankomi master's style reflect the tradition of an early sixth-century
Antiochene mosaic school? This question has already been posed by Maria
Soteriou.[632]

Now that it is becoming possible to distinguish the work of the sixth-
century silversmiths of Constantinople from that of their Syrian contemporaries, their respective figure styles must be taken into account. The round-

---

[629] But when it appears in some heads of Pelagius II's mosaics in S. Lorenzo fuori le Mura, this
can only be due to the employment of Byzantine craftsmen (cf. Oakeshott, *Mosaics of Rome* [*supra*,
note 277], 145 f.) if one rejects the view that only those of St. Lawrence and of Pelagius himself,
rendered in large glass tesserae, are in their original state (P. Baldass, "The Mosaic of the Triumphal
Arch of San Lorenzo fuori le Mura," *GBA*, 49 [1957], 1 ff.).

[630] For a detail, see Megaw, "Metropolitan or Provincial?", fig. 22.

[631] On this difference between Eastern and Western mosaic technique, see especially Nordhagen,
"The Mosaics of John VII" (*supra*, note 213), 154 ff., who, however, cites spasmodic examples of the
Eastern marble technique in Ravenna under Byzantine influence from the time of Theodoric.

[632] Soteriou, Τοιχογραφίαι μοναστικῆς τέχνης (*supra*, note 7), 246.

faced apostles on the Stuma paten and the beardless heads of Christ on the Hermitage lamp and the Cleveland chalices are considered characteristic of the iconographically backward Syrian workshops. They contrast with the more strongly modeled, more forceful heads of the Constantinopolitan silversmiths, notably those on the Leningrad reliquary of 550, including the bearded Christ, and those on the Riha paten.[633] If this distinction existed already at the beginning of Justinian's reign, before the decline of Antioch, it might be possible to relate to the provincial style of the Syrian silversmiths the preference of the Lythrankomi mosaicist for the simplified, youthful type of head which he used for many of the apostles. But the point cannot be pressed in view of the great discrepancy in scale between silverwork and monumental art.

In Antioch, as in Constantinople, no figural wall mosaics of the period have survived, but, insofar as it is relevant, we have a fairly clear picture of the figure style current there in pavement mosaics in the years before the earthquake of 526. Already in the fifth century, the Megalopsychia bust in the upper level of the Yakto complex is represented in full frontality with eyes staring into space, but not yet of abnormal size;[634] but later there were relapses both into frankly three-quarter views[635] and into slightly oblique poses, sometimes in heads basically conceived as frontal[636] like that of the Lythrankomi archangel. This contradiction is repeated in the central figure of the Worcester Hunt, approximately contemporary with our mosaic: here, despite the frontal outline of the head, the huntsman looks sideways and his blurred features are impressionistically treated. That the classical tradition died hard at Antioch is indicated no less by the stance of this bare-armed figure in the pose of a Hellenistic prince.[637] In this series, the head of Ge from the upper level of the House of Aion (early sixth century) has all the appearance of an intruder, thanks to its strict frontality and the enlarged staring eyes, heavily outlined as at Lythrankomi;[637a] while the flanking *putti* with their strongly drawn contours forcibly recall the supporting figures of Byzantine official iconography. This suggests that, like the theme and the formal composition of the Lythrankomi mosaic, the frontal iconic pose of its heads, the enlarged eyes, and the heavily drawn, stereotyped features do not represent any Syrian *penchant* for abstract forms, but were part and parcel of an official style radiating ever further from Constantinople. By the date in question, this would already have been an important influence on the workshop in Cyprus to which it is suggested the Lythrankomi master belonged.

That would leave for possible attribution to Antioch only the painterly manner in which our mosaicist used the tesserae to give a fleshy, plastic quality

---

[633] Cruikshank Dodd, *Silver Treasures*, 53 f. for Syrian examples, with figs. 3, 38, and *ibid.*, 48 ff. for Constantinopolitan, with figs. 37, 39, and 43.

[634] Levi, *Antioch Pavements*, I, 575, and II, pl. LXXVI, b.

[635] E.g., the busts in the late fifth-century House of Ge and the Seasons: *ibid.*, II, pl. LXXXIV, d.

[636] E.g., the Ktisis bust in the early sixth-century House of Ktisis: *ibid.*, I, 575, and II, pl. LXXXV, a.

[637] *Ibid.*, I, 578 f., and II, pls. LXXXVI, b, and CLXXIII, a.

[637a] *Ibid.*, I, 576, and II, pl. LXXXIV, d.

to the faces and an organic appearance to the exposed feet and arms. However, in the contemporary Antioch pavements these particular qualities of the Lythrankomi figural style cannot be matched at all closely, though this may be due to the rather coarse execution of such floors as the Worcester Hunt. Consequently, a debt to Antioch in the style of our mosaic, though probable, remains unproven, and it would be rash in the circumstances to suggest that the character, still quite unknown, of contemporary wall mosaics in that city can be seen in this village church in Cyprus.

The fragments in the Lythrankomi apse, we may conclude, belong to a mosaic thoroughly metropolitan in theme and composition, but including iconographic features which, in a work dating probably from the first years of Justinian's reign, must be counted conservative and provincial. These and the conflicts of style, for example between the stark formality of the apostles' features and the realistic rendering of the flesh areas round them, would not be surprising in Cyprus in the work of a local hand. That such it be is not necessarily gainsaid by the skill of its execution, which is of a high order, unexpected in a church of secondary importance. Indeed, while this Justinianic mosaic, one of the few surviving in the Byzantine sphere in pristine condition (as far as it is preserved), is of prime importance as a close reflection of the art of Constantinople, it is also a valuable index of the high quality of church decoration in the provinces, even in relatively remote areas, during the sixth century.

PART THREE

The Frescoes

Little remains of the painted decoration of the church and what there is is much damaged. In many places the original painted surfaces have been lost through the action of moisture and where they do survive, inevitably on the paintings of comparatively late date, the workmanship is in no way outstanding. What is preserved is of several distinct periods and, as we have already seen, it is relevant at several points to the structural history of the building. It is for this reason, rather than for their meager intrinsic value, that the principal fresco fragments from each period are presented here, together with an estimate of the date of each group based on the evidence of style. Apart from a few relatively early fragments, which are isolated from each other, there are some remains of two general redecorations to be associated respectively with the second and third restorations of the church. Something also survives of two undertakings intermediate between these: the earlier of two superimposed equestrian representations of St. George in the south aisle, and scenes from a Last Judgment composition on the north wall of the nave.

THE EARLY FRAGMENTS

There are tantalizing remains of a long painted inscription on one of the piers of the south arcade—on the west face of the first pier from the west (fig. 92). The inscription was painted in red on the white surface of a thin layer of plaster, beneath which an earlier plaster can be seen. Consequently, it is not contemporary with the first restoration of the church. On the other hand, it was painted before the pier was extended southward in the second restoration, after which the inscription was at some time plastered over. Parts of a Virgin and Child from the subsequent redecoration of the enlarged pier survive, to the right of the inscription. There are traces of a red border framing the inscription at the top, where it coincided with the fillet at the head of the pier, and down the left margin. Nothing survives of the right-hand border. The lines nearest the top margin are the best preserved, but even here only the letters near the middle of the pier are at all clear. Parts of eleven lines can now be traced, but Smirnov copied additional letters from lines 12 to 14.[638] To judge from the space available there may have been about twenty lines in all.

---

[638] Smirnov, "Mozaiki," 68. On his reckoning the now missing letters which he saw were in lines 12 to 15, but the elements which he represented as parts of lines 9 and 10 must all belong to a single line, line 10.

Smirnov copied fifty-four letters or parts of letters. In the great majority of cases these are still present and his copy can be confirmed as correct; these confirmed letters are shown black on the facsimile in figure O. A few now doubtful or entirely lost are shown hatched. Smirnov observed that there was more of the inscription than he copied, covered by the later plaster; also that when this was removed it carried most of the painted letters with it. Subsequently, some of this plaster fell, notably at the beginning and end of the first two lines. The traces of letters remaining on the original plaster in these areas are shown in outline in the facsimile, in broken outline where doubtful. In 1961 those parts of the later plaster remaining in place were removed, that covering the ends of lines 3 to 11 in one piece.[638a] In these areas some more of the inscription was found adhering to the pier, while additional letters had been transferred to the back of the later plaster. The transferred letters have also been added to the facsimile, these also in outline, or in broken outline where doubtful. Elsewhere, neither the reverse of the removed plaster nor the original surface retained any trace of paint, an indication that when the inscription was plastered over much of it had already disappeared.

Some of the letter-forms are indicative of a relatively early date: the broad *alpha* with angle-bar, the very wide *mu* with the high angle-bar, and the *upsilon* with a long hasta. This, together with the structural context, suggests that the inscription was probably painted in the ninth or tenth century.

Although more of this unusual inscription is visible than when Smirnov offered readings of short passages in lines 2, 6, and 10, much of it remains obscure. We owe the following tentative transcript and comments to Professor Mango.

Γῆ βέβλημε κ(αὶ) οὐρ(ανὸν) περι[βέβ-]
λημε κ(αὶ) τὸ ὄνομα [μ]ου (?) ΕΝ – –
ḲΜΙΕ . . . ΑΚΟ ’Ιοάνης ἁμαρτί-
αν . . ΚΗ . . μετὰ τεσάρησυν ΑΔΕ . .
5 δ . . ε̣ . ΑΜȣCA τὸ ναὸ τῆς . . . . Α Θ(εο)υ
– – ἁ]γιοτάτου ἀρχηεπησκόπου Θεο⟨δώ⟩ρου
– – – – – Σολομόνος ‘Ιεροσολίμου
– – – – – – ΟΝΑΡ . ε̣[ὐ]σταθίου
– – – – – – Ε . Θ . . . ΟΗΛ . . ε̣Κ . .
10 – – – – – ε̣ ⁝ ’Ετελ[ειώθ]η Λ .
– – – – – – – – – Ọ – CΕΚ . .
– – – – – – – – ΕΘ – – –
– – – – – – – – ΟC – – –
– – – – – – – – Η – – –

This could be interpreted as an inscription commemorating a repair (?) of the church by John, a sinful deacon (?) with the collaboration of Theodore (?), archbishop (of Cyprus ?), Solomon of Jerusalem, and one Eustathius.

[638a] Subsequently lodged in the Cyprus Museum.

1. Γῆ βέβλημε καὶ are reasonably certain; οὐρανόν (with a sign of abbreviation above it) less so. Instead of περιβέβλημε, one can think of other possibilities, e.g., περίκημε, περιτέτμημε (= I am deprived of), etc. The beginning of the inscription shows rather a high style which contrasts with the erratic spelling. It is perhaps a quotation?

2. [μ]ου: σου or του are also possible, but the lacuna seems to call for the wider M.

3. The letters AKO suggest διάκων, but if the stroke under the K makes it an abbreviation we have: A κ(αὶ) ὁ Ἰοάνης.

4. Word division uncertain. ΑΔΕ at the end of the line suggests ἀδε[λφοῖς] or perhaps ἀδε[λφ]ού[ς], taking account of the ὃ at the beginning of line 5. The reading μετὰ τέσαρης (σ)υναδε[λφ]ου[ς] should probably be rejected because, to my knowledge, συνάδελφος did not at the time have the meaning of "colleague."

5. ΑΜὃCΑ: ending of verb, first person singular? If τὸ ναὸ (i.e., τὸν ναὸν) τῆς is right, one would expect something like ἁγίας ΘΚὃ after it.

6. ἀρχηεππηοκόπου is certain. The archbishop's name presents some difficulty (unless ΘΕΟΡὃ represents the unidentifiable name of his see). The omission of δω in Θεοδώρου is not very likely. The *rho* could easily be part of a *beta*, thus giving us Θεοβού[λου], but I have not encountered such a Christian name. If we emend the *rho* into a *delta*, we obtain Θεοδού[λου].

7. A Solomon, patriarch of Jerusalem (the only one by that name), is recorded in ca. 860–65: V. Grumel, *Traité d'études byzantines*. I, *La Chronologie* (Paris, 1958), 452.

10. The three dots placed vertically mark the end of a sentence or paragraph. Ἐτελειώθη is often used for the completion of the construction, repair, or decoration of a building, usually followed by a date.

If Solomon of Jerusalem in line 7 is the patriarch of that name, the inscription can be dated approximately and acquires thereby considerable importance. Unfortunately, the episcopal list of Cyprus is extremely incomplete for this period, so that the name of the archbishop (Theodoros or Theodoulos) does not provide any confirmation.

A fragment of a painted cross in the same position on the corresponding pier of the north arcade (fig. 93) is to be connected chronologically with the painted inscription, both on account of its position and its execution on the white plaster, which here also overlies an earlier layer. The plaster is similar to that of the twelfth-century restoration, but is not continuous with that on the twelfth-century addition on the north side of the pier. The cross is drawn freely, leaning to the left; it is not central but close to the south edge of the pier. The upper arm alone is preserved, 0.22 m. high, filled with cable pattern and with antenna-like serifs at the end. One serif of the left arm is also preserved. The cable is here enclosed by a firm outline and the cross is thus distinct from the plaited crosses which became popular in the eleventh century.[639] In relief sculpture, the transition from plain to plaited crosses seems

---

[639] Typical are those on the two panels in Athens from the church of St. John Mangoutis: G. Soteriou, *Guide du Musée Byzantin d'Athènes* (Athens, 1932), fig. 31.

to have come in the tenth century, for the crosses are plain in the church of Constantine Lips (907),[640] while that on a closure panel reused in the phiale of the Lavra on Mt. Athos, which doubtless formed part of the original furniture of the Catholicon, is plaited.[641] They appear somewhat earlier in manuscript illumination.[642] The suggested dating of the inscription in the ninth or tenth century is consequently appropriate for the cross also. The painting of the cross and the inscription, though it followed one of the replasterings between the first and the second restoration for which evidence was found in the apse (fig. H), does not appear to have been part of any general redecoration of the church.

REDECORATION FOLLOWING THE SECOND RESTORATION (TWELFTH CENTURY)

The badly damaged figure of Gabriel in the south aisle confronts one on entering the south door (fig. 90). It is painted on the masonry which was added to the fourth pier from the west of the south arcade in the second restoration, to provide at this point support for the first masonry vault over the south aisle. The panel is 0.80 m. wide and the plaster on which the Archangel is painted extends up to 2.30 m. above the floor, where there is a red border with a white line within it on the black ground. Only the upper part of the figure remains; it is disfigured by drips which have etched into the plaster. Almost all the surface paint is lost. The identification is in white letters 0.04 m. high on the black ground: OAP.. on the left and ΓA.. on the right. The nimbus is yellow and has a broad red rim decorated with a double row of white dots. The loros is yellow with a red border outlined in black and overpainted with a double row of white dots.

In the north arcade are remains of other figures which evidently belong to the same scheme of decoration as Gabriel. A figure on the west face of the second pier from the west is identifiable as St. Barbara (figs. 91, 96). The plaster on which it is painted continues southward behind the adjoining masonry. This was added to carry the inner arch which reinforces that built against the north wall of the nave in the second restoration. Consequently the plaster of the St. Barbara panel continues onto the masonry which carried the initial arch and also formed part of the northwest support of the twelfth-century dome. The surface on which the damaged St. Barbara is painted would thus have been 1.42 m. wide, wide enough to contain three figures of the same width (under 0.40 m.).[643] But it seems that only St. Barbara was painted; for the

[640] C. Mango and E. J. W. Hawkins, "The Monastery of Lips: Additional Notes," *DOP*, 18 (1964), figs. 18–20, 23, and 30.

[641] Grabar, *Sculptures*, pl. XLIV, 3.

[642] Grabar (*ibid.*, 98) cites those in the tenth-century MS of the Homilies of St. John Chrysostom, Athens 211 (*idem*, in *SemKond*, 5 [1932], pl. XXIV, 2 and 3), but there is an embryonic example with "ears" reminiscent of the serifs on the Lythrankomi cross in the British Museum, MS Add. 14593, dated 817 (Frantz, "Byz. Illum. Ornament," pl. XXIV, 8).

[643] The grouping of three female saints together was a common practice: e.g., SS. Barbara, Eirene, and Catherine at Hosios Loukas: E. Stikas, Τὸ οἰκοδομικὸν Χρονικὸν τῆς μονῆς Ὁσίου Λουκᾶ (Athens, 1970), pl. 16; SS. Barbara, Marina, and Anastasia in the church at Moutoullas in Cyprus, dated 1280: Soteriou, Μνημεῖα, pl. 87a.

plaster behind the added masonry is seen to be white. It is unlikely that this figure was painted after the later masonry was added, because in that case it would have been placed centrally in the space this left exposed, which is not the case; nor would the style of this figure admit of its association with the third restoration. We may conclude that St. Barbara belongs to the same stage in the history of the church as Gabriel: a partial redecoration after the twelfth-century restoration. Only the right-hand side of the upper part of the figure survives, with some surface paint on her left shoulder. The black background is overpainted in blue and is surrounded by the usual red border with a white line; the panel was originally just over two meters high. The end of St. Barbara's name is preserved in elegant white letters 0.04 m. high written vertically and followed by a group of four dots arranged in a diamond pattern below: .. B|A|P|A|∴. The nimbus is 0.28 m. in diameter. Her costume was of red brocade with small roundels in green and yellow encircled by white dots. A larger medallion covers the preserved shoulder: a central arabesque enclosed by a border of squares, all in yellow. A white scarf with two yellow lines at the hem hangs on either side of her neck.

The pattern on St. Barbara's costume, of roundels ringed with dots to represent pearls, was popular in the twelfth century in Cyprus. It appears on the valence of the bed in the Asinou Dormition (1105/6),[644] at Perachorio,[645] and on the painted stone panels in the icon screen of the chapel in the hermitage of St. Neophytos,[646] which evidently formed part of the original furnishings of 1183.[647] The ornamented rim of Gabriel's nimbus is another distinctive feature of the same period; it can be compared with the double row of pearls round the nimbus of St. Stephen the Younger in St. Neophytos' chapel,[648] and the more elaborate jeweled edgings round those of the Pantocrator at Perachorio[649] and of St. George in the narthex at Asinou,[650] a figure now assigned to the late twelfth century.[651] Another example, precisely dated to the year 1192, is the rim of the Virgin's nimbus in the Nativity at Lagoudera.[652] Elsewhere, earlier examples of these distinctive features can be cited and they certainly survived later; but in Cyprus, coupled with the elegant lettering of St. Barbara's label, they do suggest work of the later twelfth century.

On the north wall of the nave a section of painted zigzag border has survived (figs. 94–95), which can reasonably be associated with Gabriel and St. Bar-

---

[644] *Ibid.*, pl. 79; Megaw-Stylianou, *Mosaics and Frescoes*, pl. VIII.

[645] On the altar frontal in the Communion: Megaw-Hawkins, "Perachorio," 303, fig. C, 1.

[646] Mango-Hawkins, "St. Neophytos," figs. 50 and 51.

[647] *Ibid.*, 161; for the date, p. 124; and for twelfth-century examples in Cappadocia, p. 161 note 133.

[648] *Ibid.*, fig. 41.

[649] Megaw-Hawkins, "Perachorio," fig. 4 and p. 303, fig. C, 2.

[650] Harold (Buxton), Bishop of Gibraltar, *et. al.*, "The Church of Asinou, Cyprus, and its Frescoes," *Archaeologia*, 83, pl. 97, 2; Soteriou, Μνημεῖα, pl. 83, b.

[651] C. Mango, "Summary of Work Carried out by the Dumbarton Oaks Byzantine Center in Cyprus, 1959–1969," *RDAC*, 1969, p. 103. Noteworthy also is the simple edging of pearls represented on the haloes of the Theotokos and of Christ in the lunette fresco of the Phorbiotissa in the same church (Harold [Buxton], *et al.*, *op. cit.*, pl. 95, 2; Soteriou, Μνημεῖα, pl. 82, b; Papageorghiou, *Masterpieces*, pl. XI, 2); for the narthex decoration to which it belongs is in several areas a demonstrable reproduction of the original late twelfth-century scheme.

[652] Stylianou, *Painted Churches*, fig. 30; Megaw-Stylianou, *Mosaics and Frescoes*, pl. XV.

bara. It is almost hidden by the masonry added to the fourth pier of the arcade from the west, in particular by that which reinforces the north arch of the dome. The border is on the narrow section of the south face of the original pier, between the pilaster engaged to it and its southwest corner. The plaster on which it is painted extends onto the west side of the pilaster and, further, onto the west face of the twelfth-century masonry added to carry the first dome. This face and the narrow side of the pilaster were treated as a single panel in the redecoration that followed. This panel had red borders at the left and top, 2.40 m. above the floor, and the extent of the black ground within them suggests that it contained a standing figure. The zigzag border on the narrow face at right angles to this panel is preserved only close to the springing of the adjoining arch. Above this, at a height of 2.20 m. above the floor, it is covered by the later plaster carrying the soffit decoration (fig. 102) and the fresco of the Resurrection from the Sea in the Last Judgment scenes (fig. 105), for both of which a date in the fourteenth century is proposed below. The border comprises a wavy black line down the middle of a broad white zigzag which is edged by pairs of straight lines, also in black. The triangular spaces remaining at the sides are filled with crenellated half-lozenges in red with white centers. The whole border is edged with red bands. Both zigzag bands and crenellated lozenges are characteristic of Middle Byzantine ornament. Crenellations are most common in manuscripts, enamels, and mural decoration during the eleventh and twelfth centuries.[653] The border design of crenellated lozenges is particularly well represented in wall paintings both in Cyprus and elsewhere in the twelfth century.[654]

This border and the figures of Gabriel and St. Barbara are far removed from each other in the church, but there are comparable fragments elsewhere[655] to indicate at least a partial redecoration after the second structural restoration of the church.

THE EARLIER PANEL OF ST. GEORGE

On the south wall of the south aisle and just west of the door are the scant remains of two superimposed panels containing equestrian figures of St. George (fig. 99). The earlier is 2.05 m. high and bordered by a red band with a white line inside it on the black ground. Its lower limit is 0.72 m. above the floor and the space below is occupied by a dado painted at the same time (fig. 97). Along the top, the plaster was wiped onto the masonry and the decoration at no time extended above this. The right half of the panel is covered by the plaster on which the later representation of St. George was painted, but part

[653] Frantz, "Byz. Illum. Ornament," 49.

[654] Cf. Megaw-Hawkins, "Perachorio," 340. A more complex example with the lozenges enclosed in circles decorates a window reveal in the funerary chapel at Bačkovo: A. Kostova and K. Kostov, *Bačkovski Monastir* (Sofia, 1963), pl. 37. The chapel, erected in 1083, was probably not decorated before the mid-twelfth century (cf. A. Grabar, *La peinture en Bulgarie* [Paris, 1928], 56).

[655] E.g., in the corresponding position to St. Barbara in the next bay to the east, the remains of the upper part of another figure, presumably male. A red robe below the neck and a green garment over the shoulders can be distinguished. This figure was at some time covered with a rendering of plaster.

of the earlier one remains visible to a width of 1.10 m. Near the top border a few letters of the inscription in white paint remain between a pair of incised lines 4.5 cms. apart: ΑΓΙΟ[C] ΓΕω[ΡΓΙΟC]. Nothing is left of the Saint, but the head of the white horse seen in profile is preserved, with green ears and red mane (fig. 100). The harness is red with yellow decoration of two transverse strokes alternating with large spots. Above the horse's mane is a corner of the Saint's red shield outlined and decorated in white. In the lower part, below the point where the horse's hooves would be, there are traces of three pink fish drawn in black; the least destroyed was about 0.27 m. in length (fig. 98). The water in which they swim is grey-blue with waves indicated in black outline. In this representation of the popular legend, St. George evidently slew the man-eating dragon in or by the lake which it inhabited.[655a] Horizontal scribed lines indicate the position of the red border above the dado, which is composed of alternate straight red lines and wavy black ones forming continuous chevron patterns (fig. 97).

The dado is a better indication of the date when this wall was first decorated than anything surviving in the representation above it. The same type of decoration is used on the back of the stone panels of the icon screen in the hermitage of St. Neophytos, and also in the bema and the cell, all of which are probably to be connected with the works of 1183 when the Enkleistra was painted "throughout."[656] Consequently, at first sight, this dado suggests that the St. George panel formed part of the same redecoration as the figure of Gabriel which is almost opposite it. However, on the north wall of the south aisle the upper border of the Gabriel panel is only 2.05 m. above the floor, while that of the St. George panel is 2.77 m. above it; nor are the borders of the two panels identical. These discrepancies are explained by the disparity of the two walls: the Archangel is a survivor from the decoration of the aisle in its first vaulted form, whereas St. George adorns a wall which was built *de novo* when the aisle was reconstructed with a vault at a higher level. The late twelfth-century character of the dado below St. George indicates an early rather than a late medieval date both for this reconstruction and for the painting of the first St. George panel, probably within the limits of the thirteenth century. At two points the remains of this panel are covered by small patches of painted plaster. These indicate that, after the painting of the later version of St. George, that part of the first which remained exposed was painted out.

THE LAST JUDGMENT SCENES

In the nave, the dome bay of the north wall retains a uniform plaster over most of the surface below the clerestory windows (fig. 30). This same plaster,

---

[655a] Likewise, in a fresco of 1475 at Pedoulas an equestrian St. George Diasorites rides through choppy water (Soteriou, Μνημεῖα, pl. 103). M. Chatzidakis reports an earlier representation of St. George and St. Demetrius together riding through the waves, in which fish appear. This is part of the decoration of the church of St. George Sphakiotes in the Diavaïde region (Pediada) in Crete, which bears a graffito of 1414: Κρ.Χρον. 6 (1952), 67. We owe this reference to Temily Mark-Wiener.

[656] Mango-Hawkins, "St. Neophytos," figs. 52, 60, and 100.

which was not the first on this wall, extends onto the soffits of the two arches (the third and fourth of the pier-arcade from the west), onto the west reveal of the third arch and, on the east, overlaps the zigzag border discussed above. In the soffits of the arches there are broadly painted coffer designs in red and black (figs. 102–3). The west reveal of the third arch had a dado 0.80 m. high and in the space above (1.21 by 0.63 m.), on the left side, there is the trace of an angel advancing toward the right. The background was white with a red border and a thin black line round it. The height of the angel is 0.75 m. and the red outline of the nimbus is 0.21 m. in diameter (fig. 101). The mantle is green over a blue-grey robe. The white ground and the trace of the left hand upraised suggest that this panel is to be read as part of the Paradise scene above the arch, while the positioning of the angel, so far to the left that the wing is cut by the border, also relates the figure to the decoration of the nave wall. This angel could then be regarded as one of those usually in attendance on the Virgin in Paradise scenes. Here the main representation above the arch is 1.60 m. in width, bounded at the sides by the engaged pilasters (fig. 104). The composition extended up to 0.90 m. above the top of the arch and down to the level of the springing at the sides. Virtually none of the surface paint survives. The background here also is white with a red border and a black line round it, as in the reveal below. At the center is the seated figure of the Virgin, 0.60 m. high, with hands in orant position. Her nimbus is yellow with a red outline, 0.22 m. in diameter, and her robes are black. The seat is just distinguishable, represented (in the underpaint) as a solid plinth seen in perspective. On the left is the trace of a larger seated figure, with nimbus 0.25 m. in diameter; this appears to have been Abraham with souls in his lap. On the right are the faint traces of a nude figure, with nimbus 0.22 m. in diameter, which was no doubt the Good Thief.

In the corresponding but slightly wider area (1.68 m.) above the fourth arch there is a much destroyed painting of the sea giving up its dead (fig. 105). The ocean is represented as a dark oval inset separated by low cliffs from the white surround. The personification of the sea raises a ship with mast and lateen sail balanced on his left hand and carries a rudder on his right shoulder. He is seated upon a long-necked black monster, whose head is turned back to face him. Fish disgorging the drowned are depicted here and there in the water (fig. 123). Surface paint survives only in a few small patches.

There was another zone of paintings above these two compositions, but too little of it remains even to attempt identification of the scenes. However, it may be hazarded that in the division above the Resurrection from the Sea the arrangement of the latter was reversed: the central part of light color and the surround dark. On the assumption that the clerestory windows went out of use in the second restoration, when new windows were provided in the gables, a height of 2.30 m. below the sills of these twelfth-century windows would have been available for the upper paintings. This would have been enough for two more zones comparable in height with the surviving one, which would have given good scope for other main elements of a Last Judgment.

These sadly effaced fragments are demonstrably later than the twelfth-century decoration to which the zigzag border belonged and have nothing in common with the figures of Gabriel and St. Barbara which are related to it; nor with the fragments of the first St. George panel. On the other hand, the severe pecking on the Sea scene and some fragments of later painted plaster adhering elsewhere prove that the Last Judgment scenes were concealed by a later decoration, doubtless that which followed the third restoration. These relationships and the meager indications of the fragments themselves suggest that the Last Judgment scenes were painted in the fourteenth century. The Sea scene is close to that in the narthex of the Asinou church painted in 1333; the personification is of similar scale and raises a similar ship.[657] In the Paradise scene nothing that survives is at variance with Palaeologan iconography. As for the primitive character of the soffit designs, all that need be said is that one of those in the bema belonging to the subsequent redecoration includes comparable elements (figs. 106 and 118).

THE LAST REDECORATION

The remaining frescoes are located in several parts of the bema and the nave and, though more have survived at the east end, they attest a general redecoration of the entire central part of the church. In the bema dome is a large-scale bust of Christ Pantocrator (fig. 106). In spite of the effaced condition of the painting it can be seen that the head, set high in the apex of the steep crown of the dome, is on an axis turned slightly toward the south. The right hand is raised in blessing and the left clasps a Gospel book. The nimbus is yellow and, as far as can be seen, had neither border nor cross. The dark himation was originally purple and the chiton red with a yellow clavus. No inscription survives. The background is blue-black. The circular frame (fig. 107) was possibly intended to represent marble inlay: within red borders, a folded band with alternate red and yellow faces forms a zigzag with yellow triangles in the interspaces. On the blue-black background of the drum, the *Hetoimasia*, the Preparation of the Throne, occupied the east side, but of this little more than outlines scribed in the plaster has survived. Flanking it are two medallions, that to the north containing a bust of the Virgin (fig. 108) and the other a bust of John the Baptist (fig. 109). Three more medallions with busts of archangels are placed at the other cardinal points (fig. 110), that at the south containing two figures. In the intervening spaces are four six-winged figures (fig. 111), that at the southwest with a bull's head protruding from the right side, identifiable as a tetramorph. Two Powers, pairs of interlaced three-winged circles, are preserved to the right of the south and west medallions respectively.

[657] Harold (Buxton), *et al.*, "The Church of Asinou," pl. 95, 1; Soteriou, Μνημεῖα, pl. 82, a; Stylianou, *Painted Churches*, fig. 22. The frescoes of 1333 overlie, and in some cases follow, a twelfth-century decoration, but if we compare the twelfth-century Sea in nearby Kakopetria, where the ship is lacking and the figure occupies virtually the whole ocean, it is clear that the Asinou scene represents the fourteenth-century iconography (see A. and J. Stylianou, Ὁ ναὸς τοῦ ἁγίου Νικολάου τῆς Στέγης, in Κυπρ.Σπουδ., 10 [1946], 123, fig. 76; *idem, Painted Churches*, fig. 10).

Of the inscriptions, only the first sigla of the Virgin's identification and the greater part of the Baptist's remain.

In the pendentives below, the evangelists are seated against a background of architectural features (figs. 114–17). Luke can be identified in the northeast by his inscription (fig. 116). All are writing in books, with the exception of the evangelist in the northwest, identifiable as John (fig. 117), for he holds the rolled ends of a scroll inscribed with εἶπε ὁ κ(ύριο)ς ἐαν μὴ ... taken either from John 3:3 or from John 6:53, in either case a text highly appropriate for a position above the altar table.

On the south wall of the bema are the remains of an Ascension (fig. 118); Christ in an oval mandorla, supported by two angels, occupied the lunette area at the top. Some of the surface paint toward the right at the top is preserved, with parts of the seated figure of Christ, most of the right half of the inscriptions: [IC] | XC and [H ANA] | ΛΥΨ[IC], and much of the angel on the right; but all else is lost. The soffit of the arch above was painted with a representation of marble revetments (fig. 115). The corresponding soffit in the north side is decorated with an elaborate rinceau design (fig. 107).

Across the west face of the transverse arch above the entrance to the bema is a large-scale Annunciation. It is the best preserved fragment of the series; the center and the lower parts at the sides are in a fair state, but the heads of both the Virgin and the Angel are lost (fig. 119). The background is black with a green ground below. The inscription is on the otherwise blank space at the center: O ΕΒΑΓΓΕΛΙC|M|O|C. On each side are arcades, grey on the left and white on the right, with checkered pavements in yellow and brown beneath them rendered in a somewhat confused perspective. The right-hand side is lit by three rays which are projected from the top border at the center. A dove descends from the middle ray upon the Virgin who is kneeling at a prie-dieu (fig. 113). Her right hand and that side of her body are intact but of the head there remains only a faint trace of the preliminary sketch, in red. The hand is raised in an attitude of surprise and the head was inclined toward the dove. The figure wears a dull-blue robe with a yellow cuff, and a purple maphorion. Gabriel advances vigorously from the left (fig. 112); but the whole of the upper part of the figure is lost. His right hand is extended toward the Virgin in a gesture of speech. A staff carried over his shoulder is held in the left hand. The feet are bound with thongs but there is no other indication of sandals. Gabriel wears a red himation over a dull-blue robe which is seen only at the right wrist and along the hem, where there is a white highlight at the left ankle. Just below the right foot the preliminary drawing in red is exposed where the green ground has been eroded. This green ground extended under the Angel's feet, but beneath the Virgin it is terminated a little below her prie-dieu, and a purple panel occupies the space below.

In the short barrel vault covering the east end of the nave are some remains of scenes from the Passion cycle. In the lower half on the south are two seated figures, which must have formed part of the Washing of Feet (fig. 121). Opposite, on the north side, is a fragment of the Betrayal including six of the heads: Christ receiving the kiss from Judas, two apostles to the left, and two soldiers on the right (fig. 120).

In the arches built against the nave walls to support the same vault were some figures of individual saints: in the soffits two three-quarter-length figures on either side, on the reveals below the springings of the arches a full-length figure in each case, and three more on the nave wall within the arch on either side; all of them destroyed beyond recognition. In one case only, the figure on the left of the group on the south wall, scribed lines drawing the folds of the robes can be seen.

At the foot of the same arches on the east side, the reveals of the initial arches in the nave walls, together with those of the higher added arches supporting the later vaulting, form two continuous flat surfaces of masonry between the central and the side sections of the icon screen. That on the north side has lost all its plaster, but in this prominent position on the south side part of a Nativity is preserved. On the surviving fragment two of the Magi are seen arriving on horseback at the cave in which the Virgin, robed in red, sleeps with her back to the manger, upon which the star sheds a ray of light from above (fig. 129). The scale is small (the Virgin's nimbus only 0.16 m. in diameter) and the surface heavily loaded with candle wax. Below, a dado with a wavy design with rapidly painted leaf forms is in a fair condition along the base of the wall. It is bounded above with bands of red, yellow, and green, and below with red and yellow (fig. 122).

On the reveal opposite, on the east face of the easternmost south pier, were two figures of which only the upper parts remain (fig. 130). On the left, filling an area originally 0.53 m. by 2.00 m., is St. Helena with a white cross in her left hand; the right hand is raised with palm outward. She wears a red mantle edged with pearls, clasped at the front with a brooch, over a red robe decorated with pearls in groups of five in the form of a cross. The collar and the front-piece are yellow with a red foliate design and edged with pearls. On the right, occupying a much wider space (1.27 by 2.00 m.), with only the first few letters of his inscription, is a beardless saint with a light staff carried over his right shoulder. The proportions of the panel suggest that he is mounted upon an animal. He is probably St. Mammas riding on a lion, as he is usually portrayed. A brown area toward the bottom left corner of the panel is probably one of the lion's paws.

Below the main dome, in the soffits of the arches introduced to support it, was a series of standing figures, prophets, no doubt. Something remains of three of them. That on the east side of the north arch holds a scroll (fig. 132). The other two, on either side of the east arch, are even more fragmentary.

High on the west wall of the nave, to the left of the cross-shaped window, there are the remains of two nimbed figures. These seem to have extended only down to the waists, where there is a horizontal mass of red. At a rather lower level on the extreme right are the traces of two more figures, of which only the nimbed heads remain, one above the other. These fragments could possibly have formed part of a large composition of the Dormition.

On the east reveal of the fourth arch on the south side are two standing figures, of which the lower parts are lost (fig. 131). On the left is a female saint with a red himation drawn over her head (diam. of the nimbus, 0.33 m.). Her right hand is raised with palm exposed and a cross is held in the left. No inscription remains. On the right is St. Eleazar, a bearded saint with hands in similar position, and also holding a martyr's cross. He wears a brown robe with a darker clavus over his right shoulder. In the same position in the first arch on the south side, on plaster which at one time covered the early inscription, are traces of a Virgin and Child which seem to belong to the same series of paintings.

Some of the remains of painted plaster in the narthex also appear to belong to this last general redecoration: those on the masonry blocking the doorway into the north aisle and the fragment in the extreme southeast corner.

On the south wall of the south aisle, covering the right-hand side of the earlier figure of St. George, there is a second equestrian painting of the Saint. This was probably part of the same general redecoration despite its more formal style (fig. 124). The top border is 0.16 m. lower than the earlier one, and the width of the area between the red side borders is 1.90 m. The Saint is identified by a Greek inscription, in two sections, written vertically: on the left O|A|Γ₁|O|S, on the right Γε|ω|Γ₁|O|S (visible in fig. 125, at the left). To the right of the second section are some further letters, written horizontally, but illegible (fig. 125). St. George's hair is a mass of red underpaint. His red cloak flows out behind him, decorated with white stars, and he wears yellow chain mail. The rectangular top of the shield is green with a yellow edging decorated with red and white. The horse is white, outlined in black, and the head is drawn in three-quarter view (fig. 126). On the background beside the horse's right cheek is a graffito: a monogram below the date 1598 (fig. 127).

The half-length painting of the Virgin and Child in the lunette over the south door (fig. 128) is related to the same general redecoration of the church by the rinceau on the soffit of the arch. This is of the same character as the rinceau on the soffit of the north dome arch in the bema (figs. 116–17). The painting is of the Hodegetria type but inscribed ΜΡ | ΘV and Η ΚΑΝΑ | ΚΑΡΗΑ (the Mother of God, the Kanakaria); on the interpretation, see *supra*, p. 6ff.. Christ has a cross-nimbus with the arms of the cross flaring at the rim. He sits erect on the Virgin's left arm, with his right hand extended horizontally to bless and a rotulus in his left. The Virgin's head is slightly turned toward the Child and her right hand is raised and extended toward Him.

The inscriptions are in white on a black background. The Virgin wears a red maphorion edged with yellow. This covers her other garments except the front edge of the veil covering her hair, which is blue-black and white, and the sleeve of her chiton seen on the right wrist; this is blue-black with a yellow cuff. Christ wears a light blue chiton with pale blue highlights, and over it a yellow himation with lighter yellow highlights and orange shadow lines.

In the left corner is a donor figure, a bearded man kneeling with his hands raised in prayer. He is clad in a white garment, seen on his arms and chest, which is covered by a voluminous black cloak. In front of him is a small female figure in white with her hands crossed on her breast, the position of the hands in burial.[658] This then is the donor's wife (or daughter) portrayed in her shroud, in whose memory the lunette was commissioned. Above the donor is his undated dedication in two short lines of which only a few letters are legible. It seems to start with Δέησις followed by Christian name(s) and family name (or rank).

This lunette painting is helpful in fixing the date of the last decoration, to which it belongs, and of the third structural restoration which occasioned it. The type of Hodegetria is that of the post-Byzantine icon painters. Much the closest of the published icons from Cyprus is that by the painter Titus at Tsadha, which has been dated about 1500.[659] In this the cross-nimbus has the same splayed ends to the arms of the cross and the position of Christ's hands, the left hand holding a rotulus, is the same as in the lunette.

CONCLUSION

These fresco remains of different periods, meager though they are, at least afford some aid in clarifying the involved structural history of the church. Those of late twelfth-century style attest the redecoration of many parts of the church, if not of the whole, at a time which is in line with our suggestion that the church first took its present form in a restoration occasioned by earthquake damage around the year 1160. The more extensive but hardly less effaced frescoes of the last redecoration, carried out to judge by their style in the years around 1500, confirm the architectural indications that the last general restoration, when the central dome was rebuilt, dates from just that time. The earliest fragments of painted decoration, the remains of an inscription and of a cross, adorned the church when it had the form of a basilica with pier arcades, but evidently do not belong to the time of its reconstruction as such, if this was undertaken around 700 as we have suggested, but to some reconditioning of its arcades, probably in the tenth century.

Through all these vicissitudes care was taken to preserve the apse of the original column-basilica erected in the last years of the fifth century, to judge by its capitals, which retained the steadily deteriorating (but never restored) remains of the mosaic with which it had been adorned about a generation later.

---

[658] Compare the portraits on the unusual memorial icons from the Chrysaliniotissa church in Nicosia: Rice-Gunnis, *The Icons of Cyprus*, no. 6 (pl. 1) and no. 7 (fig. 9); Papageorghiou, *Masterpieces*, pl. XLIV; idem, *Icons of Cyprus*, 38.

[659] Rice-Gunnis, *The Icons of Cyprus*, 212, no. 29 and pl. 19.

APPENDIX

A Wonderworking Mosaic in Cyprus

A mosaic representation of the Theotokos in Cyprus was included in a catalogue of fifteen wonderworking images which featured as part of the Orthodox case in the final phase of the struggle against iconoclast heresy. It was in search of this mosaic that the Russian scholar Jakov Smirnov visited Cyprus in 1895. His detailed study of what was known about it was published as an introduction to his account of the Lythrankomi and Kiti mosaics.[660] What follows is largely a summary of his conclusions.

The catalogue of wonderworking images survives in two manuscript copies of what purports to be a letter addressed to the iconoclast Emperor Theophilus by the three Eastern Patriarchs. The title at the beginning of the text which these MSS preserve gives the names of the signatories (Christopher of Alexandria, Job of Antioch, and Basil of Jerusalem) and indicates that the *Letter*, or at least the version of it which these MSS followed, was headed, somewhat provocatively in the circumstances, by a representation of the Theotokos. It also states that the *Letter* was composed at a "great synod" of 185 bishops, seventeen abbots, and 1153 monks assembled at Jerusalem in April of the year 836. Both these MSS are in the library of the Patmos monastery, one in cod. Patm. gr. 48 (item 9, fols. 379ᵛ–411ᵛ), and the other in cod. 179 (item 16, fols. 206ᵛ–230ᵛ). The text was first published by I. Sakkelion in 1864.[661] Although cod. 48 is a ninth-century MS,[662] the authenticity of the *Letter* has been questioned. It is, however, independently attested that two of the Patriarchs did meet at the time in Jerusalem, as Vasiliev has pointed out, to discuss "ecclesiastical matters," while the invalid Christopher of Alexandria was absent.[663] Nevertheless, it is questionable whether conditions then prevailing for Christians in the Caliphate would have permitted such a large gathering of Orthodox churchmen. In his discussion of the Patmos text, Vasiliev further observed that it is surprising to find in such a virtually public context a declaration of loyalty to the Emperor in the terms the *Letter* uses, frankly treasonable for subjects of the Caliph. But, whatever the precise status of this document, there is hardly any room for doubt that the list of wonder-

---

[660] Smirnov, "Mozaiki," 1–27. For an abbreviated Greek translation by A. Deliyannes, see Ἐκκλησιαστικὸς Κήρυξ (Larnaca, 1911), 43 ff.

[661] Sakkelion, Ἐκ τῶν ἀνεκδότων (*supra*, note 231), 97–112, 145–61, 193–206; Duchesne, "L'iconographie byzantine" (*supra*, note 231), 222–39, 273–85, 349–66.

[662] "Perhaps about the end of the ninth century": Sakkelion, Ἐκ τῶν ἀνεκδότων, 97, with facsimile specimen of the script on 102; "Perhaps about the middle or the end of the ninth century": *idem*, Πατμιακὴ Βιβλιοθήκη (Athens, 1890), 37. Cod. 179 is of the late twelfth or the thirteenth century: *idem*, Ἐκ τῶν ἀνεκδότων, 101.

[663] See A. Vasiliev, "The Life of St. Theodore of Edessa," *Byzantion*, 16 (1942–43), 216 ff.

working images did exist among the evidence proffered by the iconodule champions in the controversy. Indeed, the *Letter* is referred to in the *Narration on the Image of Edessa* which, though its attribution to Constantine Porphyrogenitus is questionable, was almost certainly composed in that Emperor's reign. There, the *Letter* is mentioned, together with the *Ecclesiastical History* of Evagrius, in terms that suggest they were the sources for the *Narration*.[664]

The catalogue is incorporated in the seventh section of the *Letter* and the contribution of Cyprus to it is its seventh item, immediately preceding that concerning the mosaic on the façade of the church of the Nativity at Bethlehem, to which reference has been made above.[665] It follows an account of the miraculous appearance of an image of the Theotokos in a church at Lydda, and reads as follows:[666]

Cod. 48, fol. 396ᵛ

fol. 397ʳ

ζ'. ἐν τῇ τῶν Κυπρίων χώρᾳ, ἐν μιᾷ τῶν αὐτῆς πολιχνίων, τὰ τοιαῦτα ἐνεργούμενα ἄχρι τῆς δεῦρο. Καὶ γὰρ ἐν τῇ αὐτῇ Κύπρῳ, τῷ προσνοτίῳ μέρει, εὐκτήριος οἶκος τῆς ἁγίας Θεοτόκου ἐνίδρυται, εἰκὼν ἐκ ψηφίδων. Ταύτην εἰς τὸ γόνατον ἔνθα ὁ σωτὴρ ‖ ἐγκόλποις¹ ἐγκάθηται² ἄραψ τις τοξεύσας εὐθέως ἐξῆλθε³ διαρρέον⁴ αἷμα ποταμηδὸν⁵ ἕως ποδῶν κρουνίζον⁶ καὶ ἐστὶ μέχρι τῆς σήμερον.

1 sic cod. 48; ἐγκόλπιος cod. 179, fol. 219   2 κάθηται cod. 179   3 ἐξῆλθεν cod. 48
4 διαρέον cod. 48   5 ποταμιδὸν codd.   6 κρουνίξων cod. 179

Smirnov suggested that the first sentence referred not to the mosaic but to a second image in Cyprus which it does not identify.[667] More probably, it was simply an editorial device to provide some continuity between the Lydda and the Cyprus items, which relate two quite different kinds of miraculous occurrence.

A version of the *Letter to the Emperor Theophilus*, which is regarded as "spurious and apocryphal,"[668] was ascribed formerly, and most curiously, to John of Damascus.[669] It made use of the text that has survived in the Patmos MSS, but it need not detain us; for it mentions neither the mosaic in Cyprus nor that on the façade of the Bethlehem church, doubtless because this derivative was more particularly concerned with icons.

It was evidently from the Patmos version of the *Letter* that the legend about the Cypriot mosaic was elaborated to form one of a collection of sermons in the sixteenth-century cod. Vat. gr. 1147. This wordy composition, which is accompanied by others based on stories about wonderworking images in the *Letter*, is headed as follows:

[664] PG, 113, col. 441.

[665] *Supra*, p. 73.

[666] Professor A. D. Komines has very kindly supplied this text, which supersedes those in Sakkelion, Ἐκ τῶν ἀνεκδότων, 157 (reprint, 29), and Duchesne, "L'iconographie byzantine," 282.

[667] Smirnov, "Mozaiki," 3.

[668] Vasiliev, "Life of St. Theodore," 216, following L. Duchesne, *Revue critique*, 1875 (1), 326, and V. Grumel, in *EO*, 29 (1930), 99.

[669] PG, 95, cols. 345–86, from Le Quien's edition of John of Damascus, II, 629–47, which copied the first edition in F. Combéfis, *Originum rerumque constantinopolitanarum, variis auctoribus, maniplus*, preceded by *Leonis Allati de Symeonum scriptis diatriba* (Paris, 1664), 110ff.

Λόγος διηγηματικὸς περὶ τοξευθείσης εἰκόνος τῆς ὑπεραγίας Δεσποίνης ἡμῶν Θεοτόκου καὶ ἀεὶ Παρθένου Μαρίας ἐν τῇ Κύπρῳ καὶ περὶ ἑτέρων τινῶν ὑποθέσεων. πάτερ εὐλόγησον.[670]

While embroidering the story of the Patmos *Letter* with extraneous matter, such as the claim that it was the mosaic's many miracles that provoked the Devil to assault it, this sermon gives no particulars of the mosaic or of its location other than those in the Patmos text, as Smirnov pointed out.[671]

Another version of the story, at the same time more succinct and more informative, appears in the *Thesaurus* of the monk Damascenos, a collection of sermons compiled by this sixteenth-century Thessalonian "sub-deacon and Studite."[672] Here, the twenty-fifth *logos*, which is entitled Διήγησις κοινῇ γλώσσῃ περὶ τῶν Ἁγίων Εἰκόνων, is clearly related to the text of the *Letter* as pre-served in Patmos; but that text may not have been its only source. For although in the *Thesaurus* there are again fifteen items, three of these do not feature in the catalogue incorporated in the *Letter*. Furthermore, in Damascenos' passage concerning the Cyprus mosaic there are some details not given in the Patmos text: the mosaic was outside the church, over the door; the Virgin was enthroned; angels stood on either side; the arrow pierced the Virgin's right knee; and the Arab assailant expired as he left the scene. None of these details derive from the version in the Vatican Library collection of sermons; nor, if we except the mention of the Devil, are there any features common to that version and the *Thesaurus* that are foreign to the ninth-century account. The question arises, were these details invented, perhaps by Damascenos himself, and interpolated after the story had crystallized in the form it has in the Patmos *Letter*, or do they derive from some more complete account which the writers of the *Letter* abbreviated? The relevant passage of the *Thesaurus* is as follows:[673]

καὶ εἰς τὴν Κύπρον δὲ τὴν νῆσον πρὸς τὸ νότιον μέρος, ἦτον ποτὲ ναὸς τῆς ὑπεραγίας Θεοτόκου. ἔξω δὲ τοῦ ναοῦ ἀπάνωθεν τῆς πόρτας, ἦτον μίαν (sic) εἰκὼν τῆς αὐτῆς Παναγίας ζωγραφισμένη μὲν ψηφίδας εἶχε δὲ σχῆμα, ὅτι ἡ μέν Παναγία ἐκάθετον εἰς θρόνον, καὶ ἐκράτει τὸν Χριστὸν ὡς βρέφος εἰς τὰ γόνατά της. δύο δὲ ἄγγελοι ἐστέκουνταν ἀπὸ τὰ δύο της μέρη μετὰ φόβου πολλοῦ. Μίαν γοῦν τῶν ἡμερῶν ἀπέρασεν ἀπ'ἐκεῖ ἕνας ἀράπης πηγενάμενος εἰς τὸ σπίτη του, καί, ὡς εἶχε τὸν διάβολον μέσα του, μόνον τὸν ἐφάνη καλὸν καὶ ἐδόξευσεν (ἐτόξευσεν) τὴν Παναγίαν εἰς τὸ δεξιὸν γόνατον, καὶ παρευθὺς ὡς (ὤ) τοῦ θαύματος, διὰ νὰ δείξη ἡ Παναγία τὴν ἐνέργειαν τῆς εἰκόνος της, αἷμα ἐχύθη περισσὸν ἀπὸ τὴν δομήν, καὶ ἔσταξεν εἰς τὴν γῆν. ὁ δὲ ἀράπης ὡς ἴδε τὸ θαῦμα, τρέμοντας καὶ φεύγοντας νὰ ὑπάγη εἰς τὸ σπίτη του, ἐξεψύχησεν εἰς τὴν στράταν.

Smirnov argued that both Damascenos and the compiler of the ninth-century catalogue as it was incorporated in the *Letter* made use of an earlier source, which the latter was obliged to condense. In support of this view he

---

[670] Fol. 129. The full text, which ends on fol. 130ᵛ, was transcribed by Smirnov, "Mozaiki," 6f.
[671] *Ibid.*, 7f.
[672] Damascenos, Βιβλίον ὀνομαξόμενον Θησαυρός (Venice, 1676). Later editions were printed in 1742, 1799, 1885, and 1893.
[673] As quoted from the 1676 edition, 378f., by Smirnov, "Mozaiki," 11.

cited the passages in the two texts relating to a representation of the Apostle Andrew on the wall of a church in a certain Aegean Island, the name of which was misread, and differently misread, in both. They agree that the island was in the Cyclades, but the *Letter* names it Lemnos which, as Sakkelion first pointed out, is far removed from the Cycladic group.[674] Damascenos located the church on the south shore of the island of Χειμονος.[675] Smirnov suggested that this impossible name and Λήμνῳ in the Patmos MSS of the *Letter* both represent Kimolos in the original source.[676] He clinched the matter by citing a ruined church of St. Andrew on the south coast of this Cycladic island.[677] It is difficult to resist so neat an explanation of the discrepancy. We may, then, accept as a possibility that the details of the Cyprus mosaic given by Damascenos, but lacking in the ninth-century text, are authentic elements of an earlier and more complete account of the miracle.

Some of these additional details are given also in the earliest version of the story traced by Smirnov in Russian literature: that in "The New Heaven" of Ivan Galiatovsky, first published in 1665.[678] In only one respect does this version differ from that of Damascenos: there is no indication that the medium of the image from which blood flowed was a mosaic. As his source Galiatovsky cited "the Greek synaxarion of the Sunday of Orthodoxy." Not surprisingly, Smirnov's search for this source in Greek synaxaria was fruitless, for this acknowledgment simply confirms the Russian writer's dependence on Damascenos. He must have used a MS copy of the *Thesaurus* which reached Russia before it was first printed; for in the list of contents of this work as printed the entry for the *logos* in question is ΚΕ', τῃ Κυρ. τῆς 'Ορθοδοξίας.

The circulation of such accounts in Russia inspired attempts to reconstruct on icons the appearance of the image to which they ascribed such remarkable ἐνέργεια. Like some more authentic Theotokos icon types circulating in Russia and reproducing originals located in Cyprus, these inventions were entitled the *Kypriakē*.[679] These in turn were reproduced in the nineteenth-century series of engravings of wonderworking images of the Virgin. One thing that is certain is that these engravings are wholly dependent on the texts and provide no independent evidence of any mosaic in Cyprus.[680] They illustrate no less than four iconographic types named the *Kypriakē*, but it is those that reproduce the type used on an icon commemorated on April 20[681] that were held to

---

[674] Sakkelion, 'Εκ τῶν ἀνεκδότων, 160 (reprint, 33), note §.

[675] Θησαυρός (1676) (*supra*, note 672), 383.   [676] Smirnov, "Mozaiki," 12.

[677] At the site *Ellenikā*: L. Ross, *Reisen auf den griechischen Inseln*, III (Stuttgart-Tübingen, 1845), 24. The old name of the offshore islet at this point, St. Andrew (now *Daskaliō*), is also significant; see J. T. Bent, *The Cyclades* (London, 1885), 55.

[678] I. Galiatovsky, *Nebo novoe* (Lvov, 1665), no. 36; quoted by Smirnov, "Mozaiki," 16.

[679] The earliest use of this name is recorded by Smirnov ("Mozaiki," 17) in a MS account of wonderworking images dating from the late seventeenth or early eighteenth century in the Moscow Historical Museum, no. 21061 (1890). Here, in item 35, the account of the Arab's assault on the *Kypriakē* is based on that in "The New Heaven," but it states that the image was on wood and adds that the blood which flowed from it was curative.   [680] *Ibid.*, 25.

[681] Some give the date 9 July A. M. 5900 (A. D. 392), by confusion with a half-length *Kypriakē*, which was commemorated in the cathedral of the Dormition in Moscow on 9 July, identifiable as the *Phaneromene* by the title of the Semena engraving of 1853, in which it is claimed that this icon appeared in Cyprus in 393 (*ibid.*, 19, 25).

represent the miraculous image of the story derived from the iconodule catalogue. Their engraved legends give no location for the original, probably because this was regarded as the Cypriot Virgin *par excellence*.[682] In this clearly invented type the Virgin wears a crown and is seated on a backless *thokos* with her head slightly turned toward the Child held on her left arm, somewhat as in the Hodegetria type, while the angels stand on either side, each offering a globe in one hand and carrying a lily branch in the other.[683]

Among these Russian icons and engravings purporting to represent the image of the iconodule legend, only one seems at first sight to offer a clue to its location in Cyprus. This *Kypriakē* bore an inscription suggesting that its prototype was at Larnaca, the ancient Kition; but although this would fit the indication for the location of the mosaic in the ninth-century text, no reliance can be placed on it. Only the inscription has been published: "10th of April of the year 480, in the place where Lazarus was buried,"[684] and without particulars indicating which of the *Kypriakē* icon types it concerns. *Prima facie* this inscription would be appropriate, not for a derivative from a monumental mosaic, but for a *Phaneromene* icon.[685] Further, as Smirnov pointed out, pilgrims and travelers who visited Cyprus do not mention any miraculous icon in Larnaca,[686] where they were chiefly concerned with the tomb that sheltered the supposed remains of Lazarus, until these were removed to Constantinople by Leo VI. It seems probable that by the expression "the place where Lazarus was buried" the inscription on this icon of the *Kypriakē* means just "Cyprus"; also that it concerns not the mosaic of the iconodule legend but a derivative of the *Phaneromene* icon long treasured in Nicosia.[687]

We may conclude that the Russian iconographers knew nothing of any mosaic surviving in Cyprus to which they could attach the story in their collections of wonderworking image legends. When producing a *Kypriakē* type of the Virgin to go with the story, they supplemented the scant particulars it gives by recourse to available, but quite irrelevant, copies of famous icons existing in the Island. Their imaginary creations are valueless in establishing either the location, or the iconography, of the mosaic whose miraculous powers the iconodules sought to exploit.

[682] Smirnov ("Mozaiki," 20) observed that in Russian manuscript collections of miraculous icon stories illustrated by these engravings it is this particular type of *Kypriakē* which is accompanied by an account of the Arab's assault.

[683] One of these engravings was reproduced by Smirnov ("Mozaiki," 21). He regarded as a derivative of this type one of the other three *Kypriakē* Virgins reproduced in the engravings: that identified as an icon in the village of Stromini, which he examined and found to be similar but no earlier than the beginning of the eighteenth century (*ibid.*, 23–25). However, this did not prevent it from performing, in the year 1841, a miraculous cure on the Sunday of Orthodoxy. This was appropriately timed for those who knew Galiatovsky's account of the prototype (if such it can be called) and his claim to have taken it from a Greek synaxarion of that day. But see *supra*, p. 164.

[684] D. A. Rovinskij, *Russkija narodnija kartiny*, IV = *Sbornik Akad. Nauk*, 26 (1880), 686; copied evidently from the *Klinstsevsky podlinnik* (Smirnov, "Mozaiki," 26).

[685] Though the date does not agree with that quoted for a *Phaneromene* in note 681 *supra*. Perhaps the impossibly early date for that icon's appearance was amended out of regard for the decision at the Council of Ephesus in 431, which provides the terminus a quo.

[686] Smirnov, "Mozaiki," 26.

[687] Included among the Island's wonderworking icons of the Virgin by Stephen Lusignan, *Description de toute l'isle de Cypre* (Paris, 1580), 64; cf. Papageorghiou, *Icons of Cyprus*, 50.

The remarkable ἐνέργεια which was imputed to this original *Kypriakē* need not detain us; indeed, the issue of blood from "wounds" inflicted by unbelievers is a feature of many miraculous image stories, some of them going back to the sixth century. Among those cited by Kitzinger,[688] one that is most likely to have inspired the story about the *Kypriakē* was told of an image of Christ at Beirut which produced blood and water when certain Jews inflicted on it the wounds of Christ's passion.[689] It has already been suggested that a derivative of this Beirut legend is to be seen in a similar story told of an icon of the Virgin in a Coptic source which has been attributed to the seventh century.[690]

If the story itself is legendary, it could have been told by the iconodules of a mosaic in Cyprus that did actually exist. If it did, the mosaic would have been set sometime in the period before the Arab incursions of the mid-seventh century, for these clearly provide the setting of the story. At that time, and indeed from the first half of the sixth century, compositions of the kind described in the texts were to be seen in Cyprus, as the mosaic in the apse of the Panagia Kanakaria at Lythrankomi shows. Furthermore, the iconography of the Virgin and Child in the mosaic of the iconodule catalogue would have been substantially the same as in that at Lythrankomi, if Mary was represented full-face with the Child before her; and the word ἐνκόλπιος will hardly admit of any other pose. It was indeed this pose which Kondakov believed distinguished the *Kypriakē*,[691] despite deviations from it in some of the imaginary versions followed in the engravings. This similarity is in no way surprising, for we have seen above that this formal iconography was probably the standard formula initially adopted throughout Christendom to proclaim the doctrine of the Incarnation.[692] Nevertheless, we do consider below the possibility that there could be some direct connection between the miraculous image and the Lythrankomi mosaic.

It is hardly surprising that the *Kypriakē* title does not occur in Cyprus itself. The ultimate prototype described in the *Letter* would have had no title at all, for it belonged to a time long before it was customary to include such titles in identifications of the Virgin. The practice only became common after the iconoclast controversy, when reproductions of famous images, especially icons, began to multiply and a need to distinguish them by convenient labels arose. Outside the Island it would be natural at this later stage for icons of the Theotokos based on the miraculous mosaic to be named "The Cypriot." Confusion only resulted when copies of other portrayals treasured in the Island, such as the *Phaneromene*, circulated elsewhere with the same *Kypriakē* label. Within Cyprus, icons copied from celebrated local prototypes were often

---

[688] E. Kitzinger, "The Cult of Images in the Age Before Iconoclasm," *DOP*, 8 (1954), 100ff.

[689] Related at the Council of 787 (Mansi, 13, col. 24ff.) and often subsequently, it is the twelfth item in the *Letter to Theophilus*. See E. Dobschuetz, *Christusbilder* (Leipzig, 1899), 280**ff., and on its derivatives, 281** note 3.

[690] W. H. Worrell, *The Coptic Manuscripts in the Freer Collection* (New York, 1923), 367ff. Kitzinger suggests that the seventh-century dating may be too early ("The Cult of Images," 101 note 59).

[691] N. P. Kondakov, *Ikonografija Bogomateri*, II, 316ff.

[692] *Supra*, p. 86.

identified by distinguishing titles, such as "The Kykkotissa" on those reproducing the Theotokos icon attributed to St. Luke in the monastery after
which it is named. Localizing names of this kind became attached to many
lesser images of the Virgin in Cyprus;[693] while another class of epithet indicated
characteristics of particular icons.[694] If any post-iconoclastic icon in Cyprus
was modeled on the wonderworking mosaic, it might well have been given some
such title as the τοξευθεῖσα, "Shot with an Arrow," on the analogy of the
Machairotheisa, the name given to the icon revered in the chapel of the Holy
Well in St. Sophia, to which the legend in the thirteenth item of the iconodule
catalogue was adapted.[695] As we have seen, the sermon embodying the story
about the Cypriot mosaic in the sixteenth-century Vatican MS is headed
περὶ τοξευθείσης εἰκόνος, but no such qualification of the Virgin has been recorded
in Cyprus.[696] Among those that are known, a possible name for a derivative
of the mosaic is the Αἱματοῦσα; however, this title is not understood to signify
that blood issued from the icon, but rather that it was effective in cure of
hemorrhage.[697] On the other hand, the name Στάξουσα attached to a ruined
monastery near that of Stavrouni is indeed suggestive of an image which
dripped,[698] ἔσταξεν εἰς τὴν γήν, in the words of the *Thesaurus*.

If Cyprus preserves no representation of the Virgin conveniently labeled to
establish that it was modeled on the mosaic cited by the iconodules, it remains
possible that one that is unnamed but of similar iconography does reproduce
that prototype. Talbot Rice, when studying the icons of the Island, was not
concerned with the wonderworking mosaic, but he was on the lookout for the
Kypriakē type as defined by Kondakov. In point of fact this particular
iconography is rather rare among many versions of the Hodegetria, Eleousa,
and other types. Talbot Rice published only three examples. One has attendant
figures, though these are not angels but John the Baptist and John the
Evangelist; they flank a frontal, enthroned Virgin and Child on a sixteenth-
century panel from the Chrysaliniotissa church in Nicosia.[699] In the other two

---

[693] E.g., the *Yeroskipiotissa*: Papageorghiou, *Icons of Cyprus*, 44. The practice is attested as early
as the twelfth century by the wallpainting of the *Arakiotissa* at Lagoudera: G. A. Soteriou, Θεοτόκος ἡ
᾿Αρακιώτισσα τῆς Κύπρου, in ᾿Αρχ.᾿Εφ., 1953–54, i (1955), 87–91.

[694] Such icons must have given their names to churches of the Panagia such as the *Asprophorousa*
and the *Glykiotissa* at Kyrenia, the *Galatousa* at Paphos, the *Iamatiki* at Arakapas (Papageorghiou,
Icons of Cyprus, 72), and the *Myrophorousa* (Christofides, Τὰ ἐπώνυμα τῆς Παναγίας [*supra*, note 38],
93).

[695] See G. P. Galavaris, "The Mother of God 'Stabbed with a Knife,'" *DOP*, 13 (1959), 219–33.
In the ninth-century catalogue it was an icon of Christ.

[696] See note 38 *supra* for the bibliography of this subject.

[697] Koukoules, ᾿Επίθετα τινὰ τῆς Θεοτόκου (*supra*, note 37), 433; Timotheos of Jordan (Μεγάλη ῾Ελ-
ληνικὴ ᾿Εγκυκλοπαίδεια², 19, 496) records this title at Paphos.

[698] See Enlart, *L'art gothique*, II, 424. The name *Stazousa* occurs elsewhere in Cyprus at Pissouri,
near the south coast, and at Ayios Amvrosios (District of Kyrenia): S. Menardos, Τοπουνμικαὶ καὶ
Λαογραφκαὶ Μελέται (Nicosia, 1970), 29.

[699] Rice-Gunnis, *The Icons of Cyprus*, 229, pl. 28, no. 37. As a possible representative of the
Kypriakē, Talbot Rice overlooked this example, in which both the Virgin's hands are in the downward
position, as in the Lythrankomi mosaic. He was in fact preoccupied with the position of the Virgin's
right hand and had less regard to the frontal and axial pose which is basic to Kondakov's type. He
published only the first letters of the title, and these doubtfully; on his photograph the last letters
are legible and suggestive of what one would expect: *Chrysaliniotissa*.

there are no flanking figures, though in both the Virgin's right hand is on Christ's shoulder, a characteristic of Kondakov's *Kypriakē*; neither is earlier than the seventeenth century.[700] In monumental painting there are other and earlier examples in Cyprus of this frontal and axial iconography of the Virgin and Child, and they often include the flanking archangels.[701] But we have seen above that this earliest Byzantine formula for representations of the Theotokos was once widespread,[702] and post-iconoclastic revivals of this early iconography, particularly for the Platytera in the apse, were a commonplace everywhere.[703]

If this mosaic whose legendary powers were seized on by the iconodules did in fact exist, it is to be remarked that no reference to it is made in the Chronicle of Makhairas, which has a good deal to say about the precious relics and wonderworking icons which were preserved in Cyprus. The chronicle in its surviving form was not composed before the fifteenth century, but in the relevant section the chronicler used a source, of which some elements are a good deal earlier.[704] Later writers such as Stephen Lusignan and the Archimandrite Kyprianos, both of whom have something to say about the Island's wonderworking icons, are equally silent about the mosaic. This silence would be explained if the mosaic had been destroyed and forgotten at an early date, for example in the upheavals that followed the first Arab raids. Some of the coastal towns were then abandoned and both partners in the neutralization of the Island transferred many Cypriots to their own territories, if only temporarily.[705] That no memory of the mosaic survived in the Island does not necessarily mean that it never existed.

The Russian monk Vasilij Barskij, who was in Cyprus in 1734–36 following an earlier visit in 1727, was evidently familiar with one of the accounts of the wonderworking mosaic which circulated in his country. For when he went to the village of Kiti, which is indeed on the south side of the Island, and saw the mosaic in the apse of the church of the Panagia Angeloktistos, he thought he had found it.[706] Even if one ignores the statement in the *Thesaurus* of Damascenos that the mosaic was outside, above the door of a church, all

---

[700] On one, at Ayia Varvara, the Virgin is seated on a *thokos* and is labeled *Eleousa* (*ibid.*, 221, pl. 23, no. 48); on the other, at Lefkoniko, the Virgin is unnamed and is seated on a throne (*ibid.*, 228, pl. 27, no. 60; Papageorghiou, *Icons of Cyprus*, pl. p. 112).

[701] E.g., the apse fresco of 1192 at Lagoudera (Stylianou, *Painted Churches*, fig. 36).

[702] See *supra*, p. 86f.

[703] E.g., the mosaic on the apse wall at Monreale (O. Demus, *The Mosaics of Norman Sicily* [London, 1949], pl. 63) and the fresco in the apse of the Panagia Mavriotissa at Kastoria (S. Pelekanides, Καστορία [Thessaloniki, 1953], pl. 63). The preeminence of this formal iconography is apparent in an eleventh-century icon in the Sinai monastery depicting four wonderworking images of the Virgin, individually named, with an enthroned but unnamed Theotokos in the frontal and axial formula as a centerpiece: G. and M. Soteriou, *Icônes du Mont Sinaï* (note 514a *supra*), I, 125, and II, figs. 146–48.

[704] Though the actual text the chronicler was using may not have been earlier than the fourteenth century. See *supra*, note 15.

[705] Constantine Porphyrogenitus, *De administrando imperio*, c. 47, ed. Gy. Moravcsik, DOT, I (Washington, D. C., 1967), 224, with notes by R. J. H. Jenkins, II, *Commentary* (London, 1962), 180ff.

[706] V. G. Barskij, *Stranstvovanija* ..., II (St. Petersburg, 1886), 332: "There is a beautiful church at Kiti. Therein is the wonderworking image of the Theotokos in mosaic, from which it is said that blood and tears once issued when a certain Arab wounded it."

accounts agree that the Virgin was enthroned. The standing figure of the Hodegetria type in the Kiti apse can have nothing to do with it.

The "tradition" that localizes the legend of the wonderworking mosaic at Lythrankomi is probably less than ninety years old. In 1885 a new edition of the *Thesaurus* was published in Venice, and it is surely significant that the first mention of the legend in connection with the Panagia Kanakaria is in a work published only a few years later.[707] About the same time, the lessee of the former monastery, who owned a copy of the 1885 edition of Damascenos' work, was a strong advocate for the attachment of the legend to his church, and when, in 1895, Smirnov visited him he suggested in support of it the Turkish etymology proposed for the name Kanakaria which we have discussed (see *supra*, p. 8).[708] Although the mosaic in the apse of the church conforms with the few iconographic particulars given in the accounts of the wonderworking mosaic, the Russian scholar attached more importance to the statement in the *Thesaurus* that it was located on the exterior of a church, above the door. He was satisfied that it had not survived, either at Lythrankomi or anywhere else.[709]

Since the apse mosaic (fig. 39) of the Panagia Kanakaria does not fit the legend concerning an external mosaic, a questionable "tradition" and a dubious derivation for the name Kanakaria are the only grounds for localizing the legend at Lythrankomi, and to do so would conflict with the consensus of all the surviving accounts in attaching it to a church in the south of the Island. However, those who set store by the "tradition" now current there, or prefer the Turkish etymology of *Kanakaria*, could reconcile the geographical indication, if somewhat speciously, by assuming that it refers to the position of Lythrankomi on the southern side of the Carpas peninsula. They could then proceed to the hypothesis that the fresco above the south door (fig. 128) is the successor of the mosaic at which the impious Arab was said to have discharged his arrow with such dire results.[710] They would, however, have to suppose that in the three successive reconstructions of the original south wall[711] the memory of the mosaic was never forgotten, though the fresco by which it is now represented is totally different. This is a tenuous thread by which to tie the legendary mosaic to the Lythrankomi church. It is particularly tenuous since the south door and its porch appear to be an afterthought dating from the last reconstruction of this part of the church probably in the thirteenth century; they are not related axially to any opening of the original south colonnade as it is reasonable to reconstruct it (fig. G), nor yet to any bay of the arcade which replaced it (fig. C).

In the circumstances, for those who believe that the commonplace legend became attached to a mosaic that did actually exist in Cyprus, it might be

[707] Frankoudis, Κύπρις (*supra*, note 2), 411 f.

[708] Smirnov, "Mozaiki," 66 note 1.

[709] *Ibid.*, 20.

[710] Cf. Stylianou, *Painted Churches*, 27.

[711] *Ca.* 700, in the twelfth century, and again in the thirteenth (as our examination of the structure has suggested), followed by the painting of the existing lunette fresco *ca.* 1500.

more profitable to seek clues for its localization where the Theotokos is still known by such suggestive titles as the *Stazousa* and the *Aimatousa,* and in these particular cases in quite different and, appropriately, southern parts of the Island. In the meantime, for such a search would be beyond the scope of a study limited to the Panagia Kanakaria, it would seem advisable to treat all attempts to reconstruct the appearance of the wonderworking mosaic with great reserve. Equally, the concept of a *Kypriakē* type of the Theotokos, which is based on such imaginary reconstructions, would be better ignored in serious iconographic studies.

Select Index

Since no illustrations of comparanda for the Lythrankomi mosaic have been included, this index is provided for those references where published illustrations are cited and where, if the date of such comparanda is in doubt, the chronology here adopted is indicated.

LINECUTS

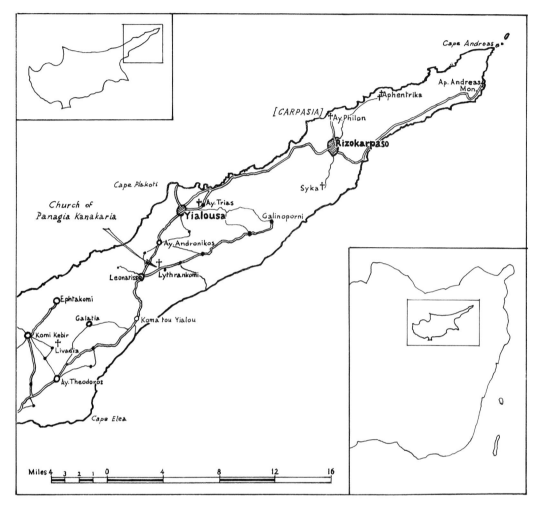

Cape Andreas

Ap. Andreas Mon.

†Aphentrika

[CARPASIA]

†Ay.Philon

Rizokarpaso

Cape Plakoti

Syka †

Church of
Panagia Kanakaria

†Ay. Trias

Yialousa

Galinoporni

Ay.Andronikos

Leonarisso
†
Lythrankomi

Ephtakomi

Galatia

Koma tou Yialou

Komi Kebir
†
Livadia

Ay.Theodoros

Cape Elea

Miles 4   3 2 1   0   4   8   12   16

A.   Sketch Plan of Carpas Peninsula

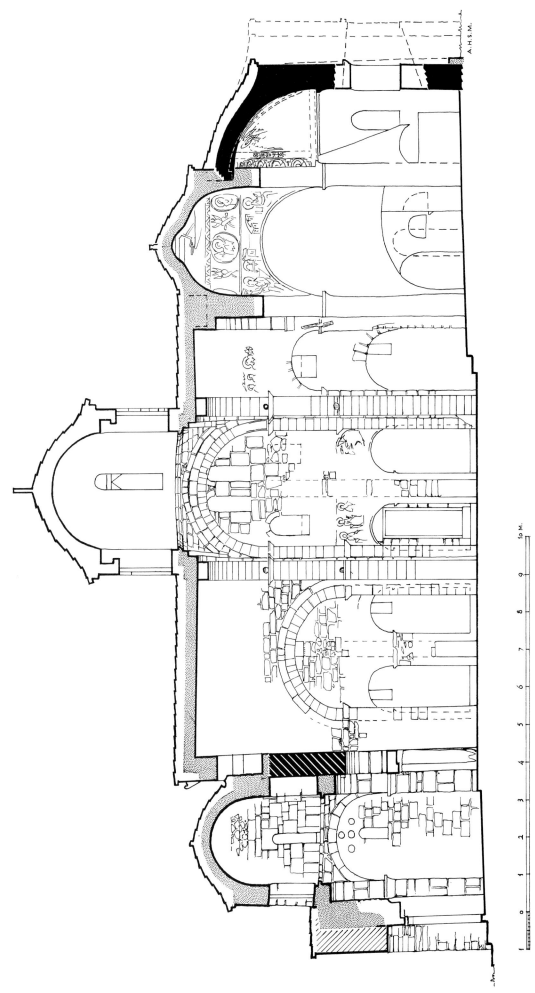

B. Section through Church, looking North. Scale 1/100 (for Conventions, see fig. C)

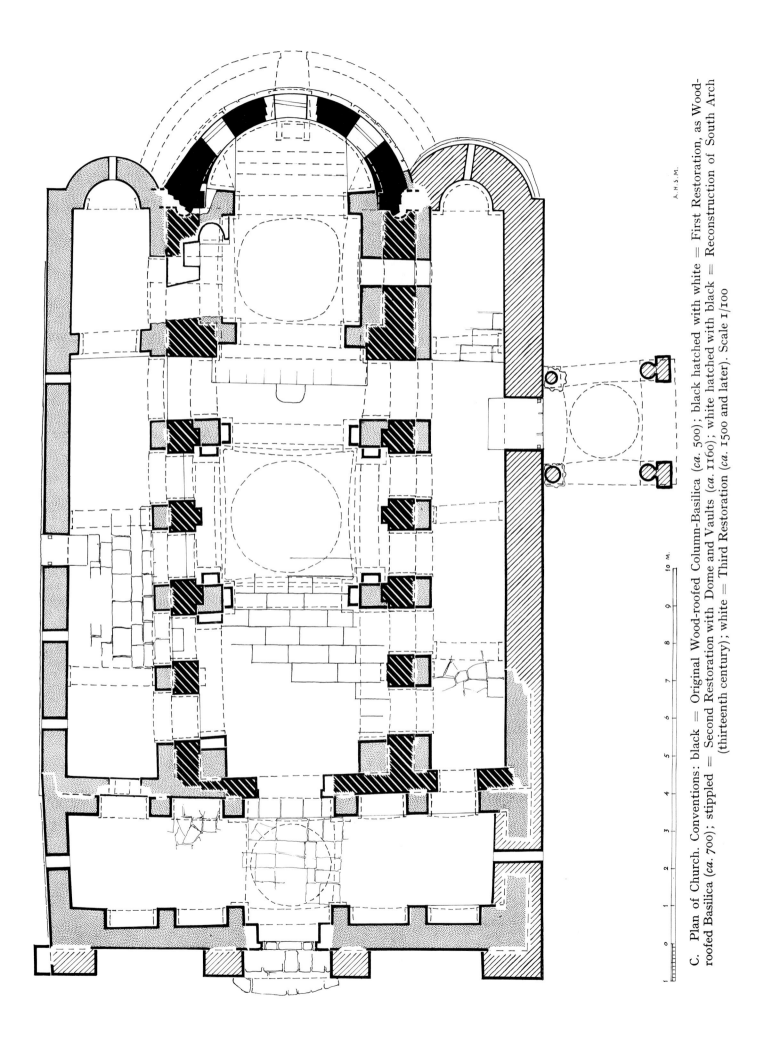

C. Plan of Church. Conventions: black = Original Wood-roofed Column-Basilica (*ca.* 500); black hatched with white = First Restoration, as Wood-roofed Basilica (*ca.* 700); stippled = Second Restoration with Dome and Vaults (*ca.* 1160); white hatched with black = Reconstruction of South Arch (thirteenth century); white = Third Restoration (*ca.* 1500 and later). Scale 1/100

A. H. S. M.

D.   Cross Section through Bema, looking East. Scale 1/100 (for Conventions, see fig. C)

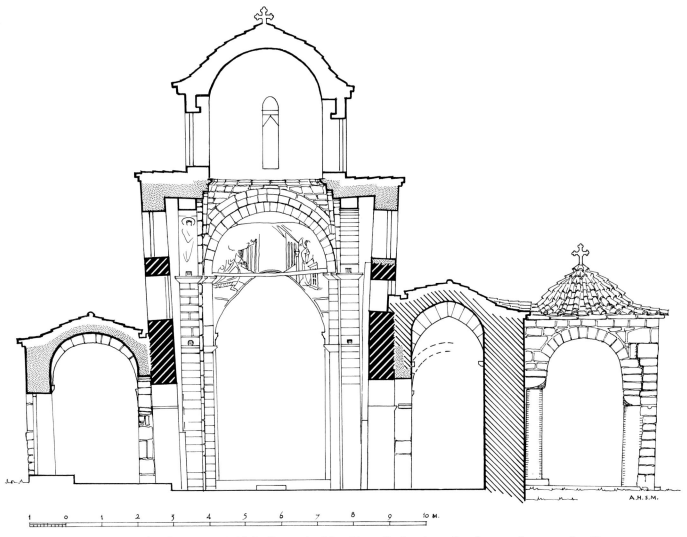

| 1 | o | 1 | 2 | 3 | 4 | 5 | 6 | 7 | 8 | 9 | 10 M. |

E.   Cross Section through Main Dome, looking East. Scale 1/100 (for Conventions, see fig. C)

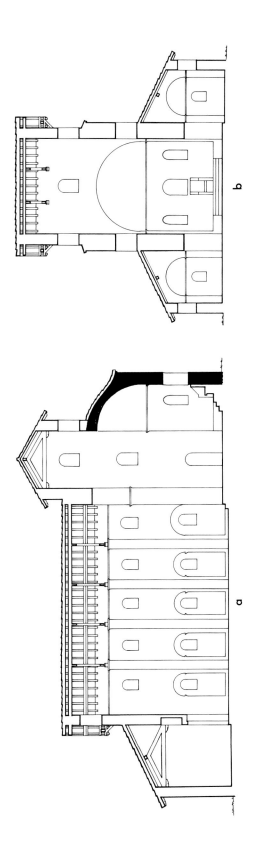

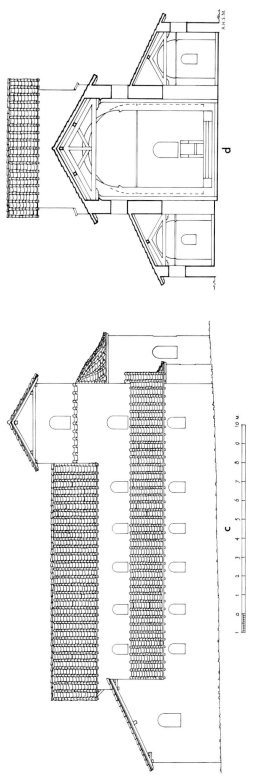

F.   Reconstruction of Pier-Basilica of First Restoration: a. Section, looking North. b. Cross Section through Bema, looking East. c. South Elevation. d. Cross Section through Nave, looking East. Scale 1/200

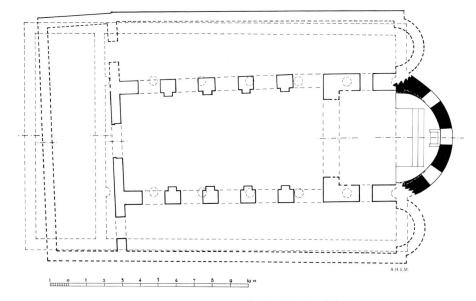

G. Composite Plan of Original Column-
Basilica (thick broken line = hypothetical)
and Pier-Basilica of First Restoration (thick
broken line = hypothetical). Scale 1/200

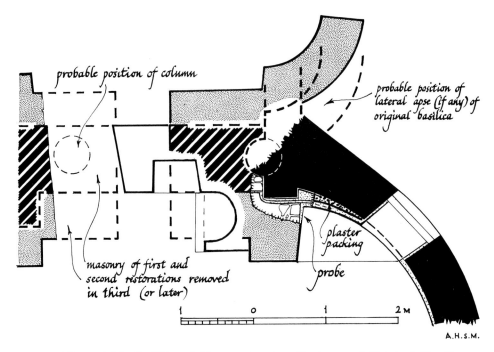

probable position of column

probable position of lateral apse (if any) of original basilica

masonry of first and second restorations removed in third (or later)

plaster packing

probe

A.H.S.M.

H. Plan of North Side of Bema, showing Features of Original Basilica
(black) found in Probe through Masonry of Second Restoration (stippled) and
of First Restoration (hatched). Scale 1/50

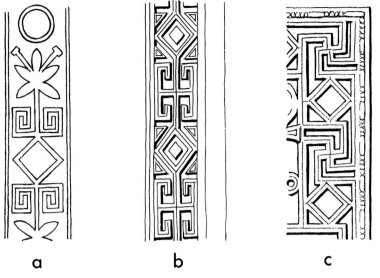

I. a. Intermediate Border. b. St. Polyeuktos, Border (restored) of Plaque Fragment. c. St. Apollinare, Border of Pierced Panel. Scale 1/10

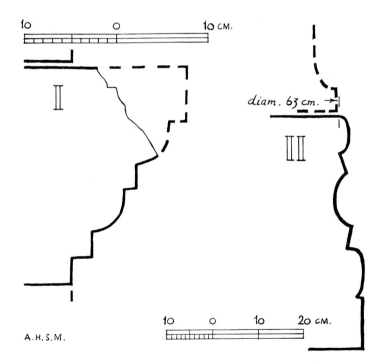

10   O   10 CM.

II

diam. 63 cm.

III

10   O   10   20 CM.

A.H.S.M.

J. Moldings of Original Basilica. 1. Archivolt of North Window of Apse. Scale 1/4. 11. Profile of Base. Scale 1/8

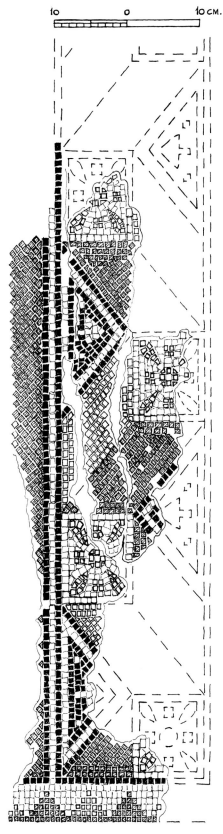

K.   Outer border, South Side.
Scale 1/5

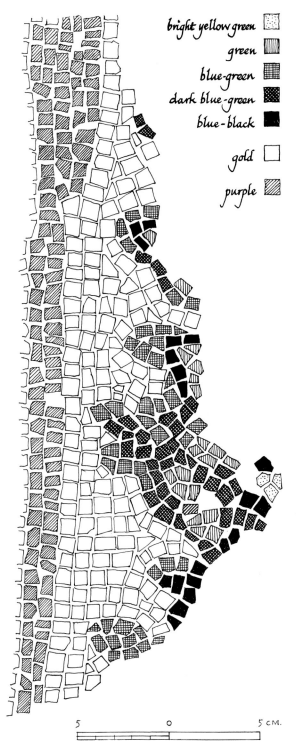

bright yellow green

green

blue-green

dark blue-green

blue-black

gold

purple

L.   Detail of Foliage beside the North
Archangel's Wing. Scale 1/2

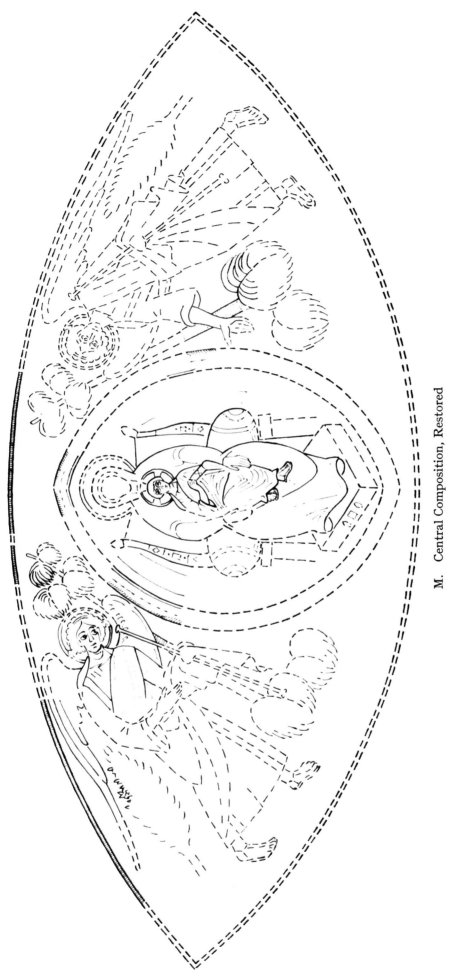

M.   Central Composition, Restored

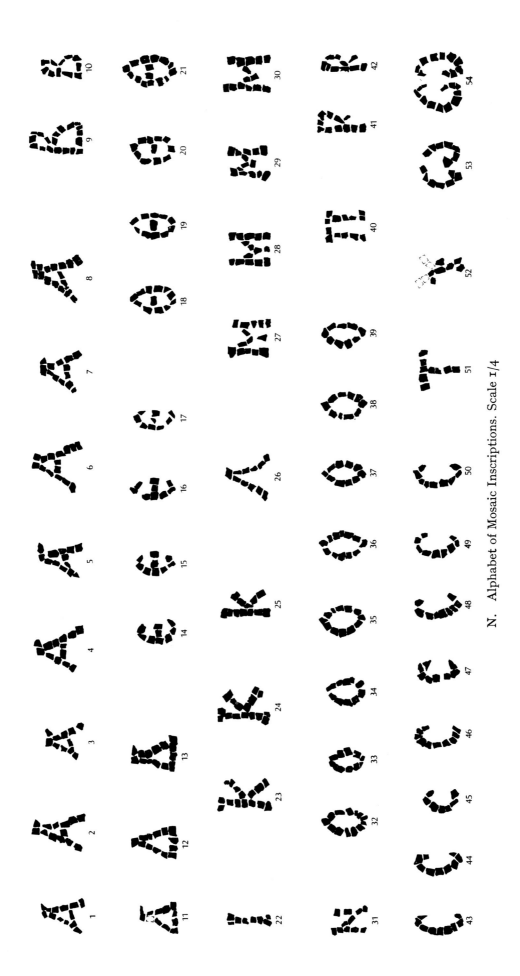

N. Alphabet of Mosaic Inscriptions. Scale 1/4

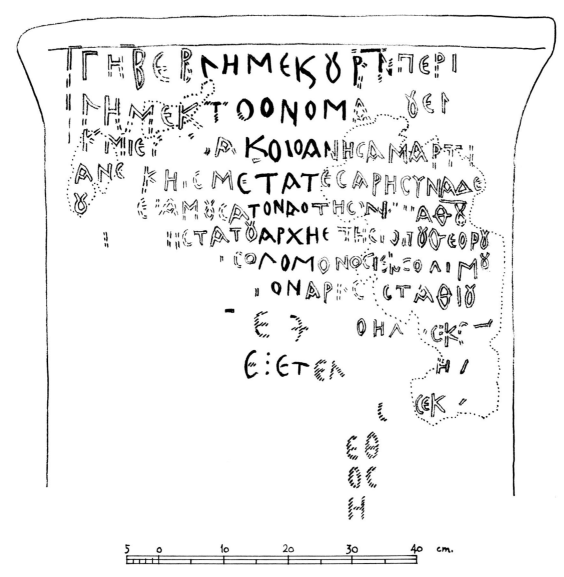

O. Facsimile of Painted Inscription. Conventions: black = Recorded by Smirnov and Confirmed; hatched = Recorded by Smirnov, Now Lost; outline = Now Visible; broken outline = Doubtful. Scale 1/5

PLATES

1. View from South

2. South Clerestory Windows

Cyprus, Lythrankomi, Panagia Kanakaria

3. View from West

4. View from Southwest

6. Interior

5. View from Southwest

Porch

8. Inscription of Chrysanthos

9. West Door, Inscription on Jamb

7. West Gable

10. View from Northwest

11. View from Northeast

12. Monastery (1970)

13. Column Base near West Door

14. Column Base reused in Altar

15. Monastery, Portico

16. Porch, Capitals used as Column Bases

17. Capital North of West Door

18. Capital South of West Door

19. Capital outside West Gate

20. Block with Mortar-Grip Channels

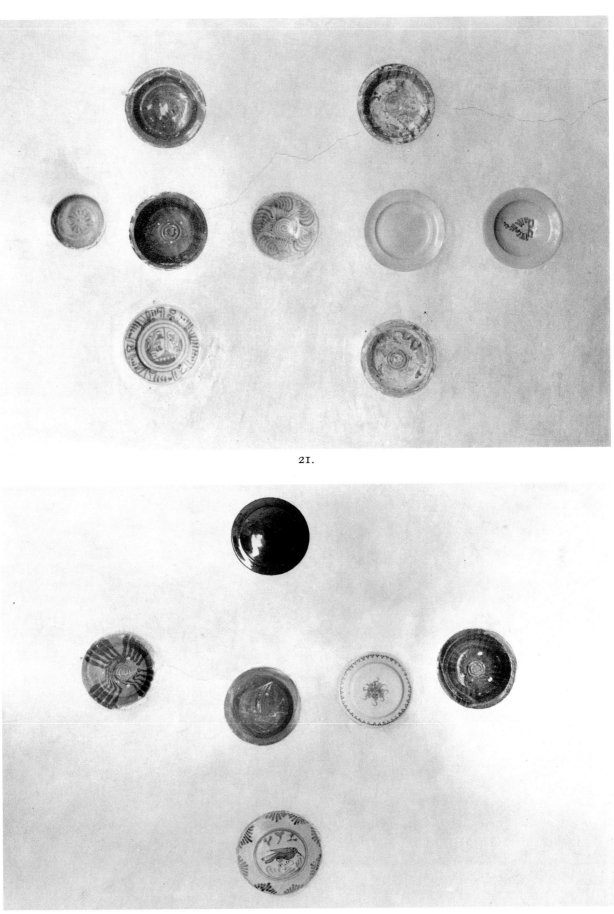

21.

22.

Narthex, Plates set in Vault

23. During Repair (1954)

24. North Window

Apse

25. Lowest Course

27. Dome Bay

Narthex

26. Looking North

29. West End

28. Dome Bay

Nave, South Side

31. East Bay

30. Dome Bay

Nave, North Side

33. Looking East

32. Looking West

North Aisle

34. Looking East

35. Looking West

South Aisle

36.   Vaulting, East End, and Bema

37.   South Arcade, West End

Nave

38.   Nave and Bema, looking East

39. Mosaic, from Below

40. Mosaic, from West

41.　North Side

42.　South Side

Conch

44. Intermediate Border, Angel's Wing, and Foliage

43. Outer and Irisated Borders, North Side

47. Intermediate Border, Tinted Tesserae Retouched

46. Intermediate Border

45. Outer Border

49. Matthew and Jude with North Borders

48. James and Bartholomew with South Border

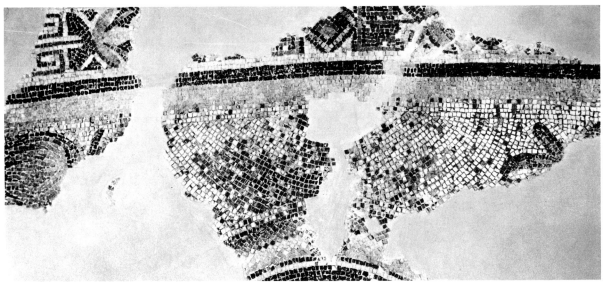

50. Intermediate Border, Summit of Conch

51. Mandorla, Apex

52. Irisated Border at South Angle

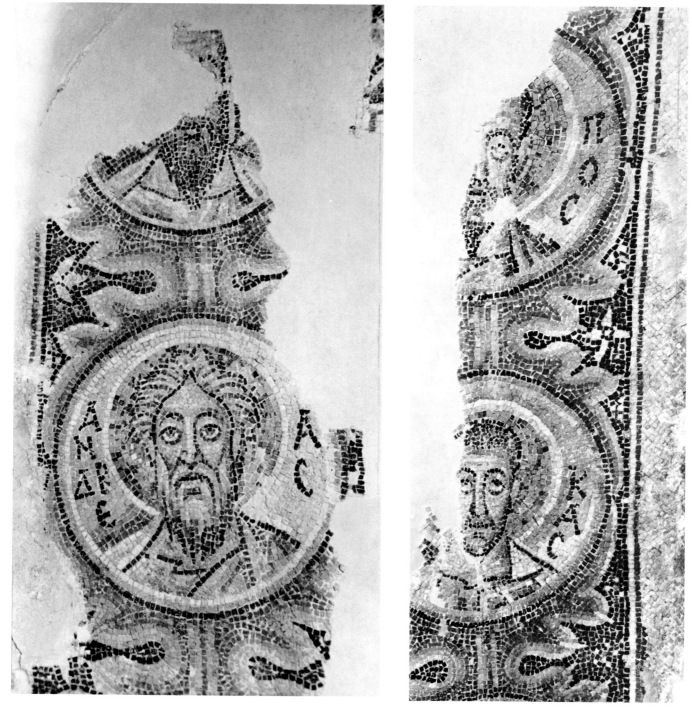

53.   Paul and Andrew   54.   Philip and Luke

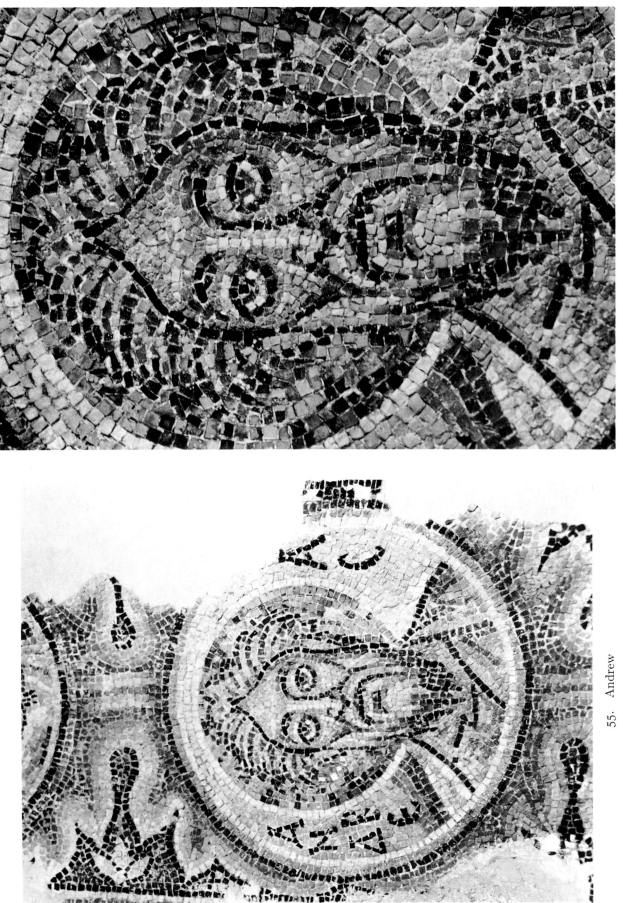

56. Detail

55. Andrew

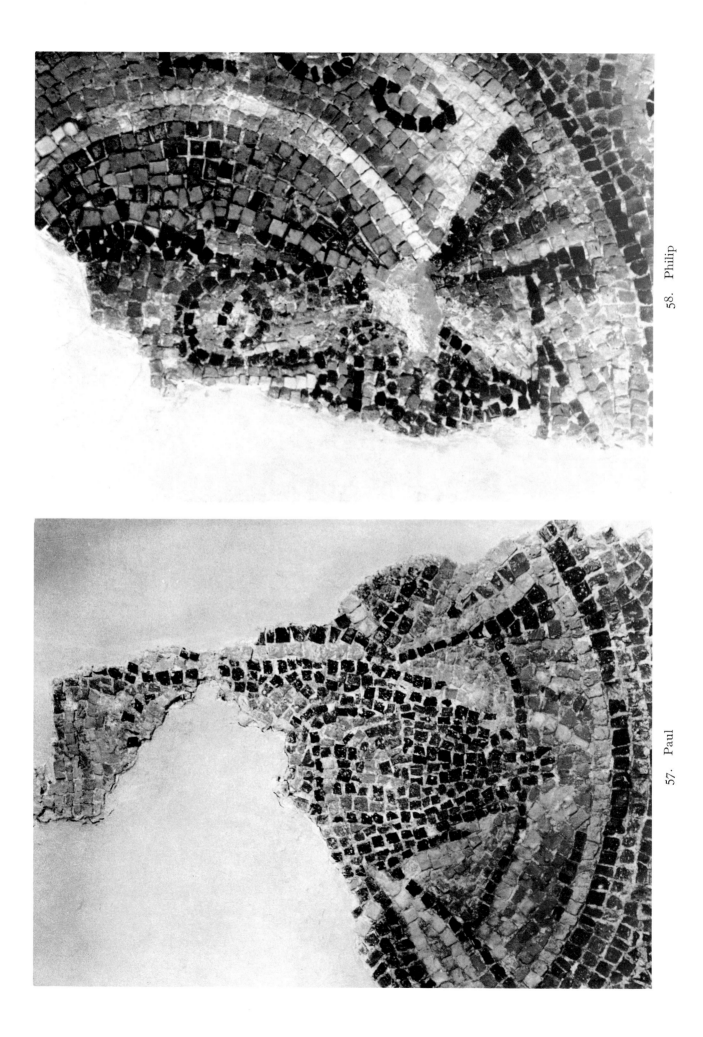

58. Philip

57. Paul

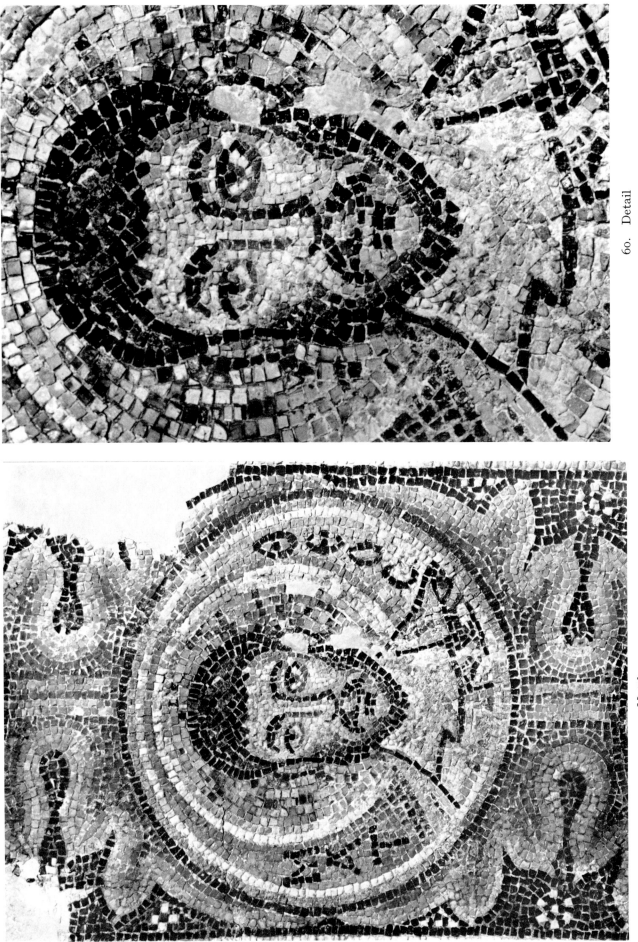

60. Detail

59. Matthew

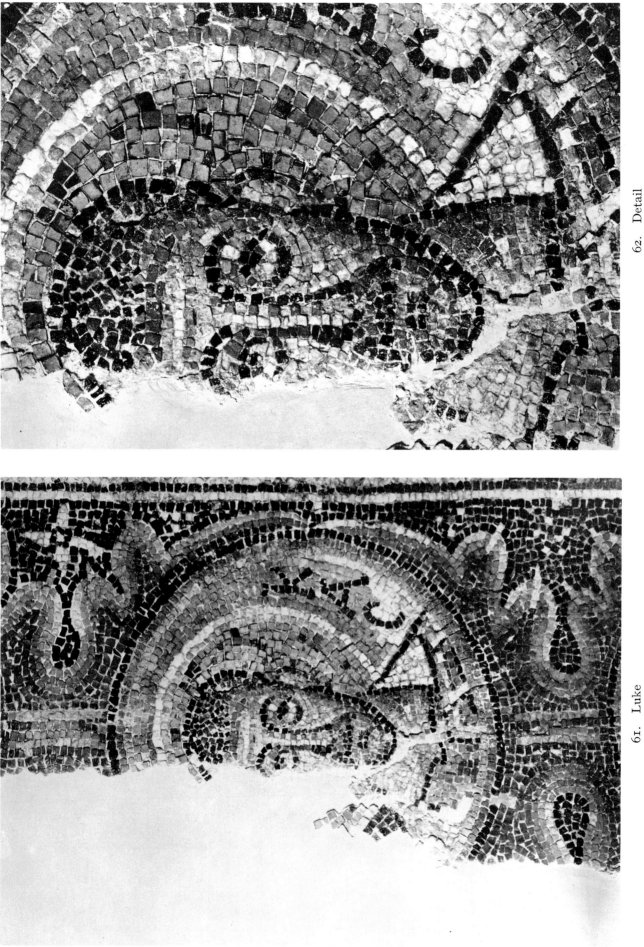

61. Luke

62. Detail

63. Jude

64. Detail

66. Detail

65. James

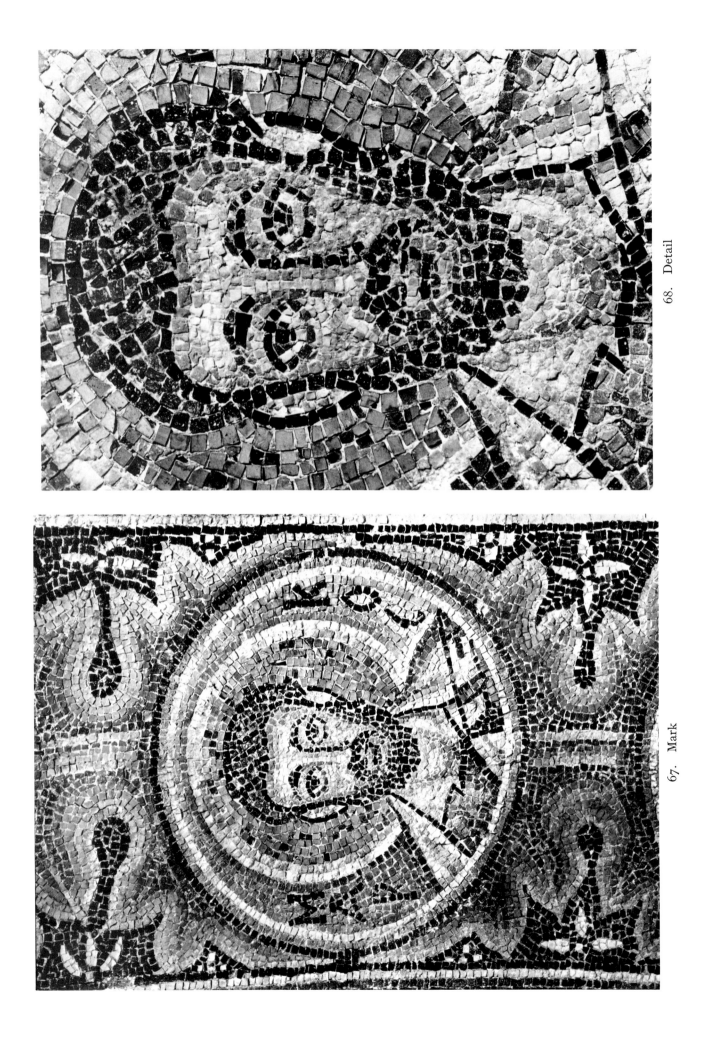

68. Detail

67. Mark

69.   Bartholomew

70.   Detail

72. Detail

71. Thomas

74. With Top of Palm Tree

North Archangel

73. With Wing

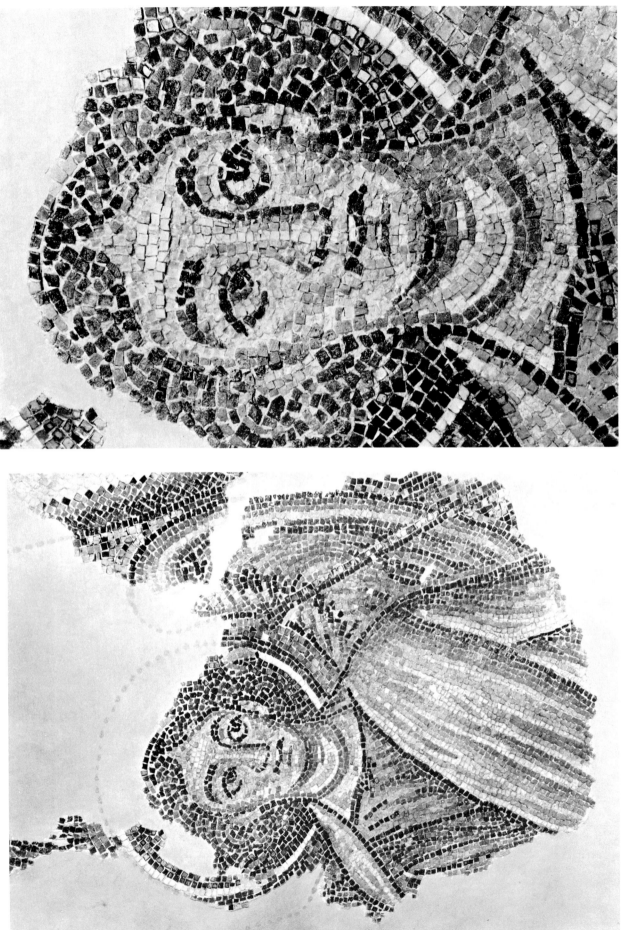

76. Detail

75. North Archangel

77. South Archangel, Forearm

78. Image in Mandorla

79.   The Theotokos

80. Area above Head of Christ

81. The Virgin's Hand, and Cushion

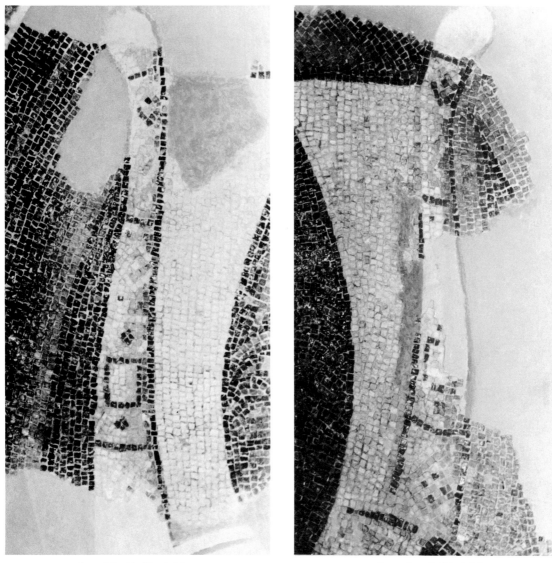

82. North Upright   83. South Upright

84. Footstool

Throne

85. Child Christ

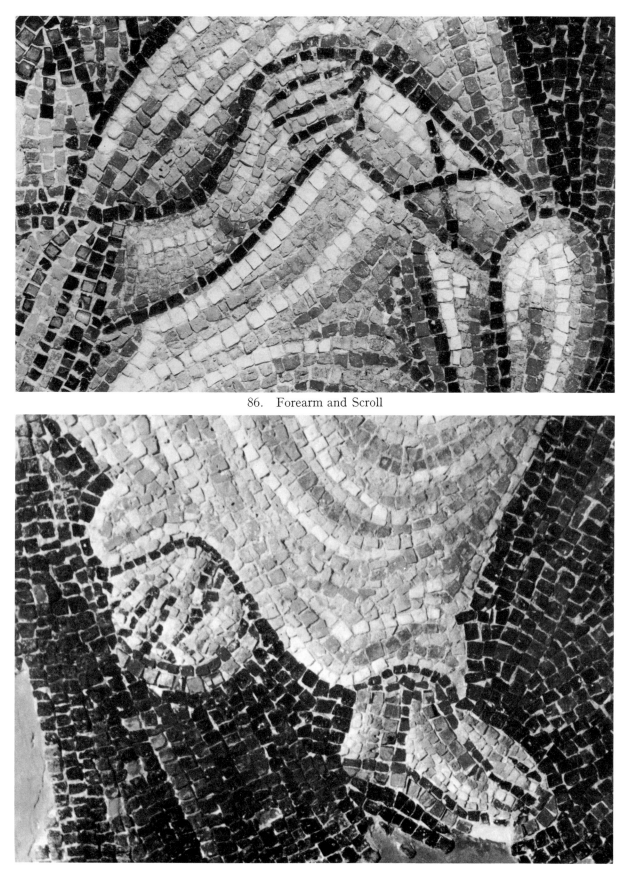

86. Forearm and Scroll

87. Feet

Christ

89. Detail

Christ

88. Upper Half

90.   South Aisle. Archangel Gabriel

91.   North Arcade. St. Barbara

92. South Arcade. Inscription

93. North Arcade. Cross   94.   95. Drawing

Nave, North Wall. Zigzag Border

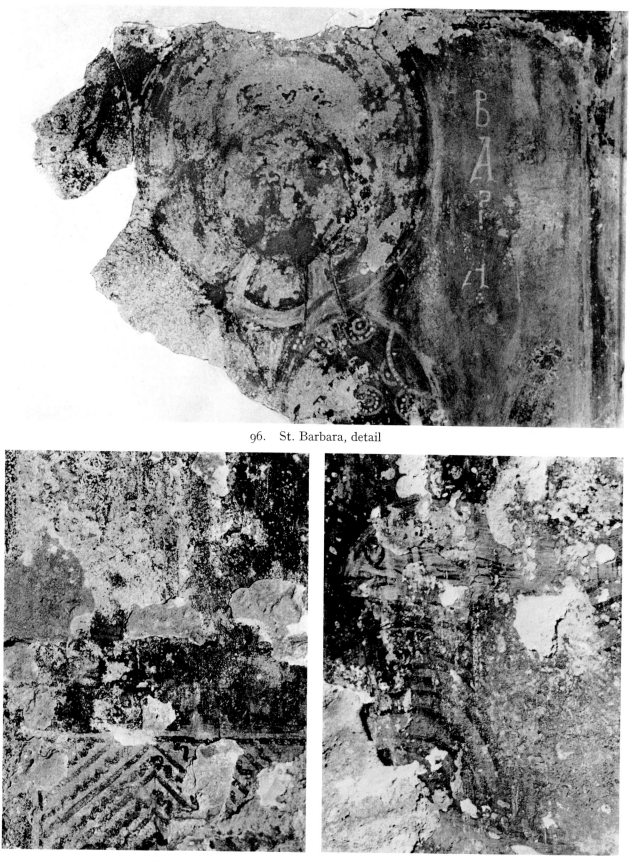

96. St. Barbara, detail

97. Dado

98. Fish

Earlier Panel of St. George

100. Earlier Panel, detail

99. Superimposed Panels of St. George

102.

103.   Soffits below The Last Judgment

101.   North Arcade. Angel

104. Paradise

105. The Resurrection from the Sea

106. The Pantocrator

107. Dome, Drum

Bema

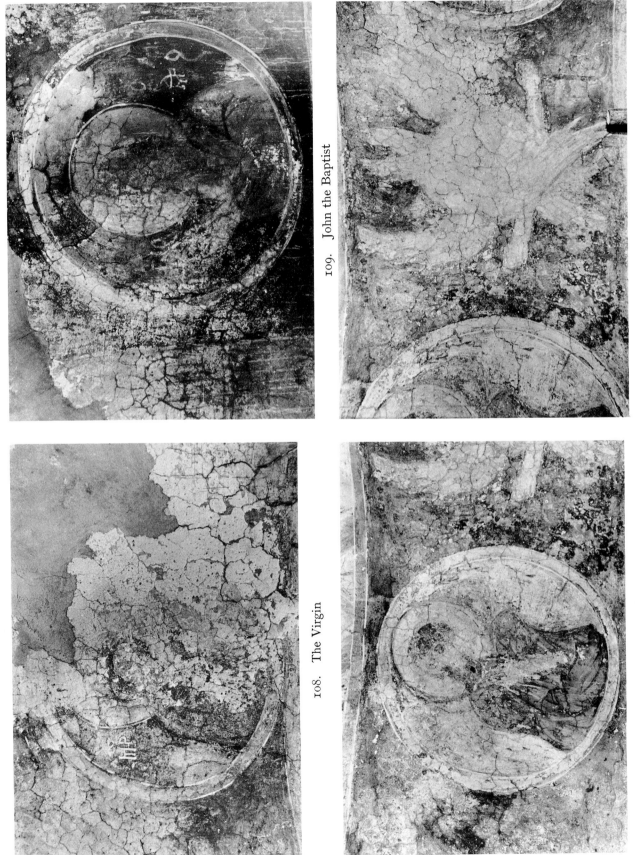

108. The Virgin

109. John the Baptist

110. Archangel

111. Hexapterygon

Bema, Dome

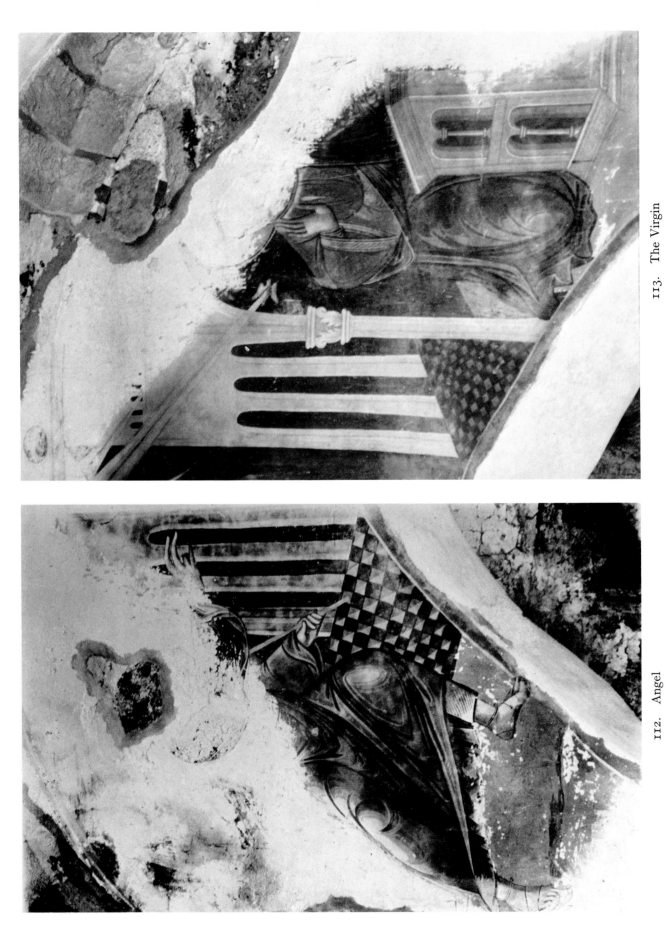

113. The Virgin

The Annunciation

112. Angel

114.

115.

Bema, Pendentive. Evangelists

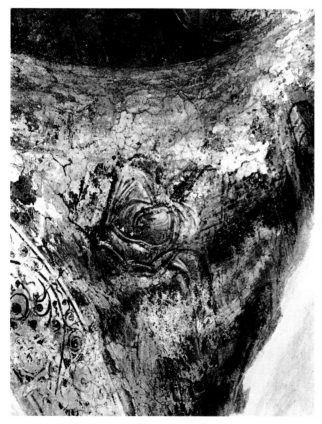

116. Northeast Pendentive. Luke

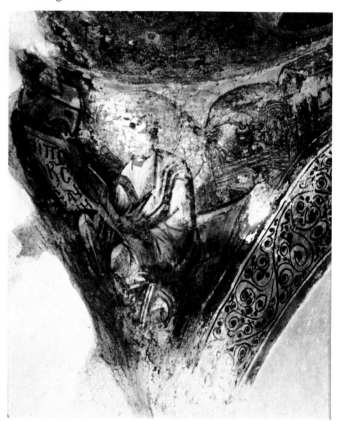

117. Northwest Pendentive. John

118. The Ascension

119. The Annunciation

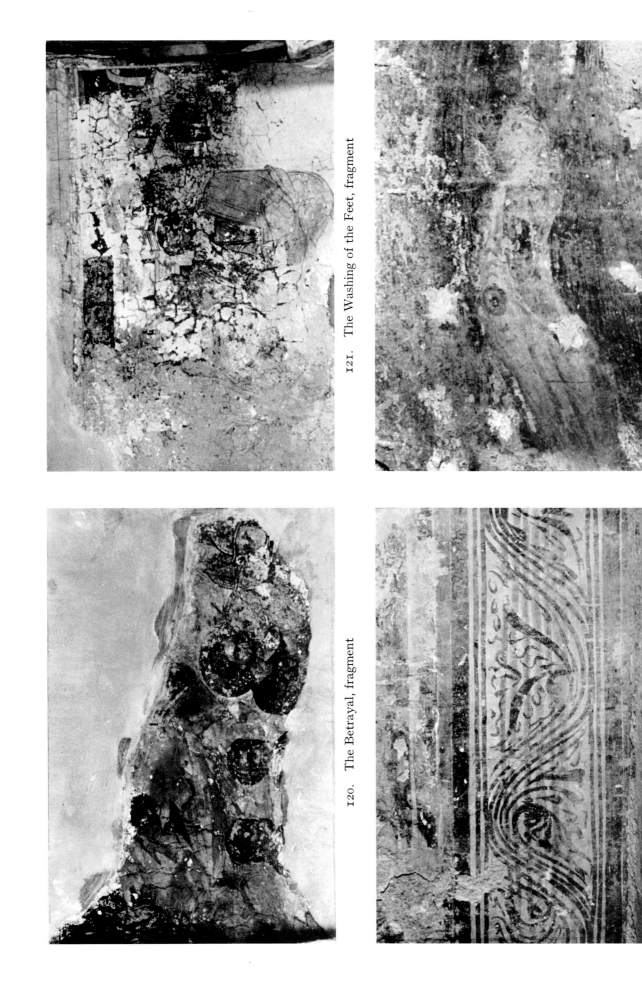

121.   The Washing of the Feet, fragment

123.   The Resurrection from the Sea, detail

120.   The Betrayal, fragment

122.   Dado below the Nativity

125. Inscription

124. Detail

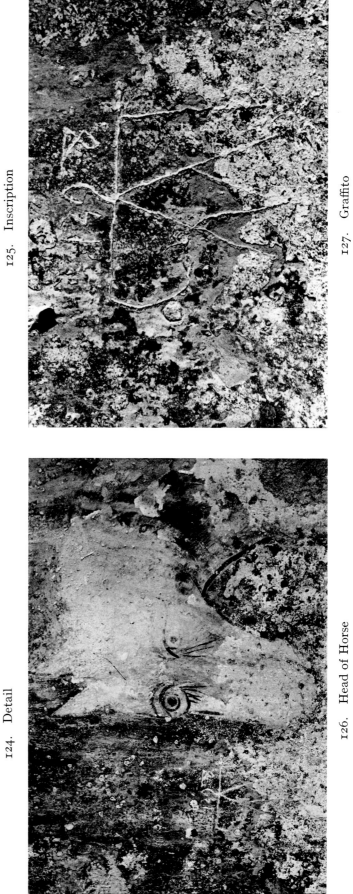

127. Graffito

126. Head of Horse

Later Panel of St. George

128. Porch. The "Kanakaria"

129. The Nativity, fragment

130.   SS. Helen and Mamas (?)

131.   Female Martyr and St. Eleazar

132.   Secondary Dome, Arch. Prophet

133. Dome, Cross

134.   North Archangel, Bust

135.   Child Christ, Upper Part

136. Christ Child, detail

137.　Apostle Border, North Side　　　　　138.　Intermediate Border

139. Matthew

141. Andrew

140. Mark

143. Jude

142. James